P9-APU-106

Lawyers' Ideals / Lawyers' Practices

LAWYERS' IDEALS / LAWYERS' PRACTICES

Transformations in the American Legal Profession

EDITED BY

Robert L. Nelson

David M. Trubek

Rayman L. Solomon

Cornell University Press

Ithaca and London

First published 1992 by Cornell University Press.

Library of Congress Cataloging-in-Publication Data

Lawyers' ideals/lawyers' practices : transformations in the American legal profession / edited by Robert L. Nelson, David M. Trubek, Rayman L. Solomon.
p. cm.
"The articles . . . were first presented at the American Bar Foundation's Conference on Professionalism held in September 1988" — Pref.
Includes bibliographical references (p.) and index.
ISBN 0-8014-2461-5 (cloth : alk. paper). — ISBN 0-8014-9710-8 (paper : alk. paper)
1. Practice of law—United States. 2. Legal ethics—United States. 3. Lawyers—United States. I. Nelson, Robert L., 1952– . II. Trubek, David M., 1935– . III. Solomon, Rayman, L.
KF300.L33 1992
174'.3'0973—dc20 91-55533

Printed in the United States of America

∞ The paper in this book meets the minimum requirements of the American National Standard for Information Sciences–Permanence of Paper for Printed Library Materials, ANSI Z39.48-1984.

To Jessica, Amy, Anne, Claire,
Hannah, Ben, William,
and Juniorette

Contents

Preface

This collection of articles is an effort to create a greater understanding of the empirical issues that lie behind the debate over whether in the practice of law the ideals of professionalism have been replaced by the demands of commercialism. This book is the most systematic attempt so far to examine what professionalism means in the various arenas of legal practice in the United States. It also seeks to advance the theoretical interpretations that lie at the heart of the scholarship on professionalism and establish a framework for analyzing the issues that is more grounded than previous idealist accounts, yet retains some of the ideas of contingency and changeability that structualist accounts have ignored.

The articles in this volume were first presented at the American Bar Foundation's Conference on Professionalism, held in September, 1988. We began to plan the conference after analyzing the American Bar Association's 1986 report on professionalism. The ABA established its Commission on Professionalism in 1984 following a recommendation made by former U.S. Supreme Court chief justice Warren Burger to then ABA president John Shepard that the bar address the decline in professionalism caused by advertising and increasing competition. The commission, known as the Stanley Commission (after its chair, Chicago attorney and former ABA president Justin Stanley), included lawyers, judges, a prominent sociologist, and two other nonlawyers. They held formal hearings and conducted informal interviews among members of the American bar. In 1986 the commission issued its recommendations in a report entitled "In the Spirit of Public Service: A Blueprint for the Rekindling of Lawyer Professionalism." The recommendations contained in the report are aspirational in character and address issues in the areas of legal education, the judiciary, organized bar associations, and legal practice.

When we examined the commission's report, we recognized that it raised fundamental questions about the relationships between the changing structure of legal practice and the set of norms associated with professionalism. Investigating the issues surrounding the status of professionalism would require historical and empirical research. We decided that the first step toward designing research in this area should be to bring together the scholars in the field to discuss the current state of knowledge and to suggest directions for future research.

This book is the result of our initial exploration in the study of professionalism. It is also the first effort of the American Bar Foundation's Program on Professionalism. The program sponsors research projects, conferences, and dissertation fellowships designed to expand our understanding of legal practice and its ideology both in the United States and abroad.

We wish to thank the authors of the articles in this volume for their cooperation in its preparation. Most important, we are also indebted to them for their various contributions to our understanding of professionalism. All the articles benefited greatly from the criticisms and suggestions offered by the discussants and other attendees at the conference, and we thank them for their participation. In addition to the authors, the speakers, panelists, and discussants were Richard Abel, H. William Allen, Ian Ayres, Robert Bell, John Coffee, Yves Dezalay, Robert Dingwall, William L. F. Felstiner, Paul Fenn, Lucinda M. Finley, Lawrence Friedman, Mary Joe Frug, Ronald Gilson, Terence Halliday, Geoffrey Hazard, John P. Heinz, David Luban, Stewart Macaulay, Robert MacCrate, Carrie Menkel-Meadow, Martha L. Minow, Michael Powell, Robert D. Raven, Deborah Rhode, Joel Rogers, Robert Rosen, Austin Sarat, Eve Spangler, Paul Starr, Randolph W. Thrower, Stanton Wheeler, and David Wilkins. Other conference participants included Robert Bennett, John B. Braithwaite, Roger C. Cramton, Robert Duncan, Janet Gilboy, John Hagan, Mark Harrison, Lincoln Kaplan, Wayne A. Kerstetter, Herbert Kritzer, Jethro K. Lieberman, Lawrence Marshall, Alan A. Paterson, John R. Schmidt, Susan Shapiro, Antone G. Singsen III, Wesley Skogan, Kent Smith, and Richard A. Salomon.

We wish to acknowledge the special assistance of several individuals. Jerry Van Hoy provided invaluable research assistance from the beginning of the conference planning through the completion of this book. His article on the Stanley Commission has been most helpful in providing background on its politics. Two past presidents of the American Bar Foundation, Randolph W. Thrower, Esq., and William Allen, Esq., were most influential in nurturing the conference from its initial conception to its completion. William L. F. Felstiner, former director of the American Bar Foundation, played an instrumental role throughout this project. He helped to conceptualize the conference, and guided, encouraged, and supported us at every step. Finally, we acknowledge the generous institutional support provided us by the American Bar Foundation, which allowed us to hold the conference and to complete and publish this book. The views expressed here are those of the authors and in no way reflect the opinions of the American Bar Foundation or its board of directors.

R.S.
R.N.
D.T.

Contributors

Eliot Freidson is Professor of Sociology at New York University. He is the author of *Professional Powers: A Study of the Institutionalization of Formal Knowledge*, recently published by the University of Chicago Press, and is completing a work tentatively titled *The Fate of Knowledge: Professionalism, Bureaucracy, and the Free Market*, to be published by Polity Press.

Marc Galanter is Evjue-Bascom Professor of Law and South Asian Studies and Director of the Institute for Legal Studies at the University of Wisconsin–Madison. His book (with Thomas Palay), *Tournament of Lawyers: The Transformation of the Big Law Firm* was published by the University of Chicago Press in 1991.

Robert W. Gordon is Professor of Law at Stanford University. He has written extensively on the history of the legal profession. His forthcoming *Lawyers of the Republic* is to be published by Harvard University Press.

Robert L. Nelson is Research Fellow and Director of the Program on Professionalism at the American Bar Foundation and Associate Professor of Sociology at Northwestern University. He is the author of *Partners with Power: The Social Transformation of the Large Law Firm* (1988), and his research interests are in the sociology of law, organizations, and inequality.

Thomas Palay is Professor of Law and Deputy Director of the Institute for Legal Studies at the University of Wisconsin–Madison. Part of the research reported here was conducted while he was a Visiting Research Fellow at the American Bar Foundation. His book (with Marc Galanter), *Tournament of Lawyers: The Transformation of the Big Law Firm*, was published by the University of Chicago Press in 1991.

THEODORE SCHNEYER is Professor of Law at the University of Arizona. He has taught at the University of Wisconsin Law School, and spent a year as a Visiting Scholar at the American Bar Foundation. His research interests include legal ethics, professional politics, and the regulation of the legal profession. His latest article, "Professional Discipline for Law Firms?" appeared in the *Cornell Law Review*.

CARROLL SERON, a sociologist, is Associate Professor in the School of Business and Public Administration at Baruch College, City University of New York. She is the coauthor with Wolf Heydebrand of the recently published *Rationalizing Justice: The Political Economy of the Federal District Courts*. In addition, she has published numerous articles on the courts. Currently she is working on a study of independent lawyers and small legal firms that focuses on how changes in business-getting techniques and the introduction of computers have affected legal practices and professional norms.

WILLIAM H. SIMON teaches at Stanford Law School and has written about legal ethics, social welfare, and economic organization.

RAYMAN L. SOLOMON is Associate Dean at Northwestern University School of Law. He is a specialist in legal history and is the author of "The Politics of Appointment and the Federal Court's Role in Regulating America: U.S. Courts of Appeals Judgeships from T.R. to F.D.R.," which appeared in the *American Bar Foundation Research Journal* in 1984, and *The History of the United States Court of Appeals for the Seventh Circuit, 1891–1941*, which was published by the Seventh Circuit in 1981.

DAVID M. TRUBEK is Dean of International Programs and Studies, Voss-Bascom Professor of Law, and former director of the Institute for Legal Studies at the University of Wisconsin. He has written extensively on social and legal theory, international law, and the civil litigation system. His most recent book is *Consumer Law, Common Markets, and Federalism in Europe and the United States* (1990).

Lawyers' Ideals / Lawyers' Practices

INTRODUCTION

New Problems and New Paradigms in Studies of the Legal Profession

Robert L. Nelson and
David M. Trubek

The American legal profession stands at the crossroads of change. The past two decades have seen profound transformations in its size and demographic composition, in the powers of bar associations, and in the structures and managerial strategies of the organizations through which legal services are provided. Although many of these changes reflect a growth in resources and diversity, the mood in most precincts of the profession is anxious rather than celebratory. The predominant sense seems to be that lawyers, both individually and collectively, have lost control over forces that are reshaping the markets in which they compete, the law firms to which they traditionally devoted their careers, the pace and quality of their work lives, and their status in society.

Emblematic of these fears was the American Bar Association's Commission on Professionalism, also known as the Stanley Commission, which was formed in 1984 to investigate whether there had been a decline in professionalism among lawyers. The announced concern of the commission was "Has our profession abandoned principle for profit, professionalism for commercialism?" (ABA 1986, p. 1). The professionalism campaign launched by the Stanley Commission was widely and swiftly embraced by the bar. A follow-up group was appointed by the ABA to deal with the professionalism problem. Most state and some local bar associations created their own committees, which issued their own reports. The Association of American

* We would like to thank Jerry Van Hoy for research assistance and for critical comments on this essay. Many other scholars gave us helpful suggestions on an earlier draft: Andrew Abbott, Richard Abel, Elizabeth Chambliss, John Esser, Eliot Freidson, Bryant Garth, Alan Paterson, Deborah Rhode, Theodore Schneyer, Carroll Seron, and Ray Solomon.

Law Schools made the issue the theme of an annual meeting. Academics and practitioners produced a significant body of writing on the subject.

To be sure, the rhetoric of decline is hardly new in the American legal profession. Observers have decried the commercialism of the legal profession for over a century (Gordon 1984a, 1988; Solomon, Chapter 4 herein). What was remarkable this time was that the leadership of the organized bar made commercialism a central concern of its rhetoric about declining professionalism and that the resulting crusade struck such a responsive chord among the bar as a whole. In the past, progressive jurists and liberal law professors have chastised the bar for becoming more of a business than a learned, public-oriented profession, and leaders of the bar have sometimes pointed out that a few lawyers ("ambulance chasers") have succumbed to the profit motive. But until the recent campaign it has been unusual for leaders to see commercialism as something affecting the profession as a whole, or for such analyses to prompt such a general response. It seems clear that economic and other forces have brought about major changes in the American legal profession. Although statistics showed that the profession as whole has benefited from these changes, their impact and their implications for professional ideals have caused widespread concern.

Concern does not, however, imply consensus about ideals or their implementation. On the contrary, sharp conflicts between various groups of practitioners have broken out in virtually every public forum in which changes in professional regulation have been proposed, including the latest revision of the profession's ethical code (Schneyer, Chapter 3 herein), debates over rules on multidisciplinary partnerships and the development of nonlegal subsidiaries by law firms (*National Law Journal* 1990a, pp. 1,46; *New York Times* 1989b, p. 27), and even in the Commission on Professionalism itself (Van Hoy 1990). Although the broad issue at the center of many debates is the "professionalism vs. commercialism" dilemma articulated by the commission, there is little agreement on the meaning of important terms or the paths to be taken. Lawyers ask whether the profession should attempt to enforce traditional limitations on the activities of its practitioners or allow them to respond freely to market opportunities. They ask whether law firms should be governed primarily according to economic criteria of profitability or defer to noneconomic factors of collegiality and mutual dependence as well (see, e.g., Gilson and Mnookin 1985, Nelson 1988, Galanter and Palay, Chapter 1 herein). Faced with increasingly divergent choices, lawyers seem uncertain about how to best serve their individual and collective interests.

Scholarship on the legal profession also appears to be at a turning point. It is no coincidence that as the professions have become increasingly significant as an occupational and economic group, the sociology of the professions has undergone a major revival. Eliot Freidson's early work (1970, 1972), which marked the first major American departure from Parsonsian functionalism, and Magali Sarfatti Larson's *The Rise of Professionalism* (1977), which proposed a new paradigm for understanding the historical expansion of the professions, began an intellectual resurgence in theories of the professions. This trend continued with another significant theoretical volume by Freidson (1986) and a major contribution by Andrew Abbott (1988), as well as several empirical accounts of the historical transformation and social organization of various professions and professional subgroups (see, e.g., Starr 1982, Blau 1984, Zussman 1985, Halpern 1988). Among the leading categories of this renaissance were studies of lawyers. John Heinz and Edward Laumann's (1982) survey of Chicago lawyers provided a comprehensive analysis of stratification within the profession. It was followed by research on bar associations (Halliday 1987; Powell 1989), particular species of lawyers, (Epstein 1981; Mann 1985; McIntyre 1987; Landon 1990), and legal services organizations (Katz 1982; Nelson 1988; Spangler 1986). Richard Abel's tour de force, *American Lawyers* (1989), and his and Philip Lewis's comparative compendium, *Lawyers in Society* (1988a, 1988b, 1989), represent the culmination of this now substantial body of research.

Despite the theoretical and empirical accomplishments of recent efforts in the sociology of the professions, a curious gap remains: we know relatively little about the professional ideologies of lawyers and other professionals (see Geison 1983, pp. 3–11). We do not know how lawyers in various organizational and institutional locations throughout the profession see the contexts in which they operate, define the interests they pursue, and perceive obligations they must honor. Do professional education, canons of professional ethics, work organizations, and community context produce the world views of practicing professionals? Does professional ideology inform and reflect the nature of professional work? How, for example, do the professional ideologies of lawyers shape and reflect the decision-making processes of the legal institutions and organizational contexts in which they practice?

The relative inattention to the "professional" consciousness of lawyers seems particularly surprising given the increasing emphasis on ideology in other fields of legal studies. Critical legal scholars treat the intellectual products of courts and other legal actors as contingent and situated cultural constructions, rather than as the outcomes of a deterministic logical system. A central problem for their approach is understanding why at certain times certain cultural constructions come to be seen as conventional or authoritative. Sociolegal scholars have begun to explain the ideology of legal actors, as well as the legal ideology of laypersons, through the analysis of the discourses these actors use in making legal claims or authoritative pronouncements (see, e.g., O'Barr and Conley 1985, Mather and Yngvesson 1981, Silbey and Merry 1986, Mertz 1988, Merry 1990).[1] This trend within legal studies is properly seen as part of a larger movement within the social sciences and the humanities to analyze how individual and institutional actors construct systems of meaning that take on the appearance of external reality and thus, self-referentially, influence the behavior of the actors that constructed them (see Wuthnow 1987, Meyer and Rowan 1978, DiMaggio and Powell 1983, Scott 1987, Coombe 1989, pp. 92–103 and references).

With few exceptions, neither critical legal scholarship nor sociolegal research has confronted the ideologies of lawyers themselves: the views they hold about the nature of their work, their relations to clients and each other, and the way they should organize their firms. As a result, we have not developed a scholarly apparatus to explain the role of professional ideology in the dramatic changes taking place in the social organization of lawyering or the reactions of various segments of the bar to these developments.

We hope to correct that oversight in this book. We believe that understanding the transformations occurring in the American legal profession requires attention to both structure and ideology. To make sense of what is occurring one must pay close attention to structural features, such as the class, status and gender characteristics of lawyers, the positions they occupy within the national political economy, and the characteristic institutions they have created to organize and manage the legal services industry. But attention to "structure" alone is insufficient. In the first place, many so-called structural features are themselves changing, as shifts in the domestic and international economy, the demography of the bar, and the economics of practice change. More important for our purposes, attention must also be paid to the ideological dimension—to lawyers' visions of themselves, their roles, and their practices. Such visions play a role in the structures and in the processes by which structural factors are changed over time, for "structure" is not a set of immanent forces operating independently of human agents. The macrolevel developments we observe are in some significant respect the product of the ideological dispositions of lawyers and the elements of society with which they interact. The internationalization of the economy, the explosion in mergers and acquisitions, the intensification of competition among corporate law firms are phenomena that correspond to microlevel shifts in the strategies and norms of governments, private enterprises, and legal actors.

Our strategy is to illustrate the promise of this approach through a set of essays on the American legal profession which propose new paradigms for

1. Also a special issue of the *Law and Society Review* was devoted to studies of law and ideology (1988).

examining the relationship between structure and ideology or which present empirical analyses of structure and ideology in theoretically interesting contexts. The unifying topic is lawyer professionalism: the set of norms, traditions, and practices that lawyers have constructed to establish and maintain their identities as professionals and their jurisdiction over legal work. From different perspectives, the chapters probe the relationship between professionalism and social change. It is not possible to provide a comprehensive account of the relationship between professionalism and the social organization of the legal profession in one book. This is an ambition that can be realized only by a program of research. We hope, nonetheless, to make some progress in this direction and suggest the value of more sustained research on the relationship between professional ideology and social structure, not only in the legal profession but for the professions generally.

In this introductory chapter we lay the groundwork. First, we offer an "interpretive account" of major changes in the collective organization and social structure of the American legal profession and speculate about the relationship between these "structural" shifts and the distinctive character of American legal professionalism. Second, we examine the place of professional ideology in three leading theories of the professions—the functionalist perspective associated with Talcott Parsons (1954), market control or collective project models associated with Larson (1977) and Abel (1989), and the knowledge-based theories of Freidson (1986) and Abbott (1988), noting the strengths and limitations of each. Third, we propose what we call an interpretive framework for the analysis of relationships between professional ideology and structural change. Fourth, we briefly describe how the essays here contribute to a better understanding of the relationship between professionalism and structural change and thereby exemplify the approach we advocate.

We should note at the outset that many of the recent developments within the American legal profession have parallels in other countries (see Abel and Lewis 1989). We decided to focus on American lawyers because the American legal community is the context we know best. We did not feel we could do justice to the analysis of these issues in other societies.

American Legal Professionalism and Its Transformation: An Interpretive Account

Our interpretive account of present concerns with legal professionalism, as well as speculations about future trends in the ideals and practices of

American lawyers, is grounded in the hypothesis that current patterns of change in the profession and the reactions they have engendered are rooted in a contradiction in the character of the professional ideology of American lawyers. Even though a variety of factors have contributed to the transformations taking place, including many exogenous to the profession, much of the current crisis *in* the American legal profession has been produced *by* the American legal profession. Three features in particular of the practice of law in America seem to be the source of these strains: (1) the entrepreneurial character of American lawyers, (2) the absence of formal differentiation within the bar and the corresponding institutionalization of the bar as a professional unity, and (3) the extreme de facto segmentation of the profession according to types of clients represented and the social and educational characteristics of lawyers. The combination of these elements has enabled the profession to grow remarkably, given rise to recurrent tensions about the nature and practical implications of professional ideals, and exacerbated these tensions to near-crisis proportions.

Legal Entrepreneurialism

As many commentators have observed, a hallmark of American lawyers has been their protean entrepreneurial spirit (generally, see Abel and Lewis 1989, Galanter 1983). They have promoted a distinct, instrumentalist conception of law as a mechanism for meeting changing social conditions (Hurst 1950; Friedman 1985), have been unusually active in local and national politics (Nelson et al. 1987) and, with some exceptions, have endorsed—and even championed—a major expansion of public legal services, examples being public defender systems and legal services for the poor (Abel 1989, pp. 130–34). American legal history is replete with examples of innovations in legal forms that private practitioners have crafted and legitimated through judicial and legislative processes (Gordon 1982, Friedman 1973, pp. 580–83; Powell 1987). Some commentators suggest that American lawyers expanded the jurisdiction of their legal work to encompass the financial needs of corporations more readily than did the legal professions of other countries (Abbott 1988, pp. 247–79; but see Sugarman 1991).

Perhaps what is most distinctive about American lawyers is the zeal with which they have developed new organizational forms for capturing particular segments of the market for legal services or for capitalizing on the economic opportunities presented by particular legal problems. Through their adaptive, expansionist approach to practice, U.S. lawyers have contributed a series of innovations to the international scene, including the large law firm, litigation networks, legal clinics, group plans, and the kind of risk-taking in the representation of injured parties encouraged by the contingent fee system (Galanter 1983; Dezalay 1990). When Paul Cravath developed his famous system for organizing corporate law practice, he did so with a keen eye toward the market for corporate legal services. Attacks on the commercialism of current practices should not mislead us into thinking that the Cravath firm was practicing law as a charity in the 1920s! The goals and managerial strategies of today's large firms may be more explicitly profit-oriented than those of their predecessors, but the current practices that have raised alarm are hardly a radical departure from an entrepreneurial tradition that goes back to the last century.

Unitary but Weak Professional Associations

Unlike in European countries, where formal distinctions are made among categories of lawyers according to education, career options, and professional privileges (such as the English distinction between solicitors and barristers), in America lawyers have adhered to the conception of a unitary bar with no formal intraprofessional distinctions.[2] Despite this insistence on unity, the profession's associations appear increasingly irrelevant to the actual organization of law practice. The basic state-licensed monopoly of lawyers over legal work remains largely intact. Although this monopoly shapes the political economy of lawyering, especially in the personal client sphere, bar associations no longer have the power to prevent lawyers from advertising or setting minimum fee schedules (Abel 1989, pp. 112–26), and in most states have lost exclusive power to discipline members (Powell 1986). The internal politics of national, state, and local bar associations have become so fragmented by the proliferation of specialized practice groups that the bar is often unable to take a unified position on issues of self-regulation (Schneyer, Chapter 3 herein; Heinz and Laumann 1982, pp. 232–73). Perhaps the most telling weakness of the organized bar has been its inability to control entry to the profession. For one hundred years, the bar has tried to limit growth by raising admission requirements. Abel (1989, p. 227) argues that these efforts were largely successful from the late 1920s to 1960 (generally, see Auerbach 1976). But nothing has curbed the steady expansion of the profession in recent years. Since 1970 the lawyer population has almost tripled (Curran et al. 1985a, p. 5).

2. Formal recognition of the split between corporate and personal client lawyers was proposed in the Reed Report in 1920, but was rejected by the American Bar Association (Auerbach 1976, pp. 110–12).

The Continuing Tale of Two Professions

Officially one, the bar is actually sharply stratified by the types of clients served. This division correlates with lawyer income and status. In their study of Chicago lawyers, Heinz and Laumann documented the existence of "two hemispheres" within the legal profession: one made up predominantly of upper-class, high-status lawyers educated in elite law schools, who represent corporations and work in high-prestige areas of law; the other composed predominantly of lawyers from the lower classes and ethnic and religious minorities, educated in local and night law schools, who represent individual clients and work in low-prestige areas of law (1982, pp. 109–18). To understand changes occurring among American lawyers, one must keep this fundamental division in mind.

Distributional Shifts across Sectors

An account of structural shifts in the legal profession is quite literally a tale of two professions, both with respect to the gap between the two hemispheres and in terms of developments within these sectors. The legal services industry as a whole has been a remarkable economic success: it added over $60 billion to the gross national product in 1987, twice the share of the national income legal services commanded in 1970. Legal services is now a larger industry than the steel or textile industry (Sander and Williams 1989, pp. 435–46). But indicators suggest that this prosperity has not been shared equally across the profession.

First, demand for legal services in the corporate client sector of the profession has increased almost twice as fast as demand in the personal client sector. Between 1967 and 1982 the percentage of law firm receipts generated by individual clients as opposed to business or government clients declined from 55 percent to 44.5 percent (Sander and Williams 1989, p. 441). While total revenue from individuals grew at a rate of 4.7 percent, the growth rate for revenue from business was 8 percent (these rates have been adjusted for inflation).

Second, the gap between the incomes of lawyers in the corporate sector and those who serve individuals has grown. Both sole proprietors and law firm partners experienced growth in real income between 1960 and 1972, with average earnings in 1972 of $37,351 and $91,874 respectively. The average earnings of sole proprietors dropped to a low of $20,069 in 1982 before rebounding to $25,339 in 1985, while partners' earnings fell to a low of $76,002 in 1981 before rebounding to $88,493 in 1985. Thus in 1961 sole proprietors (who clearly belong to the personal client sphere) made some 43 percent as much as law partners (who represent a more mixed group), but in 1985 they made only 28 percent as much.[3]

Third, the demand for lawyers to work for corporations has been strong relative to supply, whereas the demand for lawyers in the individual client area relative to supply has been weak. Richard Sander and Douglas Williams found that the decline in the incomes of sole proprietors between 1972 and 1982 was closely associated with the rapid rise in their number (1989, pp. 468–69). This evidence also suggests that in the period immediately following the low point in sole proprietor income, 1983 to 1987, an unexpectedly large number of lawyers dropped out of the profession. The clear implication is that there is substantial underemployment in the personal client sphere. At the opposite end of the spectrum, the labor market for new entrants to corporate law firms, we find the opposite picture. The shortage of graduates from elite law schools has led to startling increases in associate salaries, from an average in New York law firms of $14,000 in 1967 to over $80,000 in 1987 (Sander and Williams 1989, p. 474).

For the profession as a whole, today is truly both the best of times and the worst of times. The corporate sector is attracting a growing share of the total expenditures on legal services. This has resulted in a dramatic expansion in the size of law firms and the overall earnings of large-firm lawyers. The personal client hemisphere, in contrast, has been flooded with cohorts of young law graduates, and average earnings have declined substantially. The personal client sector is a vast and varied region and no doubt contains many successful lawyers, but there are unmistakable indications of overall economic decline. Ironically the success of the corporate sector may be directly contributing to the problems of oversupply in the personal client sector. Sander and Williams speculate that reports of high starting salaries at elite law firms have stimulated law school attendance, even though only the top 10 to 20 percent of law school graduates have realistic prospects of landing such positions (1989, pp. 465–67). Thus the social and economic distance between the two major segments of the American legal profession is increasing.

Redistribution within the Corporate Sector

Even within the corporate hemisphere, we find indications of a best/worst scenario. Although many large corporate law firms have achieved extraordi-

3. This change over time should be interpreted cautiously. Given the considerable growth of the profession during this period, particularly in the personal client sphere, there is a chance that the shifting age profiles of the two groups may have contributed to the growing divergence in their earnings. If the mean age of sole practitioners declined more than the mean age of partners, we would be comparing a younger group with an older group at the end of the period under scrutiny.

nary success, with partner earnings averaging over $1 million annually (*The American Lawyer* 1990) and rapid growth in size, number of branches, and national prestige, in many respects the once secure world of corporate law has become uncertain and acrimonious. Several prominent firms have suffered significant economic reversals (Nelson 1988, p. 49), closed, or gone bankrupt in recent years (*National Law Journal* 1990b; *Wall Street Journal* 1988; *New York Times* 1988; *Chicago Tribune* 1988). Because of the intensely competitive environment for corporate legal services, many observers anticipate that some firms will come to dominate the national market for premium corporate work, and others will be relegated to a lesser status as regional firms (Brill 1989). As a result of the increasing costs of associate salaries and major capital outlays for office space and computer technology, many firms face a squeeze on partnership profits. The Price-Waterhouse survey of law firms (1989) suggests that average partnership profits in firms of one hundred lawyers or more, after adjusting for inflation, did not increase from 1978 to 1987. Stagnant profit levels in the aggregate can only mean that partnership profits declined in many of the firms surveyed.[4]

As Marc Galanter and Thomas Palay (Chapter 1 herein) note, such pressures have had enormous effects on the professional lives of lawyers working in corporate firms. Compensation and access to participation in decision making depend more and more on one's ability to attract new business. Everyone is being pressured to bill increased hours. Junior members face declining prospects for making partner at all and longer waiting periods before even being considered for partnership. Unproductive partners face the threat of removal from partnership status. The industry as a whole is experiencing rising levels of turnover at all levels coupled with increasing reliance on lateral hiring into the associate and partner ranks and the introduction of more elaborate administrative and managerial structures for monitoring performance and coordinating work activities.

These changes alter the career prospects for all new entrants into the large corporate law firms. This generation of associates faces stiffer barriers to advancement than their predecessors did. This lessening of career opportunities is a particular hardship for women, minorities, and some graduates of lower-status law schools, who are entering the corporate law sector for the first time. Earlier generations of large law firm associates were predominantly white male graduates of elite law schools, but women are now proportionately represented at the entry level in many large firms, and

4. As we noted, in a period of rapid growth, a larger proportion of partnerships may consist of younger partners who have lower earnings levels. Ideally we should control for age effects across the time period.

minorities and graduates of lower-status schools are being hired as well. It is too soon to tell just how well these newer entrants will do in the "up or out" scramble for the top positions in corporate law firm hierarchies. There is evidence that women and lower-status law school graduates are more likely to leave large firms than other associates (Nelson 1988, p. 139; also see Hirsch 1989, Menkel-Meadow 1989, Kahler 1988, Hazard 1988). Minorities constitute a tiny proportion of the partners of large firms (Aguilar 1990). The increased hours firms are demanding from associates will probably have a disproportionate effect on women of childbearing age. Given the continuing tendency for women to shoulder more responsibility for childcare than their husbands (Hochschild 1989; Epstein 1981), women are likely to face having to choose between professional advancement and participation in family life (see also Holmes 1988).

The Demise of Professionalism?

These major changes in the legal services industry lie behind the current concerns over the "demise of professionalism." The structural changes we have outlined have created a climate in which bar leaders feel a need to question rising commercialism, yet do relatively little concrete about this concern. We think that the breadth of concern over declining professionalism and the shallowness of the response to an alleged crisis can be understood if they are placed in context.

Recent trends in the legal services industry have not changed any of the major parameters of the "political economy" of the American legal profession. It continues to be highly stratified, and all indicators are that segmentation will continue and intensify. The legal profession will continue to maintain control over its core "jurisdiction." Although lawyers face some challenges from the do-it-yourself movement at the bottom end of the pyramid and from accounting firms and management consultants at the top, the legal profession as a whole has been quite successful in preserving its monopoly over services for which demand is growing (Powell 1985; Freidson 1983). Finally, American lawyers continue—as they have for over a century—to restructure their practices and reorganize their firms to meet changing market conditions and exploit new economic opportunities.

The latter aspect of the political economy of lawyering in America is especially important for the interpretation of the current scene. It is clear that many dramatic changes are occurring within the legal services industry, but it is also the case that these changes are largely brought about by the lawyers themselves, not imposed by government policy or organized client pressure.

This is most obvious in the shifts taking place within the industry, where lawyers are clearly the agents of change. To be sure, some of these transformations are responses to client demands and altered market conditions, but they have come about through the self-conscious behavior of lawyer-entreprenuers. Whether they are managing partners of large law firms (see Nelson 1988, Galanter and Palay, Chapter 1 herein), the organizers of national legal services firms or group legal plans (Seron, Chapter 2 herein), or small-firm practitioners who rely heavily on advertising, these entrepreneurs have brought about basic changes in the way lawyers get clients, organize their workplaces, and advance their professional careers.

These efforts to restructure the legal services industry have been facilitated by a changed regulatory climate that weakened the already mild set of constraints that government and the organized profession placed on the practice of law. Although these changes occurred during a general period of deregulation, it is important to note that most of the impetus for them came from the lawyers themselves. Michael Powell has studied a variety of regulatory changes, including the collapse of prohibitions on advertising, minimum fees, and group legal service plans; the increase in legal malpractice litigation; the transfer of the power to discipline lawyers from bar associations to state agencies; and the Securities and Exchange Commission's actions to discipline infractions by lawyers. He found that lawyers were behind these attacks on traditional professional regulation and concluded that the trends were primarily the result of "competing segments of the bar [seeking] to protect their interests and promote their particular views of professional responsibility. The emergence of new, or strengthened, market, client, and government controls over legal practice was in large part a consequence of the actions of different groups of lawyers" (Powell 1985, p. 298).

As Rayman Solomon (Chapter 4 herein) suggests, the speeches of contemporary bar leaders on the topic of professionalism reflect a new, if still largely unfocused, sense that the ferment within the profession is the work of "an enemy within." We argue that this has always been the case, that the combination of entrepreneurial tendencies, weak unitary associations, and client-based segmentation continually recreates the tension between professionalism and commercialization. The profession has always, if not always willingly, attempted to adapt law and professional practice to changing social conditions. This very process brought about today's deep segmentation of the legal profession into groups of practitioners with little in common in terms of the clients they represent, the fields in which they are active, the nature of their social and educational backgrounds, and the strategies they must employ to sustain themselves economically.

The bar nonetheless has continued to portray itself as a unitary profession in the service of a unitary legal system. In an earlier era the elite of the profession may have controlled bar associations to such a degree that they could present their conception of professional ethics as that of the entire profession (Carlin 1966; Auerbach 1976). In recent years it has become apparent that no single group can lay uncontested claim to the leadership of the bar's collective institutions and thereby impose a single set of professional ideals or values. The only kind of association that can now house the diverse elements of the profession is one that imposes a minimum of collective regulation (see Schneyer, Chapter 3 herein, on the veto power of various groups within the bar concerning proposed changes in the rules of professional ethics). The organized bar has been neither willing nor able to resist the entrepreneurial pressures of the various segments of the profession "under its control."[5]

It is in this sense that American legal professionalism has brought about its own demise. The key to the economic and political success of American lawyers as a group has been their adaptiveness. But the cost has been the erosion of a distinctive professional tradition and the absence of centralized power within the profession capable of enforcing a particular vision of professional ideals.

The current "crisis" in professionalism reflects an intensification of these long-standing tendencies in response to the climate created by the broad political and economic changes of recent years. The deregulation of finance and business, the internationalization of economic exchange, the rise of litigation among corporate actors, and the continued expansion of demand for legal services by the middle class has unleashed the entrepreneurial inclinations of American lawyers. These lawyer-entrepreneurs introduced a series of innovations of scope and breadth unparalleled either in our own history or in comparative perspective. This "rationalization" of legal services has produced unprecedented wealth for the legal profession in general, but the inequality of income and opportunity it engendered has given rise to a sense of disquiet among many lawyers in particular. The very expansion of the profession has weakened its already dubious standing in the public's eye. The widely publicized complaints about too many lawsuits and too many lawyers, many of which were made by legal elites of one stripe or another (such as former chief justice Burger and Derek Bok, the former dean of

5. For example, despite the urging of former chief justice Warren Burger, the Stanley Commission chose not to denounce general legal advertising or the franchise law firms (e.g., Hyatt Legal Services) who pioneered the use of television for advertising (Van Hoy 1990, p. 20). Also see Abel 1989, pp. 240–41.

Harvard Law School)(see Galanter 1983, Nelson 1987), no doubt contributed to the fears of the leaders of the organized bar that the profession was losing the very legitimacy that protected it from attacks on key aspects of its professional monopoly. Jerry Van Hoy (1990) suggests that these concerns figured prominently in the establishment of the ABA Commission on Professionalism. The "losers" in the changing markets for legal services—the firms being eclipsed by newly emergent organizational competitors and the individuals within firms (even successful ones) being displaced by new cohorts of rainmaking partners—mourned the loss of status and income. But even the "winners" in the transformed markets and organizations, while exulting over their ascendance, might have realized that in the new era of "eat what you kill" compensation practices and "bake off" competitions for new business meant that theirs was a perilous position. Being on "top of the iceberg" today was no guarantee they would not be "pushed off the iceberg" tomorrow.

To be sure, many within the legal profession might have preferred stable markets and stable relationships guided by "professional" rather than commercial values. But this option was not available in the last twenty years—and has never really been available in recent history. The bar is too fragmented to agree on what relationships and values should be fostered. It has been too tolerant of entrepreneurship and too leery of effective professional association or governmental control to develop truly powerful regulatory mechanisms. The concerns of both the losers and at least some of the winners in the recent growth and restructuring of the industry made it important for bar leaders to say something comforting about professionalism and its value as an integrating element for the profession. The general sense that lawyers had lost control of their markets, workplaces, and careers has created a climate in which such rhetoric finds a ready audience. But a long tradition of entrepreneurship, segmentation, and weak control makes it impossible for the leaders of the bar to say or do anything significant about the trends they decry. The result is a vague and general invocation of "shared" values that really aren't shared and a symbolic and nostalgic crusade in the name of an ideology almost no one really believes in fully and which has little to do with the everyday working visions of American lawyers.

The substance of what we have presented is admittedly speculative. We hope, however, that this preliminary sketch and the other contributions in this volume suggest both the importance and feasibility of bringing together studies of structural changes in the professions—changes in work patterns, careers, income distribution, organizational forms, and so forth—with studies of professional ideology—of the epistemologies of professional groups and subgroups, of the nature of "professional identity," of the competition among various groups to define professional ideals.[6]

Professional Ideology in Theories of the Professions

Most sociological theory and research on lawyers and other professions draws on one of three theoretical perspectives: functionalism, market control, or knowledge-based professional jurisdictions. Each of these perspectives has made significant contributions to the field, but none have developed an adequate conception of the role professional ideology plays in the organization and operation of professional fields. Functionalists assume that individuals socialized into professional roles take on the appropriate ideological value orientation. Market control theorists reduce professional ideology to an instrument used by a professional elite to achieve market control. The various types of knowledge-based theorists emphasize the ability of professionals to control a body of knowledge and pay little attention to the belief systems of the professionals about their roles and responsibilities.

As we argue more fully in Chapter 5, the structural/functional conception of the professions developed by Talcott Parsons and others (Parsons 1962, 1954; Carr-Saunders and Wilson 1933) saw professional institutions as reflecting the key social functions they were intended to serve (medicine was organized to achieve health; law was organized to achieve rationality and justice). Professional ideology did not enter the functionalist account. Functionalism assumed a close correspondence between formal declarations of professional values, as in codes of professional ethics, and the values actually held by individual practitioners. The mechanisms that insured a proper inculcation of professional values were professional education, socialization and monitoring by professional peers, and the enforcement activities of

6. This book emphasizes the ideologies and practices of lawyers in their social and historical contexts. Studies of the sorts of macrolevel shifts discussed in this section are extremely valuable and very much needed. For example, we still do not understand so basic a phenomenon as the growth in number of lawyers. Sanders and William's (1989) analysis, to which we referred extensively above, is the most current and exhaustive attempt to assess rival hypotheses, but it is admittedly speculative. Moreover, they devote relatively little attention to the forces underlying shifts in the demand for different categories of legal services. Past attempts at examining changing demand patterns (e.g., Pashigian 1978) have failed to produce persuasive accounts. More promising is the work by Galanter and Rogers (1988), who have begun to explore shifting patterns of business litigation—a major source of the recent expansion in corporate law practice. They argue that the rise in business litigation is linked to a broad set of economic changes, especially the declining position of the United States in the world economy, which has had the effect of restructuring relationships among domestic economic actors.

professional associations. These processes produced a "professional role" that both reflected objective and desirable social functions and determined how the individuals occupying these roles actually behaved.

Much of the early empirical work on the professions was aimed at refuting the functionalist model. Everett Hughes and those who followed his tradition, such as Howard Becker, Anselm Strauss, and Rue Bucher, focused on medical education and professional work and debunked the myth that professional behavior was dictated by articulated professional values. Freidson (1970) offered the first systematic theoretical alternative to functionalism, arguing that the organization of the professions should be seen as a form of professional dominance. He demonstrated that the privileges enjoyed by the professions could be better explained by the power they wielded than by the functions they performed. Professional institutions often served the interests of their members better than they served their clients or society. Professionals often portrayed essentially moral or political decisions as matters of professional technique. This literature severely undermined the functionalist assertion that professional roles effectively determined professional behavior and that this behavior furthered desirable social goals. What was less clear in the wake of this critique was whether anything beyond the material interests of professionals and their immediate clients informed professional conduct. The link between professional ideology and the social organization of professional fields was left largely unexplored.[7]

Recent theoretical work has paid more attention to professional ideology. Larson's (1977) influential book proposed a significant elaboration on Freidson's professional dominance perspective by suggesting that the rise of professionalism was the product of a set of collective mobility projects by various professional groups, through which they achieved control over the market for their services. Larson wrote at length about professional ideology, but primarily in the context of her overall model of "collective mobility projects" of entire professions. In her account, and unlike the industrial bourgeoisie, which relied in its rise on the coercive power of the state, the professions depended for their ascent "most crucially on ideological persuasion" (Larson 1977, p. 54). Thus each professional group had to forge a consensus over the central cognitive base from which the group would make its claim to market control. Larson asserted that a professional ideology of individual achievement and expert knowledge was critical to the overall success of professional projects in two respects. First, it provided a mecha-

7. Obviously we are painting with a broad brush here. We do not mean to slight several excellent analyses that offer important insights into professional ideology and its broader significance. See, e.g., Bosk 1979, Lipsky 1980, Katz 1982 (discussed in Chapter 5 herein).

nism for channeling the ambitions of the middle class into the new occupational system capable of meeting capitalism's rising demand for expert labor. Second, it perpetuated a myth of individual responsibility and success in professional work, even though a growing proportion of professionals actually worked in bureaucratic contexts.

Larson's structural account portrays professional ideologies as the constructions of groups seeking to advance their collective status in a given historical period. This approach recognizes that the content of professional ideology is contestable and potentially variable across segments of the professional group. Larson thus acknowledges that "the concrete reference group of the individual professional is more likely to be a specific group of colleagues than the profession at large" (1977, p. 228). Ultimately, however, she embraces the view that the most powerful ideological force within each professional group is that of a unified profession as projected by the profession's elite. She concludes:

> But is there something besides the binding force of economic interest that allows professionals low down in the internal hierarchy to consider themselves *professionals* and thus, at least minimally, the peers of the profession's elites? . . . Professional socialization . . . takes . . . standards defined by the profession's elites and makes them part of each individual's subjectivity. Insofar as this socialization is successful, the elites will be in control not only of material rewards but also of the kind of esteem that counts—esteem granted by a reference group of major importance for the individual. While esteem is, ultimately, easier and cheaper to dispense than power or income, it holds for the recipient something more than the promise of influence; it is intimately bound up with a sense of self, precisely because professions are *ideologically* constructed as occupations that one enters by *calling*, or at least by choice. As such, they appear to express an essential dimension of the self. [Larson 1977, p. 227]

Larson offers a critically insightful reinterpretation of professional socialization: it is a mechanism through which elite definitions of the profession invade the sense of "professional self." This perspective offers market control theorists a ready explanation for the recent professionalism campaign: it is an attempt by the elite of the profession to reinvigorate this mechanism of social control.

Although Larson has identified two critical issues—the hierarchical dimension of professional socialization and the centrality of the professional self to the behavior of professionals—we are not necessarily persuaded by her conclusion that professional identity is so heavily influenced by central professional canons as she believes it to be. As we argue in Chapter 5 herein, professional ideologies are far more situational and context-specific than

Larson's elite-dominance model suggests. The processes of professional socialization are more subtle and less univalent, more fluid and conflictual, and more uncertain in terms of their consequences for how professionals organize their activities than Larson's model implies. Although she may be correct to emphasize the relationship between the instrumental interests of professional elites and the ideology of the professional group, we suggest that the determinants and effects of professional ideology are more complex than the pursuit of market control.

Richard Abel's work shows the same lacuna we found in Larson. Abel has applied Larson's framework to the study of the legal profession in the United States, England, and other common-law countries (Abel 1981b, 1988a, 1988b, 1989c). He asks "how actors seek and attain competitive advantage within a relatively free market—one structured by the state but dominated by private practitioners" (1989, p. 15). This theoretical framework allows Abel to organize an impressive amount of historical and quantitative information on the social organization of lawyers in various societies. In the introduction to *American Lawyers* Abel tells us that he purposely concentrates on quantitative indicators even though such an approach "assumes that the observer knows the meaning of a social practice without asking the actors how they understand their own behavior" (1989, p. 13). He states that he does so, not because it is superior to other approaches, but because he could only do justice to one approach in one book.

This is, however, more than an arbitrary methodological choice. It reveals that Abel shares Larson's emphasis on professional ideology as an instrument for collective control of markets. In this book and elsewhere, Abel dismisses the organized bar's interest in revising ethical codes or in mounting crusades to restore professionalism as a transparent, internally contradictory effort to legitimate the market position of the legal profession (1981a; 1989, pp. 239–45). With this perspective, he obviously has little interest in understanding the cultural frameworks that these elites (much less other lawyers or nonlawyer actors) invoke, manipulate, and reproduce.[8]

Two other major contributions to the professions field, those by Freidson (1986) and Abbott (1988), are focused on the relationship between the expert knowledge professionals hold and the institutional and workplace positions they command. Because Freidson and Abbott assign significant weight to the

8. Abel gives more attention to professional ideology in some of his other writing. In the conclusion of *Lawyers in Society* (1989), he and Lewis write of the need to "put the law back into the sociology of lawyers," which means to bring the knowledge, motivations, and actual practices of lawyers into the account. See also Abel 1985b. Despite these occasional efforts, we cannot ignore the theoretical posture of the five volumes and the numerous articles he has published on lawyers in the last decade.

conscious efforts of various actors within the professions to create and apply systems of expert knowledge, one might expect these analysts to offer a theoretical account of the professional ideologies that arise in the course of developing and deploying expert systems. They do so only to a limited extent.

Freidson argues that the power of the professions cannot be understood merely by analyzing the content of the formal knowledge they develop, but must also take account of how it is applied in the institutional contexts in which professionals work:

> Down at the level of everyday human experience, in schools, prisons, scientific laboratories, factories, government agencies, hospitals, and the like, formal knowledge is transformed and modified by the activities of those participating in its use. Thus the paradox that, while the institutionalization of knowledge is a prerequisite for the possibility of its connection to power, institutionalization itself requires the transformation of knowledge by those who employ it. The analysis of scientific and scholarly texts can be no substitute for the analysis of the human interaction that creates them and that transforms them in the course of using them in a practical enterprise. [1986, p. xi]

It is interesting that professional ideology barely enters Freidson's analysis. He speaks occasionally of the interests professionals bring to their work that may diverge from the demands organizations make of them, but gives only the briefest attention to the origins of these professional interests (see, e.g., Freidson 1986, pp. 169–71). He recognizes that professional groups are often divided internally, which weakens their ability to influence policymaking, but he does not analyze how various segments of the professions develop different agendas. Nor does he examine how the central institutions of professional groups, such as the professional schools or codes of ethics, shape the ideologies of practitioners in various institutional contexts. This is curious, for it would seem that the process central to Freidson's thesis—the transformation of formal knowledge in the practical enterprise—cannot be understood without attention to the world views that practitioners develop in response to professional training, workplace pressures, and the social and institutional context in which the workplace is embedded.

The same is true of Abbott's *The System of Professions* (1988). Abbott proposes an alternative to functionalist and monopolist models of professionalization. Arguing that earlier approaches ignored the uneven, contingent character of the rise and fall, expansion and contraction of various professions, Abbott insists that it is necessary to consider several related professions together as a linked system of potential competitors for various *jurisdictions*, which he defines as the basic sets of problems that conceptual knowledge is developed to deal with. The current structure of professionalism is thus explained as the historical outcome of professional groups making "claims" for jurisdictions before three audiences: the public (where cultural authority is constructed), the law (where the official boundaries of the professional jurisdictions are erected, interpreted, and enforced), and the workplace (where the practitioners actually confront problems). Abbott assigns greatest significance to the nature of the work itself: the success or failure of jurisdictional claims largely rests on the degree to which a professional group can develop a body of knowledge that is sufficiently esoteric that it is not readily appropriated by nonmembers, yet sufficiently systematic that it legitimates the profession's workplace practices. Shifts in jurisdictional boundaries typically begin in the workplace arena and are then worked out in the legal and public arenas. Resistance to jurisdictional changes mounted by traditional incumbents move in the opposite direction: they are initiated in the public and legal arenas to forestall encroachments in the workplace. Professional power, defined as "the ability to retain jurisdiction when system forces imply that a profession ought to have lost it" (1988, p. 136), plays a minor role in Abbott's theory. "[T]he long run of professional development reflects the equilibrating forces [of jurisdictional claims]" (1988, p. 141).

Abbott's book is an enormously creative contribution to understanding the social organization of the professions. As historical narrative it is sensitive to the specific contexts in which professional groups developed, lost, or transformed their workplace jurisdictions. As an account based on equilibrating forces in the competition for work, however, it is relatively indifferent to the ideologies of the professional actors who actually compete. "[W]hile legitimacy values have shifted markedly over the modern history of the professions, and while they differ considerably from country to country, they have surprisingly small effects on the actual history of jurisdiction. New values serve as convenient ideologies for insurgent or new groups, and that appears to be their chief role" (Abbott 1988, p. 195). Abbott explains the jurisdictional claims that professions make almost entirely in terms of external constituencies. To him, it is virtually irrelevant whether the professionals believe the claims they press.

If the content of professional ideology is unimportant in shaping the evolution of the professions, Abbott would be perfectly justified in giving it little weight. Yet there are instances in which the explanatory power of his account is weakened by his failure or refusal to analyze the intentions of historical actors. For example, Abbott devotes a chapter contrasting the fate of English solicitors and American lawyers from the early days of the twentieth century (1988, pp. 247–79). According to Abbott, both professions encountered rapidly rising demand for their services from commercial interests. The solicitors, saddled with an apprenticeship system that could not quickly produce many new lawyers, gave up jurisdictional claims on business functions to accountants and the government and concentrated instead on their monopoly on conveyancing. The American legal profession, which developed a system of legal education that could respond to an expanding demand, made good its jurisdictional claims to business functions, while giving up to title companies certain portions of its monopoly over real estate transactions. American lawyers thus preserved their jurisdictions by a strategy of client differentiation, in which very different sorts of lawyers, organized in fundamentally different ways, served the various parts of the legal services market.

Completely missing from Abbott's narrative is any attempt to examine why one strategy suggested itself to American lawyers and another to English lawyers. The account would be strengthened by an analysis that linked the institutional structures of the professions, the degree to which professional actors exhibited an entrepreneurial ideology, and the organizational arrangements practitioners developed to accommodate demand for their services. Our interpretive analysis of American legal professionalism made a partial, speculative attempt along these lines. Without a broader inquiry, Abbott's interpretation of the differences between the American and English legal professions rests on shaky grounds.

Abbott's inattention to the internal dynamics of professional ideologies may be part of a fundamental difficulty with his analysis: he emphasizes the margins of professional competition over the core of professional practices in the workplace. To be sure, Abbott gives priority to the workplace arena over the public and legal arenas, but only in the context of the argument that a profession must provide workplace solutions to maintain its place in the system of professions. The only reproduction process Abbott is concerned with is for a profession as a whole, rather than for various actors within a profession or a professional organization. Accordingly, Abbott gives little consideration to how partners make out in large law firms, to how Joel Hyatt makes out in a franchise legal services firm, or to how insiders and outsiders fight it out in the context of a local legal community. We and our coauthors contend at many points throughout this book that professional ideology plays a prominent role in the strategies of these various actors. To understand the jurisdictions they claim and their prospects for success in making these claims, one must analyze the professional ideologies that are implicated in these strategies.

An Interpretive Framework

The foregoing suggests the need for an analytic framework that integrates studies of structural and organizational changes with studies of the reactions and perceptions of the actors involved in the changing systems. Central to the approach is the concept of *agency*: that the actions of lawyers reflect choices that are neither totally unconstrained nor totally determined structurally. The choices lawyers make within their professional field, as that field has been shaped by exogenous political and economic forces, are influenced by the "objective" options presented in the current moment and the historically constructed repertoire of "legitimate" or "permissible" professional responses. Our framework links structure and individual action without resorting to the functionalist tendency to reduce individuals to players of fixed roles. The dispositions of various groups of lawyers or their organizations to perceive and act on problems in particular ways reflect, but are not ultimately determined by, the history of the professional group or subgroup. The strategies they develop will, however, "remake" the dispositions of the group for future action at the same time that strategic actions contribute to ongoing trends and developments within the legal profession.

Thus we advocate an interpretive framework for the study of the legal profession that unites political economy and phenomenology and takes into account both structure and agency. Structural accounts that cannot speak to actors or specific mechanisms of change are incomplete, for abstraction above the level of action is open to numerous interpretations and tends falsely to concretize structural features as immutable and beyond the control of human agents. Yet interpretive or phenomenological accounts that are not linked to structural features are also incomplete, for they ignore deeper patterns that shape and explain the frame of conscious action.

Research that attempts to unite these two aspects of social thought necessarily attends to professional ideology, the body of thought and practices through which a profession (or its constituent groups) develops and promulgates ideas about the nature of its work and the identities of its practitioners. Over time, the American bar has constructed an account of the nature of lawyer professionalism that constitutes a key element in the dynamic system we call the legal profession. The norms, traditions, and practices that make up this account serve a variety of purposes. They generate the claims that allow lawyers to maintain jurisdiction over work. They become part of each lawyer's professional identity, to some extent providing coherence and meaning in everyday life and allowing lawyers to respond to new situations in "appropriate" ways. They provide a set of dispositions that lawyers use to interpret their situations and orient their choices according to an internalized world view that delimits but does not necessarily determine action.

Professionalism, in this sense, relates to the overall system of action of the legal profession in two senses. It reflects overall "structural" conditions, and it contributes to the development of structural possibilities. Our understanding of professionalism thus straddles the divide between "hypothetical ideals" and "material realities." We see professional ideals partly as formed within the workplace and partly as designed, consciously or unconsciously, by lawyers for the promotion of their economic, power, and status goals. Thus lawyers' "ideals" carry within themselves heavy traces of what we have called "structure." But they also can be seen as sets of dispositions that have a logic partially independent of the structures that produced them. They may, therefore, become the object of competition among individual or collective actors who seek to appropriate (or perhaps accommodate) elements of a professional tradition in order to advance a particular mode of professional organization or pursue other objectives.

The interpretive framework we recommend has a substantial intellectual pedigree in cultural anthropology and sociolegal scholarship. We have been significantly influenced by Pierre Bourdieu's theory of practice (1977). Bourdieu assails the bright-line distinction between structure and consciousness common in social theory. His notion of *habitus* seeks to mediate between these concepts: habitus is the set of orderly predispositions actors possess as a result of their historical and social locations. While individual actors may be only partially aware of them, these predispositions manifest in many ways, including styles of dress, speech, and bodily presentation. They form a schema in which individuals instantiate the status-class composition of society. Habitus will vary across generations, can change in response to material conditions, and is indeterminate in any particular instance of strategic behavior by individuals. Yet habitus tends to produce behavior in individuals that reproduces the very system from which it emerged. "Professionalism," as we use the term, is part of the habitus of the professional field (see also Coombe 1989).

Our interpretive framework also draws on the emerging study of legal ideology and consciousness, a major development in legal studies generally. This approach recognizes that ideological predispositions account for behavior and appreciates the need to examine these phenomena in relationship to broader societal structures through the detailed investigation of micro encounters (see, e.g., Mather and Yngvesson 1981, Silbey and Merry 1986). It also presents the ideologies of legal actors as complex and contradictory, which allows considerable room for maneuver by the individual and collective actors who participate in any given domain of the legal system. This ideological approach has just begun to influence research on lawyers and lawyering. Nonetheless, the contributions of Robert Gordon (1983, 1984b, 1988), William Simon (1978, 1988), Stewart Macaulay (1979), and Austin Sarat and William Felstiner (1986, 1988) illustrate the possibilities of studying the ideologies of lawyers in practice, and we have drawn on them in our interpretation of professionalism.[9]

The Present Volume

The contributors to this book have reconceptualized the role of professional ideology in the study of the legal profession. In the chapters to follow, these authors demonstrate the heterogeneity of contemporary law practice and the variety of professional ideologies espoused by lawyers working in disparate contexts. They focus on the extent to which these professional visions *reflect as well as shape* the changing organization of law practice. These authors attend to the social construction of professional ideology and explore the institutional and organizational features that frame this constructive enterprise. They show how agency may play a role in the emerging legal profession of the future. Collectively they suggest that the "crisis of professionalism" is not, as some spokespersons in the professionalism crusade seem to argue, the result of a decline in values, but rather the reflection of complex changes that have produced a number of competing scripts for the content of professionalism. They suggest that in this context there are opportunities for entrepreneurs, moral or economic, to reshape professional organization.

The chapters in Part I examine the tensions between traditional professional ideals about how to organize law practice and the evolving realities of modern professional organizations. Galanter and Palay analyze these changes in the context of elite corporate law firms. For much of this century elite firms seemed to exemplify the highest form of legal professionalism in the United States. Although the prestige of these firms was closely connected to their representation of business interests, the law partnerships themselves were governed by principles of collegiality and professional independence. In this sense they were "above business." Galanter and Palay document how

9. The interpretive framework we have set forth here offers only a general outline of how to study the relationship between structure and ideology. In Chapter 5 we suggest a more concrete approach: the analysis of "arenas" of professional ideology.

the stable, traditional world of corporate law practice has been transformed since the 1970s. The imperative of rapid growth, which the authors assert is inherent in the promotion-to-partnership form, has led firms to engage in competitive behavior and styles of practice that would have been deemed ungentlemanly, indeed unprofessional, only a few years before. Moreover, the rush to growth has begun to put pressure on the promotion-to-partnership form itself.

Galanter and Palay look at tensions between professionalism and economic change in the context of a traditional professional organization; Carroll Seron focuses on innovative professional organizations—franchise law firms, prepaid legal services plans, and legal clinics. Seron finds that the lawyers managing and working in the "new providers" take pride in their role as mavericks within the profession. But an important component of the ideology of these new entrepreneurs is a goal to which the legal profession has long been officially committed: to increase the access of ordinary citizens to legal services. Some of Seron's findings support the view of various critics that legal training is not required to provide many kinds of rudimentary legal services to individuals, but she also shows how consumers and lawyers connected with the new providers remain attached to a traditional image of law practice in which an individual lawyer develops a personal relationship with and takes personal responsibility for the needs of his or her clients. It is ironic that while Galanter and Palay describe dramatic changes in a bastion of professional tradition, Seron finds a heavy residue of tradition in nontraditional practice settings.

The chapters in Part II examine the role that debates about professionalism play in the collective politics of the profession. Schneyer analyzes the politics surrounding the development, modification, and passage of the ABA's Model Rules of Professional Conduct. Schneyer's account cannot be readily explained by those critics of professional ethics who dismiss such codes as the product of professional conspiracies to maintain a monopoly over practice. Schneyer finds that a broad range of perspectives influenced the debates over the Model Rules. Several provisions provoked substantial conflict among different segments of the bar and were greatly modified before eventual adoption. The history of the debate on the Model Rules thus reflects the diversity of symbolic and material interests within the collective bodies of the legal profession. This diversity makes it difficult to arrive at consensus on general self-regulatory principles for the entire profession.

Solomon's chapter considers the degree to which the rhetoric of professional crisis is unique to the current period. Based upon an extensive review of publications and speeches by bar leaders from 1925 to 1960, Solomon concludes that there is a common core in the concept of professionalism as used by leaders of the bar. But he finds that in response to external crises—perceived threats to the legitimacy of the profession—bar leaders emphasize different dimensions of this common concept. Solomon sees the current anxieties about professionalism as different from those of the past. Today bar leaders consider the acquisitiveness of lawyers as the principal threat. Thus, whereas prior crises originated outside the profession, the source of the current crisis is believed to lie within the profession itself.

Part III presents three attempts to reconceptualize or reform professionalism. In the first chapter in this section we outline a framework for conducting future research on professionalism. We argue that professionalism should not be seen as a unitary or fixed set of values, but rather as an ongoing process that defines the normative orientations of lawyers. Different contexts produce different professional ideologies. We suggest that it is useful to conceive of various "arenas" of professionalism that will, depending on the political situation in the arena at any given time, generate different formulations of professional ideology. We then apply this arenas approach to the Stanley Commission's Report on Professionalism and some of the work settings of lawyers analyzed in the existing literature to underscore the initial observation that the professional ideologies of lawyers vary significantly by historical and practical context. It follows that future research on social change within the profession will benefit from analyzing the mechanisms that operate within professional arenas to create, sustain, and change the professional ideologies of lawyers.

The final two chapters argue for programs of change within the professions. Eliot Freidson, a leading sociologist of the professions, suggests that it would be valuable for professional groups to confront honestly the advantages and disadvantages of professional self-regulation compared to alternative systems: the market, on the one hand, and bureaucratic regulation, on the other. Such critical debate might force the professions to change some patterns of internal governance. But, Freidson writes, candid self-evaluation provides a better response to advocates of free market and regulatory approaches than the current tendencies of professional groups to resist change by mouthing the ideology of professionalism. Similarly, Gordon and Simon, two major commentators on the social accountability of lawyers, posit that professional ideals play a significant part in the identities of practitioners. They call for efforts by various institutions within the profession, such as law schools, bar associations, and law firms, to develop programs to reinforce and give practical effect to the ideals of professionalism.

A similar "professionalism project" articulated at the conference that led to this volume is the effort by some feminist scholars to critique dominant professional norms as "masculinist" and thus incompatible with feminist ideals and inhospitable to the aspirations of many female lawyers. This feminist project includes critiques of some forms of adversarial lawyering (Menkel-Meadow 1985) and of workplace norms incompatible with personal values and family concerns (Holmes 1987). While we were unable to secure a chapter offering a feminist perspective on professionalism, we expect that much can be learned from feminist theories of professionalism. As increasing numbers of female lawyers confront the previously male bastions of law practice, a future project for practicing lawyers and the scholars who study them will be to examine the gendered character of legal institutions.

Conclusion

To return to the metaphor with which we began, the sociology of lawyers is at the crossroads of change. It confronts a rapidly changing set of phenomena with new theoretical frameworks and new methods of research. We believe that a program of research that seeks to unify studies of professional ideals and professional practices can contribute significantly to the emerging lines of inquiry. In that sense we hope this book is not an end, but a beginning.

PART I
LAWYERS' PRACTICES IN TRANSITION

Arguably the two fastest-changing organizational contexts in the profession are corporate law firms and the so called new providers—legal clinics, national legal services firms, and group plans. Located at opposite ends of the status hierarchy of the profession, these organizations are scenes of active ferment in the definition of professionalism. The chapters in this section thus offer especially interesting insights into the relationship between professional ideology and organizational change.

Galanter and Palay argue that the apparent continuity in the traditional form of the corporate law firm belies a fundamental transformation in the principles that govern its operation. According to Galanter and Palay, the defining characteristic of the traditional corporate firm was the system of promotion to partnership, in which a select subset of associates were made partner after proving their ability for several years. They first describe the "golden age" of the promotion to partnership system, circa 1960, when law firms enjoyed stable relationships with clients and associates could look to the firm as a reliable source of increasing income, responsibility, and professional status. They then suggest that in the early 1970s a built-in imperative for exponential growth, coupled with the "external shocks" of legal and economic change, produced a dramatic rise in the demand for corporate legal services. These forces began to undermine the traditional structure. Galanter and Palay interpret several trends in the personnel policies of law firms as representing movement away from a strict promotion to partnership pattern: the increasing use of paralegals, the lengthening of the number of years to partnership, the addition of nonequity partners, and the revival of "permanent" associates as a legitimate category. These and other changes may have deleterious effects on traditional professional values of collegiality and independence from clients. Yet the authors predict that law firms will react to new pressures by developing a plurality of nontraditional organizational forms.

Seron's chapter presents a contrasting scenario, for she seems to find the continuing significance of traditional professional norms, even traditional forms of the division of lawyers' work, in otherwise explicitly bureaucratic, nontraditional legal services organizations. Seron presents the results of preliminary research into the internal organizational arrangements of new providers, organizations that became possible only in the 1970s with the dismantling of professional rules limiting advertising, price competition, and prepaid legal services. Since they are mavericks in the market for individual legal services, one would expect these organizations to espouse a view of professionalism that accentuates both entrepreneurial and consumer oriented values. Seron finds this to be the case. Both the leaders and the rank-and-file lawyers Seron interviewed saw themselves as giving a public service by providing cost efficient legal services to groups that might otherwise not have access to lawyers. Yet in many respects the organization of law practice in the new providers is not very different from what we find in traditional law firms. Some new providers, like the old, appear to rely on the ambitions of individual lawyers to generate large billings. In an attempt to counter high turnover rates, they have begun to experiment with incentive systems and career advancement programs that bear some resemblance to the opportunities offered in traditional law partnerships. Moreover, the organizers of prepaid plans discovered through market research that consumers preferred a traditional lawyer-client relationship: a lawyer with whom they could develop a personal relationship, working in a small office, in a convenient location. These plans have attempted to meet these preferences by assembling networks of already established, small law firms, who agree to provide legal services at set, discounted rates to plan subscribers.

Seron's research suggests that it is too early to tell whether the new providers will transform the way legal services are provided to individual clients. Although new organizational forms have gained a modest foothold in the marketplace, neither in their internal organization of work nor their perception of client preferences are these new providers as different from other small-firm practitioners as might have been expected. The more pervasive change in the personal client hemisphere may derive from the increasing use of advertising by small firms and the rapid diffusion of computer supported office systems. These changes could affect how traditional producers market and produce their services without significantly altering the kinds of organizations that populate the personal client sector.

CHAPTER ONE

The Transformation of the Big Law Firm

Marc Galanter and
Thomas Palay

The big law firm has been with us for almost a century. It is, in a Darwinian sense, a success story. Big firms are flourishing. There are more of them, they are bigger, they command a bigger share of an expanding legal market. The big law firm is also a success in a deeper sense, as a social form for organizing the delivery of comprehensive, continuous, high-quality legal services. Like the hospital in the practice of medicine, the big firm established the standard format for delivering complex services in the practice of law. Many features of its style—specialization, teamwork, continuous monitoring on behalf of clients, representation in many forums—have been emulated in other vehicles for delivering legal services. The specialized boutique firm, the public-interest law firm, the corporate law department—all model themselves on the style of practice developed in the large firm. Even legal professions in other countries are emulating the American big firm.

Until recently, the big law firm was not only accounted a success in terms of institutional survival and technical performance, it was acknowledged as

An earlier, more detailed version of this chapter appeared as chaps. 1–4 in Marc Galanter and Thomas Palay, *Tournament of Lawyers: The Transformation of the Big Law Firm* (Chicago: University of Chicago Press, 1991), copyright © 1991 by the University of Chicago, and the material is used here by permission of the University of Chicago Press. We thank Elizabeth Barbour, Linda Jurgella, Jacob London, and Kevin Sweeney for able research assistance and Richard Abel, James Atleson, Peter Carstenson, Neil Komesar, Scott Masten, and Michael Powell for their helpful commentary, suggestions and bibliographic help. We also received valuable guidance from participants in the symposium "Rehnquist Revisited: The Growth of Large Law Firms and Its Effect on the Legal Profession and Legal Education" held at the Indiana University School of Law, Bloomington, 9–10 March 1988. We are also indebted to Michael Morgalla for unflagging library support and Brenda Storandt for dedicated and efficient preparation of the manuscript.

the paradigm of legal professionalism. Scarcely a generation ago, Jerome Carlin studied the New York bar and found that large-firm lawyers not only had the largest incomes, served the most affluent clients, and were the best trained and most technically skilled, but experienced "maximum pressure to conform to distinctively professional standards, as well as the more ordinary ethical norms; at the same time they are insulated from pressures to violate [those professional standards]" (Carlin 1966, pp. 168–69). In technical skill, collegiality, and probity, the large firm seemed to provide a venue for the most exemplary professionalism. Ironically, Geoffrey Hazard noted in his foreword to Carlin's book (Carlin 1966, p. xxiii), the traditional badges of the profession—an independent general practice rendering personal service to all sorts of people—were no longer the marks by which the truly "professional" lawyer was identified. Instead it was large firm lawyers who embodied the professional ideal.

Since then, these big firms have continued to flourish. They have become larger, more numerous, more prosperous. There has been no decline in specialization or technical skill. Still, the sense that such firms are the chosen vehicle of the professional ideal has waned. The relationship of the large firm to professionalism now seems quite problematic.

Today, there is a palpable anxiety within the legal profession concerning the commercialization and concomitant decline of professionalism in the setting of the big law firm. Should its robust institutional success lead us to dismiss these misgivings as the tremors of the fainthearted as they experience the further development and consolidation of the big firm as an institution? Such a sanguine response is suggested by the observation that laments about commercialization and the loss of professional virtue have recurred regularly for a century (Gordon 1988, pp. 2–6, 48–59). But we submit that something this time around is different. The present "crisis" is the real thing—not in the sense of marking a decisive break from professional ideals, but in the sense that this discomfort reflects real structural changes over the past twenty years or so that are transforming big firms and their world in fundamental ways.

Our paper describes what has happened to the big law firm. We make little attempt here to explain these changes. Elsewhere we argue that as firms have grown they have simply outpaced earlier methods of monitoring and coordinating personnel, recruiting associates, and generating revenues (Galanter and Palay 1990c, 1991). To survive, they have been forced to adapt by slowing growth, generating new sources of income, remolding existing governance structures, or accepting decreased or at least different profit distributions.

We have also argued that to understand why firms have had to restructure one needs to explain why they grew so fast and why staffing and revenue constraints have begun to restrict their growth. Here too our answer is complex and encompasses changes in what corporate clients demand from law firms, changes in the supply of young lawyers, and the underlying structure of the large law firm. To us, the rapid growth of the large law firm has two components, each responsible for about one-half of the large firm's rapid growth. The first, exogenous to the structure of the firm, accounts for the rapid growth of firms after 1970. The second, endogenous to the firm's governance structure, explains the underlying exponential shape of the growth curves. This latter issue intrigues us particularly, and we have devoted considerable attention to it (Galanter and Palay 1990c, 1991).

We suggest that the big law firm, as presently structured, has a built-in "growth engine" and that roughly half of its recent growth is a by-product of the "promotion to partner tournament" used by law firms to protect the partners' human capital and to motivate the associates. This tournament is essential to the firm's structure and in order to maintain it the firm must grow exponentially. If a firm's required growth outpaces either its revenue base or the relevant supply of labor, further growth becomes impossible without internal change. A firm that does not or cannot grow will be forced to transform itself or will fail.

The transformation we describe below reflects precisely these changes and sets the context for much of the discussion to come in later chapters of this book. We shall examine the origins of the big firm, sketch a portrait of the big firm during its "Golden Age," *circa* 1960, and, finally, describe the transformation experienced by the big law firm since then.

The Emergence of the Big Firm

The big firm and its distinctive style of practice emerged around the turn of the century.[1] The break from earlier law practice can be discussed under the six headings; (1) partners, (2) other lawyers, (3) relations to clients, (4) work, (5) support systems, and (6) new kinds of knowledge. Any of these indicia of the big firm can be found apart from the whole cluster, but it is the clustering hangs of all six that gave the big firm its distinctive institutional character—a character that is changing as these features are rearranged.

Partners: In the big law firm the loose affiliation of lawyers, sharing offices and occasionally sharing work for clients, is replaced by the office in

1. We use the term "firm" throughout when discussing these developments; however, for much of the period discussed here the common term for a company of lawyers was "law office" rather than "law firm."

which clients "belong to" the firm rather than to an individual lawyer. The entire practice of these lawyers is shared by the firm. The proceeds, after salaries and expenses, are divided among the partners pursuant to some agreed upon formula.

Other lawyers: Unpaid clerks and permanent assistants are replaced by salaried "associates" (as we have come to call them) who are expected to devote their full efforts to the firm's clients. A select group of academically qualified associates, chosen on grounds of potential qualification for partnership, are given a prospect of eventual promotion to partnership after an extended probationary period during which they work under the supervision of their seniors, receive training, and exercise increasing responsibility.

Clients: Firms represent large corporate enterprises, organizations, or entrepreneurs with a need for continuous (or recurrent) and specialized legal services that could be supplied only by a team of lawyers. The client "belongs to" the firm, not to a particular lawyer. Relations with clients tend to be enduring. Such repeat clients are able to reap benefits from the continuity and from the economies of scale enjoyed by the firm.

Work: The work involves specialization in the problems of particular kinds of clients. It involves not only representation in court, but services in other settings and forums. The emergence of the firm represents the ascendancy of the office lawyer and the displacement of the advocate as the paradigmatic professional figure. The preference for office work is displayed in the advice of a partner to a young lawyer aspiring to join the predecessor to the Cravath firm: "New York is not a very good field for one who desires to make a specialty of court practice or litigated work. The business connected with corporations and general office practice is much more profitable and satisfactory and you will find that the better class of men at our Bar prefer work in that line" (Swaine 1946, pp. 554–55).

Litigation no longer commanded the energies of the most eminent lawyers. By 1900, Robert Swaine concludes, "the great corporate lawyers of the day drew their reputations more from their abilities in the conference room and facility in drafting documents than from their persuasiveness before the courts" (Swaine 1946, p. 371).[2] In 1908 Roscoe Pound remarked this shift and apprised its consequences for reform: "The leaders of the American bars are not primarily practitioners in the courts. They are chiefly client care-

2. George Gawalt dates the transition even earlier: "By the mid-1880s, the locus of the most elite practice had decisively shifted away from the courtroom to the law office and conference room. The main work of this practice was to serve as legal brokers and intermediaries between large American corporations trying to attract new capital . . . and the investment banking communities of Wall Street and Europe" (1984, p. 59).

takers. . . . Their best work is done in the office, not in the forum. They devote themselves to study of the interests of particular clients, urging and defending those interests in all their varying forms, before legislatures, councils, administrative boards and commissions quite as much as in the courts. Their interest centers wholly in an individual client or set of clients, not in the general administration of justice" (Pound 1909, p. 235).[3]

Support Systems: The emergence of the big firm is associated with the introduction of new office technologies. The displacement of copying, clerks, and messengers by the typewriter, stenography, and the telephone greatly increased the productivity of lawyers.

New Kinds of Knowledge: The proliferation of printed materials—reporters, digests, treatises—rendered obsolete the earlier style of legal research and required mastery of new areas of specialized knowledge. The acquisition of legal skills changed too. Between 1870 and 1910 the portion of those admitted to the bar who were law school graduates rose from one-quarter to two-thirds (Auerbach 1976, p. 25).

The blending of these features into the big law firm as we know it is commonly credited to Paul D. Cravath, who in the first decade of this century established the "Cravath system" of hiring outstanding graduates straight out of law school on an understanding that they might progress to partnership after an extended probationary period, requiring them to work for the firm only, eschewing practices of their own, paying them salaries, providing training and a "graduated increase in responsibility" (Swaine 1946, pp. 2–12; Hobson 1986, pp. 114, 195–203). Though most fully articulated by Cravath—who was blessed with a partner who half a century later wrote the classic law firm history (Swaine 1946) describing the "Cravath system"[4]—the elements of the big firm were also assembled by other innovators, including Louis D. Brandeis (Hobson 1986, p. 186).

The core of the big firm, we submit, is the "promotion to partnership." This is our shorthand for the organization of the firm around the expectation that the junior lawyer can cross the line by promotion and become a partner. Partners and juniors are not equals, but form a hierarchy with command and supervision exercised by partners. But the junior lawyers are neither transient apprentices nor permanent employees. They are peers, fellow profes-

3. Pound remarks the consequences of this for procedural reform: "As the interest of these clients are in the vast majority of cases defensive and procedure is one of the chief weapons of defense, the best, most vigorous and most constructive talent of the profession either neglects practice in the courts entirely or is enlisted in obstructing and defeating litigation" (1909, p. 235).

4. This term is used by his partner, Robert T. Swaine, whose history of the firm (1946) is the classic of the genre.

sionals of presently immature powers, who have the potential to achieve full and equal stature.

Firms can offer this promise only when they are confident that they will attract sufficient work to keep these young lawyers busy. That is, the senior lawyers must have either clients who produce more work than the senior lawyers can handle themselves or a reputation that will attract such clients.[5] Typically, association with a corporation or "super-capitalist" provided the necessary stream of work and "the publicity from serving such clients and the expansive contacts of these clients result[ed] in a growing network of contacts for the emergent firm" (Pinansky 1986–87, pp. 593, 605).

The big law firm—and with it, the organization of law practice around the promotion to partnership pattern—became the industry standard (Hobson 1986, p. 201). Gradually, the older patterns of fluid partnerships,[6] casual apprenticeship, and nepotism were displaced. Law firms grew. In every city, the number of big firms (as big was then defined) increased at an accelerating rate, and over time there were ever-bigger firms. First in New York, then in other large cities, then in smaller cities throughout the county there were more, bigger law firms. This can be seen in Wayne Hobson's compilation of the number of firms with four or more lawyers, which grew from 17 in 1872, to 39 in 1882, to 87 in 1892, to 210 in 1903, to 445 in 1914, to "well over 1000" in 1924 (Hobson 1986, p. 161). As firms grew, the lawyers in them became more specialized and firms began to departmentalize.

Though ascendant in the profession, these successful lawyers were subservient to and dependent on their business clients.[7] From its origins the big firm was haunted by a sense that the profession had compromised its identity and had itself become a branch of business.

By the 1930s, the scale and stability of these firms was recognized in the pejorative term "law factory." The phrase captures not only the instrumentalism, but the systematization, division of labor, and coordination of effort

5. For example, "When the law firm of Shearman & Sterling was established in 1873, Jay Gould promised Shearman that he would take his legal business to the new firm. . . . Gould was more than a rich client that assured the new firm a few large fees. At the time of the establishment of Shearman & Sterling, there were sixty-three cases pending involving Jay Gould. One year later, the figure had risen to ninety-seven" (Pinansky 1986–87, p. 610). On the Jay Gould litigation, see Earle 1963, pp. 30–31, 69–87.

6. Looking back from 1914, Theron Strong observed that "life-long partnerships . . . after all . . . are exceptional and the partnership changes which occur in the course of years are almost as great as the changes of the figures in the constantly turning kaleidoscope" (Strong 1914, p. 360).

7. One contemporary observer describes them as "little more than . . . paid employee[s] bound hand and foot to the service of [the corporation]. . . . [the lawyer] is almost completely deprived of free moral agency and is open to at least the inference that he is virtually owned and controlled by the client he serves" (Strong 1914, pp. 353–54).

introduced by the large firm.[8] The frenetic pace and intense specialization of the large firm repelled many established lawyers. The factory metaphor was felt to identify something about these offices that was profoundly at odds with professional traditions of autonomy and public service.

Circa 1960: The Golden Age of the Big Law Firm

Before the Second World War the big firm had become the dominant kind of law practice. It was the kind of lawyering consumed by the major economic actors. It commanded the highest prestige. It attracted many of the most highly talented entrants to the profession. It was regarded as the "state of the art," embodying the highest technical standards. In the postwar years this dominance was solidified.

To get a reading on the changes over the past generation, we will develop as a baseline a portrait of the big firm in its "golden age" before the transformation that it is now undergoing. This golden age of the big firm, the late 1950s and the early 1960s, was a time of stable relations with clients, of steady but manageable growth, of comfortable assurance that an equally bright future lay ahead—which is not to say that its inhabitants did not look back fondly to an earlier time when professionalism was unalloyed.

New York firms loom disproportionately large in studies of the golden age. New York City was home to a much larger share of big-firm practice then than it is now. In the early 1960s, there were twenty-one firms in New York with fifty or more lawyers and only seventeen firms of that size in the rest of the country (Smigel 1964, pp. 43, 34–35). A few years earlier, the largest firm in New York (and the country) was Shearman & Sterling & Wright with thirty-five partners and ninety associates. Three other Wall Street firms had over a hundred lawyers. The twentieth-largest firm in New York had fifty lawyers (Klaw 1958, p. 194; Smigel 1964, pp. 34–35).

To examine the golden age we compiled data from the *Martindale Hubbell Directory of American Lawyers* on two sets of firms: Group I consists of fifty

8. Some sought to wring further parallels, attributing to large firms the standardization, "robotization," and monotony thought characteristic of factories. In 1939, muckraking journalist Ferdinand Lundberg entitled the last of his series of *Harper's* articles on lawyers, "The Law Factories: Brains of the Status Quo." Lundberg explains that the "term 'law factories,' widely used in the legal profession, may be derisive, but it is accurate. The great law firms are organized on factory principles and grind out standardized legal advice, documents and services as systematically as General Motors turns out automobiles" (Lundberg 1939, p. 182).

firms that were among the largest in 1986; Group II consists of fifty smaller (but still large) firms ranked roughly between two hundredth and two hundred fiftieth in the United States in 1988.[9]

We were able to examine the sizes of thirty-five firms from each group in 1955 and 1965.[10] In 1955, our thirty-five Group I firms ranged in size from 7 to 84 lawyers, with an average size of 40 lawyers. By 1965, their sizes ranged from 13 to 112 lawyers, with an average of 62.6. The thirty-seven firms in Group II ranged from 6 to 35 lawyers in 1955, with an average of 15.8; in 1965, they ranged from 8 to 46 with an average of 25.1 lawyers. This was a period of prosperity and manageable growth for big firms. Over the decade ending in 1965, the Group I firms that twenty years later figured among the fifty largest grew at an annual rate of 5.3 percent. The Group II firms grew at an annual rate of 5.5 percent.[11]

Firms were located in and identified with a single city. An earlier wave of European and Washington offices had been largely abandoned (Smigel 1964, p. 207). "Formation [in 1957] of a nationwide . . . law firm with offices interlocking in Illinois, Washington, D.C. and New York" was startling, "so unusual that it had to be approved in advance by the Bar Association" (Levy 1961, p. 20).

Hiring: Firms were built by "promotion to partnership." Lateral hiring was almost unheard of, and big firms did not hire from one another. Partners might leave and firms might split up, but it didn't happen very often.[12] Hiring of top law graduates soon after their graduation was one of the building blocks of the big firm. Most hiring was from a handful of law schools, and walk-in interviews during the Christmas break were the norm.

9. The two data sets are described in Appendix A of Galanter and Palay, (1991) and presented in their entirety in tables B-1 and B-2 in Galanter and Palay (1990a).

As we discuss in Galanter and Palay (1991), *Martindale Hubbell* is a far from perfect source for data on the size of law firms. Unfortunately, there exists no systematic compilation of law-firm growth statistics. Published data tend to be grossly incomplete and are often constructed from two or more incompatible sources. Because *Martindale Hubbell* and the *National Law Journal* use different methods to count attorneys, the data provided by these sources should not be combined. See Appendix A of Galanter and Palay (1991). To fill the gap in the available data our research assistants have literally counted the names associated with selected firms listed in the Martindale Hubbell directory. Despite the fact that *Martindale Hubbell* systematically undercounts associates, these data sets still surpass anything previously available.

10. All calculations are based on the firms for which data were available for both years in question.

11. Our figures on growth are a little higher than those reported by Smigel (1964, p. 351). He reports that from 1957 to 1962, the number of partners in twenty large New York firms increased by 16% and that the total number of lawyers in the seventeen large firms outside New York had grown by 37% from 1951 to 1961. Since we were looking at firms that succeeded in becoming very large two decades later, it is not unlikely that our sample is biased toward greater growth.

12. The forty-two firms that responded to Siddall (1956, p. 33) had been in existence an average of fifty-eight years. He asked them to detail the "number of splits in the line of succession." Twenty-nine of the forty-two had had none; the other thirteen had undergone a total of 56 splits.

Starting salaries at the largest New York firms were uniform—$4000 in 1953, rising to $7500 in 1963 (Smigel 1964, p. 58). The "going rate" was fixed at a luncheon, attended by managing partners of prominent firms, held annually for this purpose (Smigel 1964, p. 58; Mayer 1966, p. 332).

Historically, the big firms had confined hiring to white Christian males.[13] Few African-Americans and women had the educational admission tickets to contend for these jobs. But there were numerous Jews who did and, with a few exceptions, they too were excluded.[14] This exclusion began to break down slowly after the Second World War. Jewish associates were hired, and some moved up the ladder to partner. The lowering of barriers to Jews was part of a general lessening of social exclusiveness. In 1957, 28 percent of the partners in the eighteen firms studied by Erwin Smigel were listed in the Social Register. By 1968, the percentage had dropped to 20 percent. But African-Americans and other minorities of color were still hardly visible in the world of big law firms. In 1956 there were approximately eighteen women working in large New York firms—something less than one percent of the total complement of lawyers. As late as 1968, Cynthia Fuchs Epstein estimates, "only forty women were working in Wall Street firms or had some Wall Street experience" (Epstein 1981, p. 176).[15]

Promotion and Partnership: Only a small minority of those hired as associates achieved partnership. Of 454 associates hired by the Cravath firm between 1906 and 1948, only 36 (just under 8 percent) were made partners (Smigel 1964, p. 116). Cravath may have been the most selective but it was not that different from other firms. In 1956 Martin Mayer reported that the "chance of becoming a partner . . . varies from one in seven to one in fifteen, depending on the firm and the year in which he joins it" (1956b, p. 52). The "average chance at a partnership . . . is only one in twelve" (Mayer 1956b, p. 54). Spencer Klaw, writing two years later, provides the more optimistic assessment that partnership is achieved by "perhaps one out of every six or seven" (1958, p. 142).

13. Some women and Jews were hired during World War II, when the normal supply of "desirable" candidates had dried up.

14. A *Yale Law Journal* survey found that Jewish students from the Yale classes of 1951 to 1962, especially those below the top third of their class, were less successful in obtaining work in the larger, higher-paying firms. During the 1950s and early 1960s, Jews graduating from Yale went to firms roughly half the size of their gentile classmates and earned the equivalent of classmates ranking an average of one third of a class lower in law school ranking (*Yale Law Journal* 1964). This study was based on interviews with Yale students and with hiring partners and on a survey of Yale graduates of this period who worked in New York. The exclusion of Jews and others from the big firms (and from the bar) is chronicled by Auerbach (1976, chapter 4 and *passim*).

15. Epstein reports that "[o]f the thirty four women partners on Wall Street in 1979, only three achieved partnership before 1970" (1981, p. 180).

The time it took to become a partner varied from firm to firm and associate to associate. For the New York lawyers becoming partners around 1960 the average time seems to have been just under ten years.[16] Outside New York the time to partnership was closer to seven years (Nelson 1988, p. 141). Throughout the 1960s the time to partnership dropped.[17]

One of the basic elements of the structure of the big firm is the up or out rule that prescribes that after a probationary period, the young lawyer will either be admitted to the partnership or will leave the firm. In this model, there can be no permanent connection other than as a partner. It is easy to overestimate the rigor with which the up or out rule was in fact applied.[18] In his 1958 study, Klaw observed that "[f]ew Wall Street firms have an absolutely rigid up-or-out policy, but most of them discourage men from staying on indefinitely as associates" (p. 197). Many firms had an explicit up or out rule—in some cases quite recently minted (Smigel 1964, p. 44)—but there was at work a competing and powerful norm that it was not nice to fire a lawyer. In 1956, Mayer reported that "nobody is ever fired except for immediate and specific cause" (1956b, p. 54). Smigel reports a "widespread feeling that it is not professional to fire a lawyer" (1964, p. 77). Termination tended to be drawn out and disguised. "Failure . . . is carefully disguised by the firms with the knowing help of their members and associates" (Smigel 1964, p. 78). Addressing a Practicing Law Institute forum in 1965, a Shearman and Sterling partner said of those passed over: "Naturally, we don't desert these fellows. Anybody who has been with us that long is entirely welcome to stay, and they are so few that we can accommodate them as valued "permanent" associates because they have demonstrated their ability" (PLI 1965, p. 199).

For associates who did not make partner, firms undertook outplacement, recommending them for jobs with client corporations and with smaller firms

16. In a hundred lawyer firm with twenty-six partners studied in 1956, partners had taken an average of 9.1 years to partnership (Smigel 1964, p. 137). At Simpson Thacher those who became partners between 1945 and the late 1950s had spent an average of 10.6 years with the firm (Smigel 1964, p. 79). In a firm that Smigel identifies as a "social" firm the average time to partnership was 11.7 years (Smigel 1964, p. 92). A respondent at Sullivan and Cromwell reported that "it now takes longer than ten years to become a partner" (Smigel 1964, p. 84). Compare Mayer's report that most partners felt that "ten is about right" (1956b, p. 53).

17. At the 1965 Practicing Law Institute forum, "Managing Law Offices," a Davis Polk partner observed: "In our firm . . . [time to partnership] used to be a little more than ten years, except in the rarest cases. More recently, it has been five, six, or seven years though in some cases it may still take ten years or more. The time varies with the individual, his department, and the need of the firm for another partner from a particular department" (PLI 1965, pp. 20–21).

18. Thus in a recent paper Gilson and Mnookin (1989) refer to the up or out system as "the long dominant career pattern by which employee (associate) lawyers are either promoted to partnership or fired" (p. 567) and note that it only now "appears to be changing" (p. 567).

(Smigel 1964, p. 64).[19] Ties might be maintained as the firm referred legal work to them or served as outside counsel to the corporation.

Although departure from the firm was decreed by the up or out norm, there were some lawyers who were permanent but not partners. These included managing clerks and a few specialists who because of a low-status specialty (such as immigration or labor law) or low-status origins had no expectation of being considered for partnership, although they were professionally respected and well paid (Smigel 1964, pp. 119, 231). But most permanent associates were "failures," "second-class citizens" who had not been promoted but stayed on and were assigned routine work—especially "back office" work that did not involve dealing with clients (1964, pp. 164, 231). Permanent associates were not as rare as the up or out norm might suggest. Smigel gives figures on two firms in 1956: one firm with one hundred lawyers had nine permanent associates; another with eighty-nine had twenty-two permanent associates (24.7 percent). Of all those who had started out at the Cravath firm from 1906 to 1948, sixteen remained as permanent associates—almost half as many as became partners (1964, p. 116).[20]

In the course of the 1960s, there was a decline in the number of permanent associates; or, to put it another way, the up or out norm was enforced more vigorously. In his epilogue, Smigel notes the "reduction in the number of permanent associates. The firms . . . no longer consider the permanent associate desirable" (1969, p. 375 n. 11). He suggests a number of possible reasons for this: the firms' work may have become more complex; the work formerly done by permanent associates was now being done by in-house corporate counsel; the permanent associate was viewed as an undesirable model of failure for associates (p. 375 n. 11). In the early 1970s, Paul Hoffman reported that "[p]ermanent associates are a dying breed . . . being phased out by attrition at most firms" (1973, p. 44). As we shall see, it was not to be long before they were phased back in.

Partners were chosen by proficiency, hard work, and ability to relate to clients (Smigel 1964, p. 97). In many cases there was some consideration of the candidate's ability to attract business (Mayer 1966, p. 334). And selection depended on the perceived ability of the firm to support additional partners (Lisagor and Lipsius 1988, p. 190).

Achieving partnership, the "strongest reward," meant not only status but security and assurance of further advancement: "[T]hey . . . know that they

19. In our "circa 1960" period, corporate legal work in many cases paid better than law firms (Siddall 1956, p. 107).

20. In 1934, when Sullivan and Cromwell had sixteen partners, "the firm had eight senior associates who had been there more than fifteen years and never expected to make partner" (Lisagor and Lipsius 1988, p. 108).

have tenure and feel certain that they will advance up the partnership ladder" (Smigel 1964, pp. 259, 302). There was certainly pressure to keep up with one's peers, but competition between partners was restrained. In this environment, "[a]dmission to the partnership of a leading firm was a virtual guarantee not only of tenured employment but of a lifetime of steadily increasing earnings unmatched by a lawyer's counterparts in the other learned professions" (Stevens 1987, p. 8).

But this should not lead one to conclude that the classic pattern of dividing the proceeds of the big-firm partnership was some approximation of giving each partner an equal share—or a share by seniority (the so-called lockstep system). If this was ever true, by circa 1960 the prevailing practice was to divide profits by individualized shares rather than by a norm of equal participation.[21]

Work and Clients: The work of the big firm was primarily office work in corporate law, securities, banking, and tax with some estate work for wealthy clients. Divorces, automobile accidents, and minor real estate matters would be farmed out or referred to other lawyers (Levy 1961, p. 35). Litigation was not prestigious, and it was not seen as a money-maker. Mayer estimates that "litigation occupies less than one-tenth the time of large law firm" and reports that "[s]ome firms avoid it entirely" (Mayer 1956a, p. 36). He describes large-firm litigation in the early 1960s as involving taxes, contracts, personal injury defense, and defense of corporations and directors from shareholders suits. "But to most large law firms, the word 'litigation' connotes an antitrust suit, not because the number of such cases is large but because each of them represents so enormous a quantity of work" (Mayer 1966, p. 320). The surge of antitrust litigation tended to elevate the standing of litigators, who had been "overshadowed by office-lawyer partners . . . who seldom, if ever, went near a courtroom" (Klaw 1958, p. 144). Where big firms were involved in litigation, it was typically on the side of the defendant.[22] Big firms usually represented dominant actors who could struc-

21. Siddall (1956, p. 43) reports a great variety of compensation schemes among the forty-two firms he studied. The data here do not tell us how much of the variation may be accounted for by seniority, but they cast some doubt on the notion that many or most law firms were equal partnerships. At least some of these firms attempted to apportion rewards according to the contribution of each partner to income (Siddall 1956, p. 48).

22. This tilt to big firm participation in litigation was noted by an earlier writer about Wall Street law practice: "[M]ost of the legal cases handled by the big law firms . . . place them on the side of the defense. . . . So imbued do the corporation lawyers become with a defensive psychology that they have unconsciously evolved a folklore—familiar to all newspaper men who report Wall Street—in which plaintiffs figure as racketeers or Bolshevists, in spirit if not in fact. To the average Wall Street corporation lawyer, in whose very fibre is burned the conviction that the management is always right, stockholders who bring suit against the management are simply racketeers and their lawyers are little

ture transactions to get what they wanted; it was the other side that had to seek the help of courts to disturb the status quo. Disdain of litigation reflected the prevailing attitude among the corporate establishment that it was not quite nice to sue (Macaulay 1963).

As they grew, many firms broadened their client bases, becoming less dependent on a single main client. Relations with clients tended to be enduring. "A partner in one Wall Street firm estimate[d] its turnover in dollar volume at 5 per cent a year, mostly in one-shot litigation" (Hoffman 1973, p. 72). Corporations had strong ties to "their" law firms. Many partners sat on the boards of their clients[23]—a practice that had been viewed as unprofessional earlier in the century—and would lose favor again later.[24] A 1959 Conference Board survey on the legal work of 286 manufacturing corporations found that "three fourths of them retain outside counsel on a continuing basis. . . . Companies most frequently report that 'present outside counsel has been with us for many, many years,' or that 'we are satisfied with the performance of our outside counsel and have never given any thought to hiring another' " (1959, pp. 463, 464).

We have no evidence about how many hours were actually worked or billed. Smigel reports that "[s]ome firms believe an associate should put in 1800 chargeable hours a year and a partner 1500, with the hours decreasing as the partner gets older" (Smigel 1964, p. 220).[25] It was widely believed, perhaps with some basis, that lawyers (especially associates) were not working as hard as they had in earlier times (Smigel 1964, pp. 43, 104; Klaw 1958, p. 194).

Circa 1960, New York still dominated the world of big-time law practice.

---

better; anyone who is injured in a train wreck and who sues the great and good railroad company is little more than a scoundrel. . . . Again, the bondholder who finds that he has been sold securities by means of a misleading prospectus, and who brings suit, is a knave, and his lawyer is probably more of a knave, meriting disbarment. . . . Similarly, lawyers who chase ambulances in search of clients are little better than pickpockets and their clients hardly more than criminals" (Lundberg 1939, pp. 187–88).

23. Mayer noted that "lawyers want to sit on boards because . . . it sews up the client's legal business" (1956a, p. 56).

24. Gartner reported that liability and conflict of interest concerns were leading law firms to reappraise the desirability of directorships (1973, p. 4).

25. In a detailed explication of law office organization in 1941, Reginald Heber Smith suggested as approximations of "the number of hours experience indicates [lawyers] actually will work on the average year in and year out": juniors, 1600; partners, 1520; and "older senior partners" who "are commonly devoting more time to public service, to charities," 1200 (Smith 1940, pp. 610, 611).

Subsequently, expectations about billable hours seem to have declined. In 1973, Hoffman reported that "[a]s late as five years ago [1968], associates were expected to produce 2,000 billable hours a year. The target is now down to 1,600 and the actual output is even less" (1973, pp. 130–31). It is difficult to interpret changes in these figures because "billable hours" is a product not only of actual time spent, but of recording and billing practices.

Large firms elsewhere were constructed along the same "promotion to partnership" lines, but tended to operate a bit differently. Firms outside New York tended to be more recently founded (Smigel 1964, p. 190). There was also less departmentalization, specialization, and supervision (p. 186). The organization was less formal, with fewer rules about meetings, training, conflicts of interest, and so on (pp. 184–85). The turnover of associates was lower, and there was less up or out pressure. Partnership was also easier to attain and came earlier (pp. 182, 183). There was more use of such intermediate classifications as junior or limited partners (p. 183). There was more lateral hiring (p. 181). Outside New York, firms were less highly leveraged. The ratio of associates to partners in the nineteen New York firms Smigel studied was two to one; in the firms outside New York, it was, in some instances, as low as one to one (pp. 183, 203).[26] A lawyer from a big firm in Chicago observed that New York firms "frequently employ two or three or even more associates per partner. In Chicago these ratios are lower; and there has been a well-defined trend in recent years, toward increasing the number of partners in the larger firms as compared with the number of associates" (Austin 1957, p. 16).

For big firms, circa 1960 was a time of prosperity, stable relations with clients, steady but manageable growth, and a comfortable assumption that this kind of law practice was a permanent fixture of American life.[27] Notwithstanding their comfortable situation many inhabitants and observers regarded the world of the big firm as sadly declined from an earlier day when lawyers were statesmen and served as the conscience of business (Gordon 1988, p. 48). Echoing laments that have recurred since the last century, partners complained to Smigel that law had turned into a business (Smigel 1964, pp. 303–5). No longer, Mayer reflects, do young associates regard themselves as servants of the law and holders of a public trust: "[T]hey are too busy fitting themselves for existence in the 1950s, when efficiency, accuracy, and intelligence are the only values to be sought" (1956b, p. 56).

Big law firms enjoyed an enviable autonomy. They were relatively independent vis-à-vis their clients; they exercised considerable control over how they did their work; and they were infused with a sense of being in control of

26. In late 1957, the twenty largest Wall Street firms (ranging in size from 125 to 46) had 2.28 associates for each partner. Calculated from data found in Klaw 1958, p. 194.

27. For other strata of the profession, however, there was a sense of decline from a more prosperous past. The ABA's Special Committee on the Economics of Law Practice in 1959 complained that lawyers' incomes had fallen relative to those of doctors and dentists. They saw the profession "endangered by the creeping instability of its economic status" (ABA 1959, p. 3) and "dwindling" as the percentage of national income spent on legal services fell to one third of what it had been at its all time high in the early Depression years. The solution was minimum fee schedules to be enforced by the profession's disciplinary bodies (ABA 1959).

their destinies. A sharp contrast with present practices and perspectives is implicit in the retrospective glance of a contemporary author:

> [C]ompetition was very much a gentlemanly affair. With the banks and manufacturing corporations pacing America's industrial expansion—and with the Securities Acts and New Deal legislation complicating business transactions—the workload grew faster than the firms' ability to service it. Protected by their captive relationships, the established practices had no reason to fear competitive assaults and were not, in turn, moved to encroach on their competitors' turf. Blessed with virtual monopolies in their respective markets, they focused instead on practice standards, on establishing self-indulgent compensation systems, and on perfecting the mystique and the mannerisms of elite professionals. How cases were staffed and billed, how partners were selected and paid, and how new partners were admitted to the ranks were issues based on internal considerations rather than market factors. Free to conduct their affairs as they saw fit, the established practices could all but ignore such boorish concerns as efficiency, productivity, marketing and competition. [Stevens 1987, pp. 8–9]

THE TRANSFORMATION OF THE BIG FIRM

The more numerous and more diverse lawyers of the late 1980s were arrayed in a very different structure of practice than their counterparts a generation earlier. There has been a general shift to larger units of practice.[28] The number of lawyers working in sizable aggregations, capable of massive and coordinated legal undertakings has multiplied many times over.[29] One estimate is that in 1988, there were 35,000 lawyers at 115 firms with more than 200 lawyers and a total of 105,000 lawyers in 2000 firms larger than 20 lawyers (Brill 1989, p. 10).

Growth: In the late 1950s there were only 38 law firms in the United States with more than fifty lawyers—and more than half of these were in New York City (Smigel 1964, p. 58). In 1985, there were 508 firms with fifty-one or more lawyers (Curran et al. 1985b, p. 58).

Not only were there more big firms, but they were growing faster. The firms in our Group I (fifty of the largest firms in 1986) grew from an average

28. In 1948, more than six of out of ten lawyers practiced alone; in 1980, only one third of a much larger number of lawyers was in sole practice (Abel 1989, p. 179; Curran 1985a, p. 14).

29. In 1980, there were almost fifty thousand lawyers in firms of twenty-one or more—they made up 9.2% of all lawyers, 13.4% of lawyers in private practice, and 26.1% of all lawyers practicing in firms (Curran 1985a, pp. 13, 14).

size of 124 in 1975 to 252 in 1985.[30] In this period, the average size of our Group II firms (the 200th to 250th largest in 1988) doubled from 44 to 89 lawyers.[31] The average annual growth rate over this ten-year period was 8 percent for both Group I and Group II.[32] These rates are considerably higher than the rates at which these same firms were growing twenty years earlier. From 1955 to 1965, the average annual growth rate was only 5.3 percent for the Group I firms and 5.5 percent for Group II firms.

In 1960 big law firms were clearly identified with a specific locality, as they had been since the origin of the big firm.[33] But by 1980, of the 100 largest firms, 87 had branches. Of all firms with fifty or more lawyers, 62 percent were in more than one location and 24 percent were in three or more locations in 1980 (Curran et al. 1985a, p. 53). Some of this branching was by "colonization" but most of it involved mergers with firms (or with groups defecting from firms) in the new locality. Washington has been the favorite site for branches. In 1980, 178 firms from outside Washington had branches there (Abel 1989, p. 188). But as branching activity has increased, Washington offices are a declining portion of all branches.

In the 1980s the home office and branch pattern was joined by the genuine multi-city law firm (Lewin 1984, p. 31).[34] To capture the dynamic of multi-city growth, we compared twenty of the largest firms based in New York City (NY) and twenty of the largest firms based outside New York City (ONY) for the years 1980 and 1987.[35] The NY firms had a total of 70 branch offices in

30. The range was from 50 to 198 lawyers in 1975 and from 142 to 419 lawyers in 1985. These figures are somewhat lower than those in the last paragraph, because they are drawn from our data set, based on *Martindale-Hubbell*, rather than from the *National Law Journal* Surveys. We use the *Martindale-Hubbell* data here because, unlike that from the *National Law Journal*, it permits comparisons with earlier periods.

31. The range was from 21 to 68 in 1975 and from 54 to 121 in 1985.

32. These ranges are confirmed by annual surveys of the five hundred largest firms conducted by *Of Counsel* since 1986. The reported rate of growth for all of these firms was over 9 percent for each of the three years, 1986, 1987 and 1988 (*Of Counsel* 1989, p. 1).

33. The occasional Washington or foreign branch office was anomalous (Smigel 1964, p. 207).

34. The true pioneer is Baker & McKenzie, which in the 1950s established four foreign offices, staffed largely by local lawyers, as well as a Washington office. Thirteen more foreign offices were added in the 1960s. In 1988, the firm consisted of forty-one offices in twenty-five countries (*National Law Journal* 1988, p. S-4; Lyons 1985, p. 116). On its organizational strategy, see also Stevens 1987, pp. 153–66. Another pioneer in the design of the multi-city firm was the late Robert Kutak, whose Omaha-based Kutak, Rock, and Huie, founded in 1965, was established in six regional centers by 1980 (Tybor 1981, p. 8). In the late 1970s, the firm planned to open an office in one new city each year and by the end of the 1980s to have seventeen offices around the country (Kiechel 1978, pp. 112, 113). The firm was unable to keep up this pace and experienced a severe contraction in late 1980 (Tybor 1981, p. 1).

35. This comparison is based on our "Two Twenties" Data Set, described in Galanter and Palay (1991, appendix A). For convenience, we refer to "branches," but we use that term to mean an office other than the office of the firm that contains the largest number of lawyers. In 1987, only one of our forty firms (Akin Gump) had an office larger than its "home" office.

1980 and 99 branches in 1987. The ONY firms had a total of 61 branches in 1980 and 124 branches in 1987. Thus there was a 41 percent increase in branches of NY firms over this seven-year period and a 103 percent increase in branches of ONY firms.

Not only did the number of branches increase, but so did their size. The average size of each branch of a NY firm went from eight lawyers in 1980 to seventeen in 1987. The branches of the ONY firms grew from an average of fifteen lawyers in 1980 to thirty lawyers just seven years later. The growth in branches accounted for 31 percent of the total growth of the twenty NY firms and 69 percent of the total growth of the ONY firms. The percentage of lawyers outside the largest office rose from 15 to 21 percent for the NY firms while doubling from 21 to 42 percent for the ONY firms.

We can see that branches grew much faster than main offices during this period. By 1987 there were a number of firms that had a substantial portion of their lawyers away from the largest office. Eight of the NY firms had more than 25 percent of their lawyers outside the main office (up from four in 1980); and seventeen of the ONY firms had more than 25 percent of their lawyers outside the largest office—seven had more than 50 percent outside.

Increasingly, large firms operate on an international basis. Of the one hundred largest firms in 1988, some forty-four had a total of 136 overseas offices.[36] Our comparison of the twenty largest NY and twenty largest ONY firms indicates that the largest NY firms have more overseas branches, but the gap is closing. These New York firms had thirty-nine in 1980 and forty-three in 1987. Their ONY counterparts had nine in 1980 and twenty-one in 1987. Foreign offices tend to be a larger share of the offices of the NY firms (36 percent in 1987) than of the ONY firms (15 percent in 1987).

Over the past thirty years, there has been a marked movement away from New York City as the nation's legal center.[37] In 1957, there were 21 firms with over fifty lawyers in New York City and only 17 in the rest of the country (Smigel 1964). In 1980, there were 72 firms of fifty-one or more in New York State (Curran et al. 1985a, p. 166) but in the whole country there were 287 (p. 51). In twenty years, New York City's share of large firms had fallen from more than half to less than a quarter. New York City has retained a somewhat larger but declining share of the very largest firms. In 1987, 32 of the 100 largest firms were based in New York (down from 36 in 1975)

36. The number of overseas offices ranges from one to thirty-two; eight firms had five or more overseas offices.

37. This reflects the dispersion of corporate headquarters and financial markets. In 1960, 128 of the Fortune 500 industrial corporations had headquarters in New York City; in 1988, only 50 were headquartered there. There were comparable shifts in other categories of corporations (*Fortune* 1960a, p. 131; 1960b, p. 137; 1988a, p. D-11; 1988b, p. D-7).

(Abel 1989, table 47).[38] The hundred largest firms were based in twenty-four cities (up from eighteen in 1975).[39]

Work and Clients: The kinds of work big firms do have changed. The mix of work coming into big firms has been changed by a surge of corporate litigation since the 1970s (Galanter and Rogers, 1989) and by the increase in the number, size, and responsibility of in-house legal departments. Long-term retainer relations have given way to comparison shopping for lawyers on an *ad hoc* transactional basis (Flaharty 1983, p. 1; Jensen 1988, p. 1; Couric 1988, p. 2). Corporations that view legal expenses as ordinary costs of doing business rather than singular emergencies have monitored legal costs, set litigation budgets, required periodic reporting, and awarded new business on the basis of competitive presentations from competing outside firms.

The practice of law has become more specialized. Within large firms, specialization has become more intense and the work of various levels more differentiated (Nelson 1988, pp. 147, 171). Much routine work has been retracted into corporate law departments, shifting the work of large outside firms away from office practice toward litigation[40] and deals. With more deals, higher stakes, more regulation to take into account, and more volatile fluctuations of interest and exchange rates there is greater demand for intensive lawyering. The large contested and/or risk-prone one-of-a-kind, "bet your company" transactions—litigations, takeovers, bankruptcies, and such—make up a larger portion of what big law firms do. Since few clients provide a steady stream of such matters and those that have them increasingly shop for specialists to handle them, firms are under ever greater pressure to generate a steady (or increasing) supply of such matters, by retaining the favors of old clients and securing new ones.

Competitiveness: The new aggressiveness of in-house counsel, the breakdown of retainer relationships, and the shift to discrete transactions has made conditions more competitive.[41] The practice of law has become more openly

38. A 1989 survey found that thirty-three of the one hundred firms with the largest gross revenues were based in New York (*The American Lawyer* 1989).

39. The decline in the predominance of New York based firms points to, but overstates the decline of New York City as a locus of legal activity. A significant portion of the branching activity discussed in the preceding paragraphs consists of the establishment in New York of branches by ONY firms. In 1980, only three of our ONY firms had offices in New York (average size seventeen). By 1987, ten of the twenty ONY firms had New York offices (average size thirty-nine).

40. Chayes and Chayes (1985, p. 295) report that major corporations responding to a small survey reported half of all legal fees paid to outside lawyers were for litigation.

41. During this period, the profession's traditional means of suppressing intraprofessional competition, minimum fee schedules, was struck down by the Supreme Court as a violation of the Sherman Act (*Goldfarb v. Virginia State Bar*, 421 U.S. 773 [1975]). Two years later the traditional ban on advertising fell (*Bates v. State Bar of Arizona*, 433 U.S. 350 [1977]). The demise of minimum

commercial and profit-oriented, "more like a business."[42] Firms rationalize their operations; they engage professional managers and consultants; their leaders worry about billable hours, profit centers, and marketing strategies. "Eat what you kill" compensation formulas emphasize rewards for productivity and business-getting over "equal shares" or seniority (Heintz 1982, p. 24; Gilson and Mnookin 1985, p. 313; but see Nelson 1988, pp. 202–4). There is more differentiation in the power partners wield and the rewards they receive; standing within the firm depends increasingly on how much business a partner brings in.[43] Rising overhead costs and associate salaries put pressure on partners. In many firms, partners work more hours, but their income has not increased correspondingly.[44]

The need to find new business has led to aggressive marketing. Some firms have taken on marketing directors, a position that did not exist in 1980. In 1985, there were forty such positions (Galanter 1985, pp. 1, 28).[45] By 1989 "almost 200 law firms ha[d] hired their own marketing directors."[46] The push for new business also brought about increased emphasis on "rainmaking" by more of the firm's lawyers (Haserot 1986, p. 15; Jensen 1987b, p. 1). Those lawyers who are responsible for bringing in business enjoy a new ascendancy over their colleagues.[47] The need to find new business has

---

fee schedules did not directly affect the big firms, but the encouragement of competition and particularly the freedom from restrictions on self-promotion provided them with new means to adapt to the changing marketplace. On the indirect effects of *Bates*, see Galanter and Palay (1991, chapter 4).

42. Recall that similar observations have been made ever since the early days of big law firms.

43. Reflecting on Smigel's contention that law firms lack the hierarchy, rules, and conflict characteristic of other organizations because they are organized around professional norms, Nelson concedes that if this was so in "the stable professional community of New York law firms in the late 1950s . . . [i]t is clearly not accurate today. Large firms are the regimes of client-producers, and this stratum of partners dictates the policies of the firm and projects the ideology of professionalism that justifies the structure of the firm and the client-producers' role in it" (1988, p. 276).

44. A survey by Altman & Weil of median earnings of partners in 700 large (75-plus lawyers) firms found earnings in 1986 had increased by 78% over those ten years earlier, but inflation had raised prices 93%. Average hours billed were up 8% to 1,685 hours annually (Jensen 1987a, p. 12). A Price-Waterhouse survey of medium and large firms found that from 1978 to 1988 partner earnings rose only 1% after accounting for inflation (cited in Brill 1989, p. 6).

45. The next year it was reported that "more than 60 law firms, ranging in size from 14 lawyers to nearly 600 . . . [in] about 25 cities . . . had hired a marketing administrator." A National Association of Law Firm Marketing Administrators was established in the same year (Schmidt 1986, p. 15).

46. Merrilyn Astin Tarlton, former president of the National Association of Law Firm Marketing Administrators, quoted in the *New York Times*, 2 June 1989, p. 86.

47. "Rainmaker" is a term of fairly recent vintage. None of the 1960s material we used employed it. For example, Mayer spoke of "the business-getters [who] eventually refused to put up with . . . [equal shares]" (1966, p. 336). The idea of a lawyer who specializes in obtaining business has been part of the large-firm scene for a long time. The older term was the straightforward "business getter." As early as 1907, a practitioner observed that "[i]n nearly every large firm in our great cities the indispensable partner is 'the business getter.' " (Andrews 1907, p. 608). An extended 1925 satirical sketch describes the business-getter as a type that "has waxed and swelled, until his work constitutes

shaken the traditional structure of the big firm. A description of big firms in the Southeast reports that the "shift from a traditional reliance upon a small number of rainmakers to the aggressive stance that everyone must make rain has resulted in a reduction in numbers of associates receiving a vote for partnership as well as—in many cases—a redivision of partners' profit pie. Many firms also go a step further by eliminating non-producing partners and restructuring or jettisoning non-productive departments" (Bellon 1988, pp. 19, 20).

The search for new business has been directed not only toward would-be clients, but to existing ones. In a setting where corporations are more inclined to divide their custom among several law firms, firms engage in "cross-selling" to induce the purchaser of services from one department to avail itself of the services offered by other departments (Weklar 1988, pp. 22, 26; O'Neill 1989, p. 17).

Lateral Hiring and Mergers: In the classical big firm, almost all hiring was at the entry level. Partners were promoted from the ranks of associates. Those who left went to corporations or smaller firms, not to similar large firms since these adhered to the same no lateral hiring norm. But starting in the 1970s, lateral movement became more frequent. At first, firms made an occasional lateral hire to meet a need for litigators or to fill some other niche. But soon lateral hiring developed into a means of systematically upgrading or enlarging the specialties and localities they could service and of acquiring rainmakers who might bring or attract new clients. As lateral movement increased, a whole industry of "headhunter" firms emerged, gaining respectability as it grew.[48] The number of legal search firms grew rapidly from 83 in 1984 to 167 in 1987 to 244 in 1989 (Abel 1989, p. 188; *National Law Journal* 1989a, p. S-3).

The flow of lateral movement widened from individual lawyers to whole departments and groups within firms and to whole firms. Mass defections and mergers became common, enabling firms at a stroke to add new depart-

---

a profession in itself, and he bestrides the legal world like a colossus." Technically a lawyer, "[a]ctually he is a peripatetic electric signboard, a prospectus that walks like a man, a barker with a modulated voice, a glorified sandwich man, a solicitor in more senses than one, broadcasting the virtues of his law firm in waves more subtle than those of Marconi" (Smith 1925, pp. 199–200). Nelson recounts a humorous folk categorization of big-firm lawyers into "finders, minders, and grinders" (1988, pp. 69–70)—those who acquire new clients, those who attend to existing ones, and those who grind out the work.

48. Legal headhunter firms emerged in New York in the late 1960s in response to the constriction in the supply of lawyers. At first such activity was regarded as a discreditable departure from professional decorum. "In 1967 when Lois R. Weiner . . . decided to specialize in finding jobs for lawyers, the publishers of [the] Martindale-Hubbell [Directory] refused to sell her a copy" (Stevenson 1973, pp. 12, 13).

ments and expand to new locations. A casual search of the legal press from 1985 to 1989 produced a list of seventy-one mergers involving eighty-three firms with more than fifty lawyers; in fifty-eight of these mergers, at least one of the merging firms had one hundred lawyers—a sizable portion of the whole population of firms of that size.[49] Mergers were not only a way to grow; they also provided a convenient device to shake out or renegotiate terms with less productive partners.

Firms hired laterally not only by mergers but by inducing specific lawyers to change firms, "cherry picking" as it came to be called in the late 1980s. A 1988 survey of the five hundred largest law firms found that over a quarter reported that more than half of their new partners were not promoted from within but came from other firms.[50] Lateral movement was not confined to the partner level. The same survey found that one quarter of the responding firms reported that more than half their associates were hired laterally (Smith 1989, p. 6). Increasingly, associates move from one big firm to another. A recent survey of promotions at thirty-five large firms in seven localities reveals thirty-three of the thirty-five firms hired some associates laterally and that of 2227 associates who entered in the late 1970s, 500 (22 percent) had not come to those firms directly from law school, but "arrived at their current firm later in their careers" (Wise 1987, pp. 1, 32).[51] A recent *New York Law Journal* survey found that at twenty-three of the thirty largest firms in New York, an average of 24 percent of the associates being considered for partnership were lateral hires (Adams 1989, pp. 1, 6).

The other side of this movement was splits and dissolutions of firms.[52] As firms grew larger the task of maintaining an adequate flow of business often

49. Compiled from data supplied by Holly Moyer of Hildebrandt, Inc. According to the *National Law Journal* annual surveys, there were only 218 firms with one hundred or more lawyers in 1985 and fewer than 300 in 1988.

50. A survey in *Of Counsel*, reported in Smith 1989, p. 6. Approximately four hundred firms provided information on lateral hiring. The figures in this survey were close to those in a 1986 survey.

51. We use "late 1970s" here to include the few instances in which the data cover years as late as 1981. It is not clear whether these associates arrived in the years stated or arrived later but were assigned to an earlier associate "class." The data presented do not permit us to distinguish between lateral hires arriving from clerkships and government service and those who were leaving other firms, but it seems safe to assume that there were at least some of the latter.

52. According to Hildebrandt, Inc., about one hundred law firms dissolved in 1987, including about a dozen with more than thirty lawyers (*Wall Street Journal* 1988; Abel 1989, pp. 186–87). Although there have been some spectacular breakups of large firms, such as the dissolution of Finley Kumble in 1987, the pressure to merge or dissolve was thought to be most severe for midsize firms. In 1988, a Hildebrandt consultant reported that "[i]n the past two years, more than 60 midsize firms—more than 10% of the total nationwide—have either dissolved or merged. . . . Though midsize firms make up 10% of all law firms they accounted for 25% of the field's mergers and closing in the past two years" (Dockser 1988, p. B-1).

became more difficult. Firms were more vulnerable to defections by valued clients or the lawyers to whom those clients are attached. Size multiplies the possibility of conflicts of interests resulting in tension between partners who tend old clients and those who propose new ones that can induce a breakaway. Surrounded by other firms attempting to grow by attracting partners with special skills or desirable clients, firms are vulnerable to the loss of crucial assets. So dissolution may be catalyzed by lateral movement and merger activity and such break-up in turn stimulates a new round of lateral movement.

Hiring: As firms grew, thus requiring larger numbers of qualified associates, recruitment activity intensified. Recruiting visits to an increasing roster of law schools, extensive summer programs, brochures, and expense-paid "call-backs" of candidates have become familiar parts of the big law firm scene.[53] Starting salaries have increased dramatically, beginning with a great contraction of the supply of associates in the late 1960s. The Vietnam War draft diverted law graduates to occupations in which they could obtain deferments, just when 1960s activism inspired a disdain for corporate practice among students seeking work in poverty law and public-interest law. The percentage of elite law graduates entering private practice dropped precipitously.[54] Confronted by criticism that their work was unfulfilling and inimical to the public interest, many firms acceded to demands that recruits be able to spend time on "pro bono publico" activities (Berman and Cahn 1970). The *Wall Street Journal* reported that "now it's common for [the big corporate law firms] to permit their attorneys to spend substantial portions of their time in noncommercial work" (Falk 1970, p. 1).

Firms responded to their supply problem not only by accommodating their recruits' public-interest impulses but by sharply increasing their compensation. In 1967, the starting salary for associates at elite firms in New York was $10,000; scheduled to increase to $10,500 for 1968 recruits. In February 1968, the Cravath firm, breaking with the "going rate" cartel (Smigel 1964,

53. This trend has transformed the law school scene by linking law students early and tightly to the world of law practice, a development that has been described by Roger Cramton as "the new apprenticeship" (1981, p. 521).

54. "From 1964 through 1968 . . . the number of Harvard Law School graduates entering private law practice declined from 54 to 41 percent." Yale graduates entering private practice dropped from 41 percent in 1968 to 31 percent in 1969; the percentage of Virginia graduates entering private practice dropped from 63 percent to 54 percent from 1968 to 1969 (Berman and Cahn 1970, pp. 16, 22–23). "[I]n 1970, none of the thirty-nine law review editors graduating from Harvard expects to enter private practice" (Green 1970, pp. 658, 659). A similar drop among Michigan graduates is documented by David Chambers, who found that those entering private practice dropped from 74 percent in the classes of 1965 and 1966 to about 60 percent for the years from 1967 to 1970. Chambers shows that most of the decrease was due to diversion into teaching and graduate work to secure draft deferments (Chambers 1989a, pp. 8–11).

p. 366), raised the salaries for incoming associates to $15,000, setting in motion a new competitive system of bidding for top prospects.[55] Firms that wanted to be considered in the top stratum had to match the Cravath rate. The change in New York starting salaries reverberated throughout the upper reaches of the profession. The salaries of more senior associates had to be raised to preserve differentials; the take of junior partners had to be adjusted accordingly; firms outside New York, though paying less, had to give corresponding raises to maintain parity with their New York rivals. Unlike later increases in compensation, the one in the late 1960s was not accompanied by pressure to bill more hours. In fact, it appears that hourly billings were dropping during this period.[56]

In 1986, when the highest-paid beginning associates were getting $53,000, Cravath administered a second shock by unilaterally raising salaries to $65,000 (Lewin 1986, p. 33). At the time of the first "Cravath shock" the big-firm "going rate" referred primarily to a few dozen firms, most which were located in New York; by the time the second occurred the big-firm world consisted of several hundred geographically dispersed firms, many national in scope. Long-accepted city differentials have been eroded by branching, especially by recent moves by New York firms into other legal markets, causing some firms in those localities to match the higher New York salaries.

As the number and size of large firms has increased, recruitment has become more competitive and more meritocratic, leading to changes in the social composition of the new recruits.[57] The range of law schools from which the big firms recruit has widened, and recruitment has gone "deeper" into each graduating class.[58] Religious, racial, and gender barriers have been swept away. The social exclusiveness in hiring that was still a feature of the world of elite law practice in 1960 has receded into insignificance. Performance in law school and in the office counts for more; social connections for less.[59]

55. Observers also saw the move as a response to the declining popularity of practicing in New York, as opposed to other locations, and a Cravath partner attributed the increase to the high cost of living in New York (Zion 1968a, p. 45; 1968b, p. 31).

56. In 1973, Hoffman reported that "the associates' work load has fallen greatly throughout the blue-chip bar" and suggested that the reduced hours reflected both interest in pro bono work and a new unwillingness of recruits to sacrifice their private lives (1973, pp. 130–31).

57. Consider Bernstein's analysis that demand for new associates by the 250 large firms outruns the total production of the "top twenty" law schools, however generously defined (1988, p. 20).

58. This is frequently described as a dilution of quality, but it should be recalled that since the golden age law school has attracted a much more talented pool and law school admissions have become more selective (Abel 1989, table 4).

59. But even absent deliberate exclusion, selection on the basis of educational credentials and the candidates' social affiliations, personal preferences, and career expectations will maintain some degree of association between legal roles and the social origins of lawyers (Heinz and Laumann

By the late 1980s the population of lawyers in big firms included a significant number of women and members of minority groups. A 1989 survey of the 250 largest firms found that 24 percent of their lawyers were women: 9.2 percent of the partners and 33 percent of the associates (Jensen 1990). A 1987 survey of these firms reported that women were "40 percent of the associates hired in the last two years, the same percentage as women in law school" (Weisenhaus 1988, pp. 1, 48). The percentage of women partners increased at almost one percent a year throughout the 1980s.[60] These numerical gains took place even as many women have expressed dissatisfaction with working conditions and career lines in large firms, especially as these obstruct and penalize child-rearing (Klemesrud 1985, p. 14; Mairs 1988, p. 1; Kingson 1988, p. 1; Holmes 1988). Women have been less satisfied than their male counterparts with law practice in general and with practice in large firms specifically (Tucker, Albright, and Busk 1989; Hirsch 1985; Nelson 1990).

African-Americans remained underrepresented in the world of large law firms. In 1989 they composed 2.2 percent of associates and less than one percent of partners (Jensen 1990). The ratio of partners had doubled since 1981, but the percentage of African-American associates declined slightly after 1981 (from 2.3 percent to 2.2 percent), while the percentages of other minorities rose (Weisenhaus 1988, p. 50; Jensen 1990).

Leverage: Firms have become more highly leveraged—that is, the ratio of associates to partners has risen. Using the data from our Group I set of fifty of the largest firms in 1986[61] we calculated the change in associate to partner ratios at five year intervals from 1960, the midpoint of the golden age, to 1985 (Galanter and Palay 1990b, table 3). During that period these firms grew from an average size of 48 to 239 and the ratio of associates to partners increased 28 percent from 1.16 to 1.49.[62] The ratio of associates to partners

---

1982, p. 332). Abel argues that the inclusion of women and the erection of higher educational hurdles have worked to "narrow the class background of lawyers, whose origins have grown even more privileged" (1989, pp. 109–10).

60. Women were 2.8% of partners in 1981 and 9.2% in 1989 (Jensen 1990).

61. This data set is discussed in Galanter and Palay (1991, appendix A).

62. We also used the data from our *National Law Journal* "Two Twenties" Data Set" (described in Galanter and Palay, 1991, appendix A) to calculate the change in associate to partner ratios from 1980 to 1987. We found that between these years the associate to partner ratio increased 31% from 1.72 to 2.25.

The trends here are the same as reported in the text; the magnitudes of ratios differ because of the different way that the various sources counted their data. Our assumption is that the various figures provided by the *National Law Journal*, and the data reported by *Business Week*, *Juris Doctor*, and Klaw (see the discussion of these in Galanter and Palay, 1991, appendix A), are more accurate representations of absolute firm size than those in our data set, which is based on *Martindale-Hubbell*. But our data set, because it goes back much further and was gathered in a consistent manner, provides a more accurate representation of trends. Here, as elsewhere, we are more

rose consistently during the successive five year intervals, with the exception of the period from 1965 to 1970. The slight drop in the associate to partner ratio in this period is consistent with the initial phasing-out of permanent associates and the tightening of the labor market, both of which occurred about this time.[63]

Because of the well-known (but less well explained) difference in the leverage of large New York firms and those elsewhere, we also divided our firms into two groups: those whose principal office is located in New York and those whose principal office is found elsewhere. Between 1960 and 1985 the average size of New York's biggest firms increased almost 375 percent from an average of 45 lawyers to 214 lawyers. The increase in size of firms based elsewhere was somewhat greater, growing 425 percent from 50 to an average of 261 lawyers; still, the New York firms continued to be more highly leveraged. In New York the average ratio of associates to partners increased from 1.36 in 1960 to 1.82 in 1985. The firms in other cities, by contrast, had only an average of 1.05 associates per partner in 1960 and 1.18 in 1985.[64] This means that New York firms were not only more heavily leveraged than other firms, but that the differences were increasing. The average number of associates per partner in New York grew by 34 percent between 1960 and 1985 while outside the New York it increased by only 12 percent. Moreover, in 1960 only 20 percent of firms based outside New York had associate to partner ratios exceeding that of the average New York firm. By 1985 none of them did.[65]

---

interested in the change in leverage than in its absolute amount at any given time in any given firm. We report the *National Law Journal* data here only to give the reader a sense of the absolute size of the ratios. Once again, the reader is cautioned not to mix data from the different sources.

63. This dip appears in another data set that we can derive by combining a report in *Business Week* (1968, p. 79) on the twenty largest firms and a report in *Juris Doctor* on the twenty-five largest firms (de Tocqueville 1972, p. 56). Both of these reports, apparently based on information supplied by the firms, list numbers of partners and associates. Comparing the *Business Week* 1968 figures and the *Juris Doctor* 1971 figures, the decrease in leverage is even more pronounced, from an average ratio of 1.99 associates per partner in the 1968 top twenty, to 1.72 associates per partner in the 1971 top twenty-five. The greater decrease might be due to the different dates (1968 and 1971 in the combined set, and 1965 and 1970 from our *Martindale Hubbell* set) or from some disparity in the way in which the *Business Week*, and *Juris Doctor* surveys were conducted.

64. At least part of the difference between New York firms and firms elsewhere probably lies in the different meanings attributed to the term "partner." If firms designate as partners those lawyers who have been given that title (and a promise of permanent tenure) but not a share of the firm profits, then they would display lower associate to partner ratios than if the partner designation were reserved to lawyers who had a share of the profits. There is reason to think that in at least some cities outside New York the designation partner is used more expansively (Wise 1987). Since this practice would simultaneously reduce the number of associates and increase the number of partners used in calculating these ratios, our comparisons would overstate the difference in leverage.

65. Again comparing the *National Law Journal* data with ours, we see that the trends are basically consistent, though the absolute numbers differ. Using our "Two Twenties" Data Set, we found that

Promotion and Partnership: Over the two decades preceding 1980 the period during which lawyers served as associates before becoming partners became shorter. Robert Nelson found that the average time spent as an associate by those promoted to partnership in large Chicago firms during the 1950s was 7.5 years; this fell to 7.21 in the 1960s; to 6.19 for those promoted between 1970 and 1975; to 5.64 for those promoted between 1976 and 1980 (Nelson 1988, p. 141). But in the 1980s time to partner seems to be stretching out. A study of five large New England firms found that associates had to wait eight or nine years instead of seven (Spangler 1986, p. 55). A *National Law Journal* survey of thirty-five firms in seven localities found that some two-thirds of associates hired in the late 1970s had spent seven to eight "years to partner" (Wise 1987).[66] Many partners anticipated further increases (Nelson 1988, p. 141).

Generally, increases in leverage suggest that a smaller percentage of associates will be promoted to partner. Nelson studied associates hired by nineteen large Chicago firms from 1971 to 1983 and determined which of them were still with these firms in 1984. If we assume that anyone who was there after nine years had become a partner, we see that fewer than half of those hired before 1975 had departed by 1984, so that more than half had become partners (Nelson 1988, p. 139, table 7). But Nelson suggests that "if we project current annual rates [of departure] over a six-year period [the normal period to partnership in Chicago], little more than one-quarter of the lawyers starting with firms would be expected to make partner" (Nelson 1988, pp. 138–39).

---

between 1980 and 1987 the associate to partner ratio at the twenty largest New York firms grew from 2.16 associates per partner to 2.82. Over the same period the ratio of associates per partner in the firms outside New York jumped from 1.2 to 1.63. The "Two Twenties" data shows a slight convergence in the ratios of the two samples. According to the "Two Twenties" data the firms outside New York have increased their ratio of associates to partners by about 36%, while the New York firms have risen by only 31%; however, in neither 1980 nor 1987 was any firm outside New York more leveraged than the average New York firm.

In addition, Klaw reports the total number of associates and partners at the twenty largest firms on Wall Street in 1957 (1958, p. 194). From this we calculate that the average associate to partner ratio at that time was 2.27. The percentage difference between Klaw's lawyer counts (apparently based on information from firms) and ours (based on *Martindale Hubbell*) is roughly the same as the difference between our counts in later years and those of the *National Law Journal*. On the assumption that both Klaw's and the *National Law Journal*'s counts are roughly equivalent and disregarding the fact that Klaw is counting Wall Street as opposed to New York city firms, we can combine these two data sets to get a rough second approximation of the change in associate to partner ratios in New York between the golden age and today. The trends are quite similar to those we report in the text, though again the absolute numbers differ, with an increase of roughly 25% in the average ratio of associates to partners in New York firms.

66. A survey of 150 medium-sized firms found that the median time to achieve partnership had increased between 1975 to 1985 from five years to six years (telephone interview with D. Weston Darby, Jr., of Cantor & Co., August 1989; reported in Darby 1985).

A 1987 *National Law Journal* survey (Wise 1987) of promotion at the five largest firms in each of seven localities revealed both regional and inter-firm disparities. The portion who made partner varied from the lowest range of 10 to 35 percent in New York to the highest of 29 to 64 percent in Los Angeles. The portion making partner at the five largest Chicago firms ranged from 33 to 48 percent, higher than the percentage Nelson anticipated for the coming years, but lower than what he reported for the period just past (Wise 1987, p. 32). Similarly, lowered estimates of the percentage of associates who will make partner are suggested by an account of large-firm practice in the Southeast, which reports that "[m]anaging partners at many major firms speak openly of their expectations that no more than 10 percent of any incoming class eventually will make partner" (Bellon 1988, pp. 19, 20).

A constriction of promotion to partnership, anticipated elsewhere, seems to have arrived already in New York's largest firms. A *New York Law Journal* survey computed the chances of achieving partnership at twenty-two of the thirty largest firms in New York City in 1980 and 1989. Some 25.1 percent of the "associate classes" of 1968, 1969, and 1970 (including laterals assigned to those classes) had become partners by 1980; but only 18.8 percent of the classes of 1978, 1979, and 1980 had become partners by 1989 (Adams 1989, pp. 1, 6).[67] These lower figures seem in the neighborhood of the chances of become a partner back in the 1950s (Mayer 1956b, p. 52; Klaw 1958, p. 142; see also Smigel 1964, p. 116).[68]

We noted earlier that in the 1960s firms applied the up or out norm with increasing stringency. Permanent associates were described as "a dying breed." But before the end of the decade, the institution was reinvented (Bodine 1979). Firms modified the promotion to partnership model by creating a new stratum of permanent salaried lawyers (Graham 1983, p. 3; Hallam 1983, p. 1; Galante 1983a, p. 1; 1983b, p. 1; Singer 1987, p. 12; Freeman 1987; Blum and Lobaco 1988). This is done under various names: nonequity partner, special partner, senior attorney, senior associate, participating associate, etc. As a Washington legal headhunter recently observed, "Everyone is studying this because everyone is running against the same economic realities. The larger classes of associates are coming up, and there is just not enough room at the top" (Griggs and McNeill 1987–88, p.

67. These figures should not be overinterpreted. Not only is the time interval for the more recent group one year shorter than for the older group, but the findings are equally consistent with lengthening of time to partnership.

68. Contemporary associates have their own "golden age" myth of a time when young lawyers were trained as generalists rather than being pushed early into a specialty, received intensive mentoring, and "could expect to make partner after a certain number of years" if they "performed well and committed no egregious blunders" (Holmes 1988, p. 20).

4). But permanent associates need not be those who failed to make partner. The managing partner at Cravath noted in 1983 that "[w]e now have about 24 what we call 'permanent associates,' who almost all were specialists in one sort of work or another. Most, but not all, had been hired laterally with their specialties already in hand."[69] After a hiatus of some years, Sullivan & Cromwell resumed the hiring of permanent associates: "Of the sixteen . . . in 1987, nine or ten worked in the area of clearing securities registrations, and others in oil and gas taxes, wills, and litigation" (Lisagor and Lipsius 1988, p. 258).

Firms also have increased the use of personnel who are not eligible to be partners. This is most evident in the increasing delegation of work to paralegals—that is, lower-salaried nonlawyer employees performing routine legal tasks under the supervision of lawyers (R. Simon 1988, p. 1).[70] The number of paralegals working in law firms increased from 14,000 in 1972 to 32,000 in 1977 to 58,000 in 1982 (Sander and Williams 1989, p. 442 n. 24). Paralegals can be found in law firms of all kinds and sizes, but they have become an important and growing presence at big law firms. In 1980 at the twenty largest firms in New York, there were 23.4 paralegals for every hundred lawyers; by 1987 this had increased to 30.9 paralegals per hundred lawyers—an increase of 32 percent.[71] Outside New York, paralegals were almost as numerous, 20 per hundred lawyers in 1980 and 25.5 per hundred in 1987—a 32 percent increase. In short, the paralegal population of the big-firm world seems to be growing slightly faster than the lawyer population. The presence of paralegals has been growing at the same time that the ratio of associates to partners is increasing, giving firms additional leverage without additional pressure to create partners.

The search for leverage without "the pressure created by regular associates eager to make partner" is also evident in the hiring of associates on a lower-paid nonpartnership track (Orey 1987, p. 20). Programatic two-tier hiring was initiated by Jones Day in 1984. The second tier was drawn from less prestigious law schools, and the academic performance of these associates was generally lower than that of those on the partnership track. Second-tier associates are paid less (in 1986 starting staff attorneys at Jones Day received $30,000 per year, as opposed to $52,000 for starting associates). The presence of these low-paid lawyers enables firms to compete for "low

69. As noted, the up or out norm had rarely been applied with absolute rigor. A Davis Polk partner observed that the new senior attorney program "just regularized what's been the fact for some time in the past" (Graham 1983, p. 3).

70. As Simon points out, definitional problems abound.

71. This is drawn from analysis of our *National Law Journal* "Two Twenties" Data Set.

end price sensitive business," including routine work that might have been done in-house by corporate law departments (Orey 1987). A 1988 survey found that twenty-three of the five hundred largest law firms had added "staff attorney" positions outside the partnership track during the preceding year (Nelson 1989, p. 14).

Another device for enlarging capacity without engaging new associates is the use of "temporary" lawyers. These "legal temps" are not employees of the firm, but are supplied by agencies who screen and certify them. Use of temporaries enables firms to respond to fluctuations in demand (often but not always, in connection with litigation) without the increase in overhead to accommodate additional regular employees. Such jobs attract lawyers who wish to work part time or irregularly. Temporaries are used frequently by smaller firms to enable them to handle more business without expanding, but they are another tool for big firms to enlarge capacity without adding to the partner/associate core. The first legal temp agency opened in 1983; in 1988 there were about a dozen agencies that, between them, operated in about as many jurisdictions (Labaton 1988, p. 26; Berkman 1988, p. 24; Mansnerus 1988, p. B-10).[72] Instead of bringing temporaries in, excess work can be sent out to "satellite firms." And other services, such as "litigation support" can be purchased from outside suppliers,[73] enabling firms to achieve enlarged capacity without bringing additional lawyers into the partner/associate core of the firm.

In these ways the classic big-firm notion of "promotion to partnership"—that all the lawyers were potentially members of a fraternity of peers—is attenuated. But if all lawyers are no longer potential peers, some nonlawyers are being invited into the core of the firm's operations. We have noted the drive to cover more specialities and more locations. The movement to build on successful relations with clients to sell them new kinds of services is not limited to legal services. Since legal services are often consumed in conjunction with other services, some firms have adopted strategies of hiring nonlawyer professionals. "Firms have brought in engineers, teachers, lobbyists, regulatory economists, banking regulators, nurses, doctors, and business managers (MBAs) to help provide client services" (Haserot 1987, p. 16;

72. The New York City Bar Association's reproach of these agencies' percentage fees as violating the ban on fee-splitting chilled the business there, engendered heated protest, and was withdrawn (Mansnerus 1989, p. 19).

73. These include not only computerized document retrieval but can extend to "taking over case management, tracing the whereabouts of defendants and witnesses, writing briefs and researching issues, providing expert witnesses and making visual presentations for trial" (Middleton 1984, pp. 1, 26).

Lauter 1984, p. 1). Other firms have established coordinate "nonlegal" businesses (investment advice, economic consulting, real estate development, consulting on personnel management, marketing newsletters, etc.) (Stille 1985, p. 1; Saltonstall and Lane 1988, p. 25; Siconolfi 1985, p. 33; Marcus 1986, p. A-1; Silas 1986, p. 17; Lewin 1987, p. 25). A lawyer whose firm branched out into office support services said that acquisition of this business was "like a company that makes peanut butter buying a company that makes peanut butter jars" (Stille 1985, p. 22). Others project a grander vision of the evolution of law firms into diversified knowledge conglomerates: "If the railroads had asked themselves what business they were in and had answered 'Transportation,' they might be in the airline business [today]. . . . We realized we were in the business of selling knowledge, whether we were advising legal clients, giving seminars, doing investment banking, making video tapes, or publishing newsletters" (Stille 1985, p. 20).

A partner at Arnold & Porter, which has established three consulting subsidiaries, anticipates that

> by the end of the century . . . large firms will become immensely more diversified in the services they offer. They will become more oriented toward problem-solving than traditional law firms, assemble teams of experts—lawyers and non-lawyers—and offer their clients "one stop shopping." . . . By the end of the century, legal services will be provided broadly in the context of a diversified service firm that will draw upon the talents of many disciplines with financial, economic and scientific resources available within a single institution. [Fitzpatrick 1989, p. 465]

In the meantime it is clear that the notion of the law firm as an exclusive and specialized repository of distinctively legal knowledge and skills has been loosened, if not abandoned.[74]

As the firm copes with the exigencies of its new competitive environment, the situation of the junior lawyer is more precarious and more pressured, although it is also more lucrative. But the partnership core is even more affected. Partners are under mounting pressure to maintain a high level of performance—and performance that fits the business strategy of the firm. Many new features of the law firm world such as mergers and lateral movement amplify the power of dominant lawyers within a firm to sanction their errant colleagues—and the prevalent culture endorses such sanctions.

74. The shift in perspective is succinctly put by one general counsel reflecting on the change in the nature of professionalism: "Most lawyers think of themselves first and foremost as lawyers, when in reality, they are a very small part of a much larger profession or industry. That industry is the industry of information management" (Liggio 1984, p. 106).

So partners worry about having their prerogatives or shares reduced or even being "pushed off the iceberg" or "de-partnerized" (Fisk 1988, p. 50). There are now real possibilities of downward movement. "[W]ith profits being squeezed and competition on the rise," reported one consultant, "many firms can no longer afford to support these [unproductive or disaffected] partners. Firms are trying to 'rehabilitate' these partners, decreasing some partners' incomes and asking others to leave" (Heintz 1983, p. 15). Thus a long-established 87 lawyer Seattle firm recently dismissed eight partners and six associates, on the grounds that "the firings were necessary to increase profitability and keep talented attorneys from being hired away."[75] The unassailable security of partnership is no longer assured. "Partnership used to be forever, but it is no longer" (Bernstein 1982, p. 100).

As the world of big law firms undergoes these dramatic structural changes, many of its inhabitants experience considerable distress about commercialization, the decline of professionalism, (see, e.g., ABA 1986) and the loss of the distinctiveness of law practice. To some extent this distress about lost virtue is a constant feature of elite law practice. But what distinguishes current worry about commercialism and professionalism from that of a generation ago is that the latter was combined with stable expectations about the large firm as an institution. If the inhabitants of the golden age thought the large firm was already too big,[76] they harbored few doubts about its durability.

Conclusion

For a long time, those who inhabited the world of the big firm could expect that the years to come would not be terribly different from the years just past. But this sense of stability has been shaken.

By choosing the "promotion to partnership tournament" as a form of governance the big firm committed itself to a dynamic of exponential growth. The environment allowing, growth comes in ever-larger increments and eventually changes the character of the firm and, by the conjoint growth of its companions, of the legal world in which it is situated. This is not to say that

75. "Mass Firing in Seattle," *National Law Journal* 1989b, p. 2. Cf. the report that in the early eighties, "[d]issatisfied with the performance of some of its partners, Willkie, Farr and Gallagher of New York has asked about a half dozen to leave" (Bernstein 1982, pp. 84, 100).

76. Smigel reports that in the early 1960s most lawyers in firms of one hundred or more lawyers "feel they have reached or passed their optimum size" (1964, p. 367).

the classic "promotion to partnership" firm is doomed. Undoubtedly many such firms will continue to exist. If it starts small enough and has good luck in obtaining clients, such a firm can have a long run. But the world of legal practice will cease to be dominated exclusively by firms of this type. This is because the most "successful" and enduring (and hence the largest) of these firms are likely to turn into something quite different from the firms of the recent past.

Those who cannot manage exponential growth or who seek to avoid its unattractive accompaniments will devise other institutional forms more to their liking. Some of these will flourish, changing the mix of firms that populate the corporate hemisphere of the legal world in the near future. We anticipate pluralization—both that big firms will be less similar to one another and that some of the work they presently do will be done by firms (or non-firms) that are not big firms at all.

What kind of setting will these successor forms of practice provide for the admired qualities associated with professionalism such as self-governance, independence of judgment, and individualized treatment? There is no reason to believe that the big firm is the only possible vehicle for these qualities. The transformation and displacement of the big law firm is not necessarily a danger to professionalism; indeed it may present an opportunity for new forms of pursuing professionalism.

Looking back, we see the relationship of the big firm to professionalism as ambivalent. Law practice, or at least that part of it that serviced large organizations, departed a century ago from the individual practice format for doing legal work. But it never arrived at the great bureaucratic corporation as a format for practice (on the specter of practice by corporations, see Bristol 1913, p. 590, Dawson 1930, p. 274). Perhaps the promotion to partnership firm should be credited with averting such developments by permitting development of sufficient size to undertake the most large-scale and complex work.[77] The big firm form carried an inadvertent commitment to exponential growth, but that growth was sufficiently slow to be compatible for a long period with "professional" forms of governance. Law practices never suffered the separation of ownership from control. Compared to other business services, law remained relatively unconcentrated, decentralized and unbureaucratic. As the big firm becomes a less congenial vehicle, lawyers confront new challenges to use their institution-shaping skills to reorganize the formats of professional work to make it produce the services and protections desired by the society while making it fulfilling for those who do the work.

77. Apparently the big firm enjoyed some comparative advantage over internal law departments within corporations (Pinansky 1986–87).

CHAPTER TWO

Managing Entrepreneurial Legal Services: The Transformation of Small-Firm Practice

Carroll Seron

Today, lawyers have various avenues for getting business. Beginning in the early 1960s, the Supreme Court held that private associations may advise members on legal claims.[1] In 1977, the Court held that lawyers may "advertise prices at which services are performed."[2] The impact of these decisions has been notable. Direct mail companies offer prepaid legal plans through credit card companies, direct sales, and telemarketing, which creates a stable client base for participating attorneys. Unions negotiate the provision of a full-time legal services unit as part of a fringe benefits package. National legal services firms open storefront offices in a variety of cities and use

I am particularly grateful for the helpful comments and support of Marie Provine at various stages of this project and to Robert Nelson for his substantive and editorial suggestions. In addition, it is a pleasure to thank John Flood, Eliot Freidson, Wolf Heydebrand, and Daniel Poor for their perceptive comments. The American Bar Foundation, the National Science Foundation (Grant No. 88–08754) and the PSC-CUNY Research Foundation provided funds for this study; I greatly appreciate their generous support.

1. See NAACP v. Button, 371 U.S. 415 (1963), Brotherhood of Railroad Trainmen v. Virginia State Bar, 377 U.S. 1 (1964), United Mine Workers of America, District 12 v. Illinois State Bar Assoc., 389 U.S. 217 (1967), United Transp. Union v. State Bar of Mich., 401 U.S. 576 (1971).

2. Bates, et al. v. State Bar of Arizona, 433 U.S. 350 (1977). Also see Goldfarb v. Virginia State Bar, 421 U.S. 733 (1975). The issue of lawyer advertising and solicitation remains one of consideration by the Court; see Ohralik v. Ohio State Bar Assoc., 436 U.S. 447 (1978) 22, *In re* Primus, 436 U.S. 412 (1978), *In re* R.M. J., 455 U.S. 191 (1982), Zauderer v. Office of Disciplinary Council, 471 U.S. 626 (1985); and Shapero v. Kentucky Bar Association, 486 U.S. 466 (1988). *Shapero* considered the question of mail solicitation where an attorney contacted individuals facing foreclosure to advise them of their need for an attorney. Although the Court has held that in-person solicitation is not protected (see *Ohralik*), in *Shapero* the Court held that direct mail solicitation does not present the same problems. Over Justice O'Connor's strong dissent, Justice Brennan's opinion in *Shapero*, by striking down the virtually universal ban on "subjective predictions of client satisfaction" (at 4535.35) eliminates one of the last instruments through which state bar associations could regulate advertising.

television advertising to market services. Local for-profit legal clinics with several branch locations in a metropolitan area advertise in the *Yellow Pages*, on buses, and in newspapers. Thus, in addition to the traditional small law firm, there are now "clinical" storefront law firms, "national" legal services firms, prepaid legal providers, and not-for-profit law firms seeking the business of the individual client (Menkel-Meadow 1979; ABA 1982; Singsen 1984, 1985; Pfennigstorf and Kimball 1977).

When lawyers market and sell their services in these new ways, they enter relatively uncharted waters. It is unclear, however, if these developments represent an extension of the professional's traditional prerogative to control his or her work or a more fundamental transformation in the legal practice of the "individual-client hemisphere" (Heinz and Laumann 1982). I intend to explore this issue by mapping the emergent organizational structure, politics, and culture of the work settings of the "new providers" (Singsen 1984) and to speculate about the implications of these developments.

New providers incorporate some traditional aspects of professional service, perhaps most notably the very private and personal relationship between practitioner and client. At the same time, however, these new forms of legal practice introduce an entrepreneurial twist: attorneys take risks by experimenting with new strategies to cope with an increasingly competitive environment. The new providers rely on close managerial oversight in the belief that it will ensure a high rate of productivity. These developments exhibit many characteristics of traditional small-firm and solo practice, but they also suggest the potential to transform the delivery of individual-client legal services.

This essay is one of the first close looks at how these new lawyer-entrepreneurs operate.[3] Because the new providers represent a notable departure from traditional practices, I first describe in detail the organizations studied. Then I turn to the concerns of a sample of practitioners and consider the skills they report to be essential for solo or small-firm practitioners in the world created by new providers.[4] Finally, I analyze the tensions between

3. Singsen (1984, 1985) has also examined the impact of these changes on legal practice. His primary focus was whether these new forms of legal services are meeting the needs of working-class people. In other words, he is concerned with a more evaluative question.

4. I conducted twenty-nine open-ended interviews with five managers of plans and twenty-four practitioners to ensure a cross section of respondents in various types of practice settings.

Interviews with managers took from one to three hours. Interviews with practitioners took from thirty-five to ninety minutes, though the great majority lasted between forty-five and fifty minutes. Prior to interviewing the practitioners, I met with the manager or supervisor of the program to develop a baseline for describing the goals, history, and organization of the program.

Questions focused on respondents' backgrounds, expectations, aspirations, and reasons for participating in one of the programs as well as the organization's techniques for socializing new recruits

professional, entrepreneurial, and managerial value orientations in various practice contexts.

A Descriptive Overview: The Delivery of Legal Services

In the last decade three key developments have transformed legal services delivered to individuals: (1) the advertising of legal services, (2) the marketing of prepaid plans, and (3) the computerization of a host of legal forms and management tasks. Indeed, every plan manager interviewed for this study spoke unabashedly about the importance of borrowing techniques from the world of business. Furthermore, attorneys in private practice in all types of settings studied echo the sentiment that delivering legal services is a business. The one clear theme to emerge from the preliminary phase of this project is that business strategies—advertising, sales, efficient management, computerization, and productivity evaluation—have become part of the repertoire of individual-client legal practice.

To understand the impact of these organizational patterns, I interviewed providers representing various types of work arrangements. On the not-for-profit side, I selected DC 37 Municipal Employees Legal Services Plan (MELS), which serves the members of the American Federation of State, County, and Municipal Employees (AFSCME) of New York City, one of the first union in-house legal services plans. On the for-profit side, I selected Hyatt Legal Services and Jacoby and Meyers, the major national legal services firms (also see Singsen 1984). In the area of prepaid legal services plans, I selected Signature Group, Hyatt Legal Services,[5] and Nationwide Legal Services. The discussion that follows is drawn from interviews with the managers of each plan. I interviewed practitioners to confirm or clarify the organizational picture presented by managers. Over the course of these

---

and managing and monitoring the work of practitioners and relations with clients and peers. I wanted to determine whether the introduction of business techniques had fundamentally altered the way lawyers think about their work and designed my questions to elicit an understanding of how practitioners constructed a professional identity in light of an openly cost-conscious, business-oriented approach to the delivery of services.

Nonmanagerial respondents were assured that their responses would be kept confidential. Only two refused to allow their interviews to be taped for transcription. Names of practitioners were provided by the managers of each of the new providers.

5. In addition to its storefront law offices located in twenty-five midsize media markets, Hyatt also markets prepaid plans. Because they sell legal plans through credit card companies, they compete with Signature and Nationwide. Because they also arrange packages for associations and unions, to some degree, they compete with MELS.

interviews it became apparent that managers and practitioners alike believe that they are bringing an important service to an underserved population, working and middle-class Americans.

Non-profit, In-house Legal Plans

In 1974, the Ford Foundation and AFSCME undertook a pilot program to explore the feasibility of providing legal services to union members as part of a benefits package. This was the first nonprofit, in-house legal services plan. Drawing on the models developed by the legal services and community action programs of the Office of Economic Opportunity, MELS was created to meet the legal and social needs of a largely lower-income population of union members. It is overseen by a board of trustees that is responsible for the policy and direction of the program, to include the types of cases covered. Board members are selected by the executive board of AFSCME, often with suggestions from MELS staff.

MELS captures much of the ethos and values of the Great Society programs of the 1960s. Gerald Mann, the director, was the first employee; Sheila Manashe, a social worker, was the second; and both are still a part of this organization. Mann and Manashe both report that they came to MELS from Great Society programs in the belief that unions composed of lower-income members provided a vital arena for expanding social services. By including social workers in the plan, they sought to develop a more comprehensive or diagnostic approach to the problems facing lower-income individuals. When members come to MELS with a legal problem such as a conflict over a custody issue or landlord-tenant dispute, they may, depending on the situation, be advised to see a social worker as well as a lawyer.

The organizational history of MELS is divided into two rather distinct periods. During the pilot phase (fron 1974 to the early 1980s), professionals were organized into two "specialized" teams—Wills and Administrative matters—and two generalist teams that were viewed as mini–law firms. Each team was composed of a supervisor, a senior attorney, staff attorneys, and social workers. Similar to traditional small-firm practice, each generalist team handled the range of civil cases covered by the program.

In the early 1980s the team structure was modified. Nine specialized legal units were established: Housing, Wills, Matrimonial, Family court, Change of name/adoption, Consumer matters, Bankruptcy, Real estate, and Administrative matters (see Figure 1). Teams still consist of supervisors, senior attorneys, staff attorneys, and social workers, although the size of each varies depending upon caseload and some teams do not have an assigned

Figure 1. Overall organizational structure of MELS

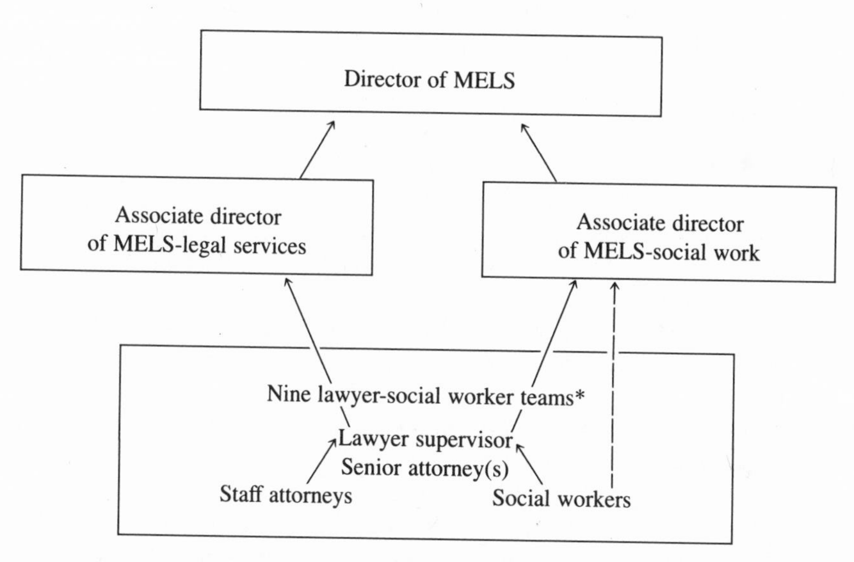

*These teams include 1. Housing, 2. Matrimonial, 3. Wills, 4. Change of name/adoption, 5. Consumer matters, 6. Real estate, 7. Bankruptcy, 8. Family court, and 9. Administrative matters.

social worker. Wills, for example, is a rather small team without an assigned social worker while Matrimonial has two supervisors. MELS currently employs about seventy attorneys and twelve social workers.

The specialized team model was developed in response to the problems caused by large caseloads and high turnover rates. First, specialization was thought to produce economies of scale. MELS management believes that lawyers are more efficient in handling a large caseload if they can concentrate on one field. Second, specialization helped minimize problems caused by a fairly high turnover rate among staff attorneys. Although many supervisory attorneys have been with the program since the beginning, staff attorneys tend to leave, largely because of the limited opportunities for mobility in a relatively flat organization. An organization of specialized teams eases the transition when a member resigns.

There is a bureaucratic cast at MELS that echoes the organizational contours of government legal services (Meadow and Menkel-Meadow 1982; Menkel-Meadow and Meadow 1983; Katz 1982). Within each team staff attorneys report to their supervisor; in turn, supervisory attorneys report to the associate director of legal or social services, depending on the nature of the problem. Although the team concept moderates the hierarchical aspects of this chain of command, and supervisors reported that they sometimes poll the group on an administrative matter, rank in the organization determines who makes the ultimate decision. Yet, there are important factors that humanize this work setting. First, the doors of administrators are open. An attorney who had been there for less than one year reported that he would feel perfectly comfortable going into the directors's office to share a concern. Second, the social workers on the staff at MELS begin from a therapeutic mind-set. These professionals start with the assumption that the problems of their clients require much more than a technical, legal solution. Finally, a sense of political commitment to the role that the plan plays in the lives of working people softens some of its harsher bureaucratic characteristics. Attorneys work at MELS because it comports with their political values.

The political cohesiveness of the organization may be weakening, however. A number of attorneys with more seniority reported that political commitment growing out of the legal services movement is less and less of a bond. They noted that in the not-too-distant future (and in distinct contrast with earlier years) none of the staff attorneys will have had legal services experience. In this environment, the high-status teams are those which prepare the practitioner for work in private practice, especially on matrimonial matters. Often, the next job a departing staff attorney takes is in private practice geared to individual clients, perhaps with Jacoby and Meyers or Hyatt Legal Services.

For-Profit, National Legal Services Firms

Currently, Jacoby and Meyers and Hyatt Legal Services dominate the national, for-profit legal services market. Briefly, national legal services firms have a management company in place that is responsible for the purchase of equipment, real estate expansion into new areas, training, customer relations, and all advertising. Jacoby and Meyers is headquartered in Los Angeles and New York; Hyatt, in Cleveland. In addition, these firms have each developed a network of storefront offices that is responsible for the day-to-day delivery of services. Jacoby and Meyers opened law offices in shopping centers beginning in 1972 and began to expand the reach of the market after the *Bates* decision in 1977, which permitted lawyers to advertise. Hyatt Legal Services opened in 1977 in Cleveland immediately following *Bates*.

Both of these firms rely on the techniques of business and marketing to provide legal services for lower-income and working-class Americans. Drawing on the imagery of the legal services movement, the founders of

Jacoby and Meyers and Hyatt Legal Services claim that the goal of national legal services firms is to fill a void for those in the middle. Lawyers interviewed at both firms pointed out that the rich have always had access to legal services and, with the development of government legal services program during the 1960s and 1970s, the needs of the poor were being met. These firms target the working person with limited resources and time.

Managers at each firm anchor their organizations in the legal services movement. At Jacoby and Meyers the story is that Jacoby and Meyers had the idea for legal services while in school together and blazed the trail of establishing multiple law firms before the 1977 Supreme Court decision. At Hyatt, the story is that on the day the Supreme Court handed down the *Bates* decision, Joel Hyatt resigned from the prestigious law firm of Paul Weiss, Rifkind, Wharton, and Garrison and returned to Cleveland to open a storefront law office. Such stories function as legitimating and, in some sense, as personalizing narratives for these nontraditional organizations (see Meyer and Rowan 1978, Bolman and Deal 1984).

Equally important, both firms proceed from the claim that television advertising informs and educates consumers of their rights to reasonably priced legal services. Advertising informs consumers of their legal rights and, it is argued, puts them closer to an equal footing in a very private relationship with an attorney. The opportunity to advertise is the step that made it possible to discuss openly the marketing of legal services. One might claim that advertising professional services brought the discussion of business out of the closet.

Access, availability, and fair fees are seen as essential to success in this new market. To this end, law offices are situated in convenient locations such as malls and shopping centers; offices are open in the evenings and on Saturdays. A contract for the cost of a legal service is spelled out at the first visit, but all fees must be paid prior to the delivery of the service. The initial consultation costs are very modest. Standardized forms make subsequent transactions increasingly cost efficient. Interviewees in both firms pointed out that these obvious and necessary techniques were borrowed from the world of business, but were considered "radical" when first applied to legal services.

Although competition for individual clients is not a new phenomenon (Carlin 1962), these firms clearly have recast the parameters of the game and the tools for gaining an edge. Competition between Hyatt Legal Services and Jacoby and Meyers remains somewhat indirect. The size of a market is the basis upon which both firms have made decisions to expand, and each firm has tended to move into new markets that resemble its initial niche. Jacoby and Meyers has expanded into the largest. Following its L.A. roots, it has moved to New York and to the major population centers in New Jersey, Arizona, and Pennsylvania. By contrast, Hyatt first expanded in smaller markets such as Denver, the Buffalo-Rochester-Syracuse triangle, and Atlanta. Currently, Jacoby and Meyers is located in five of the six largest market areas; Hyatt in twenty-one markets, most of them midsize. San Francisco is the only city where both firms have opened offices.

The workhorse of these firms is the law office in a "convenient location." Here attorneys handle a general-practice caseload. Tasks are divided between a managing attorney, who is responsibile for the administration and profits of an office, and associates. The number of associates in each office is determined by the demands of the location.

Figure 2 describes the organizational structure and tasks of a local office. As the figure suggests, the structure of these firms is similar. A primary task of managing attorneys is to train new associates. Indeed, in four of the five offices of both firms that I visited, the managing attorney was in the process of training or hiring a new attorney. Both firms have decentralized attorney recruitment from headquarters to regional offices because experience suggests that this is more efficient. In the spirit of the benefits to be gained by a well-designed division of labor, both firms have brought the concept of specialization to "shop floor" management. At Jacoby and Meyers, bankruptcy, criminal, and personal injury cases are assigned to specialists who, depending on demand, are either in the direct employ of Jacoby and Meyers or work on an of-counsel basis for the firm. For example, in the New York area Jacoby and Meyers employs attorneys who handle all bankruptcy and criminal cases, but turns over all personal injury matters to a firm that specializes in such work. At Hyatt, they tend to refer major criminal and personal injury cases to outside firms because they do not feel they have adequate in-house resources or expertise.

There is a consensus about what is required to be a successful attorney at a national legal services firm. One must be able to carry a high-volume practice of individual-client cases—wills, bankruptcies, divorces—from an early stage.[6] Many commented that the caseload at a national legal services firm is very similar to that of a legal aid office. As one interviewee put it,

6. Most of the attorneys interviewed from Hyatt and Jacoby and Meyers had been there a number of years or viewed themselves as successful in this type of practice. Because there is a very high turnover rate—a point made by managers and practitioners alike—it is reasonable to assume that the successful attorney is hard to find. Managers at both firms reported that the hardest part of their job has been finding "good" attorneys to employ. "High" and "low" values are reported here as perceptions of practice. I am not using these terms in any absolute sense. Both firms use training manuals and other teaching devices to inform attorneys of procedures. Once this is done, however, attorneys begin to carry a caseload.

Figure 2. Organizational Hierarchy of For-Profit Legal Services

Hyatt	Jacoby and Meyers	General description
Regional attorney	District manager	Advertises openings. Screens candidates. Provides support for training. Base salary plus profits of region.
Managing attorney	Managing attorney	Oversees office. Hires new attorneys. Hires support staff. Handles cases. Trains attorneys. Base salary plus bonus from office.
Staff attorney	Staff attorney	Entry-level position. Handles general cases. Base salary plus bonus.

working at a national legal services firm is an "extension of legal aid," but geared to the needs of working- and middle-class consumers. This theme typifies the description of the founders as well, and captures an important cultural element of national legal services firms.

The legal work at a national firm may be an extension of legal aid or MELS, but organizational aspects of these work settings appear notably different. As one interviewee at one of the national legal services firms summed it up, during the first ten years of practice most decisions from headquarters concerned ensuring profitability and efficiency. Managing attorneys were responsible for keeping up with tight reporting procedures from their offices to headquarters. They learned to keep an eye on statistics and case flow; to think of cases in terms of dollars and cents; to supervise and evaluate the work of associates; and, to incorporate support staff into the organizational culture of the local office.

Despite the presence of various types of accounting and case-tracking procedures, attorneys also commented that their day-to-day work setting is akin to any solo or small-firm practitioner. They are in their offices by themselves, or with one or two associates. A managing attorney runs the office with support from headquarters, but much of this involves ordering materials or equipment and supervising accounting. Echoing the sentiments of Jerome Carlin in 1962, these attorneys report that they find legal practice to be lonely; elaborating, many commented that they look forward to meetings as a time to swap ideas, share administrative problems, commiserate about work situations, and tell war stories as a way to deal with the isolation.

Profitability through systemization is one theme that emerges from the first decade or so of these firms, but equally important to an attorney's success is the degree to which he or she can be an "entrepreneur" in a managed environment with a very high volume practice. When asked about the kinds of people they seek to hire, managers at headquarters underscored the need to be "entrepreneurial." Attorneys in the field often used the same word. Still, two comments on what they seem to mean by this term are in order. First, as one attorney suggested, one may be only so entrepreneurial or these settings will be too confining. Thus, these firms look to hire people who will bring in new business but who are also willing to work within a framework established by someone else. Second, with regard to gender, one person put it this way: It is hard to locate women who are "very entrepreneurial" because being an entrepreneur means working long hours, "hustling," and taking risks—traits one does not find in women.[7] Thus, the attorney who is successful at Hyatt or Jacoby and Meyers seems to be, in general, a male who can work with managed reporting systems, can endure the isolation of a small-firm practice, can handle the caseload needs of individual clients, can meet the demands of working very long hours, and has the spirit to build on the advertising provided by headquarters.

Many attorneys who come to work at Hyatt and Jacoby and Meyers do not stay in this "sink or swim" environment. Recognizing the need to address the problem of turnover, both firms are experimenting with new personnel practices. Attorneys at Jacoby and Meyers described a new mentoring program where more senior attorneys are assigned to associates to share the tricks of the trade; this program supplements the formal training of associates by managing attorneys. In 1985 Jacoby and Meyers also instituted a partnership program where attorneys who have been with the firm for at least five years may be asked to join the partnership and thus participate in a more lucrative profit-sharing arrangement. These are different ways to deal with the problem of turnover.[8] The mentoring program is designed to help keep attorneys. The partnership program is designed to engender a sense of commitment to Jacoby and Meyers at the point that a successful attorney

7. I interviewed one woman lawyer at a national law firm. I was, however, told that there are women who have been quite successful at these firms, but that on balance there is a notably larger proportion of men. At this stage, I am not sure if this is disproportionate to the profession at large. In weighing this factor, also keep in mind that many of these attorneys appear to be younger than the median age for the profession as a whole, and thus we should expect a larger proportion of women than is found in the profession generally.

8. One managing attorney at one of the national law firms commented that successful associates (those who make it through the first year or so) are very sought after by other, small general-practice firms because they know how to handle a high volume of work. Though I was not able to weigh the accuracy of this point, it makes intuitive sense because these associates have "social skills," they can move cases, they know the local legal culture, and they have been in court a lot.

Again, the reader should keep in mind that I am assuming that the attorneys interviewed for this project are, on balance, the success stories of Hyatt Legal Services and Jacoby and Meyers.

might be considering a position elsewhere. What is perhaps most interesting about both programs is that they are quintessentially lawyerly. These "innovations" are traditional in large law firms.

Paralleling this theme, a managing attorney at Hyatt reported that he has suggested to headquarters that attorneys in local offices be encouraged to participate in quite traditional routes to bringing in clients, such as speaking at luncheons and joining civic organizations. In theory, bringing in clients through advertising is the task of headquarters. But, this attorney suggested, it is equally important to develop more traditional routes because advertising may not be sufficient and because it is helpful for morale when attorneys feel a part of the local legal community.

Prepaid Legal Plans

The future of legal plans is the issue around which Hyatt Legal Services and Jacoby and Meyers part philosophical company. Jacoby and Meyers has done some marketing of legal services plans, but they are not convinced that this strategy is feasible. Hyatt, on the other hand, is deeply involved in the business of selling legal plans and has become one of the major players in this segment of the market.

As with advertising, a number of key Supreme Court decisions permitted the marketing and soliciting of prepaid legal plans. Most managers agreed that legal services plans would not have came about without the Court decisions because of the generally traditional posture of the legal profession toward business-getting practices.[9] The marketing of legal plans has also enjoyed the benefits of major changes in the direct mail industry. Advances in technology in the last ten years have transformed the direct mail industry from a few small firms run out of homes or small offices into a major industry. As one interviewee commented, ten years ago a graduate of a prestigious business school would not "be caught dead" working in direct mail; today, it is a "hot" area because it is so technologically sophisticated.

The concept of legal plans may also be traced to the labor movement. As Gerald Mann commented, as far back as the 1920s it was not unusual for a

9. For example, even the Signature Group (discussed later in this chapter) claims that they would not have proceeded without the Supreme Court decisions. They began to explore the feasibility of marketing prepaid legal plans, just as they might any other service, when the *Wall Street Journal* picked up the item. The *Journal* story caused great concern among the board of directors of Mobil Corporation, which at the time held a controlling interest in the stock of Montgomery Ward and Signature Group. This event lead Signature Group to request a letter of opinion from the Department of Justice commenting on whether the plan violated antitrust statutes. Today, the legal plan has an individual in the office of Signature's general counsel assigned full-time to the program.

lawyer to hang out at the union hall, give advice, and in the process pick up a few cases to help support his practice. In this sense, legal plans attached to unions simply formalized an older practice. Underscoring the union connection, another attorney reported that labor lawyers explored the development of "closed" plans for members to be paid for by the welfare fund as early as the 1950s. Here too, the development of legal plans was an expansion of an individual's labor law practice, though the practice terminated when it was found to be unethical by the New York state bar association. Indeed, Hyatt began with the premise that "legal plans would be the next fringe benefit," and they have been providing coverage for the Sheet Metal Workers for many years.

Today, marketing legal plans for unions is only one part of a bigger picture. I will focus on the approach taken by Hyatt Legal Services, Signature Group, and Nationwide. By most accounts, these companies are the major players in the business.[10] Each firm begins with the premise that it is possible to market a prepaid legal services package, that this service meets the needs of a working- and middle-class market, and that being responsive to the needs of consumers is a key to success. Yet, each firm puts these premises to work in different ways, many of which are new and build upon clever combinations from the world of business. Understanding these developments is essential for understanding this tier of the legal profession.

Hyatt's Prepaid Plan

Hyatt markets plans tailored to a specific union; group plans as part of a fringe benefits package; "cafeteria plans" where an employee may elect legal services through an automatic payroll deduction; and, most recently, individual plans marketed through credit card companies. A major task of the central office is to develop legal plans to fit the needs of new corporate clients. Thus, the range of services provided may vary from plan to plan.[11] Nevertheless, the procedure between individual and attorney is essentially the same across the plans: When individuals enter into a Hyatt plan, they are given access to a toll-free number. Should they need an attorney, they call

10. One interviewee suggested that he might add Mid-West Mutual Insurance to the list of competitors. Interviews with attorneys disclosed that many of them participate in a number of plans, though none reported participating in Mid-West's.

11. The range of services varies from the plan worked out for the Sheet Metal Workers, which covers all legal needs, to more limited variations where some services (e.g., real estate closing, name change) are covered by simply joining the plan and then all other services are covered at a reduced fee. Participating attorneys receive a reference manual outlining the coverage of each plan; all attorneys interviewed who participate in this program reported that the variation across Hyatt plans does not pose a problem.

this number, and, depending on their location, they are given two or three choices. To meet this demand, Hyatt has developed open panels of "participating Hyatt lawyers" who work in areas where Hyatt does not have a branch. When a participating attorney is used for a service, the attorney is reimbursed by Hyatt according to the standard fee schedule; when an in-house Hyatt attorney is used for the service, the attorney is given credit toward his or her bonus.

Signature Group's Prepaid Plan

By contrast, Signature Group, a wholly owned subsidiary of Montgomery Ward, developed legal plans as part of its direct response approach to selling "continuity" products, such as auto and travel clubs and homeowners' insurance. One point of interest, lawyers were not involved in the development, nor are there any lawyers in the ongoing management, of the Signature program.[12]

One morning the former president of the company came to work and suggested that they begin to test the market to determine the feasibility of selling a legal services package.[13] The company used their usual methods of market testing—altering the "creative" piece, the cost, and the exact services covered—to see which package generated the largest response. Through this process of market testing and refinement, Signature crafted a product to meet the desires of consumers.

Signature research showed that consumers want to go to "regular" lawyers, that is, lawyers who are older, work in their own offices, and are conveniently located. Signature also learned that consumers are fearful of not knowing how much a service will cost. Signature marketed a product that fits this profile. For a very small monthly charge, an individual is assigned a lawyer who has been matched to the purchaser by zip code; the lawyer has agreed to perform services at a reduced hourly rate.[14] By simply joining the

12. A direct response business is built on a model where it tests consumers until the details of a product, reasonable cost, and rate of return are known in advance of actual marketing; using the Montgomery Ward customer file as a test market, the Signature Group constantly explores the feasibility of selling new "continuity" products. While testing a product, the "creative" pieces will contain a disclaimer stating that the company will not, in all likelihood, go forward with the exact product.

13. The structure of the corporation reflects this responsiveness. Signature works on the concept of "profit centers" where the head of a division, for example legal services, is responsible for his or her own budget, profit and loss, investments, hiring, etc.

14. Underscoring Signature's commitment to consumer satisfaction, a participant may change lawyers by simply calling a toll-free number and requesting a reassignment. Consumers are also encouraged to seek second opinions from other participating attorneys.

plan, a consumer may receive a simple will, telephone consultation, review of legal documents, basic letter-writing, free initial consultation on a legal matter, and access to a set of services at a fixed fee.[15] Should a consumer decide to use a lawyer's services, all arrangements are worked out privately between the individual and lawyer. Signature sees itself, then, as the liaison between lawyer and consumer.

Signature began marketing this product in 1982 in Illinois, Pennsylvania, and Colorado. Today, the product is sold in forty-six states and the District of Columbia. The basic package—a monthly fee in exchange for access to an attorney at a reduced hourly rate—has not changed in the last five years, nor has it been modified to fit the perceptions of attorneys in various states.[16]

Once Signature decides to enter a state they develop an adequate attorney network to meet consumer demand. Before attorneys are accepted into a program, they must meet a number of basic requirements and agree to sign a contract that they will provide service at the reduced rate set by Signature.[17]

Although Signature is very concerned with "quality" of service, this amorphous concept is *only* tested and measured from the standpoint of the consumer.[18] Thus, they keep an eye on retention rates, and they monitor closely all consumer complaints. Should a consumer complain, the attorney is called immediately. If an attorney receives too many reasonable complaints, he or she is phased out of the program, that is, the attorney is not

15. On balance, the programs are pretty similar in structure, providing a set of "free services," a set of services at a reduced rate (e.g., name changes, real estate closings), and a reduced charge for other services.

16. Before entering a state, Signature must, of course, determine compliance with state insurance regulations. In some states, this product is defined as "insurance" because it includes a free will; where this occurs, modest adjustments are made. They do not, however, alter the hourly rate to reflect the customary fees of a community; thus, regardless of location, a subscriber to the Signature Plan pays $50.00 per hour for any legal service.

Because Signature was so successful at marketing continuity products to their own file, a number of years ago they decided to expand by marketing to other credit card files, such as those of Chase Manhattan Bank and oil companies. Within the Signature Legal Services Plan there is a director of marketing who is responsible for selling this product to other credit card companies.

17. All participating attorneys must be in a firm composed of at least two partners who provide a general service practice; attorneys must have at least three years of experience; they must carry their own malpractice insurance; they may not have had any disciplinary actions taken against them by the state bar association; and they must provide references. All attorneys must submit their names to the state bar for an annual review to determine if any disciplinary actions have been taken. Further, if an attorney's situation changes (e.g., if he or she severs a partnership), he or she is to notify Signature within thirty days. Recognizing that attorneys may not always take this step, the managers at Signature who serve as the liaison with attorneys constantly monitor this aspect of the program.

18. Should a customer complain to Signature about the quality of an attorney's service, he or she is advised to report it to the state bar association. They draw a very clear division between their job to manage a service and the profession's job to monitor quality through peer review. Indeed, it is for this reason that there has been a self-conscious decision to not have any lawyers manage this program from headquarters.

assigned new clients. In fact, if a client feels that he or she has been charged for a service that was not performed, Signature may, depending on the situation, simply pay the attorney's bill. In their view, a dissatisfied customer may purchase next year's refrigerator from Sears rather than from Montgomery Ward, the parent company. They plan to develop strategies for documenting the monetary impact of good management practices, such as returning telephone calls (the single largest complaint from consumers across all of the programs), keeping appointments, and maintaining a polite support staff. Through careful tracking of complaints from consumers, they can then pass this information along to attorneys to help them improve their business.

Nationwide's Prepaid Plan

The Nationwide Legal Services Plan is a publicly held corporation that markets a number of products. Much like Hyatt and Jacoby and Meyers, Nationwide is the personal product of one man, in this case William Kirschner. In 1977, Kirschner received a telephone call from a friend in New Jersey, asking him if he would like to be a participating attorney in a legal plan negotiated for the Retail Clerks' union. He said "sure," got off the phone, and went to find out what a legal plan was. He learned that the Retail Clerks had negotiated a legal benefits package where members could use the services of designated attorneys in their state. In exchange, participating attorneys in this semi-closed plan agreed to provide services at a reduced fee that was paid by the welfare fund of the union. While continuing to practice law, Kirschner expanded on the union benefit concept and began to market legal plans to other groups. In September 1984 Nationwide became a publicly held company, and he gave up the practice of law to work for Nationwide full-time.

Using direct mail, telemarketing, and direct sales Nationwide sells legal plans in thirty-seven states. They market two products for individual consumers, the "one will" and "two will" packages. Essentially, for a small monthly charge, services include a simple will and trust plan; unlimited advice and consultation on the telephone; unlimited review of documents up to six pages in length; unlimited letter writing; one half hour of face-to-face consultation; and access to an attorney at a discounted rate. The rate of discount depends on the plan taken, but ranges from 25 to 33 percent off an attorney's normal hourly charge.

The link between purchaser and attorney is decentralized. Within each state, Nationwide retains a "lead firm" who handles all clients in that state and in exchange receives a percentage of the monies collected from participants. In Kirschner's view, this structure has the advantage of making the "lead firm" into a "corporate partner," thereby encouraging a commitment to the program. A consumer is given access to a toll-free number to contact the lead firm; he or she presents the problem, and the firm takes it from there. In the vast majority of cases the problem is solved on the telephone. But, if this is not sufficient, the lead firm uses an attorney data base, matching expertise and zip code, to assign a local practitioner. In order to participate, attorneys must carry malpractice insurance, agree to sign a contract that they will work within the arrangements established by Nationwide, and receive high ratings from clients.

Like Hyatt Legal Services and Signature Group, Nationwide constantly stays abreast of consumers' complaints. Client satisfaction is seen as the key to success. Clients are surveyed to rate the quality of service on a regular basis. Further, consumers are given a toll-free number to report complaints, or they may contact the lead firm in the state. All complaints are investigated. If the complaints are with the lead firm itself, the problem is investigated immediately. If necessary, the lead firm in a state can be changed within a matter of days, since Nationwide owns the toll-free number. In addition, Nationwide monitors all attorney logs to determine case types, demand, and hours expended on a case. If an attorney is taking too long and therefore charging too much for a service, he or she is notified.

Nationwide is somewhat smaller in terms of in-house personnel than Signature or Hyatt. Between twelve to fifteen people handle marketing, administration of plans, and customer relations. The marketing division sells plans directly and works with a marketing company as well to enhance access to a broader group of consumers. Like Hyatt, the types of plans offered vary from employee benefits to payroll deductions to direct sales.

Currently, Nationwide is exploring the feasibility of marketing a new plan for small businesses.[19] The plan is being tested in California where commissioned representatives have been engaged to sell the plan directly, in much the same way that insurance policies and investment packages are sold. Prior to the actual undertaking, Kirschner suggested that market testing showed that this is a logical arena for expansion, but that it is still in the earliest stages of development.

Although discussions of market-testing and solicitation are part of all of these stories, the leaders of new provider organizations incorporate the small-firm tradition of legal practice and preserve the private relationship

19. This plan will include telephone consultation; "free" collection letters up to a specified number and $15.00 per letter thereafter; a 25 percent discounted hourly rate; a legal services plan for the individual owner; and, for an additional fee, legal plans for all employees.

between lawyer and client. By claiming to make legal services available to traditionally underserved clients, they allude to the concerns of the consumer movement and remind the profession at large that they perform an important service. Yet, an open embrace of management and risk-taking is also a direct challenge to the traditional organizational contours of the profession. Many of these new providers see themselves as both lawyers and businesspersons, and they are equally proud of both roles. Before considering the full implications of this combination of managerial, entrepreneurial, and professional orientations among leaders of these organizations, it is important to assess how these new arrangements are seen by practitioners working on the "shop floor."

From the Bottom Up: The Views of Practitioners

Although the organizational structures of these "new providers" vary in interesting and important ways, these practitioners share the experience of working in or with larger organizations. Whether one goes to work at MELS, a national legal services firm, or joins a prepaid plan, attorneys of the "individual-client hemisphere" are learning to fit into larger organizations and, in this sense, modifying the "collegiate" tradition of this sphere of practice (see Abbott 1989). This pattern is not unique to the new providers. The demographics of the profession show a decline in the proportion of solo practitioners and an increase in the total population of lawyers. Summarizing her findings, Barbara Curran writes that "the most notable change has been the decline in the proportion of lawyers engaged in the private practice of law on a solo basis and the increase in the proportion engaged in firm practice or employed in settings other than private practice" (1986, p. 20; also see Abel 1986, 1988b).[20]

The new providers are distinctive, however, in their emphasis on managing the work of lawyers. The managers of these programs require that attorneys fit into their scheme; managers of new providers, like managers of all occupational professionals (Elliott 1972), are concerned with the efficient, productive, and cost-effective delivery of service. Thus, these practitioners are confronted with a set of role expectations different from those facing other small-firm lawyers. They must learn how to promote themselves within an otherwise structured context. By marketing their services, more-

20. The decline in small partnerships and solo practitioners parallels data for England (Abel 1988a).

over, they must pay special attention to the wishes of consumers. Despite all the manifest changes in context and tactics, the "new provider" settings incorporate many traditional elements: these attorneys report that they have control over their cases and clients; when a client enters an attorney's office, the door is closed, the case is theirs, and the relationship is private. These lawyers in new providers do not see a conflict between the innovations of self-promotion and attention to customer satisfaction and the traditions of the private lawyer-client relationship.[21]

Promoting Oneself

Marketing one's professional services through advertising and participation in direct mail prepaid plans contradicts the ideology of a passive, service orientation associated with traditional law practice. Yet, ten years after the Court's decision on advertising, there was a notable consensus among these practitioners that it is an accepted and necessary part of legal culture. Expressing the sentiments of many, one attorney suggested that "advertising is good for the industry" because it raises the level of consciousness of one's right to sue.

Many practitioners in small-firm settings (who may or may not be affiliated with a prepaid plan) reported that marketing one's services can be very expensive.[22] Without adequate resources, many turn to more limited promo-

21. When you consider the findings reported in this section, you should be aware of a number of caveats. First, although the findings suggest interesting developments, they must be read cautiously: Twenty-five interviews provide a sound basis for speculation, but it is impossible to estimate precisely how and whether this group of attorneys reflects the larger population of metropolitan, small-firm practitioners. Second, the attorneys interviewed for this phase of the project were chosen by the providers. Though I requested names of individuals at various ages and stages in their careers, it is reasonable to assume that these attorneys represent successful role models in these programs. Third, and in keeping with the exploratory emphasis of this study, I modified the questions put to attorneys over the course of this initial phase; consequently, I do not have comparable data on all questions. Finally, it is very difficult to demarcate absolutely between various forms of legal services plans. Indeed, the competitive nature of this market appears to create an environment where some attorneys have experimented with multiple strategies to expand their clientele—borrowing and reshaping organizational forms from competitors and other business arenas as resources permitted.

With this in mind, this discussion is based on four interviews with attorneys at MELS, seven attorneys at national legal services firms, ten attorneys affiliated with a prepaid plan, and four attorneys who were contacted through the *Yellow Pages*.

22. In order to get some sense of the actual costs of advertising, I contacted the *Daily News* and *New York Post* in the summer of 1987. A one-year contract to run a daily ad costs about $73,000.00 at the *Daily News* and about $93,000.00 at the *New York Post*. During interviews with attorneys, I gained the general impression that the *Daily News* is the preferred newspaper for advertising legal services. As of this writing, I do not have any information on the range of costs for radio and television advertising, which is, no doubt, much more variable.

tional efforts, such as advertising in local newspapers and participating in prepaid legal plans. Thus, short of mass-market advertising on television, practitioners may experiment with more modest attempts at self-promotion. For example, attorneys may begin by placing an advertisement in the *Yellow Pages*, the size of which will depend on their resources.[23] Further, a group of attorneys reported that they have experimented with advertisements in newspapers that are directed to a particular community, for example, gays, Haitians, Jews, or widows. According to those who have experimented with the ethnic-specialty newspaper strategy, it has the advantages of getting one's name into a specific community and, of course, being considerably less expensive.[24]

Underscoring the theme of self-promotion, attorneys associated with legal plans suggested that they agreed to join as a way to secure a small toehold for building a business. Yet, these attorneys were quite clear that legal plans are not a sufficient basis for building a practice. Rather, these attorneys tend to view legal plans as a mechanism for access to other clients; as a way to bring in one or two "big" cases, such as negligence disputes, that will make the other cases worth the effort; or, as a way to gain access to cases that are not covered under the plan so that a "regular" fee may be charged.

Finally, a key ingredient of self-promotion is social poise. Consistently, practitioners emphasized the importance of the "social skills" of attorneys and support staff alike. As one attorney put it, social skill is "more important" because legal skill can "always be bought." Further, a key figure in storefront law firms is the receptionist, who must have a pleasant telephone voice, know whether the person has come to the right place for help, and indeed bring in that client through the initial inquiry.[25] Thus, the first step to success in this new world of legal services appears to be marketing and selling oneself. This is not new per se (see Carlin 1962); what is different is the overt, systematic, and self-conscious effort directed at this matter.

23. A basic listing in the *Yellow Pages* costs about $125.00 per year whereas a three-inch color box runs about $6700.00 per year.

24. Linking one's name to a specific ethnic community as a strategy for getting business is not an especially new idea. Carlin (1962) described the efforts of attorneys to participate in the activities of an ethnic association as a way to secure clients. Advertising in ethnic newspapers is, in many respects, an extension and systemization of this strategy. In fact, the parallel with the experience of the attorneys studied by Carlin can be taken one step further, for many also reported that the clients who arrive at one's doorstep in response to small newspaper advertising are not necessarily the most desirable prospects. As a number of attorneys suggested, one has to be careful because ethnic newspaper advertisements tend to bring in more clients with smaller cases, thereby reinforcing the market already available.

25. In one interview, a managing attorney at a national legal services firm described an incident where someone was sent from headquarters to help during a period of staff shortage. When he asked if he might answer telephones, the local manager made it clear that he could answer the phone only if he could do as good a job as the receptionist.

Consumer Satisfaction

Equally, one may not overlook the other side to self-promotion, that is, concern that the consumers are satisfied. Quality service is equated with how consumers rate their treatment by an attorney on criteria they deem important—tidiness, responsiveness, and courtesy. As one industry representative put it, all of these precautions to insure consumer satisfaction are simply "good business sense."[26]

Yet, consumer satisfaction goes beyond market-testing. There is a shared perception among the entrepreneurs and practitioners that their work blends the values and ethos of the consumer movement with the movement to provide legal services to the poor (Abel 1988b). Reflecting the values of the consumer movement, respondents claimed that prepaid plans clarify fee arrangements in advance of service; that advertising informs prospective clients of their rights and thus puts consumers on a more nearly equal footing when they enter a law office; and, that managing the work processes of attorneys protects clients because matters are completed in a timely fashion. Not surprisingly, respondents also described a strong identification with the goals of the movement to provide legal services to low-income Americans. Recall that most of the founders of these programs came of political age during the 1960s. They described their work as a strategy for expanding the reach of legal services to middle-class and working people that has been tempered by realism and maturity. This vision is shared by the lawyers working in these organizations.

Old-Fashioned Lawyering

The full picture of the legal services industry is still more complicated, because many practitioners also report that in many respects their work is organized in the same fashion as traditional practice. Managers report and practitioners corroborate that attorneys have their own cases, contact clients directly, go to court, and argue their fair share of trials. Although they recognize that many cases are perhaps "boiler-plate" matters, they also note that many of their age-peers in other legal practice settings have much less control over an entire case than they do (see e.g., Spangler 1986, pp. 28–70).

26. Clearly, service professionals, such as doctors and lawyers, have always had to pay some attention to the elusive dynamics of client satisfaction in order to stay in practice. What is interesting about these developments is that the "industry" has taken steps to formalize this aspect of the professional-client relationship.

Further, the experience of practitioners in for-profit legal services is of a piece with their counterparts of an earlier era to the extent that their client base is not secure or predictable (see, e.g., Carlin 1962, Heinz and Laumann 1982). It is interesting that attorneys in offices at national legal services firms shared this sentiment with attorneys in private practice. The advent of individual legal plans, as well as advertising, have had a direct effect on the market for clients who bring in individualized, "one-shot" cases,[27] rather than the market for corporate clients who are far more likely to be "repeat" players in the legal system (Galanter 1974). My interviews suggest that the new providers—like the traditional solo practitioners—are attorneys for the "one-shot players" and suffer all of the corollary difficulties. These attorneys do not receive retainers. Their clients tend to come for a specific need (e.g., a house closing, a will, or a divorce) and thus do not generate a solid client base.[28] It is not surprising that these practitioners also report that although they may be making more money than they expected, they do not feel financially secure.

The elements that describe the work settings of new provider legal services clearly include a belief in the value of applying managerial techniques to professional service. Of equal importance, these developments rest on entrepreneurial self-promotion while preserving some features of a tradition of professionalism. How then are we to explain the organizational dynamic of these developments?

Toward a New Paradigm of Professional Service

During the twentieth century, the legal profession secured a quite powerful niche as the "gatekeeper" to a body of formal and esoteric knowledge (Freidson 1986; also see Abel 1988b, Auerbach 1976, Heinz and Laumann 1982, Halliday 1987, Larson 1977, Szelenyi and Martin 1989) and with it control over how and where legal work may be done. Reflecting this control, the profession's code of ethics sets standards of appropriate behavior that

27. Two caveats are in order. First, Nationwide's attempt to develop a prepaid legal plan for small-business people may expand the parameters of this market. Second, one interviewee who is also the attorney for a number of "closed" union plans reported that these are much more lucrative than "open" plans. At this stage, it is not feasible to comment further on the accuracy of this point; in fact, it is impossible to develop an accurate picture of the number of attorneys who are involved in closed plans without a systematic survey of the population.

28. "One-shot" attorneys may have relatively lucrative practices (especially those who have developed successful personal injury practices), but there is considerable variance in income within this group, reflecting the uncertainties of client relationships (see Heinz and Laumann 1982).

limited attorneys' creativity to solicit work. But the developments described here suggest that delivering legal services to individual clients revolves around three relatively distinct tasks and value orientations that do not all complement the traditional professional model (also see Abel 1986, 1988b). These tasks are those of the (1) manager, (2) entrepreneur, and (3) professional.

In this milieu, many of the traditional distinctions between for-profit and not-for-profit practice begin to break down. First, a number of the for-profit firms have marketed plans for unions that present a direct and competitive connection across these spheres of practice. Second, while MELS presents a philosophy of legal practice quite different from that of most for-profit organizations,[29] more and more young practitioners at MELS seem to view their work as training for one of the for-profit firms, which suggests an important, if informal, link. Finally, the founders of these programs all know each other and serve on the same boards, for example the American Prepaid Legal Institute (a quasi-independent arm of the American Bar Association). They describe themselves as part of a common, if competitive, network.

If we listen closely to the words used by these respondents to describe their organizational culture, it is clear that they draw a distinction, perhaps only an implicit one, between a manager and an entrepreneur. Yet, this distinction is key to understanding the full implications of the new provider movement.[30] Figure 3 presents a schematic overview of these value orientations and the contradictory dynamic at their core. The combination of a managerial and professional orientation is risk-averse, but undermines the importance of expanding the business of lawyering. The combination of a managerial and entrepreneurial emphasis is needed to survive in a competitive environment, but seems anti-professional. The resolution, or lack of resolution, of this contradiction is central to the new provider movement.

The Manager's Task

American popular culture continues to equate the principles of management with Taylorism (Bendix 1956). Good managing is simply a matter of supervising tasks that have been broken down to their simplest common denominators. The central managerial function is to work out the most

29. In all the programs selected for study, the person who began the program is still at the helm. In many respects, the personality and entrepreneurial style of these individuals continue to play an important role.

30. I am grateful to Wolf Heydebrand for pointing out the importance of defining these two tasks as quite distinct aspects of this undertaking.

Figure 3. Contrasting value orientations within legal services

MANAGER
- Supervision
- Accounting
- Efficiency
- Stability and predictability
- Automation

ENTREPRENEUR
- Innovation
- Getting business
- Social skill
- Networking and politiking
- Risk-taking
- Political commitment

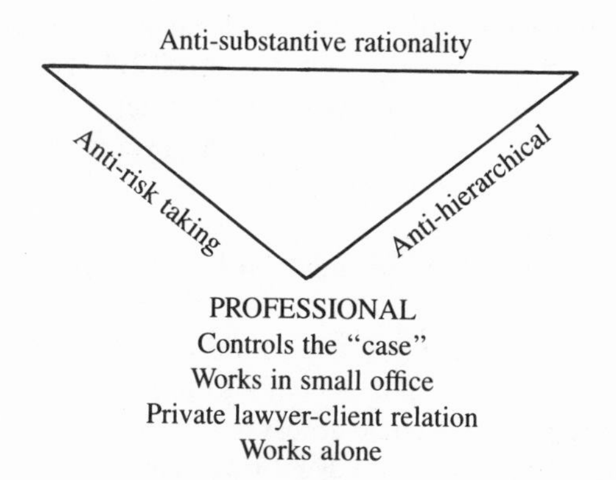

appropriate structural arrangement for insuring the efficient completion of assignments (Braverman 1974; Edwards 1979; Hirschhorn 1984; Zuboff 1988). Of course, when this model of management is applied to overseeing the work of professionals, some tensions are inevitable, even where supervision is by professionals (Freidson 1986, pp. 85, 134–55).

Yet, a Taylorist model must have been one of the dominant images of managing that shaped some of the leaders of the new provider movement. When the founders at MELS, Hyatt Legal Services, or Jacoby and Meyers describe the process of creating high-production legal offices, they elaborate on a process of rationalizing—standardizing, systematizing, and simplifying—legal work, a direct application of Taylorist principles. The introduction of computers extended rationalization by automating steps that had once been performed in a labor intensive manner. Automation was an essential step toward implementing their vision of a storefront law office, a vision that was based on the application of a factory model of production to the delivery of a professional service—a novel, but not a radical, idea.

These firms developed a detailed division of labor in terms of the supervisory structure as well. Top management assumes that the attorneys in direct supervisory positions will do nothing more than oversee the work of other professionals, and that "headquarters" will handle the riskier creative issues.

Yet, lawyer-managers on the shop floor have a somewhat more nuanced understanding of supervision. At national legal services firms, managing attorneys describe the constraints imposed by this Taylorist mind-set and the ways in which their job entails more than a concern for dividing tasks efficiently. It is most interesting that local-area managers of national legal services firms describe how they must balance social relations between lawyers and support staff within an office because they have learned that *everyone* is key to making a profit. The same observation was made by small-firm practitioners who rely on prepaid legal plans to expand their client bases. Senior attorneys in charge of teams at MELS also underscored the importance of learning to balance dynamics between attorneys, paralegals, and social workers in a relatively formal managerial environment. At a private law firm, a secretary[31] is as likely to bring in a client through an initial telephone contact as any of the attorneys. At an organization such as MELS, all employees share in helping the client through the difficult initial moments of seeking help.

Thus, in each of these settings, albeit for different reasons, it is essential that all employees understand the tasks of the office—a demand that is eased through computerization and equal access to information. At the local level, managers balance structural demands to insure an efficient, rationally organized system that takes interpersonal realities into account and recognizes that all employees are essential for a successful operation.[32]

At a more analytic level, these managers are balancing the realities of a relatively flat organization where the gap in the knowledge and skills of lawyers and support staff is necessarily reduced (Hirschhorn 1988). This dynamic is, of course, exacerbated as many forms and techniques of lawyering are made "explicit" through computerization (Hirschhorn and Farquhar

31. Managers at headquarters claimed that they will not redesignate the legal staff as "paralegals" because, they claim, such a relabeling would raise too many unrealistic expectations about their work. Yet, it is exactly this "expectation" and identity with the organization that a local-area manager seeks to instill in order to develop a profitable office.

32. In light of the tension between professional and supervisory demands, managers must be sensitive to the play of interpersonal dynamics (Mintzberg 1973). Underlying this view is a more dynamic model of supervision that echoes Occhi's (1984) notion of a "theory *Z*" manager, which builds on McGregor's (1960) model of "theory *X*" versus "theory *Y*." McGregor claimed that an approach to management based on controlling the structural arrangement of work (theory *X*) will alienate a labor force and that a more effective approach must respect the interpersonal and individualistic needs for fulfillment from work (theory *Y*). By contrast, Occhi claims that an effective manager must balance "theory *X*" and "theory *Y*."

This approach, moreover, builds on two key assumptions: (1) externally, the political-economy of the organization is relatively stable and predictable (Heydebrand 1989); and (2) internally, the organization is a basically harmonious or homogeneous work unit. In this world one may be a good manager, but one need not take risks; in fact, the image of a good manager is someone who is risk-averse and "sticks to the knitting" to accomplish the job at hand (Bolman and Deal 1984).

1985). From the standpoint of the lawyer, computerization can "de-professionalize" day-to-day work because knowledge is no longer controlled at one source (see, e.g., Abel 1985a, Ehrenreich and Ehrenreich 1977a, 1977b, Freidson 1986, Haug 1973, 1975, 1977, Derber 1982, Halliday 1987, MacDonald and Ritzer 1988, Nelson 1988, Oppenheimer 1973, Powell 1985, Ritzer and Walczak 1988, Rothman 1984, Larson 1980, Spangler 1986, Szelenyi and Martin 1989). From the standpoint of support staff, however, computerization can enhance responsibility (Hirschhorn 1984, 1988).[33] The manager is actually working in an uncertain setting, balancing the flux generated by a rationally "automated" and a creatively "informated" work environment (Zuboff 1988). There is, in the final analysis, a degree to which management practices and the traditional limitations on professional certification may act as a drag on the entrepreneurial business of expanding this service.

The Entrepreneurial Task

Entrepreneurs are celebrated, if slightly mistrusted, figures in American popular culture, for they are "change-masters"—people who bring a new vision to their work, develop a new product, or realize a new insight for bringing in business (Kanter 1983). An entrepreneur thrives on uncertainty by shaking up the established ways of doing things.[34] One can sense this dynamic among the leaders of the new provider movement. Leaders of the for-profit programs are very proud of their accomplishments and the business they have developed, but they are also well aware of how they have been misunderstood by the traditional segments of the legal profession.

This tension is hardly a surprise when one realizes that these entrepreneurs

33. Clearly, this aspect of new provider work settings presents a powerful challenge to the traditional foundation for controlling expertise. At this stage it is not clear, however, the extent to which there is an explicit recognition of the potential powers of automation. On the other hand, attorneys were clear to note that their "real" expertise was of an affective nature, i.e., being able to work well with people. One might speculate that this concern reflects an implicit recognition of shifting realities and an unconscious attempt to define their "expertise" in new ways.

34. In the last few years, students of management have begun to study stories of founders and entrepreneurs to understand the successes and failures of organizations (see, e.g., Meyer and Rowan 1978, Alvesson 1987). One interesting theme to emerge from this work is that entrepreneurial firms—particularly in high-tech areas—incorporate this spirit into their organizational structure: individuals may be encouraged to campaign for their favorite new products (Kanter 1983); work may be organized around teams, so that "reporting" may take place at multiple "hubs" through various matrices (Hirschhorn 1984); or, electronic mail may be used to expand the reach of informal exchange of ideas (Zuboff 1988). From the standpoint of a rationalized management model, these organizations often appear to thrive on complexity, chaos, and confusion.

have creatively capitalized on the "calling" of professional service. First, for-profit new providers have transformed an "ideal" of equal access to legal service from a public to a private sector activity. Second, these practitioners are quite clear that their activity *at* work—solving people's problems—is their calling. That is, they do not distinguish between public service and "regular" work. Thus, the founders of national legal services firms recast the political symbols of the legal services movement, such as available lawyers, and those of the consumer movement, fair, reasonable, and standard pricing, to market and advertise their business (Edelman 1971). In like manner, the developers of prepaid legal services packages transform the political concerns of the consumer movement into a commercial venture. In this endeavor nonprofit organizations like MELS play an important role by keeping this political language alive. Clever advertising; finding a good location; developing, packaging, and marketing the right packages all require continual change, innovative shifts, and risk taking to survive in a highly competitive market. In the field, practitioners share these concerns and present themselves as part of this new social movement to extend the reach of legal services.

Although the new provider movement commercializes the language and deed of a calling, more appears to be at stake. For a good entrepreneur must also be able to "sell" ideas. The task of selling requires networking with others, communicating ideas, and presenting oneself well. Often, these "action-centered," "tacit," or "ambiguous" skills (Zuboff 1988) are more important than substantive knowledge of an area. Indeed, the importance of "network building . . . based on . . . sociability in direct oral communication as he or she nurtures the goodwill of others" (Zuboff 1988, p. 104) is key to success in corporate culture (see, e.g., Kotter 1982, Kanter 1977, Mintzberg 1973). It is not surprising that these appear to be the essential, if at times ambiguous, skills that the founders of these movements use to "communicate" their message.

What is interesting about this change in lawyering, however, is that good social skills are equally important for the success of a local office. In many corporate organizations, midlevel managers tend to be "locals" who focus on the task at hand. Upper-level managers are the "cosmopolitans" who negotiate corporate position (see, e.g., Zuboff 1988).[35] This distinction in style or value orientation does not, however, describe the division of skills in

35. This point bears some parallels to Nelson's (1988) discussion of "finders, minders, and grinders" in large law firms which, in turn, draws upon Gouldner's (1950) earlier description of a division of professional labor between "locals" and "cosmopolitans"—or those who mind the shop and those who take care of the larger world (also see Merton 1968).

the new provider movement. Rather, the success of this undertaking requires that all participating personnel bring "good social skills," that is, that they know how to communicate the story of this undertaking. Politicking, networking, listening, and communicating are key factors in the success of local offices. This is the message that Signature Group, the most openly business-oriented of the providers, sends to its participating attorneys through its newsletter. MELS began with a recognition of the importance of this "tacit" skill when they included social workers in the development of teams. In a flattened organizational structure, managing attorneys must cultivate this constellation of skill in *all* personnel who may have contact with the public, support staff and attorneys alike. Thus, this emphasis on sociability acts as an additional force to destabilize the importance of substantive legal knowledge, that is, the importance of being a "good" lawyer in the traditional sense of this term.

The Professional Dimension

The managerial and entrepreneurial dynamics of this undertaking undermine the professional core of practicing law. The managerial push standardizes legal work so that a high-volume practice is feasible. Computerization has been absolutely essential, a point emphasized by the founders of all of these programs. The entrepreneurial push makes good social skills the essential job requirement for all personnel, again a point that was implicitly recognized by respondents. If legal work can be standardized and social skill is more important than legal expertise, then is this project professional in name only?

In the "old" model of the profession, individuals were both the managers and authors of their labors. Where individuals worked alone or in very small groups, there was almost absolute autonomy. This imagery has often been closer to an ideal than to any actual practice, particularly in newer professions (see, e.g., Auerbach 1976, Carlin 1962, Freidson 1986).

Thus, the push of the professions to demand the right to work autonomously must be examined in light of the equally powerful trend toward the consolidation of work into large-scale, managed organizational settings (see, e.g., Hall 1968, Montagna 1968, Noble 1977, Larson 1977, Scott 1965, 1969, Wiebe 1967). The two trends are parallel and, in fact, part of a common, if conflicted, theme in many arenas of work (e.g., engineering, teaching, social work). Newer, occupational professionals (Elliott 1972) evolved with the expansion of large-scale organizations at the turn of the century and have sought to maintain control over technique within managed settings.[36] The empirical evidence suggests, therefore, that autonomy has at least two dimensions. One aspect of professional autonomy refers to its structural elements or the degree of control over the setting where one works. The second aspect of autonomy refers to control over knowledge required to carry out one's job, or the technical dimensions (Heydebrand 1973). The pivot of control has, for most professions, resided with the claim to control the gates to "formal knowledge" (Freidson 1986).

In the case before us, however, lawyers attached to new provider work settings appear to be experiencing diminishing control over the technical dimensions of their work, but not over key elements of the structural dimension.[37] A professional's claim to technical autonomy includes the authority to define the services to be performed, the "formal knowledge" that is required, and what constitutes good service. As we have seen, many aspects of these technical components have begun to erode. The range of services, such as divorces, wills, or real estate, is defined by management. Computerization has begun to transform access to the "formal knowledge" of lawyering. Finally, management has established control over quality by emphasizing the importance of consumer satisfaction rather than legal expertise.

On the structural side, however, these work settings recall those of earlier generations. The offices are physically small, relatively isolated organizations. Here, the "organization" of these providers, whether national legal services firms or prepaid plans, is actually a computerized telephone network that makes it possible to centralize and de-centralize simultaneously. Communication, oversight, and coordination of work are facilitated through information networks that render more centralized bureaucratic techniques obsolete (Hirschhorn 1988) and permit day-to-day work to be completed by relatively autonomous work units. Further, the client's relationship with an attorney is very private. At this pivotal axis of what it means to be a professional, these practitioners are actually doing their work in a most traditional manner. Although they may report that clients ask more questions, the clients ask those questions behind closed doors where the individ-

36. Some "new" professions (Etzioni 1969) have succeeded in retaining autonomy over standards and performance within large-scale organizations, for example, engineers (Noble 1977; Zussman 1987), scientists (Kornhauser 1962), and business managers (Chandler 1977). Others have been notably less successful, for example, social workers (Lubove 1965; Scott 1969) and teachers (Bowles and Gintis 1976).

Yet, a similar tension between structural and technical autonomy has been documented for the elite of the legal profession (Heinz and Laumann 1982; Nelson 1988), doctors (Freidson 1975; Starr 1982), and architects (Blau 1984).

37. In this sense, developments within this "hemisphere" of legal practice appear to be taking a markedly different direction from that of the corporate hemisphere.

ual attorney is on his or her own. There is a certain irony in all of this. The organizational contours of a traditional, solo practice are being used as a mechanism to motivate professionals to meet quotas set by management. In fact, it is in this context that some of the familiar concerns described by these individual-client attorneys—particularly the loneliness and insecurity of practice—begin to fall into place. Though attorneys associated with new providers must adjust to the demands of a managerial voice, where these lawyers work and how they interact with clients have not changed in twenty-five years (Carlin 1962).

CONCLUSION

The story of the new providers is that of three contending sets of value orientations. At its core, the professional orientation is defined by the desire to control one's work. The managerial orientation is defined by a concern to streamline, standardize, or rationalize the substance of work to make the process as efficient and simple as possible. Finally, the entrepreneurial orientation is defined by a willingness to shake up the established ways of organizing tasks. Clearly, the tension between a managerial and professional orientation is a familiar theme in the sociology of the professions (see, e.g., Freidson 1986). The introduction of an entrepreneurial dynamic complicates this tension by adding another challenge to a professional model.

Each of the new provider work settings shares some dynamic within each of these value orientations. Though MELS is the least entrepreneurial in the business sense of the term, it is a constant reminder of the political symbols of this movement. National legal services firms began with a relatively traditional managerial orientation, but advertising their services has demanded that they relax the boundaries of entrepreneurship and encourage all employees to learn to take risks and sell services. Finally, developers of prepaid plans, particularly the Signature package, are at the cutting edge as they turn legal services on its head by beginning with questions of consumer demand. To date, however, they must negotiate within a world constructed by the legal profession.

A reading of the many new trade journals discloses that the organized bar is aware of the implications of these developments. Bar associations have organized programs to guide young lawyers in the development of small-firm practice so that they may learn to advertise effectively, and manage their practice efficiently. The use of computerized programs is advocated as a way to streamline preparation and increase productivity. Such activities have introduced a fundamental uneasiness to the profession. Computer programs tend to demonstrate the increasing feasibility of executing many legal tasks, such as wills, bankruptcy, and divorce, without the aid of an attorney; this development underscores a managerial voice. Creative advertising and business solicitation undermine the passive posture of the professional and emphasizes an entrepreneurial voice. To date, the profession has successfully co-opted these managerial and entrepreneurial developments. Whether it will be able to continue to control them remains to be seen.

PART II

Lawyers' Ideals in Historical Perspective

These chapters provide a historical view of the diversity and changing character of lawyers' professional ideals. The studies illustrate the way both conflicts among groups of lawyers and perceived threats from outside the legal profession impel lawyers to redefine and pluralize notions of "professionalism."

Theodore Schneyer's account of the passage of the ABA's new Model Rules of Professional Conduct provides a unique analysis of the contemporary politics of the ABA and the difficulties it faces in attempting to maintain a unified ethical code for American lawyers. Schneyer reviews an extraordinary amount of material, including all records and notes compiled by Geoffrey Hazard, the reform commission's reporter. Schneyer reports heated conflicts among lawyers during the drafting and passage of the new rules. The original draft, surprisingly oriented toward a public audience (particularly the press), was significantly amended late in the process, at the insistence of particular groups of lawyers, such as corporate counsel. Before final passage, supporters of the draft rules faced significant dissent from various state and specialty bar associations. The public display of divisiveness and lobbying efforts by specific lawyer interest groups drew considerable criticism from the press and politicians. Schneyer concludes that the process of passing the new rules effectively accommodated the plurality of interests in the bar and was, in that sense, legitimate. His analysis clearly demonstrates, however, the disunity that exists within the profession on fundamental questions about self-regulation and professional responsibility, and thus that "professionalism" is truly a contested terrain.

Rayman L. Solomon presents a systematic examination of the professionalism projects of past leaders of the organized bar between 1925 and 1960.

He finds that the core of that concept remained relatively unchanged over that period; however, social, political, and economic events created various crisis periods. In each crisis period, bar leaders argued that some aspect of professionalism was endangered, and pushed for restoration. The crisis periods Solomon identifies are marked not only by an increase in the number of speeches that address a particular issue (such as delivery of legal services during the Depression), but also by an almost formulaic expression of concern that the public holds lawyers in disrepute and the profession is in grave danger. In each, the rhetoric of professionalism was used to hold the profession to the norms embedded in the concept and, thus, to reestablish the legitimacy of the profession. The five periods of crisis cover most of the period Solomon studied. He suggests that the profession is almost constantly in crisis because bar leaders are hypersensitive to threats to the bar's monopoly position. The leadership realizes that in a liberal democracy this privilege is suspect, and is always subject to removal by the state. Finally, Solomon points out that although professional leaders have always worried about commercialism, until now it has never been the explicit focus of a crusade to restore professionalism. This suggests a difference between prior professionalism "campaigns" and the current "crisis of professionalism." In the past, campaigns have been waged against threats to the wealth and power of the profession, but today that wealth and power appears to be the very source of concern.

CHAPTER THREE

Professionalism as Politics: The Making of a Modern Legal Ethics Code

Theodore Schneyer

In 1977, the president of the American Bar Association, William B. Spann, Jr., asked Omaha lawyer Robert Kutak to chair a special committee to review "all facets of legal ethics." Six years later the ABA House of Delegates approved a comprehensive new ethics code (ABA 1983), completing the process Spann and Kutak had set in motion. As if to underscore the length and intricacy of that process, both men had died in the interim.

However applicable Robert Michels's (1949, p. 401) famous "iron law of oligarchy" may be to the organized bar in other respects, it does not describe the ABA's production of the Model Rules of Professional Conduct, which amounted to the most sustained and democratic debate about professional ethics in the history of the American bar. Compared to the making of the ABA's earlier codes—the Canons of Professional Ethics (ABA 1969) and the Code of Professional Responsibility (ABA 1979), adopted in 1908 and 1969, respectively—the Model Rules process was an extravaganza. The Kutak Commission alone cost the ABA nearly $700,000. Other ABA entities, along with over a hundred state, local, and specialty bar associations, spent considerably more to participate in the process.[1] Two specialty groups,

An earlier, more detailed version of this chapter was published under a similar title in *Law & Social Inquiry* 14 (1989): 677–737. Readers who are interested in the many, often unpublished primary sources on which this chapter is based may consult the footnotes of that article for the appropriate references. I thank Deborah Rhode for comments on an early draft. Research was supported by a Meyer Grant from the American Bar Foundation and by summer grants from the University of Wisconsin Law School and Graduate School and the University of Arizona College of Law (from funds donated by the law firm of Streich, Lang, Weeks and Cardon, P.A.). Thomas Hartzell, a student at the University of Arizona College of Law, provided valuable research assistance.

1. The Wisconsin State Bar, representative in this respect of many state and metropolitan bar associations, spent $20,000 to have a committee analyze Kutak Commission proposals and suggest changes.

the Association of Trial Lawyers of America (ATLA) and the National Organization of Bar Counsel (NOBC), prepared full-blown codes of their own (ATLA Commission 1980; NOBC 1981) as rivals to the Model Rules. And two published drafts of the Model Rules—the Discussion Draft and the Proposed Final Draft—each triggered hundreds of written comments and scores of articles in law reviews, bar journals, and newspapers.

Because it is so rich in primary sources, the Model Rules process offers a rare opportunity to study the internal politics of the bar.[2] The political account of the Model Rules process presented here is based on news articles; early drafts of the Model Rules; Kutak Commission correspondence, memoranda, agenda books and journals; comments submitted to the commission or the House of Delegates; and several interviews.[3]

One of my aims is to advance an ongoing policy debate on the extent to which courts and administrative agencies should defer to the ABA when they adopt rules to govern the practice of law in their jurisdictions. A majority of the state supreme courts have already adopted the Model Rules, usually with amendments (Schneyer 1989, p. 679). Others may follow suit. As they did with the Code of Professional Responsibility and to a lesser extent the Canons of Professional Ethics, the courts appear to be treating the ABA not as a private pressure group but as the "preliminary arena . . . of public government" in which the law of lawyering is "first formulated" (Gilb 1966, p. 140). Whether this deference is wise depends at least in part on how open the ABA's process was to public opinion and to the views of all segments of the bar. By describing the process in some detail, I intend not only to show how open it was but, more generally, to inform judgments about the merits of a surprisingly common phenomenon: de facto delegation of public lawmaking to private groups (see Jaffe 1937, Macaulay 1983, pp. 3–10).

My more fundamental aim is to contribute to the sociology of the legal profession. In this essay I approach this task in four ways. I weigh the influence of various bar groups on the Model Rules and examine how they wielded their power. I compare the Model Rules process with the production of the two earlier ABA codes in order to highlight changes that have occurred over the century in the structure of the organized bar. Without trying to

2. There have been surprisingly few studies of the internal politics of private associations. Two of the best are Lipset, Trow, and Coleman (1956) and Garceau (1961).

3. Outside comments and internal ABA documents pertaining to the Model Rules were collected by Kutak Commission reporter Geoffrey Hazard and placed on file at the American Bar Foundation in Chicago. Comparable documents from the process that led to ABA adoption of the Code of Professional Responsibility in the late 1960s were deliberately destroyed. The preservation of Model Rules documents suggests that ABA leaders may now accept a greater degree of public accountability than they did for the earlier ABA codes and their preparation.

measure the Model Rules themselves against any objective standard of professionalism, I use the Model Rules debate to sketch what one might call the bar's "professionalism-in-fact"—the set of values and styles of ethical reasoning that, for better or worse, lawyers today appear to have in common.

At the same time, however, I wish to speak to the range of ethical opinion—the ethical pluralism—that presently exists in the bar and to suggest how the distinctive ethical concerns and views of certain subgroups may relate to their work settings, political environment, or clientele. This pluralism is not always apparent from reading the Model Rules, which like all codes strives for at least a surface coherence; but it would be a mistake to view the ABA's final product as its only product. Tentative drafts, as well as comments submitted to the ABA during the Model Rules process, remain in the profession's ethical stockpile, as is clear from the frequency with which state supreme courts, when they adopted the Model Rules, rejected some of the ABA's final provisions in favor of earlier versions (Schneyer 1989, p. 680).

To identify the range of ethical views within the bar, I compare the positions that various specialty groups took in the Model Rules debate (e.g., ATLA, which is composed mainly of personal injury lawyers; and NOBC, which is composed of lawyers who investigate and prosecute other lawyers in disciplinary cases). Assuming, as I do, that these positions accurately reflect the views of group members,[4] one can use them not just to sketch an ethical picture of "the bar" or "the average lawyer," but to paint a whole gallery of professional sensibilities.

The story of the adoption of the Model Rules can be seen as a three-stage process. The first stage began with the ABA decision in 1977 to form the Kutak Commission and ended with the publication of the Discussion Draft in early 1980. Here the commission focused on the ABA's "foreign relations." It tried to promote lay participation, respond to scholarly criticism of the earlier ABA codes, and garner favorable press coverage, while paradoxically using secrecy to stave off pressures from within the bar. The second stage began in early 1980 and ended shortly after the publication of the Proposed Final Draft in May 1981. Central here are the intense hostility within the bar to early drafts of the Model Rules and the resulting shift in Kutak Commission rhetoric. In the final stage, which culminated in ABA adoption of the Model Rules in August 1983, the center of activity was no longer the Kutak Commission (a drafting body) but the relatively faceless

4. For the contrary view that codes of professional ethics are primarily addressed to the public, express values professionals think the public will accept, and may not be reliable evidence of professionals' own views, see Newton, 1983, p. 32.

House of Delegates (a voting body of nearly four hundred). This stage was marked by backstage negotiations between commission leaders and various bar groups, many of them concerned not with the overall tenor of the Model Rules but with rules that would particularly affect them.

Besides providing a chronological account of the Model Rules adoption process, I shall explore some of the pervasive themes in the Model Rules policy debates. These were the constant resort to "legalism" as the idiom of ethical discourse, the persistence and centrality of the concept of role in lawyers' ethical thought, the stress on perceptions of comparative institutional competence (what the Model Rules should address, what should be left to other regulatory techniques), and the widespread fear among lawyers that acknowledging ethical duties in a code would expose them not just to professional discipline but to malpractice liability and other legal fallout.

Introduction

I focus on the formulation rather than the content of the Model Rules in order to supplement and challenge other scholarship on professional ethics generally and the ABA codes in particular. Scholars in many fields have been interested in codes of professional ethics since the remarkable flowering of those codes at the turn of the century. Until the late 1960s, most saw the codes and other specialized machinery for regulating the professions as a healthy development.[5] Since society as a whole has no real interest in professional ethics, Durkheim (1958) held at the turn of the century, specialized bodies must adopt rules of ethics and see to it that they are observed. And these bodies "can only be formed by bringing together individuals of the same professions" (1958, p. 7). For Durkheim, neither the market, nor general morality, nor all-purpose legal institutions such as the criminal law

5. Scholars today are apt to see things the other way around; many exhort professionals to rely on their own consciences and not to adhere slavishly to codes, which are politically suspect because private professional associations produce them and ethically suspect because they allegedly displace moral reflection or, at a minimum, promote reflection of a rule-bound, legalistic sort. I believe, however, that society stands to benefit from a dynamic process, if we can create it, in which professionals regularly test their subjective judgments against an external, less idiosyncratic set of ethical principles *and* test those principles against their own judgments.

The Kutak Commission never regarded the Model Rules as a complete moral guide for the perplexed lawyer. But even if the Model Rules did short-circuit the moral thought of some who consulted them for guidance, on balance they might still promote ethical reflection. After all, they generated broad debate among lawyers during the drafting process and continued to do so in the local-adoption process. "Articulation of the professional ethic," as philosopher Lisa Newton (1981) puts it, is "what makes a profession a moral enterprise."

could play superego to the practitioner's id; only professional associations and their codes were up to the task.

Economic conditions encouraged Durkheim's American contemporaries to see things his way. After 1870, as the economy grew more complex and the cities larger, expertise became more specialized and had to be marketed to strangers (Larson 1977, p. 6). Institutions that could vouch for a specific calling through licensing, codes of ethics, and specialized disciplinary bodies became attractive. They amounted to institutional advertising, assuring the public that a calling was ready and able to shoulder its corporate duty to hold practitioners to standards.[6]

New York county bar leader Julius Henry Cohen may have mixed his metaphors, but he caught the spirit of the times when he told fellow lawyers in 1916: "We are all in a boat. The sins of one of us are the sins of all of us. Come, gentlemen, let us clean house" (1924, p. 109). Cohen was influenced by Felix Adler, a philosopher and founder of the Ethical Culture Societies, who felt that ethical problems in industry, business, and the professions must be solved by the people who "live with those problems." It is not enough to have a general philosophy of ethics, Adler said, there must be daily application of philosophy to fact, and this "can best be done by the experts in the line" (quoted in Cohen 1924, p. 158).

Like Cohen and Adler, Herbert Harley, the reform-minded patriarch of the American Judicature Society, believed that by writing, interpreting, and enforcing codes of ethics, professional associations were not usurping the role of the state or the market but were on the contrary filling a regulatory vacuum. Focusing on the legal profession, Harley wrote

> There must be somewhere in the state or society power to establish standards of professional conduct with responsibility for enforcing them. It is easy to understand the practical failure of the courts in this field. And it is too delicate a matter for legislative control. . . . The public generally is most concerned with mere honesty and wants only to hold the lawyer to the standard for the lay fiduciary. . . . But the public suffers a thousand times more from less conspicuous infractions than from plain dishonesty. . . . This is the situation in a measure with respect to all professions. Their practitioners deal in mysteries. They are not safely judged except by their colleagues. [1922, pp. 34, 37]

This functionalist analysis held sway for years, although the rationale for a professionalism package consisting of ethics codes and other self-regulatory

6. A related idea, always popular with bar leaders, is that professional associations, by developing, publicizing, and fostering the enforcement of ethical standards, enhance their members' reputations or "human capital" and are thus entitled to their support.

machinery oscillated between two poles. Scholars such as Kenneth Arrow (1963) thought the package functioned to protect clients from experts who had the power to manipulate the demand for their services and who alone could judge the quality of those services.[7] Others, ranging from progressives Herbert Croly (1965, p. 136) and Louis Brandeis (1914, pp. 319–24), to sociologist Talcott Parsons (1954), to legal scholars Lawrence Friedman and Zigurds Zile (1964) in the mid-1960s, felt that at least in the bar's case the package functioned as a corrective to the practitioner's natural economic bias *in favor* of clients and against other interests.[8]

Since the late 1960s, however, scholars have more often derided than defended professionalism, and the ABA ethics codes have been under constant attack. Yet the attacks vary so widely that they may say more about fashions in political criticism than about legal ethics.

Some critics of the ABA codes have emphasized the process and setting in which they were developed. Writing just as the Model Rules process began, Jethro Lieberman acknowledged the need for a new code of legal ethics but argued on the basis of certain provisions of the Code of Professional Responsibility that the ABA could never overcome the "conflict of interest inherent in balancing self-interest against public and client interest" (1978, p. 217; see also Wolfram 1978). Lieberman thought a more neutral body such as the Judicial Conference of the United States should draft the new code. Similar views were expressed during the Model Rules process by legal scholar Deborah Rhode (1981) and by Thomas Lumbard (1981), a leader in ATLA's effort to derail the Model Rules project. Though these critics insisted on the importance of the process, none looked in detail at how the ABA was developing the Model Rules or had developed its earlier codes. None compared the ABA process with a concrete alternative.

Other attacks focused on the substance of the ABA codes. The first wave of such attacks crested shortly before the Code of Professional Responsibility went into effect in 1970. Positing a sharp conflict between two lawyer classes, these critics read the Canons of Professional Ethics as a degradation ceremony enhancing the status of the elite corporate bar that allegedly controlled the ABA, at the expense of an underclass composed largely of urban, ethnic, solo practitioners (Carlin 1966, chap. 3; see also Auerbach

7. Other economists, however, have long questioned the benefit to society of professional licensing and rules of ethics. See, e.g., Friedman 1962, pp. 137–60, Kessel 1958.

8. "Since the state's control [over lawyers in the United States as opposed to the Soviet Union] is so weak, one danger is that lawyers will tend to neglect the interests of society in favor of the exclusive interests of clients. . . . Thus, in the United States, the urge to professionalize, to increase standards, to inculcate morality on the part of the lawyer, is necessary" (Friedman and Zile 1964, pp. 35–36).

1976). "[W]hether by design . . . or mere peradventure," Philip Shuchman wrote, the Canons outlaw the tactics "Little Lawyers" must use to drum up business (solicitation, personal loans to clients, fee-splitting, below-minimum fees, etc.), yet tolerate and thus legitimate the tactics of "Big Law Firms" (intra-firm referrals and meeting prospective clients at the country club) (1958, p. 268). These conflict critics had little to say about the many provisions of the Canons that were unrelated to business-getting. Nor did they come to grips with the possibility that some restrictions on these "Little Lawyers" actually *benefited* them at the consumers' expense by restraining competition among them.[9]

Other critics, riding the same wave of consumerism that swept Ralph Nader into prominence, viewed the ABA codes not as arenas of intraprofessional conflict but rather as the conspiracies of a monolithic profession against an unprotected public. Some faulted the codes for doing too little to correct the maldistribution of legal services. For example, Marna Tucker argued that although the ABA supported federally funded legal services for the poor, unmet needs remained so great that the Code of Professional Responsibility's description of the lawyer's duty to do pro bono work as an unenforceable aspiration was an indefensible bow to self-interest (1976, pp. 27–28). Many others focused on all-too-enforceable duties outlined in the code that arguably distorted the market for middle-class legal services. Thomas Morgan (1977) claimed, for example, that the code regularly placed lawyers' economic interests above client and public interests. Morgan saw this pattern not just in the rules on fees, advertising, and group legal services—matters that clearly implicate lawyers' pocketbooks—but even in strict limits on taking on clients with potentially conflicting interests. Morgan regarded such limits as featherbedding, requiring two lawyers when one might well suffice (1972, pp. 727-28).

Besides its arguable inconsistency with Shuchman's intraprofessional conflict theory, Morgan's lawyers-versus-consumers analysis shares with all the criticisms a weakness stemming from its exclusive focus on code text. Morgan never makes it clear whether he means to criticize the code's effects on legal services, the aims of those who produced the code, or both. In either case, he offers and perhaps could offer no corroborating evidence from outside the text itself—no data on the impact of ethics rules on lawyers and

9. Ironically, one neo–conflict theorist (Heinz 1983, p. 907) recently suggested that court decisions in the 1970s hurt the "hemisphere" of lawyers who represent individual clients by striking down minimum fee schedules and restrictions on advertising and solicitation, and also suggested that the courts may have rendered those decisions because the elite corporate bar provided no "inter-hemispheric" support.

nothing about the code's legislative history (information the drafting committee had largely destroyed).

More recently, moral philosophers and some legal scholars have mounted a third and quite different attack.[10] They argue that the Code of Professional Responsibility coheres around a 'standard conception' of the lawyer's role (see, e.g., Goldman 1980, Luban 1983). This brand of "role morality" boils down to two principles: neutrality and partisanship. The first requires the lawyer to practice without regard to his or her own views concerning a client's character or aims. The second commits the lawyer to pursue client aims using every effective tactic within the law. The philosophers find the standard conception or "hired gun" ethic unacceptable because it prompts lawyers to disregard their own values and the welfare of third parties. As a remedy, some (Simon 1978; Wasserstrom 1975) propose "deprofessionalization" (a concept no clearer than the endlessly contested "professionalism"); others (Postema 1980, p. 82) call for the abandonment of an ethics code in which lawyers' duties are "fixed" or "entirely predetermined."[11]

This criticism is marred by the existence of provisions in the code that do not square well with the standard conception. The code permits lawyers to decline cases they find morally objectionable (Ethical Consideration [EC] 2–26), and to forego the use of "offensive" but otherwise lawful tactics in a client's behalf (Disciplinary Rule [DR] 7-101[A][1]). In many cases, it also allows lawyers to withdraw from representing a client who refuses to take their advice, including moral advice (DR 2–110[C][1][e]). These counterexamples suggest that the standard conception is a *mis*conception; it represents one major theme in the bar's ethical tradition but cannot fully account for the content of the ABA codes. They also suggest that legal ethics may be a discipline with no paradigm, only fragmentary and often incompatible conceptions of the lawyer's role continually vying for dominance: the lawyer as client's "hired gun," yes, but also as "officer of the court," as "lawyer for the people" (Brandeis 1914, pp. 319–24), or "counsel for the situation" (see Frank 1965, p. 698), as "friend" (Fried 1976), and as "minister" (Shaffer 1981, pp. 35–104).

The view that the Code of Professional Responsibility rests on a standard

10. This attack may be part of a broader criticism (Drew 1973; Melone 1977; Payne 1977) of the organized bar's role in lawmaking, namely that lawyers use the bar as a "front" to pursue client objectives at societal expense, even in the face of the traditional exhortation to work through the bar to improve the law "without regard to the general interests or desires of clients" (ABA 1979, EC 8–1).

11. The very fact that the Code of Professional Responsibility is a code undermines the argument that it completely "fixes" or "predetermines" a lawyer's role. Each rule in a code must be understood in the context of all the others, which inevitably gives the addressee some leeway; the text being interpreted is always richer and more complex than any one rule (see Fletcher 1981).

conception of the lawyer's role is also at odds with the final systematic attack on the ABA codes. Critical legal scholar Richard Abel argues that the ABA codes are too vague and inconsistent to constrain lawyers or give them any real guidance (1981b, p. 642). Because the codes are in the parlance of critical legal studies "indeterminate," Abel considers them merely a tool to legitimate the bar's relative freedom from outside control (p. 667). He thus criticizes as providing *no* guidance or restraint the very rules philosophers have lately criticized for "entirely predetermin[ing]" the lawyer's role! That critics can view the same rules at the same time in such contradictory ways suggests how little we really know about the link between rules of ethics and professional conduct.

For all their disagreements, the early supporters and the later critics of codes of professional ethics all search for the deep function, overarching theme, or grand design of the codes. They all jump quickly from modest evidence to broad political or sociological conclusions. And they all take their evidence primarily from the codes themselves; even the critics who question on procedural grounds the ABA's legitimacy as a source of rules of ethics fail to examine just how the ABA has produced its codes, who was involved in the process, what the participants thought they were doing, and why *they* said they were doing it.

By looking closely at the Model Rules process and taking seriously the views of those who participated in it, I hope to resolve some of the questions raised but not fully answered in the existing literature. Were the Model Rules affected by public opinion and the scholarly criticism of the earlier ABA codes? If public opinion and scholarly criticism were brought to bear on the Model Rules, at what stage and through what channels did this happen? Did lawyers view the Model Rules as a public relations stunt with no regulatory significance? Were there intraprofessional conflicts in the Model Rules process and, in particular, did an elite corporate bar try to distance itself from other lawyers by labeling their practices unethical? Did lawyers approach the issues in terms of "role morality," and if so, did they agree that the Standard Conception defines the lawyer's proper role?

A Chronological Account of the Model Rules Process

The Decision to Develop a New Code

The Kutak Commission was created only a few years after the Code of Professional Responsibility went into effect. Although Robert Kutak publicly hedged at first about his mission, telling state and local bar presidents that the commission might decide to "leave well enough alone," it seems clear that he and ABA president William Spann were out from the beginning to produce a new code, which immediately raises the question, Why the haste to replace a seven-year-old code that had not come into being itself until sixty-two years after its predecessor? In part the impetus was, as Richard Abel suggests, a felt need to shore up the profession's public image in the wake of the Watergate scandal, in which many lawyers were implicated. Spann's charge to the commission says as much.[12] But it also suggests that the project had much to do with shoring up among lawyers and regulators the ABA's image as lawgiver for the practice of law.

The ABA's primacy in this respect, established by 1920,[13] was confirmed as recently as 1972. By then, most of the state supreme courts had adopted the Code of Professional Responsibility, often verbatim, to govern the lawyers in their jurisdictions. But by 1977, two developments had thrown the ABA's primacy into doubt. First, the Supreme Court narrowed on First Amendment grounds the permissible scope of bans on lawyer advertising (*Bates et al.* v. *State Bar of Arizona* 1977) and banned on antitrust grounds the use of ethics rules and professional discipline to enforce local minimum-fee schedules (*Goldfarb* v. *Virginia State Bar* 1975). These rulings, along with earlier ones protecting group legal services plans, federalized issues lawyers had long considered to be within the preserve of the ABA and the reliably deferential state supreme courts. Second, while the state supreme courts had swiftly adopted the Code of Professional Responsibility, neither the ABA's subsequent amendments to the Code nor its opinions construing the Code were faring nearly as well. This was notably the case with respect to two issues prominently mentioned in Spann's charge, issues well below the threshold of public consciousness but of great interest to elite law firms.

One of these issues involved the "revolving door" through which lawyers move in and out of government. Read literally, the Code seemed to say that when a government lawyer went into private practice, neither that lawyer nor his or her new partners and associates could participate in a matter he or she had worked on while in government.[14] This ripened into a serious problem for firms that recruit government lawyers. Some courts and agencies were

12. On the use of other bar projects and programs to shore up the legal profession's public image, see Halliday 1987, pp. 92–93.

13. By 1920, all but thirteen states had adopted the Canons of Professional Ethics, but in most cases only by bar association resolution.

14. DR 9–101(B) prohibits former government lawyers from working on matters they had worked on in government; DR 5–105(D) prohibits all lawyers in a firm from taking cases that other DRs prohibit any lawyer in the firm from handling.

barring entire firms from cases in which one lawyer was disqualified by virtue of former government service. This threatened to make former government lawyers extremely unattractive hires in firms with substantial administrative practices. And so, in its strained Formal Opinion 342 (1975), the ABA Standing Committee on Ethics and Professional Responsibility held that if the disqualified lawyer was properly screened, others in the firm could handle the matter he or she had worked on in government. The trouble was that the ABA could not assure law firms that courts and local disciplinary bodies would accept this reading. While the ABA had formed a special committee to lobby for local adoption of the Code of Professional Responsibility, there was no committee to lobby for local adoption of ABA ethics opinions or piecemeal amendments.[15]

The other exotic issue mentioned in Spann's charge to the Kutak Commission was of special concern to securities lawyers. DR 7–102(B)(1) of the Code originally required a lawyer whose services had been used by a client to defraud others to take steps to rectify the fraud, if necessary by "blowing the whistle" on the client. The SEC used this rule in 1972 to bolster its complaint in the National Student Marketing case against two leading law firms that failed to notify shareholders or the SEC when they got wind of fraud in the merger transaction they were working on (see Karmel 1972). In 1974, the ABA House of Delegates countered by amending the CPR to subordinate the whistle-blowing duty to the lawyer's duty of confidentiality. As the Standing Committee later construed the amendment, it gutted the disclosure duty. The trouble was again that a large majority of states had never adopted the amendment (Kramer 1979).

The Model Rules eventually solved the revolving-door and whistle-blowing problems to the satisfaction of the elite firms that cared about them (see Model Rules 1.11[a]; 4.1[b]). Still, the question remains, Why were ABA leaders so responsive to the corporate bar's immediate ethical "needs," and why did they care enough about reasserting the ABA's primacy on such rarefied matters to commit the organization to producing a new code? A new code, after all, was not only expensive but risky. The uncertain factors that had kept piecemeal amendments to the Code of Professional Responsibility from being widely adopted might doom a new code as well. Perhaps the state supreme courts were now taking their regulatory duties so seriously that they would no longer rubber-stamp ABA rules in any form;[16] if so, the Model

15. On the balkanization of provisions dealing with larger advertising after the Supreme Court struck down the absolute ban on advertising, see Wolfram 1978, pp. 635.

16. On the relatively recent opening up of state judicial rule-making proceedings to interest groups other than the organized bar, see Grau 1978, pp. 49–70.

Rules, though intended to restore uniformity in legal ethics, might end up balkanizing the field even more. Moreover, if a new code turned out to restrict lawyer competition in some way, that might expose the ABA or the participants in the drafting process to antitrust liability.[17] And there was always the risk that the Model Rules project would prompt other bar entities, unhappy with the ABA's approach or hoping to increase their own visibility at ABA expense, to produce a rival code and seek its adoption at the state level—to work, one might say, to "decertify" the ABA as the ethical voice of the bar.[18]

To understand why the ABA went forward in the face of these risks, one must understand the link between the making of professional ethics codes and the making and maintenance of professional associations. Organization is not, as Durkeim supposed, essential to systematic ethical thought; American doctors knew the Hippocratic Oath and read Thomas Percival's treatise on medical ethics well before the AMA existed (Berlant 1975, pp. 64–127). When a professional association is born, however, promulgating an ethics code is often its first order of business. (The AMA turned Percival's treatise into a code in its first year.) Unlike a treatise or an oath, a code takes collective effort to produce and thus helps to justify the association's existence; it is also enforceable, if only by ousting violators from the association.[19]

Since the American polity is not run on corporatist principles (Salisbury 1979; but see Schneyer 1983), and the ABA thus enjoys no official designation as *the* voice of the legal profession, its position is never completely secure.[20] It has never been able to claim more than half the country's lawyers as members, and new specialty groups have increasingly become self-aware and spun off their own organizations, fragmenting not only professional loyalties and resources, but ethical and political perspectives as well.[21] To maintain its authority inside as well as outside the bar, the ABA must in a time of professional ferment display its authority. One way to do so is to refurbish its image as lawgiver for the entire profession.

17. In 1976, the Justice Department sued the ABA for conspiracy to restrain trade by adopting, distributing, and (through ethics opinions) aiding in the enforcement of the Code of Professional Responsibility, which severely restricted lawyer advertising and solicitation. The suit was dropped in 1978, but only after the ABA promised no longer to promote or aid in the enforcement of the code.

18. This risk materialized in 1979, when ATLA decided to draft a rival code. In most states, however, the ATLA code has never received serious consideration as a comprehensive alternative to the Model Rules.

19. In medicine, ouster from the AMA and local societies could have real economic consequences; for many years membership was a prerequisite for hospital privileges (Starr 1982, p. 168).

20. Since 1936, the ABA has been organized partially as a federation of state, local, and some specialty bars. To this extent the ABA is at the apex of the bar structure in the United States (see Johnstone and Hopson 1967, p. 38).

21. In 1982, for instance, corporate house counsel formed their own professional organization.

The First Stage: Responsiveness to Lay Opinion and Scholarly Criticism

The answer to the question of whether the Model Rules process was open to lay opinion and responsive to criticism of the earlier ABA codes depends on the stage of the process one focuses on. The first stage, from the creation of the Kutak Commission in 1977 to the circulation of its Discussion Draft in January 1980, was surprisingly sensitive to public opinion and scholarly criticism, surprisingly closed to bar insiders.

The Kutak Commission

To weigh the ABA's responsiveness to outside opinion and criticism, one should first consider the makeup of the Kutak Commission. All nine charter members were lawyers, but only three were private practitioners—Kutak himself, a partner in a rapidly expanding Omaha law firm; Robert Meserve, a member of the prestigious American College of Trial Lawyers (ACTL) and former ABA president; and Richard Sinkfield, a black lawyer in a large Atlanta firm. This was in sharp contrast to the committee that drafted the Code of Professional Responsibility in the late 1960s. Nine members of that committee were in private practice and six were ACTL fellows. If the ACTL—indeed, the private bar generally—was to have a major impact on the Model Rules, it was not going to come through any stacking of the commission in their favor.

Some of the Kutak Commission's charter members, though lawyers, were either on record as critics of the earlier ABA codes or had special ties to a lay constituency. Judge Marvin Frankel was an outspoken critic of the client-above-all mentality he found common among trial lawyers and embodied in the earlier code but inconsistent with the truth-finding function of the courts (Frankel 1975). Jane Lakes Frank worked in the Carter administration and had been counsel to a Senate subcommittee that had investigated the impact of legal fees on the availability of legal services. She was a staunch consumer advocate, on record (1976) as a critic of the Code's restrictions on lawyer advertising and group legal service plans. Tom Ehrlich, a former law school dean and then president of the Legal Services Corporation, also wanted to draw new attention to problems in the delivery of legal services to the poor. Kutak himself was on the board of the Legal Services Corporation.[22] The

22. Being so well represented, the legal services community was able for the first time to make an ABA ethics code responsive to its distinctive problems. Model Rule 1.8(e)(2) provides, for example, that a lawyer may pay litigation costs for an indigent client. Also, early Model Rules drafts contained

first meetings considered how to inject lay opinion into commission deliberations. A subcommittee recommended that three nonlawyers be added as voting members.[23] Meserve dissented on the ground that an already low and now dwindling percentage of private practitioners on the commission would make for rough sailing when the time came to navigate the commission's product through the House of Delegates. It was decided to add two nonlawyers, but also another practitioner. President Spann had no objection to adding "public" members, as long as they did not represent any particular constituency.[24] According to Kutak Commission reporter Geoffrey Hazard, Spann wanted a critical and outward-looking drafting committee in order to counteract the narrower and more traditional views that would prevail in the House of Delegates. In other words, Spann expected the Model Rules to be forged in something akin to an adversary proceeding between two ABA entities.

Some names bandied about as potential lay members of the commission were David Cohen of Common Cause, anthropologist Laura Nader (but not her brother Ralph), Bess Meyerson, McGeorge Bundy of the Ford Foundation, and philosopher Charles Frankel. The nonlawyers finally added were Lois Harrison, active in the League of Women Voters, and Alan Barth, an editor of the *Washington Post*. Barth died in 1979 and was not replaced, but his selection was a sign of the ABA leadership's interest in the press as an audience for the Model Rules project. Harrison's only discernible impact was to keep alive for several drafts a requirement that lawyers' fee agreements be in writing.

The lawyers' group most dissatisfied with the makeup of the commission

---

a "good samaritan" rule that would have allowed lawyers to provide service, "despite limitations" on their competence, in situations of "emergency or special [client] need." Legal services lawyers succeeded in removing the term "special need," fearing that administrators in legal services offices might use it to force them to provide second-class representation.

Other charter members included Robert McKay and Samuel Thurman, law professors who (like Ehrlich and Hazard) may have exposed the commission to the charge of being too "academic," and Howell Heflin, just off the Alabama Supreme Court and well enough connected in Democratic politics to leave the commission a few months later for the U.S. Senate. Heflin was replaced by Arno Deneke of the Oregon Supreme Court. Having a state supreme court "seat" on the commission was perhaps a concession to the ultimate goal of getting the Model Rules adopted at the state level. Other lawyer-members added later were William Spann, from the end of his ABA presidency till he died in 1981; Robert Hetlage, an ABA leader and private practitioner who was appointed along with two nonlawyers; and L. Clair Nelson, house counsel for a large company and onetime ABA treasurer.

23. This meant that what had so far been an ABA committee had to be reconstituted as a commission. Under ABA bylaws nonmembers could not serve on ABA committees.

24. Adding public members to its committees has become the bar's preferred way to bring lay opinion into bar deliberations. The practice is open to the charge of "tokenism" precisely because the lay members, in addition to being far outnumbered, typically have no clear constituency (see Kariel 1961, pp. 264–65).

was probably NOBC, the emergent association of lawyers who investigate and prosecute disciplinary cases. NOBC lawyers felt they had a new and important enforcer's perspective to bring to the Model Rules deliberations, but the commission refused to add an NOBC member, since the addition would further dilute the private practitioners' strength. This may be why NOBC eventually prepared its own code as an alternative to the Model Rules rather than working solely within the Model Rules Process.

Publicity

Not only did the public members of the commission prove inconsequential, but lay groups completely ignored the series of public hearings the commission held in 1980. Yet there was one mechanism that brought lay opinion more effectively into play. The commission's early work, culminating in the publication of the Discussion Draft in January 1980, was designed to garner favorable reviews from the lay press.

There is considerable evidence of the Kutak Commission's interest in press coverage and, less directly, of its vision of the Model Rules as a professional covenant with the public, not simply a covenant among lawyers. Believing it would "send a message" to the public, the commission put its client-protection rules concerning lawyers' fees,[25] competence, promptness, and communication with clients right up front where reporters and consumer advocates could see them; it also banished to the final sections what was left of traditional bans on lawyer advertising and solicitation—bans once considered consumer protections but now under a constitutional cloud and widely regarded as self-serving restraints on competition. Moreover, Hazard and Kutak talked in 1980 about hiring a public relations consultant. "If we could get key elements of the news media and corporate and civic leadership to understand what this is all about," Hazard wrote to Kutak, "we might create a climate in which the proposal could be given the kind of serious consideration it deserves" (letter, 23 December 1980).

Finally, the commission ruminated in early 1979 on what its product would say to the "larger public," and more pointedly, to the *New York Times*. Some hoped the *Times* would call the Model Rules an authoritative statement that lawyers are responsible to demands "beyond those of their immediate clients." Others hoped the *Times* would stress the seriousness with which the ABA was approaching the task of regulating a private

25. By requiring that all legal fees be "reasonable" rather than requiring only that they be less than "clearly excessive" as the code had done, the proposal that eventually became Model Rule 1.5(a) was meant to place a bit more restrictive ceiling on fees.

profession in the public interest. Still others hoped the *Times* would stress the shift in legal ethics from a preoccupation with the courtroom lawyer to a recognition of lawyers' other "functions and roles." All hoped the press would regard the commission's product as a significant departure from the earlier ABA codes.

When the Discussion Draft was published, the press reacted largely as hoped. The *Times* welcomed the draft as a proposal "fundamentally to alter" the lawyer's relationship with clients by requiring lawyers to weigh client obligations "against the duty to be fair and candid toward all other participants in the legal system, even adversaries" (Greenhouse 1980, p. 6). The *Times* also supported the unprecedented attention to lawyers' out-of-court roles as adviser, negotiator, and intermediary. The Discussion Draft also played to favorable reviews in the *Washington Post* (Robinson 1980, p. 1).[26]

Not every newspaper review was favorable, however, which suggests that nonlawyers are as divided as the bar on issues in legal ethics. A critical *Wall Street Journal* editorial homed in on proposed Model Rule 1.13, a rule addressed to lawyers representing corporations and other organizations ("A License to Squeal?" 11 February 1980, p. 20). The proposal made it clear that such lawyers represent an entity, not its management. The point had already been made in the Code (EC 5–18), but proposed rule 1.13 elaborated on it in a way that ruffled the *Journal*'s pro-management feathers. The rule contemplated situations in which a lawyer who reasonably believes it would serve the company's interests could blow the whistle on managerial wrongdoing, not just by going to higher-ups in management or to the company board, but if necessary even to outsiders such as the Securities and Exchange Commission. The *Journal* called the proposal an effort to usurp management's role in defining the corporate interest and a wedge that would drive management and legal counsel apart.[27] The bad press prompted Kutak to send the *Journal* a four-page response.

Secrecy

During the nearly two and a half years before the Discussion Draft was published, the commission was outward-looking not only in its concern about press reaction but in another sense: It sought out the opinions of some of the profession's harshest critics. For instance, the commission invited Mark Green to its February 1978 meeting. Green had recently coedited with

26. The *Post* emphasized the draft's positive treatment of consumer protection issues.

27. In a 1980 speech, Otis Smith, vice-president and general counsel to General Motors, took the similar position that Model Rule 1.13 was crossing over the line between legal ethics and corporate governance. In his view the proper relationship between company and counsel is a matter for each company and its counsel to work out.

Ralph Nader a muckraking book (*Verdicts on Lawyers*, 1976) about the bar and especially the ABA. In April 1978, the commission hosted Jethro Lieberman, whose new book, *Crisis at the Bar*, had not only attacked the Code of Professional Responsibility but called the ABA an inappropriate forum for devising a legal ethics code. The commission also welcomed comments on its "precirculation" drafts from a committee of the Society of American Law Teachers. This committee was in sympathy with the scholarly critics who considered the Code of Professional Responsibility too client-oriented and too little concerned with the lawyer's fidelity to his or her personal values and to the legitimate interests of third parties. It proposed that lawyers be permitted to limit the scope of their undertaking for a client in order to avoid legal tasks inconsistent with their own values, and be permitted also to withdraw from representing a client whose position they find repugnant. These proposals found their way into the final version of the Model Rules (see Model Rules 1.2[c], 1.16[b][3]).

While the commission was reaching out to the ABA's sharpest critics, its early relations within the bar were standoffish. In an October 1977 letter, Robert Kutak told bar leaders that the commission was open to "any and all suggestions." Yet Kutak cautioned commission members not to show early drafts to others. There was a select list of forty-two readers inside and outside the ABA to whom early drafts were sent for comment; but half of those readers were academics, not practitioners, and few could keep pace with the completely revised drafts Geoffrey Hazard was cranking out for commission meetings every other month.

In this climate of secrecy few bar entities were able to form or press their positions before the Discussion Draft was published. The only bar group to make an immediate impact was a special committee created by the ABA's forty-thousand-member Corporation, Banking, and Business Law Section in response to the *National Student Marketing* case. Donald Evans, chair of that committee, attended the Kutak Commission's December 1977 meeting and offered in February 1978 to have his committee draft the rules that would address issues of special interest to the corporate bar. Although Kutak never took Evans up on the offer, the Evans committee, and especially Loeber Landau of Sullivan & Cromwell, came to play a major role in the Model Rules process because of their persistence and the technical quality of their submissions.

Kutak Commission member Robert McKay, attesting to the corporate bar's perceived clout, reported that there was a "felt need" on the commission to have the ABA Corporation Section as an ally when the time came to move the Model Rules through the House of Delegates. The Evans committee was interested above all in the provisions that would deal with the representation of a corporation or other organization. Though not completely satisfactory, the whistle-blowing provisions of Discussion Draft Rule 1.13[28] were more acceptable to the Evans committee than to the *Wall Street Journal*, at one extreme, or, at the other, to the Georgetown Institute for Public Representation,[29] a public-interest law firm. The Evans committee and the corporation section were never absolutists on questions of confidentiality, as trial lawyer groups proved to be. They recognized, according to Geoffrey Hazard, that in extreme cases corporate lawyers might need the discretion to disclose otherwise confidential information in order to protect themselves from liability and "beat their client into rectitude." Over breakfast at the August 1980 ABA meeting in Honolulu, Hazard, Kutak, and the Evans committee began to fine-tune Rule 1.13 so that it would still permit whistle-blowing outside the company, but only if the board of directors' handling of corporate improprieties is based on personal interests at odds with company interests. As Evans wrote Kutak in August 1980, "[I]t is presumptuous and inappropriate to permit the lawyer to override the judgment of the duly constituted highest authority of the organization if they make a good faith (though perhaps incorrect) assessment of the best interests of the corporation. The possibility of personal conflict between directors . . . and the organization itself is the only unique attribute of the organization client warranting a special disclosure rule."

What can we make of the curious combination of openness and secrecy in the Kutak Commission's initial work? One critique of private lawmaking is that it often violates the norms of openness and accountability we associate (perhaps naïvely) with public lawmaking. And the commission's early proceedings could certainly have been more open. Yet the secrecy here was not meant to shut out lay interest groups or the press, secrecy's putative victims. It let the commission consider their task from a lay or critic's perspective before being overwhelmed by pressures from within the bar.

28. The Discussion Draft provided that if the highest authority in an organization insists upon action or a refusal to act that is "clearly a violation of law and is likely to result in substantial injury to the organization," the lawyer may take further remedial action, including disclosure of confidential information as necessary, if the lawyer reasonably believes such action will be "in the best interest of the organization."

29. In the late 1970's the Georgetown Institute for Public Representation proposed that the SEC adopt rules requiring corporate counsel to report violations of the law to the agency. In 1980, the SEC rejected the institute's proposals pending the ABA's adoption of ethics rules on the subject.

The Kutak Commission always took Rule 1.13 as a statement of duty to organizational clients, which as artificial entities acting solely through agents sometimes present difficulties analogous to those lawyers face in representing mentally disabled clients whose guardians may be acting against their clients' interests. The Georgetown Institute, on the other hand, sought to impose disclosure duties on corporate lawyers in order to protect the investing public and perhaps the general public from corporate wrongdoing.

The Critics

To see how the Kutak Commission's makeup and receptivity to critical opinion colored its early drafts, one need only examine a few provisions. The commission's draft of 25 January 1979 provided that a lawyer presenting a case to a tribunal must disclose facts adverse to the client's case if "disclosure . . . would probably have a substantial effect on the determination of a material issue of fact." This departed from the traditional view that lawyers should inform a tribunal of adverse legal authority, but not of adverse evidence, which may be left to one's adversary to present or not to present. The departure was sure to be unpopular with the trial bar, but was precisely the position commission member Marvin Frankel (1975) had taken before the Model Rules process began.

The same draft (and later ones) revived Louis Brandeis's famous concept of the "lawyer for the situation," allowing lawyers to act as "intermediaries" between clients, even at some risk that a conflict of interest might later materialize. This reflected substantial commission "hesitation" about rules that "might seem chiefly designed to make more work for lawyers by drawing the strictures on independence and candor too tightly," precisely the criticism consumer-oriented critics had leveled at earlier rules on conflict of interest.[30]

The August 1979 draft barred lawyers from drawing up or negotiating for a client an agreement containing terms a reasonable lawyer would know to be unconscionable as a matter of law. This duty to third parties went well beyond the Code's rule (DR 7–102 [A] [7]) that lawyers may not counsel or assist a client in conduct they know is criminal or fraudulent. The extension was in response to the general criticism that the Code of Professional Responsibility unduly subordinated third-party to client interests and specifically to legal scholar Murray Schwartz's criticism (1978) that the Code unwisely extended to office work the courtroom lawyer's unaccountability to adversaries.[31]

Finally, there was the matter of mandatory pro bono. The Model Rules process gave little attention at any stage to the distribution of legal services.

30. Comments in the January 1979 draft made a crucial reference to uncontested divorce as an area in which an intermediary would sometimes be appropriate. The intermediary concept survived the Model Rules process; the divorce reference did not. It was opposed by the NOBC on the ground that it would complicate enforcement of the conflict-of-interest rules, and by divorce lawyers in the ABA Family Law Section on the ground that it is nonsense to speak of "representing" two clients in their dealings with one another if they are at least formally adversaries.

31. The counselor's and negotiator's stepped-up duty to third parties was dropped by 1981 on the ground that unconscionability is so vague a standard that its use in a disciplinary rule might chill appropriate conduct and give lawyers too little notice of what could subject them to discipline.

But, responding to critics such as Marna Tucker (1976), the August 1979 draft did require lawyers to devote forty hours a year, or the dollar equivalent, to improving the legal system or providing legal services to those who cannot afford them. (A pro bono requirement with teeth soon proved to be an idea on which commission members, relatively sensitive to public opinion, were way out in front of the rank and file.)

The Second Stage: The Retreat to Legalism

In early 1979, though its drafts were still under wraps, the commission began to map its strategy for moving the Model Rules through the House of Delegates. The formulation of an ABA ethics code was too rare an event for anyone to have a clear idea about how to proceed. But as a first step, Kutak set up a "showcase" program for the ABA meeting in August. The idea was not to unveil a draft of the Model Rules (that was scheduled for January 1980), but to familiarize bar leaders with the project and make the case in principle for a new code. Apparently Kutak had not considered the absurdity of a "showcase" with nothing to display.

Commission consultant Ray Patterson urged that the program not only kick off the campaign for a new code, but also celebrate the Code of Professional Responsibility's tenth birthday by praising it as a "land-mark" in legal ethics. "The main idea we want to get across," Patterson wrote, "is that the new code is not to be a radical document, but a product that is grounded in the same basic ideas as the current code" (memorandum to Robert Kutak, 30 January 1979). The strategy, in other words, was to introduce the Model Rules to the bar in terms quite different from the "significant departure" rhetoric that was being used to tout the Model Rules to the public and to the critics of the bar. The new rhetoric would not necessarily make the Model Rules a conservative code; but it did mean that any reforms would have to be grounded in traditional principles.

The Bar's Reaction

Among those invited to review the August 1979 draft and discuss the Model Rules at the showcase program was legal scholar Monroe Freedman, long-time advocate of a nearly absolute duty of confidentiality running from lawyer to client. Just before the program, Kutak asked Freedman not to disclose the details of the August draft. This turned the program into a fiasco. Because he had not agreed to keep anything confidential when he was invited to be on the panel, Freedman (in his words) "declined to follow Mr. Kutak's instructions that the bar and the public be kept in ignorance of what the commission had wrought after two years of intensive, secret deliberations" (letter to the editor of the *National Bar Journal*, 2 September 1979). At the program, Freedman called the draft "radical and radically wrong," and disclosed some of the "disclosure" rules to illustrate his point. He also gave the draft to the press. Trade journals quickly published it. Many lawyers were outraged both by the substance of the draft and by the secrecy in which it had been developed.

Amid the uproar, ABA leaders wondered whether to keep the Model Rules project alive or wind up the commission's affairs. President-elect David Brink agreed to continue the project only if Kutak gave bar groups time to review and respond to the Discussion Draft. The commission adjourned for nine months and solicited comments on the Discussion Draft.

Those comments, and the ones on the later Proposed Final Draft, were voluminous. They varied widely in subject and point of view. Some came from public-interest groups, government agencies such as the Justice Department and the SEC, and companies such as General Motors with large in-house legal staffs. Most came from individual lawyers and bar groups in roughly equal numbers, which meant that the vast majority of lawyers' views were channeled through groups. One partial but representative list of commentators on the Proposed Final Draft had 129 entries, of which 76 were organizations. Twenty-five of those were ABA subunits; 34 were specialty groups such as the ABA Patent Law Section.

The comments reflected a bar vastly more organized and differentiated than the bar that responded in 1908 to an ABA call for comments on the proposed Canons For Professional Ethics. That call produced a few hundred responses, but most were brief letters from ABA members, and the remainder were from general-purpose state and local bar associations; specialty groups did not exist. The sentiments expressed in those early comments were remarkably uniform; only the treatment of contingent fees engendered any serious disagreement. It appears that in 1908 the chief issue was whether lawyers were going to join the professional bandwagon and "get" ethics; the precise content of the canons seemed secondary.

Kutak's Response

In December 1980, after the initial comment period was over, Kutak, sent bar leaders a "Dear Colleagues" letter in an effort to win back support. The letter offered his assurances that the commission had no radical agenda and would weigh all the comments received, even at the cost of delaying the project. It also identified recurrent themes in the comments, including fears that the Discussion Draft could destroy both the adversary system and traditional norms of confidentiality in lawyer-client relations.

"Dear Colleagues" was written in an idiom known as legalism, which addresses in purely legal terms issues that might instead be considered ethical or political (see Shklar 1964, pp. 1–2).[32] The letter encouraged lawyers to support commission proposals as necessary concessions to existing law. Thus, in response to the charge that his commission was out to destroy the adversary system, Kutak observed that some lawyers believe they owe their clients a legal duty not to reveal "a client's surprise perjury, a client's concealment of material evidence, or an opposing advocate's failure to apprise the court of legal authority directly adverse to a client's position." In fact, Kutak asserted, lawyers have no such duty. But he did not assert that the law left the commission with *discretion* to accept or reject such nondisclosure duties; that would have forced the commission to make overt policy judgments. He insisted instead that the existing law gave the commission no choice but to recognize *disclosure* duties in these areas. The commission's hands were tied, Kutak said, because the "great weight" of legal authority "makes it clear that lawyers have traditionally been required by the courts to speak truthfully and to bring to the court's attention any false or misleading facts or law that have been knowingly or unwittingly presented to it."

Kutak cited no legal authority to support these assertions, and unless one adopts a circular definition of legal authority—one that counts the earlier codes and bar association ethics opinions as law—there was little authority to cite. Kutak was presumably aware of this. One might infer that his legalism was a rhetorical move, not a fully internalized ideology.

As for confidentiality, Kutak used a similar argument to defend a Discussion Draft rule not only allowing, but requiring, lawyers to reveal confidential information when it "appears necessary to prevent the client from committing an act that would result in death or serious bodily harm." Kutak claimed that judicial "pronouncements" supported this unprecedented ethical duty.[33] The key pronouncement he had in mind was probably the well-known *Tarasoff* decision (1976), which holds that, notwithstanding the

32. To many outsiders, the lawyer's tendency to be "legalistic" is not an endearing characteristic. Yet legalism as a style of discourse has its uses in bar politics. For example, sociologist Terry Halliday has shown (1987, pp. 227–45) how the shared idiom of legalism enabled liberal and conservative Chicago Bar Association members to coalesce in fighting against certain legislative infringements on civil liberties during the McCarthy era. Lawyers joined ranks on the ground that these infringements were unconstitutional, not that they were bad policy. Conservative lawyers would not have joined a campaign based on policy arguments, and the public would have been less apt to accept such arguments as within the organized bar's expertise.

33. The Code of Professional Responsibility permitted but did not require lawyers to disclose a client's intention to commit any crime (DR 4–101[C][3]).

social value of professional confidentiality, tort law sometimes requires therapists to warn the known targets of their patients' violent threats. It is far from clear, however, that courts would apply the *Tarasoff* doctrine to the lawyer-client relationship. Besides, the *Tarasoff* court justified its imposition of a tort duty by citing a rule in the AMA *Principles of Ethics* that permitted the disclosure of otherwise privileged information in order to protect the welfare of the community. Since disclosure was ethically permitted, the court saw no reason not to make it legally required. This interplay underscores the "mirrors within mirrors" relationship that often exists between rules of professional ethics and the law.

Though Kutak's legalism may have won back some support, it also ran into a fascinating obstacle. His brand of legalism regarded other law as cause and legal ethics as effect, but the lawyers most passionately interested in the Model Rules often saw things the other way around. Their approach to legal ethics was as legalistic as Kutak's, but they rejected his characterization of the Model Rules as codifying a preexisting "law of lawyering." For them, the law of lawyering was largely inchoate, and the Model Rules process was either an opportunity to shape that law, or more often, a dangerous source for new malpractice theories, new grounds for disqualification and denial of legal fees, and new liability under the securities laws.

One example of the affirmative use of the Model Rules process to shape other law was the strategy of the ABA Corporation Section, and especially the Evans committee, for whom the Model Rules process was often SEC politics by other means.

The Evans committee was created in response to the SEC's use of a Code provision, DR 7–102(B)(1), to bolster its *National Student Marketing* complaint against two law firms that learned the merger documents they had drafted were fraudulent but let the merger close without telling stockholders or the SEC what they knew. In 1980, the SEC tabled a proposal that the agency codify the theory of the *National Student Marketing* complaint. The SEC found the proposal premature because the ABA was then considering the same issues in the Model Rules process.

This meant that the ABA—the Corporation Section's home court—was where the action would be. An Evans committee memorandum in 1978 pointed out that ethics rules no longer served simply as a guide to lawyers and a basis for professional discipline. The memo declared that the Code of Professional Responsibility had become "the basic *source of law*" from which courts and agencies "draw the responsibilities of lawyers." Armed with this insight, the Evans committee sought whistle-blowing rules for corporate lawyers that would be tough enough to reassure the SEC, yet hedged enough to keep lawyers' relations with management comfortable.

But whistle-blowing was not the only matter on which the Evans committee tried to use the Model Rules to influence other law. In January 1982, committee member Loeber Landau sent Robert Kutak a memo and report on the impact of *Garner* v. *Wolfinger* (1970) in shareholder derivative suits. *Garner* holds that although the lawyer-client evidentiary privilege applies to relations between corporations and their counsel, courts in shareholder derivative suits may order corporate counsel to disclose otherwise confidential information to the plaintiffs, even over the objection of management, whenever "good cause" can be shown.

Landau was disturbed that nothing in the Code of Professional Responsibility had discouraged the *Garner* court from reaching this conclusion. The Code merely notes that the lawyer for a company represents the entity itself, not its officers or other constituents (EC 5–18). Since management was not the client, and shareholders no less than management were constituents, the Code left the *Garner* court free to decide that the policies supporting the attorney-client privilege did not necessarily apply to derivative suits. The Corporation Section hoped to trump *Garner* with Model Rules commentary to the effect that the lawyer for a corporation may not reveal privileged information to shareholders in derivative suits. Although the section never got quite those words, the final Comments to Model Rule 1.13 do state that the lawyer for an organization "may not disclose to constituents information relating to the representation" unless disclosure is "authorized by the organizational client."

Legalism and the 'Standard Conception'

The Kutak Commission did not use legalism merely to justify its rules. More and more, legalism came to be reflected in the rules themselves. By the time the Proposed Final Draft was published in May 1981, several provisions in the Discussion Draft had turned into rules that defined a lawyer's ethical duties in terms of other law. For example, Rule 3.7(b) in the Discussion Draft forbad lawyers to seek "improperly" to influence a judge or a witness, but Rule 3.5(a) of the Proposed Final Draft barred attempts to influence a judge "by means prohibited by law" and Rule 3.4(b) barred the offering of inducements to a witness that are "prohibited by law." And whereas Discussion Draft Rule 3.2(b) forbad lawyers to "improperly" obstruct another party's access to evidence, the Proposed Final Draft's Rule 3.4(a) forbad them to "unlawfully obstruct another party's access to evidence"[34] (or to "alter, destroy or conceal" documents relevant to a judicial proceeding).

With each of these changes, the later version permits the lawyer to go to

34. "Unlawful obstruction" here presumably referred to laws on obstruction of justice as well as the rules of civil discovery.

the "limits of the law" for a client. For that reason and because the Proposed Final Draft is more likely than the Discussion Draft to reflect the views of practitioners, one might interpret the changes as expressions of the so-called standard conception of legal ethics. Yet if one looks beyond the rules themselves, one finds that lawyers usually pressed for the changes on grounds other than duty to client. Take, for example, a committee report from the Association of the Bar of the City of New York (ABCNY) that criticized Rule 3.4(a) of the Proposed Final Draft for not adding a *second* "unlawfully" before the words "alter, destroy or conceal." Whether and when documents must be retained, the report noted, is already a complex legal question. Even the hint of an "additional standard will exacerbate the complexity that already exists and distract the lawyer's attention from the need to consider the applicable law."[35] In other words, the ABCNY committee defends the equating of ethical with legal duty not by appealing to client interests, as the standard conception would dictate, but on the basis of clarity and fair notice to lawyers.

Earlier in the Model Rules process, both legal services lawyers and some members of the Kutak Commission argued that, if the Rules were to impose on lawyers a duty to "expedite litigation," that duty should require of lawyers no more than the law of civil procedure did. The legal services lawyers who took this position did seem to be endorsing the client-partisanship mentality of the standard conception. As one lawyer put it, the power to expedite must never be used to "expedite a disadvantageous result for the client" (letter from Alan Houseman to Geoffrey Hazard, 29 November 1979).[36] The commissioners, on the other hand, did not argue that clients are entitled to lawyers who will do anything for them within the bounds of the law of civil procedure. Their argument was based on perceptions of institutional competence: Rules of ethics that speak to this point should track the rules of civil procedure because "delay and burden are uniquely amenable to regulation by court rule and judicial oversight, without the mischief of interjecting into the adversarial process the invitation to file a grievance with disciplinary authorities in the course of a trial."

Work from Within or Go Outside?

Once the Discussion Draft was published, bar groups had to decide how to respond. They could try to influence matters directly by participating in the

35. The extra "unlawfully" found its way into the final version of Model Rule 3.4(a).

36. This hired-gun stance may sound strange coming from lawyers who are not even dependent on their clients for fees. But perhaps, lacking any fee nexus with their clients, the greatest professional problem these lawyers face is to convince their clients (and themselves) of their adversary zeal.

ABA process, thereby confirming the ABA's status as a fountainhead of ethics; or they could react through other channels. Groups working within the ABA process but unhappy with the Discussion Draft had to decide whether to oppose the Model Rules outright or chip away at specific rules. As a matter of organizational courtesy, ABA committees and sections could neither "go outside" nor oppose the Model Rules in toto. State and local bars directly represented in the ABA House of Delegates (organized partly as a federation) also felt obliged to work from within, but could work to defeat the Model Rules in their entirety—which the California State Bar and New York State Bar Association did. These bodies have perhaps grown too big for their ABA "breeches."[37]

The most important decisions to "go outside" were those of ATLA and the NOBC, organizations fairly new to bar politics and anxious to become more visible. Like other specialty groups, they found it easier to reach a consensus on ethics than the general-purpose state and local bars did. But neither had a strong voice in the ABA House of Delegates.

NOBC members thought the Discussion Draft contained many provisions that would let lawyers "equivocate [enforcers] to tears." Also, since they used the Code of Professional Responsibility constantly, they had invested more time than most lawyers in learning it and were afraid of losing their expertise. Their chief complaint was that the Discussion Draft used an untried restatement format (black-letter rules and explanatory comments), not the Code's three-part structure (basic canons, aspirational ethical considerations, and enforceable disciplinary rules). They doubted that the new format would catch on and warned that the Model Rules would promote less rather than more uniformity among the states. Reluctant for all these reasons to junk the Code and the extensive body of cases and ethics opinions interpreting it, they drafted a new version of the Code as an alternative to the Model Rules, using some of the Kutak Commission's substantive ideas.[38]

37. Government agencies had to make similar decisions. A few including the U.S. Department of Justice filed comments on the published Model Rules drafts, but none made a sustained effort to influence the development of the Model Rules. The Federal Trade Commission and the Antitrust Division of the Justice Department had a special interest in rules on fees, advertising, solicitation, group legal services, and law firm ownership, yet they did little lobbying. Perhaps they were reluctant to participate in making rules they might later have to challenge, the Antitrust Division saved its criticisms for a 1984 letter to the state supreme courts, which were then considering the Model Rules for local adoption. The letter expressed concern about Model Rule 1.5, which requires legal fees to be "reasonable." The division thought the rule might stifle competition. When an ABA ethics opinion read Rule 1.5 to impose a fee ceiling but no floor, the division withdrew its criticism.

38. When the ABA House of Delegates approved the Kutak Commission's restatement format in early 1982, NOBC was able to shift gears and work within the ABA to shape the rules of special concern to enforcers. Though it failed in its efforts to save a proposed requirement that all lawyers' fees agreements be in writing, it successfully argued that the Model Rules should retain the "catch-all" provisions of the Code of Professional Responsibility proscribing illegal conduct involving "moral turpitude" and conduct involving "dishonesty, fraud, deceit or misrepresentation."

ATLA's decision to "go outside" was more momentous. Founded in 1946, ATLA consists mostly of plaintiffs' personal injury lawyers, a substantial percentage of whom are the urban, ethnic, solo, and small-firm practitioners that the conflict critics of earlier ABA codes of ethics considered a professional underclass. Though its present membership of more than sixty thousand is only about a sixth of the ABA membership, ATLA is the second largest national bar organization and lately has been growing at a faster rate than the ABA. Its decision to draft a rival code undoubtedly reflected real ideological differences with the Kutak Commission,[39] but ideology was not the only motivation. ATLA leaders apparently felt that the hostility of many lawyers to early drafts of the Model Rules gave ATLA a chance to increase its stature at ABA expense. Announcing in September 1979 that ATLA would draft its own code, President Theodore Koskoff likened the ABA to a dinosaur, pointing out that a bar association's size "doesn't guarantee survival."[40]

ATLA had not gone outside at first. But as soon as the Kutak Commission's August 1979 draft was leaked and stirred up a fuss, Koskoff seized the opportunity. Monroe Freedman was named reporter for the ATLA project, and by June 1980 ATLA published the discussion draft of its own American Lawyer's Code of Conduct.

Kutak tried to nip ATLA's rebellion in the bud by publicly welcoming ATLA's ideas but dismissing ATLA's perspective as too narrow to yield a comprehensive and balanced code. ATLA must remember, Kutak said, that "trial is an adjective before lawyer and the ABA is working to write not just a code for a specialized area, but a code for all lawyers." "Writing a code is easy," Kutak added; "I'm only perplexed at how they [ATLA] would enforce it."[41] Kutak's arrogance on this point was repaid by Thomas Lumbard, director of the National Board of Trial Advocacy and co-reporter on a later draft of the American Lawyer's Code of Conduct. Lumbard chided Kutak for presuming that all fifty states would "bow down before the infallible pope of legal ethics and adopt what he says ought to be the rules" (Schneyer 1989, p. 711).

ATLA's code and its critique of the Model Rules are of especially interesting because ATLA brought a conscious ideology to the subject. The creed has two tenets. One is consumerism—the customer is always right. The discussion draft of ATLA's code, for example, abandoned the traditional rule

39. But not the sharp differences over business-getting activities such as solicitation that the "conflict" critics of the earlier ABA codes might have predicted.

40. Through the 1970s ATLA and the ABA had often disagreed on another political front—federal no-fault automobile legislation (see Heymann and Liebman 1988, pp. 309–35).

41. Kutak was implying that only the ABA could successfully promote an ethics code for adoption by the state supreme courts.

allowing lawyers to use client confidences to recover a fee. Consumerism does more than subordinate lawyer interests to client interests. It equates client interests with the public interest; each citizen's interest in the legal system is solely a matter of how the system treats him or her as a present or potential client.[42] Describing the views of the nonlawyers who served on the committee that drafted ATLA's code, Koskoff said: "They were shocked by the concept that a lawyer would reveal a client's secrets except in the most extreme circumstances. They reminded us . . . that what we were writing was not just a Code of Conduct for lawyers, but a Bill of Rights for clients. As one of the nonlawyers . . . put it, 'When I need a lawyer, I need him to be my lawyer. And if he isn't going to be my lawyer, I don't need him' " (Koskoff 1980, pp. 46–47).

The second tenet in the ATLA creed, suggested by the description of a code of legal ethics as a clients' "bill of rights," is (liberal) constitutionalism, that form of legalism which grounds the lawyer's ethical duties in clients' (generously defined) constitutional rights. This tenet extends the imagery and values associated with criminal defense work to other forms of law practice, especially civil litigation. Thus, Koskoff invokes as an appropriate ethic for all lawyering Lord Brougham's famously exorbitant statement in his criminal defense of Queen Caroline: "[A]n advocate, by the sacred duty which he owes his client, knows, in the discharge of that office, but one person in the world, that client and none other." This view is upheld in the preamble to the American Lawyers' Code of Conduct in passages that reaffirm the value of the adversary system by appealing to the rights to counsel, trial by jury, and due process.

Reviewing the Model Rules Discussion Draft from ATLA's perspective, Koskoff gave it two thumbs down for embracing the "essentially totalitarian view, now popular with many who strangely call themselves liberals, that the public interest is best served by serving the public wholesale, and by making lawyers servants of the system, rather than the bulwark between organized power and the individual" (Schneyer 1989, p. 712).

There was no greater gulf between the discussion drafts of the Model Rules and the Code of Conduct than on the issue of confidentiality. For example, the Model Rules draft required lawyers to disclose a client's confidences to prevent him from killing or seriously injuring someone, and permitted disclosure to prevent, or rectify the consequences of, a client's "deliberately wrongful act." The American Lawyer's Code of Conduct had two positions on the issue, but even the less extreme of the two had no

42. Thus, the preamble to the discussion draft of ATLA's Code of Conduct defines the public as "the actual and potential clients whom we serve."

provisions that required disclosure and permitted it only to avert imminent loss of human life.

With time, the ABA moved much closer to ATLA on the issue of confidentiality. Yet ATLA leaders never reconciled themselves to the Model Rules or to the ABA's primacy in matters of legal ethics. Thomas Lumbard suggested that the ABA abandon the Model Rules project and get out of the business of codifying ethics. He proposed that a code be drafted instead by a new interstate agency controlled by "the courts" (Lumbard 1981, p. 271).

This suggests how badly ATLA leaders wanted to decertify the ABA as the unofficial voice of the legal profession on matters of ethics. The "courts" that would control this interstate agency are, after all, run by judges; and judges are as hostile as any interest group in the legal profession to the nearly absolute protection of confidentiality favored by ATLA. Recall Judge Marvin Frankel's opposition to what he called the "client above all" mentality of trial lawyers. Note also that when state supreme courts adopt the ABA's Model Rules, the rules they most commonly amend are those protecting client confidences almost absolutely.

A more bizarre sign of ATLA's interest in decertifying the ABA came in the final phase of the Model Rules process. At the February 1983 ABA meeting where the black-letter Model Rules (but not the Comments) were finalized, the House of Delegates voted 207–129 to amend the commission's proposed Rule 1.6. The amendment narrowed the cases in which a lawyer may reveal a client's confidences in order to prevent the client from committing a crime. As amended, the rule allowed disclosure to prevent a crime likely to result in imminent death or substantial bodily harm, but not to prevent or mitigate the effects of economic or property crimes. Believing the amendment created a haven for white-collar criminals, Senator Arlen Specter, a former prosecutor, introduced a bill in Congress that would make the disclosure standards of the unamended Rule 1.6 binding on lawyers under federal criminal law. Even the bar leaders who had opposed the amendment to Rule 1.6 in the ABA House of Delegates opposed the Specter bill, arguing that lawyers are and should be regulated at the state level and by courts, not legislatures.

Given the importance they attach to confidentiality, one might have expected ATLA leaders to mount an even more ferocious attack on the Specter bill. Yet Koskoff merely sent a letter to other opponents of the Model Rules suggesting that Robert Meserve, who replaced Robert Kutak as commission chair when Kutak died in January 1983, might have put Specter up to introducing the bill in order to instigate an ABA reconsideration of the House of Delegates' amendment to Rule 1.6.[43] And Monroe Freedman, the reporter

43. Meserve denies this. Koskoff charged in the same letter that the Kutak Commission regularly

for the American Lawyer's Code of Conduct and long-time champion of confidentiality, testified in *support* of the Specter bill! He did so not because he favored the bill on the merits (he didn't), but because ABA "efforts at self-regulation of the legal profession through a comprehensive code" have "failed consistently." Freedman wanted Congress to govern the conduct of lawyers before federal courts and agencies.

The Third Stage: Endgame

It was clear by fall 1982 that the Model Rules process would produce a new code. Those on record as opposing the Model Rules in toto began to speak wistfully about what might have been. In a 25 May 1982 letter to NOBC's Charles Kettlewell, ATLA's Thomas Lumbard complained that their organizations lacked the money to produce the materials needed to combat "the great sea of crap coming out of [ABA headquarters in] Chicago." A self-styled "consortium" of opponents to the Model Rules tried to coordinate their efforts to amend the rules that most concerned them, but there was little talk now about sinking the whole project. Kurt Melchior, an ABA delegate from the California State Bar, urged delegates from other disenchanted groups—the ABA General Practice Section, NOBC, ATLA, the New York State Bar Association, and ACTL—to seek authorization from their organizations to be flexible at the February 1983 ABA meeting in New Orleans, where the House of Delegates would debate and vote on the Model Rules, rule by rule. "Clearly," Melchoir wrote, "some form of new rules will be adopted. Let's try to make these rules of a kind that our profession and the public we serve can live with."

Behind the Scenes

Since the House of Delegates meets only twice a year, it was an awkward forum in which to debate a proposal as complex as the Model Rules. The commission forwarded its final draft to the House of Delegates for consideration at the August 1982 meeting, but when that meeting adjourned, the House had only discussed and acted on one of fifty rules! The House did much better at its February 1983 meeting, when it acted on all the other rules. Still, this final stage necessarily featured behind-the-scenes negotiation. Hazard, Meserve, and Kutak (until his death in January 1983) sought support among the delegates by accommodating a number of "special interests."

---

tried to get ABA delegates to accept its positions by arguing that failure to do so would invite outside intervention in the regulation of the bar.

A seemingly key accommodation involved Rule 1.13, on which the commission had been negotiating with the Evans committee from the beginning. When he announced the Corporation Section's endorsement of the Rules in August 1982, Loeber Landau of the committee called Rule 1.13 one of the "most important rules our Section had a hand in shaping." He was pleased with the rule's new attention to the special problems of representing organizations, with its clear statement that the lawyer for an organization represents the entity and not its various constituents, and with its careful hedging in, but not complete removal, of the lawyer's discretion to blow the whistle outside the corporation on managerial wrongdoing that jeopardized company interests. Rule 1.13 had been honed, Landau said, to the point where the lawyer's relations with management would be comfortable, yet in an extreme case involving both managerial wrongdoing *and* an inadequate internal response occasioned by conflicts of interest on the board of directors, the lawyer could "go outside," if need be, to protect the company. Calling proposed Rule 1.13 a sensible "resolution of questions which the SEC and others have raised in recent years," Landau added that if the bar did not provide such a resolution, the SEC would fill the void, and the result was not likely to be as "considered and desirable as proposed Rule 1.13."

Negotiations produced language responsive to the special pleading of many other groups, some of them quite small. For example, an organization of state attorneys general succeeded in having passages included that made it clear that government lawyers are often authorized to make choices that in private practice must be left to the client—such as whether to sue or whether to accept a settlement offer.[44] Similarly, the ABA Administrative Law Section negotiated more latitude in case selection for former government lawyers and their private firms. All this made for a code that in the end had little more coherence than its predecessors but, unlike those codes, had words added or removed to accommodate lawyers practicing in almost every imaginable setting. In the ten years between the drafting of the Code of Professional Responsibility and the Model Rules, practice setting, field of specialization, and clientele had become, along with lawyer's role, crucial variables in the making of rules of ethics.

Although L. Clair Nelson, an in-house lawyer, was appointed to the Kutak Commission in late 1980, the only perceptible impact of house counsel on the Model Rules came in this final frenzy of special pleading. House counsel appear to have convinced the commission to abandon a new requirement that lawyers who work on salary for organizations other than law firms extract

44. This language went into the introductory "scope" section of the Model Rules after Meserve wrote to Hazard on 17 February 1983: "I think we are going to have to do something for our friends who are attorneys general, etc. I would be glad to have your ideas as to how we can keep them happy."

from their employers a written commitment to respect their independent professional judgment. They argued that however sensible the rule might be for legal services lawyers, to prevent their superiors from driving undesirable wedges between them and their clients, it made no sense for lawyers whose employers *are* their clients (see Schaefer 1982). Besides, as a matter of professional status, house counsel wanted to be treated like outside corporate counsel, not like lawyers in government agencies and legal services offices (see Schneyer 1988, pp. 481–83).

Since over 10 percent of the bar are now house counsel (Curran et al. 1985a, p. 19), their relative lack of involvement in the Model Rules process calls for explanation. Before 1982, house counsel had neither an ABA section nor an association of their own. This was a substantial political liability given the extent of the structural differentation of the organized bar, where influence is exercised through organizational channels. Recognizing this too late to have much impact on the Model Rules, house counsel in 1982 formed the American Corporate Counsel Association (ACCA). Leaders of the ABA Corporation, Banking, and Business Law Section reportedly greeted this development "with dismay"; they considered their section the "proper and logical home" for lawyers in corporate law departments as well as for outside corporate counsel.

Since one of house counsel's most important duties is to monitor the work of outside counsel and control legal expenses, ACCA is likely to become a strong voice for tighter controls on frivolous actions, dilatory tactics, discovery abuse, and other practices that inflate corporate legal costs. If so, ACCA may find itself in the future at ethical odds with trial lawyers. There are already signs of this. In 1985, an ACCA committee, in what might be called an act of ethical proliferation, developed litigation guidelines that corporations can adopt to govern in-house and outside counsel alike. Among other things, the guidelines bar the inclusion of any cause of action in a civil complaint that would not itself be an adequate basis for a lawsuit. Outside firms, which still take the lion's share of corporate litigation, may be discomfited by such restrictions.

Strange Bedfellows

Not all the commission's last minute efforts consisted of accommodating specialty groups through changes nobody else cared about. There were issues so contested that they could only be resolved by a formal vote in the House of Delegates. The first of these matters was the writing requirement for lawyers' fee agreements. The commission's Proposed Final Draft required the basis or rate of every fee to be explained to the client in writing.

Commission member Lois Harrison supported the requirement as a way to protect consumers; NOBC, as a way to avoid lawyer-client misunderstandings and make a record in case a fee dispute should arise later.

The requirement was opposed by two groups who seem light-years apart in other respects. The ABA General Practice Section opposed it on behalf of small-town and rural lawyers reluctant to formalize their relations with clients. The Corporation Section saw it as an affront to sophisticated business clients, and was aware that large law firms make some fee arrangements not easily reduced to writing (see Stewart 1983, p. 23). By House vote, the general writing requirement soon became a mere "preference" (Model Rule 1.5 [b]). Those who view the formulation of legal ethics codes as an arena of conflict between Big Law Firms and Little Lawyers or between the two "hemispheres" of lawyers representing companies and lawyers representing individuals could not have predicted the alignment of bar interests on this issue.

The Showdown

There were still other issues, touching on confidentiality, which not only had to be decided by House vote, but also set up a showdown between the Kutak Commission and the group that ultimately emerged as its most formidable antagonist—the American College of Trial Lawyers (ACTL). The showdown came at the February 1983 New Orleans meeting where the black-letter portions of the Model Rules were debated, amended, and approved.

ACTL membership is by invitation. Most ACTL members concentrate on civil litigation, where they often represent insurers and other companies against clients represented by ATLA lawyers. Though ACTL has no direct representation in the ABA House of Delegates, Robert Meserve, himself an ACTL fellow, estimates that one-sixth of the delegates are members. He also thinks the House defers to the ACTL fellows far more than their numbers might suggest.

In April 1982, ACTL released a report highly critical of the Kutak Commission's Proposed Final Draft. The report urged that the House of Delegates reject the Rules and resubmit them to the commission, and that the commission be reconstituted to increase the number of members with "a full appreciation of the realities and goals of legal practice." Most criticism of the Rules by this stage was rule-specific; ACTL had broader concerns. It still found the Rules "permeated by a philosophy that is inimical to the adversary system and to effective legal representation" (American College of Trial Lawyers 1982, p. 7).

Kutak was upset that ACTL was not "on board." In two letters to ACTL president Alston Jennings, he carefully responded to each ACTL criticism, often conceding that they had force. He told Jennings that a few amendments could make the Model Rules satisfactory from ACTL's standpoint. Although their differences with ACTL were too fundamental to iron out in negotiations, Kutak, Hazard, and Meserve convinced ACTL to think in terms of amendments, not outright rejection.

ACTL was worried about four rules above all, each touching on confidentiality. One was Rule 1.6. As proposed by the commission, Rule 1.6 allowed lawyers to disclose otherwise protected information to prevent a client from committing a crime or fraud likely to cause substantial bodily harm or substantial injury to financial interests or property; it also allowed lawyers to make disclosures to rectify the consequences of a crime or fraud that their services had been used to further. ACTL argued that so broad a hedge on confidentiality would make clients less candid and thus reduce lawyers' opportunities to discourage client wrongdoing (an argument, notice, based on public rather than client interests). At the February 1983 ABA meeting, ACTL proposed an amendment allowing disclosure only to prevent crimes likely to cause "imminent death or substantial bodily harm" (crimes ACTL lawyers apparently do not *want* a chance to discourage!). The House adopted the amendment 207 to 129.

Some opponents called Proposed Rule 1.6 a "radical assault" on professional traditions. The fact is that its analog in the Code of Professional Responsibility, DR 4–101(C), had permitted lawyers to disclose confidential information as needed to prevent a client from committing any crime, however trivial. And ironically, ACTL's amendment to Rule 1.6 was an assault on its own ethical "tradition," which was quite in keeping with the Proposed Rule. As drafted in 1972, ACTL's Code of Trial Conduct, an early example of ethical proliferation, provided that a lawyer is not "bound to respect" confidences concerning his client's intention to commit *any* crime; on the contrary, the lawyer may make whatever disclosures are needed to prevent a crime and "should do so if injury to person or property is likely to ensue" (Sec. 5[b]).

ACTL's about-face here may reflect a shift in values from the gentleman lawyer to the hired-gun orientation, perhaps occasioned by a new competitiveness for clients and thus a new urgency to reduce client fears of lawyer betrayal. But such a transformation of values in a mere decade seems unlikely. The change more likely reflects a fear that, unlike the earlier ABA codes or ACTL's own guidelines, the Model Rules were going to have real legal bite, so that ACTL could no longer afford the luxury of rules that sound good to critics but do not reflect a trial lawyer's real practices and values.

The second key rule ACTL sought to amend was 1.13. As proposed after long negotiation between the Kutak Commission and the Evans committee, Rule 1.13 posed two problems for ACTL. Rule 1.13(c), discussed earlier, permitted a lawyer in unusual circumstances to reveal confidential information to outsiders in order to protect the organization, even over the objection of the organization's highest authority. ACTL considered it presumptuous for lawyers ever to "play God" by disclosing information the highest authority in the corporation was determined to keep confidential. If counsel is troubled by the board's resolution of a legal problem, ACTL argued, let counsel withdraw.

The other troubling section was 1.13(a), which provided that the lawyer for an organization represents the organization "as distinct from" its directors, officers, employees, members, shareholders, or other constituents. ACTL considered "artificial" the distinction between the organizational client and its various constituents, especially management, since most lawyers who represent companies are retained by and work closely with management. Lawyers in this position are often expected to treat management if not precisely as the client then at least as the most vivid embodiment of the client. That is precisely why the Evans committee welcomed Proposed Rule 1.13(a). ACTL, however, sought to change "as distinct from" to "including," implying that the lawyer for an organization should normally think of him or herself as representing its various constituents as well.

The House adopted both ACTL amendments to Rule 1.13, this time by a vote of 185–113. But after the February 1983 meeting, as Geoffrey Hazard worked with ACTL leaders to harmonize the Model Rules commentary with the amended Rules, he convinced ACTL leaders of something the Evans Committee had understood all along: that if the lawyer representing a corporation also represents its constituents—including shareholders—that would support the *Garner* v. *Wolfinqer* requirement that company lawyers reveal otherwise privileged information to the plaintiffs in some shareholders' derivative suits. ACTL leaders, in whose hierarchy of values confidentiality was tops, saw the light and accepted a friendly amendment. As finally adopted, Model Rule 1.13(a) provides that the corporate lawyer represents "the organization acting through its duly authorized constituents."

Until the final stage of the Model Rules process, Rule 1.13 was understood to be in the ABA Corporation Section's bailiwick, where the reigning perspective was that of the "transaction lawyer," not the litigator. The Evans committee had worked and reworked the rule, largely in hopes of convincing the SEC not to revisit the issues involved. But in the end, ACTL came along, the proverbial bull in a china shop, and substantially changed it. ACTL's attention to a rule with only passing application to litigation suggests that it sees itself as the steward of a confidentiality-centered ethic applicable not just to trial work but to all lawyering. And ACTL's power to remake a rule of such direct interest to another bar entity, especially one as powerful as the ABA Corporation Section, was remarkable.

The other two provisions of special interest to ACTL were Proposed Rules 3.3 and 4.1. These concerned the lawyer's rights and duties upon learning that the client has used the lawyer's services in perpetrating a fraud on a tribunal (3.3) or a person (4.1). The Code of Professional Responsibility had treated these situations in DR 7–102(B)(1), which required lawyers to take steps to remedy both kinds of fraud. As first promulgated, DR 7–102(B)(1) did not indicate how the duty to rectify could be squared with the duty under DR 4–101 to keep a client's confidences. A 1974 ABA amendment (adopted in only a minority of states) made it clear that confidentiality overrode the duty to rectify. The Kutak Commission addressed the problem in two separate rules because it was committed to structuring the Model Rules according to the lawyer's various roles, something the Code had only begun to do. Fraud on a tribunal involved the lawyer's duties as advocate (Rule 3.3); fraud on a person involved the Lawyer's duties as drafter or negotiator (Rule 4.1). In each case, the commission proposed that the duty to rectify frauds should override the duty of confidentiality as defined by Rule 1.6. And in both cases, ACTL members or their allies proposed amendments subordinating the duty to rectify to the duty of confidentiality. The commission won by a 209 to 101 vote on Rule 3.3 (duty to the tribunal), but lost by a 188 to 127 margin on 4.1 (duty to a third person). Why the different outcomes on such similar issues? One answer is the continued resonance among lawyers of the notion that as "officers of the court" they owe a special duty of candor to judges, a duty unmatched by any responsibility to a client's out-of-court victims. The officer-of-the-court argument was raised in the floor debate on Rule 3.3, and raised with particular force by William Erickson of the Colorado Supreme Court. ACTL may have been able to hold its own against the Kutak Commission and the ABA Corporation Section, but for trial lawyers the judiciary is apparently an interest group of a different order.

Geoffrey Hazard suggests another explanation for the outcome in the debate over Rule 3.3. ACTL members in the House were actually split on their own amendment. Some wanted, like ATLA lawyers, to privilege confidentiality over the duty to rectify; but others were attracted to the rule as proposed, for reasons having to do with their particular practice and clienteles. They considered personal injury plaintiffs more likely to commit perjury (i.e., fraud on a tribunal) than the clients they usually represent. In their view, if Proposed Rule 3.3 did reduce perjury or mitigate its effects, that would work to the advantage of ACTL clients.

The House of Delegates' Failure to Read the *Times*

Only a month or so before the showdown in New Orleans, the *New York Times* and *Wall Street Journal* printed stories about a multimillion dollar business fraud involving a computer-leasing firm (OPM). Perhaps unwittingly, a New York law firm—Singer, Hutner, Levine, and Seeman—had helped OPM close many fraudulent deals, so many that for several years OPM accounted for 60 percent of the firm's billings (Gandossy 1985, p. 221). Eventually, the firm withdrew from further representation. But it did not tell OPM's new law firm why it had withdrawn. Perhaps as a result, there were additional fraudulent transactions.

The news stories dwelt on Singer, Hutner's seemingly willful blindness to fraud and its later refusal to share its concerns with the successor firm. Ethical questions were raised: When is a law firm on notice of a client's wrongdoing? To what lengths should it go to monitor a client's conduct? At what point should it resign? When should it blow the whistle on a client who has used the firm's services to perpetrate frauds? The *Times* indicated that the ABA was in the throes of an "acrimonious debate" on these issues and would take action at an upcoming meeting.

In its response to the ACTL amendments in New Orleans, the Kutak Commission was as sensitive to the press coverage of the OPM scandal as it had been to coverage in the first stage of the Model Rules process. It supported on the House floor an amendment to its proposed Model Rule 1.16 that made it clear that a lawyer may withdraw from representing a client who has used his services to carry out a crime or fraud. Geoffrey Hazard also drafted comments that weakened the thrust of the ACTL amendments to Rules 1.6 and 4.1. Those amendments, remember, took away the lawyer's *right* to disclose confidences in order to rectify a fraud in which his services had been used, and subordinated the lawyer's *duty* to rectify a client's out-of-court fraud to the duty of confidentiality. Hazard's commentary permits a lawyer, when he withdraws from representing a client who has used his services for purposes of fraud, to publicize the withdrawal and "disaffirm" any opinion or document he prepared for the client. Although the lawyers for future OPM's would not be permitted to blow the whistle on their clients, they could "wave the red flag" (Rotunda 1983).

The House of Delegates, however, responded to the OPM publicity with indifference, adopting the ACTL-sponsored amendments to Rules 1.6 and 4.1 by a substantial margin. "Forced to choose starkly between models of the lawyer as client's mouthpiece and as caretaker of the law," barked a follow-up *New York Times* editorial (1983, p. A26), the ABA House of Delegates "has opted for mouthpiece." Robert Meserve, who became commission chair when Robert Kutak suddenly died two weeks before the New Orleans meeting, reacted more poignantly. Meserve was upset about the amendments to Rules 1.6 and 4.1 because they seemed to ratify much of what Singer, Hutner had done. "Whatever our opinion of the ultimate result of [Robert Kutak's] work," Meserve said, Kutak "had no doubt, nor do I, that it was a most important endeavor to set the lawyer right before the court of public opinion." The trouble was that although that court had jurisdiction over the commission, it could not reach the House of Delegates, which in the final stage of the Model Rules process was the more important body.

Professionalism-In-Fact: Some Pervasive Themes

The account to this point has stressed the variety of ethical perspectives and concerns that came into play in the Model Rules process. When one attends to trial lawyers for plaintiffs and defendants, to in-house and outside corporate lawyers, to legal services lawyers, to ethics code enforcers, to judges, to law professors, and to other lawyer "types," it becomes apparent that the bar does not speak with one voice. Still, many lawyers at all stages of the Model Rules process shared certain values and styles of ethical argument. One of these, the idiom of legalism, has already been discussed. Three more will now be considered: the bar's preoccupation with what I call "defensive ethics," its penchant for arguments based on notions of institutional competence, and its persistence in addressing ethical issues in terms of role. These themes add up to a mind-set that for better or worse probably animates many American lawyers today.

Defensive Ethics

The least attractive of these themes is a preoccupation with matters of self-protection. Insofar as lawyers design the rules of legal ethics to protect themselves from *legal* mishaps, "defensive ethics" is a species of legalism. It is also the flip side of a pattern some critics thought they saw in earlier ABA codes. That pattern involved the use of rules of ethics to aggrandize lawyers at the expense of their clients. In the Model Rules process, there is little sign of lawyers pressing for rules that serve their own interests in this positive sense, and some evidence of forbearance,[45] even in documents

45. Thus, in response to the criticism that some code restrictions on representing clients with potentially conflicting interests amounted to featherbedding, Model Rule 2.2 expressly permits lawyers to serve at times as "intermediaries" between two or more clients.

lawyers would not have expected to come under public scrutiny. But if self-aggrandizement was out, self-defense, as Deborah Rhode has observed, was in (1985, p. 616). The process was rife with pleas for rules that would curb or at least not foster malpractice claims, motions to disqualify, denials of legal fees, or exposure under the securities laws.

One manifestation of this defensiveness was the ABCNY view that the Model Rules Comments should identify "safe harbors"—courses of action that would "avoid any question as to whether there has been compliance with the Rule." Taken far enough, safe harbors could transform a code of lawyers' duties into a bill of lawyers' rights. Perhaps this is why Geoffrey Hazard did not draft the Comments with the safe-harbor function foremost in mind. But Hazard (1979) displays considerable sympathy for the argument that the Model Rules should, above all, give lawyers fair notice of what they may or may not do. One of the few unsympathetic groups on this point was NOBC, whose members apparently hoped that the *in terrorem* effects of including some vague catch-alls in the Rules (e.g., forbidding "dishonest" conduct) would nicely supplement their meager disciplinary enforcement budgets.

Another instance of defensive ethics involved Model Rule 1.6, which defined a lawyer's duty of confidentiality. That duty sometimes collides with disclosure duties embodied in laws aimed at a far broader class than the bar—laws, for example, requiring professionals to report instances of child abuse or large cash transactions with clients. Such laws are typically silent about how they should be reconciled with confidentiality duties. Hoping to convince judges to relieve lawyers of duties under these general laws whenever the issue should arise, the liability-averse got Hazard to insert this sentence into a comment to Rule 1.6: "Whether another provision of law supersedes Rule 1.6 is a matter of interpretation beyond the scope of these Rules, *but a presumption should exist against such a supersession*" (Emphasis added). The general counsel of the SEC quickly saw this for what it was: "[F]ederal securities laws may impose disclosure responsibilities on lawyers which transcend the requirements of confidentiality imposed by ethical rules," wrote Daniel Goelzer to the Special Committe of the D.C. Bar studying the Model Rules. "That the lawyer must obey the law where the law requires disclosure should be noncontroversial; a 'presumption' to the contrary seems inappropriate" (letter, 25 January 1984).

Defensive ethics found a place even in Kutak Commission deliberations. At their meeting on 25 August 1978, for example, the commission debated the merits of a rule requiring lawyers to communicate with their clients at reasonable intervals and to convey all the information their clients need to make the decisions that are rightfully theirs. Commission members saw the merit of such a rule, which responded to a very common complaint about lawyers. But they worried that by creating such a rule with the intention that it be enforced through the disciplinary process they might "unwittingly be writing a negligence per se standard for some future civil claim."[46]

No provision was more closely examined for its potential legal fall-out than Model Rule 1.1, which deals with lawyer competence. As a result of efforts to weed out all the language that could create new liabilities, Rule 1.1 never came to say much more than that a lawyer must be competent. For example, the Discussion Draft version of Rule 1.1 permitted a lawyer to work only on matters in which he or she "can act with adequate competence," that is, the competence displayed in "acceptable practice by lawyers undertaking similar matters." On the ground that it might imply that general practitioners are incompetent to handle some tasks, this language was dropped. The commission feared that the provision would invite malpractice litigation and wanted especially to protect sole practitioners and small-town lawyers, who are not apt to specialize. In this and other matters, according to Geoffrey Hazard, the commission was solicitous of "Little Lawyers,"[47] despite its relatively elite composition and the social gulf that continues to exist between the "hemispheres" of the bar (Heinz and Laumann 1982).

The emphasis on defensive ethics gave the ABA Committee on Professional Liability more than a cameo role in the Model Rules process. The committee went through the Proposed Final Draft with a risk manager's fine-tooth comb and found a number of disturbing provisions. For example, on the ground that it "invit[ed] lawyers and the courts to use the Rules for civil liability purposes," the committee disapproved of this already guarded language in the introductory "Scope" section: "Violations of the Rules should not necessarily result in civil liability, which is a matter governed by general law. The Rules . . . may have relevance in determining civil liability, but they should not be uncritically incorporated into that context."[48]

Defensive ethics is a clear concession to self-interest, but can it be justified as responsible self-interest? There has certainly been an increase in the past decades in malpractice claims and insurance premiums, but its magnitude and the significance of codes of ethics as cause or cure are far from clear. Bar defensiveness in the absence of data on these matters seems no more responsible than the defensiveness doctors have displayed in pressing for "good

46. Such a provision was ultimately adopted in Model Rule 1.4.

47. The solicitude may have been unnecessary. Working through the ABA General Practice Section, sole practitioners and small-firm lawyers had enough clout to kill a proposed rule to facilitate the delivery of legal services by allowing lawyers for the first time to form law partnerships with nonlawyers. They did so by raising the specter of department store lawyers replacing the traditional forms of small-firm practice.

48. The final version provides that the Model Rules "are not designed to be a basis for civil liability. . . . [N]othing in the Rules should be deemed to augment any substantial legal duty of lawyers or the extra-disciplinary consequences of violating such a duty."

samaritan" laws relieving them of liability for negligence in providing voluntary service in an emergency; apparently no doctor has ever been successfully sued for such a thing.[49]

In any event, the defensiveness that lurks behind this maneuvering takes us far indeed from the purely ethical merits of rules on, say, confidentiality and disclosure. Perhaps lawyers would accept broader ethical discretion to protect third parties through disclosure if they could be sure that non-disclosure would not then result in tort claims against them. That this and many other Model Rules debates turned on defensive considerations thus raises an issue of public policy: In the interest of promoting the development of sound ethical standards, should the law prohibit the use of rules of professional ethics to establish malpractice liability, just as in personal injury cases it excludes evidence of subsequent repairs and settlement negotiations in order to promote desirable negotiation and repairs?

Arguments Based on Institutional Competence

Another striking feature of the Model Rules process is the frequency with which lawyers grounded their decisions and arguments on comparisons of institutional competence. Such arguments focus on which of two or more institutions should take the lead in making and enforcing rules on the subject at hand.

Trivial examples of this phenomenon are Kutak Commission decisions not to delve into subjects being addressed by other ABA entities. The commission spent relatively little time on lawyer advertising and solicitation because another special ABA commission was looking into that subject in the wake of the *Bates* decision (1977). The commission did grapple with the criminal defense lawyer's perennial problem of how to deal with a client who intends to commit or does commit perjury, because other ABA bodies expected it to.[50] But it spent little time on other issues that arise in criminal practice, issues already addressed in ABA Criminal Justice Standards. And when it did look at such issues, its proposals were derived from those standards:

49. According to a major report from the U.S. Department of Health, Education, and Welfare, physicians' fears of potential liability for rendering emergency aid are "undoubtedly real," but "appear to be based on little more than rumor or hearsay" (1973, pp. 15–16).

50. In early 1979, the chair of the ABA Standing Committee on Association Standards for Criminal Justice informed Hazard and Kutak that his committee would propose no changes in ABA Defense Function Standard 4.7–7, dealing with the problem of client perjury, until the commission had time to tackle the problem. For the commission's solution to the problem see Model Rule 3.3(a),(b).

Comments to Model Rule 3.8, which concerns the responsibilities of prosecutors, treat the ABA Standards Relating to the Prosecution Function as the final word on the subject, since those standards came after "prolonged and careful deliberation by lawyers experienced in both criminal prosecution and defense." In other words, it was on grounds of relative competence that the commission and the House of Delegates left the ethics of criminal practice largely to the more specialized Standards. But the commission never considered similarly deferring to ATLA or ACTL on the ethical questions that arise in civil litigation. It is not clear whether this was because of the perceived demerits of ATLA and ACTL positions, because those associations are not ABA entities, because there was no balance of plaintiff and defense lawyers in either association, or all the above.

Other arguments based on perceptions of institutional competence have been touched on earlier in the essay. When the Evans committee pressed for a detailed rule on the duties of the lawyer for a corporation, it did so on the ground that an alternative regulator, the SEC, would be too apt to design and enforce standards promoting agency goals at the expense of the rights of the parties being represented. And when ABA officials went to Washington to testify against the Specter bill, they spent little time on the merits of the bill's disclosure standards, arguing instead that a state supreme court, not Congress, is the appropriate institution to regulate the bar. On the other hand, when the Kutak Commission considered how, if at all, to address the problem of dilatory and harassing tactics in litigation, a majority took the position that Model Rules on these subjects should simply track the pertinent passages in the Federal Rules of Civil Procedure. This again was not so much a debate about what the rules should be as about which institution should be the frontline rule maker or enforcer in a given area.

There is a pattern in these arguments. Bar self-regulation and regulatory alternatives that rely heavily on the judiciary (as in the formulation and enforcement of rules of civil procedure) are favored; alternatives that involve legislative or administrative oversight, as with the SEC and the Specter bill, are not.[51] The disfavor with which so many lawyers look upon regulation by Congress, state legislatures, and public agencies like the SEC has itself given rise to a common phenomenon in bar politics: liberal bar leaders trying to cajole the rank and file to accept an unpalatable ethical duty such as mandatory pro bono by suggesting that if the bar does not impose the duty then less

51. This general bias became quite explicit at the ABA's midwinter 1989 meeting, when the House of Delegates approved a resolution sponsored by the ABA Special Coordinating Committee on Professionalism. The ABA resolved to oppose "all regulation of the practice of law by executive or legislative bodies, whether national, state or local."

reasonable regulators will impose a less palatable duty.[52] Robert Kutak sometimes used this tactic in the Model Rules process. After the bar's hostile reaction to the Discussion Draft, Kutak told the *Wall Street Journal*: "If we don't get our house in order, . . . somebody is going to write our rules for us. I don't think anybody wants that" (Curley 1981, p. 44).

Finally, the dramatic increase in the number, size, and organizational complexity of law firms (and other law offices) appears to have started ABA leaders thinking about the relative competence of the individual lawyer and the law firm *as a collectivity* in maintaining ethical standards in practice. By drafting and adopting Model Rules 5.1 through 5.3, the Kutak Commission and the House, respectively, acknowledged the ethical significance of a law firm's "culture" and structure, if only by directing senior lawyers to put proper procedures into place and to supervise subordinate lawyers and lay employees. They did not, however, make a centralized decision concerning the structures and monitoring procedures that firms must adopt (e.g., new-business committees to guard against conflicts of interest). Perhaps again on grounds of institutional competence, they left that to the experimentation of individual firms. Whether this development ultimately leads to rules subjecting law firms qua firms to professional discipline for structural and procedural shortcomings remains to be seen.

The Persistence of Role Morality

One criticism of legal ethics in recent years has been the moral philosopher's claim that the Code of Professional Responsibility instilled in lawyers or at least legitimated an overly deterministic "role morality." The role supposedly embodied in the Code was that of the lawyer as an advocate committed to achieving the client's objectives by every lawful means. This role is said to require a lawyer to disregard nonclient interests and conceivably his or her own off-the-job values.

Evidence from the Model Rules process suggest that the bar responded to this criticism, but not by abandoning a role-based ethic in favor of "ordinary morality," as some of the critics had prescribed. The response was rather to develop a more elaborate set of lawyers' roles and subroles in order to make role morality more wholesome. The bar's faith in ethical progress through

52. In 1976, ABA president Chesterfield Smith crusaded for a bar-administered mandatory pro bono program. His pitch for the program ended this way: "[T]imely actions by the organized bar recognizing that each and every lawyer must do some public service are essential if substantial self-regulation by lawyers is to continue" (Smith 1976).

role differentiation goes back to a 1958 ABA/AALS report that distinguished between the lawyer's roles as advocate and counselor, a distinction recognized though not emphasized in the Code. In the Model Rules, lawyers took the faith to new lengths.

The Kutak Commission wanted from the beginning to build the Model Rules around an elaborate set of roles. By August 1978, the commission had "arrived at a working hypothesis that the requirements of professional responsibility in the rendering of legal services vary with the particular roles in which the lawyer is acting. That is, the . . . rules of the attorney-client relationship should reflect whether the lawyer is acting as adviser, advocate, negotiator, intermediary, legal auditor, or administrator—those being the general role categories which previous Commission sessions have identified as significant" (Kutak Commission Journals, 25 August 1978). Besides attempting to specify the proper conduct of the lawyer as advocate, counselor, intermediary (e.g., between two would-be partners trying to work out a partnership agreement), and evaluator (e.g., preparing for a corporate client a prospectus on which third parties are likely to rely), the commission also recognized subroles within the traditional role of advocate. Rule 3.3(d), for instance, differentiates between the advocate's role in *ex parte* matters and in other cases; the *ex parte* advocate must disclose all material facts to the tribunal, including facts adverse to the client's position. And Model Rule 3.9 lays out the advocate's duties in legislative and administrative, as opposed to adjudicative, proceedings.

Several commentators objected to the commission's plan to flesh out the Model Rules on a skeleton of lawyers' roles. But their objection was not the philosophers' view that role morality unduly narrows one's ethical perspective. Rather, it was a practical objection: that the Model Rules would be unwieldy if separate rules on general matters had to be provided for each role; that the Model Rules would be difficult to enforce and useless to consult for guidance if they involved a complex grid of lawyers' roles; that lawyering involves frequent, imperceptible role shifts; and that it is too difficult to draft rules that demarcate these various roles from one another.

The commission heeded these criticisms and made the final product a less dramatic departure from the earlier codes than it might have been. On grounds of drafting economy, it developed rules on competence, confidentiality, and conflict of interest that apply to all client relationships, and abandoned separate rules for the lawyer as negotiator and as administrator. But it refused to retreat to the point where no legal work would be ethically distinguishable from advocacy. Retreat would have left the advocate's role too dominant and the commission unable to present the Model Rules as a conceptual advance.

Conclusion

I have not emphasized policy issues in this essay, but some of what I have written here pertains to whether state supreme courts should defer to the ABA when they adopt disciplinary rules to govern the lawyers in their jurisdictions.

If one's basis for such a judgment is the degree to which the ABA was open to the full range of *professional* opinion in the Model Rules process, then deference makes considerable sense, particularly if the alternative is a process in which the courts, ill-equipped to legislate from scratch, would take the lead. True, some bar entities had more influence on the Model Rules than others, perhaps even disproportionate influence, but a broad enough array of lawyers' groups participated to ensure that the Kutak Commission and the House of Delegates heard opinion and counter opinion on the big issues. Trial lawyers took a near-absolutist position on confidentiality, for example, but judges, many law professors, and the commission itself took a contrary view. The trial lawyers often "won" at the ABA, but the expression of opposing views in comments and early drafts paved the way for adoption of less absolute provisions when the Model Rules were considered in the states. The ABA to which the courts are deferring is no monolith.

It is likely of course that bar entities structured differently than the ABA would produce different rules. ATLA did, for example, and there are signs that the American Law Institute may soon produce a *Restatement of the Law Governing Lawyers* (see ALI 1989) that diverges from the Model Rules in important respects.[53] This, however, does not imply that the ABA's process for eliciting a cross section of professional opinion was deficient.

If one's basis for judging the wisdom of state court deference to the ABA is instead the degree to which the Model Rules process was open to *lay* opinion, the evidence is much more equivocal. The lay press emerged as an important source though never a galvanizer of public opinion, and the Kutak Commission was quite sensitive both to the press and to scholarly criticism of earlier ABA codes. The House of Delegates, however, seemed impervious to these forces.

If one believes (as I do not) that no private bar association could be a legitimate codegiver unless legal ethics were a purely technical subject—one the public found uninteresting and impenetrable, but on which lawyers widely agreed—then the ABA's legitimacy is doubtful indeed. Two of the

53. These points of divergence include the role of the attorney-client privilege in shareholder derivative suits and the scope of the lawyer's discretion to disclose confidential information to prevent crimes by their clients.

most salient features of the Model Rules process were the attention it received from the lay press and the range of professional opinion that surfaced, a range comparable to what one might expect with any controversial piece of legislation.

Finally, if one considers the ethical debate that goes hand in hand with producing a professional code as a good in itself, and thus as a criterion for judging the wisdom of deferring to the ABA as codegiver, as I confess I do, then the Model Rules story again supports deference. One cannot imagine American lawyers participating as extensively in an ethics debate conducted under other auspices. And if lawyers had not expected the ABA's product to be adopted as law, they would surely have been less motivated to participate in the Model Rules process.

Policy matters aside, what does this detailed account of the Model Rules process tell us about the values and structure of today's legal profession? For one thing, it shows that at the collective level no less than in individual practice the profession has become vastly more differentiated than it was when the ABA adopted its first ethics code in 1908. Most lawyers' views are now transmitted to the ABA drafting body or House of Delegates, and possibly shaped as well, by mediating organizations. Moreover, specialty groups like the ABA's Corporation, Banking, and Business Law Section (recently renamed the Section of Business Law) or the ACTL, nonexistent when the ABA first produced an ethics code, now seem to have more influence on the ABA's product than the older, general-purpose state and local bar associations, perhaps because the latter find it harder to achieve a consensus among their diverse memberships (see Schwartz 1980a).[54]

For another thing, this study shows that while the lawyers participating in the Model Rules process shared certain values and styles of ethical discourse—legalism, defensive ethics, a preoccupation with institutional competence, and a commitment to role morality—they also differed on many central issues in legal ethics. Taking trial lawyers, corporate counsel, legal services lawyers, code enforcers, judges, private practitioners in large and small firms, law professors, and others properly into account, and considering how divided the House votes were on key issues, one is struck by the heterogeneity of ethical views in today's profession.

54. Of course, when it comes to adoption of the Model Rules at the state level, the support of the state bar association remains crucial. The ABA was able to produce the Model Rules despite full-scale opposition from the California State Bar and the New York State Bar associations, but the Model Rules are unlikely to be adopted in California and New York. In 1982, when the board of governors of the California State Bar resolved to oppose the Model Rules in toto and forwarded their resolution to the ABA House of Delegates, they assumed that without state bar approval California would never adopt the Model Rules. They took an interest in the Model Rules because "such rules will have an impact upon the California lawyer who practices in other state jurisdictions and in federal courts."

One is struck also by how often the ethical concerns and viewpoints of bar groups can be traced to the peculiarities of their workplace, clientele, or political environment. Special pleading now abounds. Legal services lawyers want rules that guarantee their zealous commitment to clients and special attention to the problem of advancing litigation expenses for the indigent and the problems of maintaining professional independence from lay employers. Securities lawyers want ethics rules that buffer them from an aggressive SEC. Small-town lawyers do not want to formalize their ongoing client relationships by putting fee agreements in writing. Bar counsel want the easiest rules to enforce. Trial lawyers want to minimize the perception that they might have to betray their clients' trust, even at the risk of having to blink at perjury. And so on.

Finally, this study shows that none of the substantive criticisms scholars leveled at earlier ABA ethics codes accounts for very much of what happened in the Model Rules process. First, the process was in no sense an arena of conflict between powerful law firms and powerless "Little Lawyers." ABA leaders did show special concern for issues of interest to elite law firms, such as the revolving door and the duty to blow the whistle on (or more precisely, for) a corporate client, indicating that elite firms may have special power to mobilize the ABA for particularistic purposes; these matters, though, were simply of no concern to "Little Lawyers." Small-town practitioners and lawyers from elite urban firms joined to oppose a requirement that all fee agreements be in writing. The Kutak Commission and the House of Delegates showed sensitivity to general practitioners when they ensured that the Model Rules did not imply that those lawyers were incompetent to handle matters in which other lawyers specialized. And small-firm and solo practitioners working through the ABA General Practice Section displayed considerable clout of their own, killing a rule that would have facilitated the growth of new group legal services plans by allowing nonlawyers to own an interest in law offices.

Second, although defensive exercises of self-interest were common, one cannot fairly describe the Model Rules process as a collective effort to aggrandize lawyers at their clients' expense. True, the House of Delegates rejected the rule that would have spurred competition by allowing lawyers for the first time to work for firms in which nonlawyers are investors. The House also approved an anti-competitive rule (Model Rule 7.3) barring solicitation of new clients even through the mail.[55] But there was no concerted push for rules restraining competition among lawyers, if only because

55. The Supreme Court has struck down on First Amendment grounds the restriction on direct-mail solicitation of clients known to have specific legal needs (*Shapero* v. *Kentucky Bar Association* 1988).

Supreme Court decisions had taken the subjects of group legal services, lawyer advertising, and minimum fee schedules largely out of bar hands. One large bar group, ATLA, even purported to treat consumer interests as an ethical cornerstone. And though the upper limit on lawyers' fees remained vague, the Model Rule 1.5(a) made a shallow bow to consumer interests by lowering the Code of Professional Responsibility's "clearly excessive" ceiling to one of "reasonableness."

Third, the moral philosophers' "hired gun" criticism of the earlier ABA codes seems largely inapplicable to the Model Rules. That criticism asserted that rules of legal ethics have forced lawyers into an advocate's role that places client interests above all others, and have done so by forbidding lawyers to let their own values or the interests of third parties affect their decisions about whom to represent and how to represent them. Yet the Model Rules recognize that lawyers play several roles, not just that of advocate. They also invite lawyers in *any* role to take their own values into account. They permit lawyers to refuse to represent a client on moral grounds (Model Rule 6.2, Comment); authorize lawyers to "limit the objectives" of representation by excluding client aims they find "repugnant or imprudent" (Model Rule 1.2[c]); and in a remarkable concession to lawyers' sensibilities allow them to withdraw whenever "a client insists upon pursuing an objective the lawyer considers repugnant or imprudent"—even if the client's interest will be "adversely affected" by the withdrawal (Model Rule 1.16 [b][3])! These rules were meant precisely to resolve the "potential conflict between the lawyer's conscience and the lawyer's duty to vigorously represent a client" (ABA Center for Professional Responsibility 1987, p. 103).

One other point about the moral philosophers' critique: When lawyers sought language that was consistent with the so-called standard conception of legal ethics, they often gave reasons that had nothing to do with that conception. Instead, rules that permit lawyers to go to the limit of the law for their clients were defended on grounds of fair notice to lawyers or, in the case of the ethics of civil litigation, on grounds of institutional competence.

Fourth and finally, however indeterminate the Model Rules might seem to Professor Abel and other critical scholars, participants in the Model Rules process did not understand themselves to be engaged in a public relations charade that would legitimate the bar's tradition of self-regulation but have no regulatory bite. True, the Kutak Commission and other ABA leaders were vitally interested in the public reaction to the Model Rules. Still, if one starts not with Professor Abel's reifying question, "Why Does the ABA Bother?" but asks instead why the participants in the Model Rules process bothered, then one must conclude that lawyers expected the Model Rules to have real significance as a guide to lawyers with ethical questions, enforced in the disciplinary process, and as a source of other law. Ironically, the group that fought hardest to insert (certain) intentionally vague provisions into the Model Rules was NOBC, whose members were bent on making enforcement *easier*.

That no criticism of the earlier ABA codes can in itself account for the motives and discourse of those who participated in the Model Rules process does not mean, of course, that the older, functional theories of codes of professional ethics are more satisfactory. As with the critical theories, there is little evidence that the participants in the Model Rules process generally saw themselves as the functionalists might have supposed—protecting an unsophisticated clientele from professional exploitation and incompetence, or protecting society from the overzealous pursuit of client aims. In short, if one looks closely enough at the process in which the Model Rules were developed, no single grand theory, critical or functionalist, comes close to accounting for it. Detailed study of the making of a professional code may thus be a useful corrective to the soaring theories scholars have so far brought to the subject.

CHAPTER FOUR

Five Crises or One: The Concept of Legal Professionalism, 1925–1960

Rayman L. Solomon

The leadership of the American legal profession recently expressed its concern about a crisis in professionalism through the report of the ABA's Commission on Professionalism (1986) and through the work of the committee to implement that report (ABA 1986). To speak about a crisis in professionalism implies that change has occurred, and thus requires that professionalism be placed in its historical context. In fact historical comparisons abound in the report of the commission, as well as in public statements by leading practitioners. The first page of the commission's report states the fundamental question to be "Has our profession *abandoned* principle for profit, professionalism for commercialism?" When discussing the question of commercialism many practicing lawyers explicitly compare today's practice and notions of professionalism with those when they entered the profession. What, however, is this "professionalism" that lawyers have abandoned, and what previous "crises" has the legal profession experienced? In this essay I will examine conceptions of professionalism between 1925 and 1960 and present a comprehensive description of how twentieth-century bar leaders described what professionalism meant during a period of rapid political, economic, and social alteration. Linking the content of the concept

I thank Lawrence Friedman for his support and imaginatively insightful comments as the discussant on this paper at the American Bar Foundation Conference on Professionalism in September 1988. I also thank the following for their assistance and advice: Ben Brown, Steve Diamond, Jim Grossman, Gordon Hylton, Art McEvoy, Beth Mertz, Chris Tomlins, David Trubek, Jerry Van Hoy, Richard Zansitis, and members of the Social History Workshop at the University of Chicago. I am indebted to Ethan Cohen for his research assistance. Greg Lind, David Futrelle, Aaron Epstein, and Brice Prince also made significant contributions to the research. Carol Avins's support and suggestions improved the clarity of both the style and substance of the essay. All errors remain unfortunately my own.

with social, political, and economic conditions external to the legal profession can add to our understanding of the symbolic uses of the rhetoric of professionalism.

The major argument of this article is that professionalism, as conceived by the elite of the bar, is a set of symbolic rhetorical and normative concepts that was remarkably stable over the period of this study. The individual strands of the concept are constantly present; i.e., in any given year there was a speech or speeches invoking one or all of the components of the set. The content of these speeches resembles that of previous or subsequent years. What does change is the appearance of crisis periods during which certain aspects of professionalism appear to be challenged. During these crisis periods some components of the concept are discussed with greater intensity and frequency than others. This alone does not mark the periods as "crisis." The rhetoric at those times also conveys the bar leaders' perception that the profession is under attack or held in disrepute by the public. Speeches and articles about professionalism by these leaders were aimed at both the profession itself and the general public, and were attempts to reestablish the legitimacy of the profession. These periods are also marked by competing visions and interpretations of the measures necessary to restore that legitimacy. While bar elites shared a belief in what professionalism entailed, they differed politically on how the concept was to be realized.

The period 1925 to 1960 is marked by nearly continuous crisis for the legal profession.[1] These are related to Prohibition, the Great Depression, court-packing and the growth of federal regulation, McCarthyism, and the specter of federally funded legal services. To understand how these events relate to the concept of professionalism in the practice of law, one must raise and attempt to answer several questions. Were these five events separate crises, or were these thirty-five years one constant crisis with different triggering events? Were there periods of equilibrium and disequilibrium or was disequilibrium the equilibrium? Are these crises "real" or entirely self-created by the profession? And finally, what does the history of these earlier periods of crisis reveal about the present concern over the commercialization of law practice?

Before we turn to an examination of the content of the speeches, a brief description of certain analytical issues surrounding the study of legal professionalism is in order. *Professionalism* has no commonly accepted definition.

1. The boundaries of the period studied are somewhat arbitrary. I begin with the period between 1870 and 1925 because these years have received detailed study by sociologists and historians, a subject I shall treat more fully in the course of the essay. The cutoff date of 1960 was selected to provide for examination a period sufficiently long to observe different patterns, yet not too long to research and discuss.

Historians and sociologists tend to describe it in terms of the attributes that scholars of the legal profession commonly recognize as central to our construction of the concept of a profession. Conceiving of professionalism in this manner was the approach of the recent American Bar Association's Report of the Commission on Professionalism. The report acknowledged the difficulty of defining the concept, and then gave a working definition of a "**profession**" based on a historical observation by Roscoe Pound and a contemporary analysis derived from the work of Eliot Freidson, himself a member of the commission (ABA 1986, pp. 10, 11). The elements of the commission's definition (1986, p. 10) are

1. The profession receives special privileges from the state.
2. Its practice requires substantial intellectual training.
3. Clients must trust the professional because their lack of training prevents them from evaluating his or her work.
4. "The client's trust presupposes that the practitioner's self-interest is overbalanced by devotion to serving both the client's interest and the public good."
5. The profession is self-regulating.

Embedded in these elements are two core sets of claims that demarcate it: one involving knowledge and the other autonomy. Knowledge, in part, encompasses the academic training and expertise that comprise the profession's claim to be "learned," to have mastered the esoteric and inaccessible (to the general public) substantive and procedural rules of law. This formal knowledge is supplemented by the experientially based practices employed on behalf of clients—knowing how "legal things" are done in the real world. It is the combination of these sources of knowledge that has been described as a major determinant of the power exercised by the legal profession (Friedson 1986; Heinz 1983). The third element of the commission's definition captures this in its claim that clients must rely on their lawyers because the lawyers possess an expertise that the clients do not have.

There are four principal aspects to the autonomy of the legal profession—two of which concern the profession's relations to "politics" and two, its relations to "the market." Individual lawyers are to be politically independent from both their clients and the government. The bar, as a collective, is to abstain from partisan politics. Both of these statements are derived from the fourth element of the commission's definition—that the lawyer is to stand between his client and the government and not be openly identified with either. These assertions about a lawyer's political independence, as Robert

Gordon has explained, are central to the ideal of advocacy in American legal culture:

> Proponents of the Advocacy Ideal emphasize lawyers' nonsubordination to the officers and purposes of the state. Believers in the ideal of lawyers as engaged in a public profession, on the other hand, stress that lawyers should remain independent of all the particular factional interests of civil society, *including those of their clients*. . . . If lawyers generally get overidentified with one set of client interests, they won't be credible advocates for the opposing position in the next case. If lawyers generally get identified with client causes, moreover, they won't be able to take on disgusting or unpopular ones. . . . [A]lthough lawyers' services and technical skills are for sale, their personal and political convictions are not. . . . The loyalty purchased by the client is *limited*, because a part of the lawyer's professional persona must be set aside for dedication to public purposes. (Gordon 1988, p. 13)

Claims about market autonomy overlap but are distinct from political autonomy. These are derived from the fourth and fifth elements of the commission's definition—that the lawyer's self-interest is subordinated to that of his client, and that the profession is free from state regulation. Individual lawyers are to reject the business ethic of profit maximization, as the interests of the client and the public are to take precedence over the lawyer's economic self-interest. The commission's charge of the commercialization of practice, incorporates these notions that law has become a business subject to market demands (as well as the concept that lawyers have lost political independence from their clients). The commission accused the bar of becoming subservient to their corporate clients for the sake of more business and greater wealth.

In the second of the two aspects of market independence, the bar, as a collective, is to be free of both governmental regulation and the full effects of market forces. The bar enjoys a monopoly over the practice of law; it controls the supply of lawyers by determining and administering the requirements for entry into the profession. Additionally, the bar controls the machinery for disciplining the members of the profession, and had been completely exempt from antitrust provisions until the U.S. Supreme Court's decisions of the early 1970s that struck down some of the bar's restrictions on advertising and other anti-competitive measures.[2]

Thus, professionalism can be conceived of as an ideology of bar elites that seeks to establish the various claims about the nature of the legal profession

2. *Goldfarb v. Virginia State Bar* 1975; *Bates and O'Stern v. Arizona State Bar* 1977.

as behavioral norms for both individual lawyers and the bar as a collective. Knowledge and autonomy are the cornerstones of this elite construction of the profession, and their development and preservation are the defining characteristics of the rhetoric of being a professional. Bar leaders invoke the concept of professionalism to lament the decline of some aspect of this normative universe and to exhort their audience to reestablish the norms.

This sketch of professionalism and its constituent parts conforms to earlier historical and sociological descriptions of the concept. Scholars addressing the subject have examined the rhetoric of bar elites to piece together a description of professionalism as it developed during the late nineteenth and early twentieth centuries. The major elements of these descriptions are calls for higher educational qualifications, independence from the government and clients, greater control over the qualifications and regulation of the profession, and the need for law practice to avoid commercialization—to avoid becoming a business subject to market pressures. Throughout Jerold Auerbach's monograph (1976) or the articles of Robert Gordon (1984a, 1983) numerous examples of speeches containing these themes can be found. Auerbach describes the debates surrounding Elihu Root's ABA committee's recommendation in 1921 that educational requirements be raised for admission to the bar. The leading elite lawyers of the day supported the idea and voiced sentiments similar to those of the dean of Columbia Law School who advocated "a 'new and enlarged conception of legal education' as the prerequisite for a socially responsible profession" (Auerbach 1976, p. 100). William Howard Taft "pleaded for higher standards 'for the good of society.' . . . Only lawyers highly trained . . . could comprehend 'the present thinking of the people' " (Auerbach 1976, p. 100). The eminent historian of the Progressive Era, Richard Hofstadter, noted that at the turn of the century many bar leaders complained that "law had lost much of its distinctly professional character and had become a business." He quotes a leading Chicago attorney who wrote that "the profession is commercialized" and that this accounted for the bar's loss of status (Hofstadter 1955, pp. 158–59). Auerbach, Hofstadter, and Gordon all quote Louis Brandeis's lament that "[i]nstead of holding a position of independence, between the wealthy and the people, prepared to curb the excesses of either, able lawyers have, to a large extent, allowed themselves to become adjuncts of great corporations and have neglected the obligation to use their powers for the protection of the people. We hear much of the 'corporation lawyer' and far too little of the 'people's lawyer' " (Hofstadter 1955, p. 161; Auerbach 1976, p. 34; Gordon 1988, p. 2).

Despite this convergence among scholars on the descriptive content of the rhetoric of professionalism, there is no consensus on the *effects* of this rhetoric. Critical scholars such as Abel, Larson, or Auerbach have examined the elite bar's calls for greater professionalism during the late nineteenth and early twentieth centuries and have argued that these rhetorical outpourings had no effect on the behavior of lawyers. They view them instead as disguised attempts to establish and retain the elites' monopoly of the practice of law. According to this perspective, the effects of such monopoly power are to enhance the economic interests of legal elites (Abel 1985a; Larson 1977), to enable those elites to control the social composition of the bar (Auerbach 1976, p.34), and/or to reinforce the legitimacy of class divisions in the existing order. The purpose of demands for higher entry requirements, Auerbach argues, was to exclude religious and racial minorities from entry into the profession, and those individuals who were able to overcome these barriers were to be relegated by ethical codes and other regulations (prohibitions against solicitation and minimum fee schedules, for example) to practice among their "own kind" (Auerbach 1976, pp. 41, 42).

Other scholars, both noncritical and critical, acknowledge the monopolistic consequences of the concept of professionalism, but argue that the rhetoric of professionalism has other behavioral and social effects as well. Burton Bledstein shares the view that the requirements of training, expertise, and autonomy from government and clients characterized the development of "the culture of professionalism," but saw professionalism as a path of vertical mobility for the middle class, not a vehicle for maintaining class domination (Bledstein 1976). Terence Halliday has recently challenged the monopoly thesis by arguing that, although monopolistic motives may have driven legal elites during the formative era of professionalization, currently the autonomy of the profession and the substance of its expertise allows the bar to play a mediative role between the demands of clients and the state (Halliday 1987, chap. 12). He describes the bar's collective professionalism as a "never stable tension between civic and monopolistic values" (Halliday 1987, p. 370). Stephen Botein, writing about the ABA's role at the turn of the century in fighting against judicial recall, examines how the bar's concept of the separation of law from politics created not only the bar's initial opposition to public control over judicial decisions, but later shaped its tactics against Franklin Roosevelt's plan to "pack" the Court (Botein 1983, p. 49). Robert Gordon has developed the most forceful argument for the behavioral consequences of the ideology of professionalism. In a series of articles he has described lawyers as having " 'ideal interests' as well as material ones, and as struggling to work out a relationship between their beliefs and their practices—between the ideal and actual—with which they could live in comfort" (Gordon 1984b, p. 53). He has analyzed the rhetorical claims for the independence of lawyers—from both political and economic control of the state and from their clients—and shown how these have led to rhetorical and behavioral strategies for maintaining that independence during the first quarter of the twentieth century.

This investigation of the conception of legal professionalism through an examination of the rhetoric of bar elites shares with the work of Gordon, Halliday, and Bledstein a belief that the speeches and articles of these lawyers were intended to affect the actions of the members of the bar through the restoration of norms that defined the profession. I do not claim to address the question of whether prior generations were more professional, as the materials studied are not what one would study to measure the level of professionalism in any period—if indeed that task is even possible. Neither do we describe how the ideology of professionalism affects the actual practice of law. Any such efforts would require a comprehensive history of what lawyers do in their daily work life, not how they describe what it means to be a professional.

Unlike earlier commentators, however, I focus on the period from 1925 to 1960. Most of the previous historical and sociological work has concentrated on the last quarter of the nineteenth century, as that was the "take-off" period of professionalization in the United States. During that time lawyers, along with doctors, college professors, engineers, and others, established the structures that promoted and legitimated their status as professionals by founding national organizations, establishing university training in their disciplines, raising the minimum requirements for entry into practice, devising ethical codes that dictated how practice was to be carried out, and gaining the power both to design these regulations and to enforce them without the intervention of public authority. I examined the concept of legal professionalism from 1925 to 1960 by analyzing a sample of published speeches and articles that appeared in legal periodicals during that period.[3] I identified 729 articles from listings in the *Index to Legal Periodicals*, which is a comprehensive index of law reviews and state and local bar journals. The articles examined were those in which authors were reflecting on the legal profession as a whole, and not the numerous substantive articles on the various formal ethical codes or other subjects such as administrative law. As will be seen, these articles might focus on contemporaneous problems facing the organized bar, lawyers as a profession, or individuals in practice. Forty-three of the articles were found to be not relevant—most of these being anecdotal reminiscences from practice or stories of the early bench and bar.[4] The sample appears to have a broad geographic base with most authors being urban elites. Approx-

3. I reviewed articles from 1925 to 1930, then from every third year between 1930 and 1960.

4. I examined all articles indexed under "Legal Ethics" or "Legal Profession." Those of little interest or use included historical accounts of bar leaders of the previous century (for example,

imately 30 percent of the articles came from national journals such as the *American Bar Association Journal (A.B.A.J.)*; 30 percent from midwestern journals; 16 percent from the northeast; 17 percent from the south; while only 8 percent were from the west. A tentative composite analysis of the authors shows that almost three-quarters were elites. Ten percent were national elites (national bar leaders, federal officeholders); 35 percent had appeared in *Who's Who*; and 28 percent were local elites (local bar association officers). Nineteen percent were practitioners who did not appear to hold or have held any bar leadership position. Twenty-eight percent of the authors identified lived in cities of under 100,000 people; 24 percent in cities of 100,000 to 500,000; and 38 percent in cities of over 500,000.

A continuity in the contents of the concept of professionalism across the entire period emerges from these articles. Moreover, the elements of that concept are exactly those that the studies of the late nineteenth and early twentieth centuries have described. Articles similar to the ones Auerbach and Larson point to that emphasize the bar's autonomy over the market appear in each year of the sample and from each region of the country. These advocate raising or tightening entry requirements, eliminating the unauthorized practice of law, and disciplining those engaged in solicitation. Others of this type simply protest that the profession is overcrowded. In the 1920s an Oklahoma practitioner denounced those who hitch their wagons to an ambulance rather than to a star (Thrift 1927). Missouri and Kentucky bar leaders in the early 1930s called for higher entry requirements; the president of the ABA addressed a group of New York lawyers in 1933 and cited overcrowding and the entrance of unqualified lawyers as two of the most serious problems facing the profession (Kemp 1933; Ragland 1933; Martin 1933). A New Jersey judge addressing his state's bar association in 1936 devoted his talk to the dangers of lay encroachment (Brogan 1936). A 1942 speech by a Boston lawyer decried the loss of business to lay persons and urged lawyers to expand their expertise and practice to new areas of administrative law (Salter 1942). Three years later a similar address was given by an Ohio lawyer to the state's junior bar association (Taggart 1945). A 1948 article by an estate specialist warned of the dangers of the encroachment of insurance agents in the field of estate planning. He pointed out that the dangers to the public resulted from the fact that the insurance agents—unlike lawyers—were not disinterested parties, and had an inadequate code of ethics (Otterbourg 1948). A speech to the Nevada bar association in 1954 described the unauthorized practice of law as the central problem facing the bar, and urged more vigorous enforcement of ethical canons (Dickerson 1954). In 1957

Crawford 1925, pp. 140–51); descriptions of the the foreign bar (*Solicitor's Journal* 1926, p. 991); and several that were merely anecdotal (for example, Hutchens 1926, pp. 61–78).

ABA president David Maxwell vigorously defended the bar against charges of laxity in enforcement of ethical codes. He argued that the organized bar had a fundamental commitment to disbarring the unethical and ensuring that only those qualified by training and character could be admitted to the bar (Maxwell 1957). These are only a few, but representative, examples of the constant refrain of bar elites invoking increased control over the supply of lawyers and the market for lawyers' work as a necessary tenet of professionalism.

The independence of lawyers from the profit concerns of the market is also a consistent theme throughout these years. From the 1920s on one can see the continuation of the denunciations of the commercialization of practice that historians such as Richard Hofstadter describe occuring since the end of the nineteenth century. In a 1926 speech to the Rhode Island Bar its president lamented the fact that economic conditions had turned the energies of the ablest and best-trained lawyers into seeking and retaining clients rather than serving the public interest (Cohen 1926). An Oklahoma City bar leader in 1933 accused lawyers of pursuing money and failing to dissuade their clients from breaking the law (Gibson 1933). That same year a Houston lawyer criticized lawyers for being too absorbed in business and representing the special interests of their clients at the expense of the public (Huggins 1933). A 1938 article in *Harper's Magazine*, following the court-packing controversy, attacked lawyers for, among other things, their identification with the interests of corporations and their inability to serve the public (Lundberg 1938a). Similarly, in 1942 a Connecticut judge protested the fact that lawyers "had become businessmen, not professional men" (Quinlan 1942). Surveying the changing world of law practice in 1948, a prominent lawyer cited as the greatest danger to law its becoming more like big business. He lamented that young lawyers were pursuing the high salaries of the large "businesslike" firms (Ash 1948).

The statements of Louis Brandeis and others, which scholars such as Robert Gordon have used to illustrate the ideal of the political autonomy of the bar, are found in this sample as well. A justice of the Wisconsin Supreme Court published an article in 1927 entitled "An Ancient and Honorable Profession" in which he stated that the lawyer "is charged with a dual function: to serve the public in aid of the administration of justice, and to promote the interest of his client. The latter must be subservient to the former" (Doerfler 1927). A 1942 article by a Denver judge lamented the bar's loss of leadership, and blamed that loss on its refusal to address the great social issues of the preceding decade. He claimed that lawyers were going into large firms where they disdained "human" problems, instead spending all of their time advising corporations (Johnson 1942). In that same year a Kansas lawyer alerted his fellow members of the state bar to the danger that the "lawyer has degenerated into a mere employee of its client," and at the same time implored them to remain independent also of the government in order to safeguard the country from the perils of fascism (Stone 1942). Justice William O. Douglas in a 1948 article in the *A.B.A.J.* called for lawyers to be policymakers, as their training "should have given them some inkling of the bold and comprehensive strokes of . . . action" needed in the United States and the world. He regretted, however, that after the war too many had slipped back to concern only for their clients (Douglas 1948). A Ford Motor Company attorney told a Milwaukee bar group in 1954 that lawyers must assume responsibility for counseling business ethically as well as legally. He implored them to use their training for leadership in making public policy (Reid 1954).

These themes within the concept of professionalism do not, however, exhaust the picture that emerges from the sample of the articles between 1925 and 1960. There were crisis periods in which debate raged over a topic and then subsided or disappeared almost completely. These were times when major social, political, and economic events brought into focus gaps between the normative ideals of professionalism and the perceived realities of lawyers' practices. Bar elites responded to these gaps by exhorting their audience to reestablish the normative ideals. The volume of articles about a specific aspect of professionalism thus increased dramatically. Yet a crisis can be measured by the quantity of articles alone. Articles during such periods were almost formulaic. Typically, they expressed the public's disenchantment with the bar, and then explored the sources of that disfavor. The latter was linked to the relationships between external social, political, and economic events and the bar's responses to them. The solutions were not proposed in one voice. Apologists saw the public as misinformed about the bar, and urged public relations campaigns to explain why the various actions of the bar were necessary and desirable. Critics, on the other hand, saw the bar's behavior as falling short of the ideals of professionalism; they urged structural reform. An examination of the crisis articles themselves provides no definitive explanation for their form, but the emphasis on public antagonism toward the bar is suggestive. Central to the definition of the profession (which also appears as the ABA commission's first element) is the assertion that the profession receives special privileges from the state. Commentators have explained this as a bargain between the bar and the state in which the bar is granted professional autonomy in exchange for dissociating itself from the commercial market and from partisan politics. Fear that public anger at the bar could force the state to revoke this bargain transforms the speeches of these bar leaders from isolated laments to a chorus calling attention to perceived crises.

Five crises in the legal profession have been identified between 1925 and

1960. They are related to Prohibition (1925 to 1932); the Great Depression (1929 to 1938); court-packing and the growth of federal regulation (1936 to 1945); McCarthyism (1948 to 1958); and the specter of federally funded legal services (1954 to 1960). The dates associated with these crises are not strict chronological boundaries, but rather mark the periods of maximum intensity of debates surrounding the effects of these events on the bar's conception of professionalism. The difference between a crisis period and simply an increased attention to a subject is clear when one considers World War II. The literature of that time contained a vast outpouring of support for the war effort and exhortations for the bar to assume leadership in the fight against fascism, but no questioning of the public's attitude toward the profession or criticism of the bar.

Prohibition: Autonomy from the Client

During the late 1920s and early 1930s the criminal justice system was the prodominant topic of the speeches and articles published by the leaders of the bar. These authors usually began by decrying the decline in prestige of the legal profession or by seeking to refute public criticism leveled at the bar. In a typical example a Maryland judge speaking to the local bar association in 1925 started his address, "Certain Lay Critics," by surveying the history of anti-lawyer sentiment. He quoted remarks by Shakespeare, Swift, Franklin, and Jefferson, then he turned immediately to an analysis of the lawyer's role in representing criminal defendants (Parke 1925). Similarly, a 1926 editorial in *The Docket* contained references to articles and an editorial in the *Saturday Evening Post* that criticized lawyers for contributing to the crime wave overwhelming the nation (*The Docket* 1926). The 1926 presidential address to the Wisconsin State Bar Association examined the declining prestige of the lawyer, and linked it to law's having grown more like a business and to the misperception that the bar was responsible for high crime rates (Wilcox 1926). A 1927 South Dakota bar leader also began his address by denying that lawyers were responsible for the crime wave (Hubbard 1930). This sudden concern over criminal justice is related to Prohibition and the state of law enforcement in the 1920s.

Prohibition led to the development of organized crime, which prompted the public to perceive a crime wave. The failure of federal and state authorities to enforce the laws against the manufacture, sale, and consumption of alcohol led to public investigations and private studies of corruption in the police, the courts, and the legal profession (Solomon 1985). Public dissatisfaction with the law's ability to control the growth of crime threatened the legitimacy of law itself. The public perceived lawyers as defenders of criminals and believed them to be involved in the politics of organized crime. Film historian Andrew Bergman captures this point in his analysis of six "shyster" films—all made in 1932. He writes: "A further note on films about lawyers. They are clearly marked 'Depression' not only by the gross caricature of social dislocation, but by the laughing-stock image they conveyed of the law. . . . [The films' lawyers] by operating through the loopholes of the law, used legal codes as the straight man for an ongoing joke . . . the law again came off as a vacuum" (Bergman 1971).

Bar leaders responded to such public criticism by attempting in several ways to reestablish the norm of political autonomy—the independence of lawyer from client. The defenders of the bar argued that the public did not understand what Robert Gordon has labeled, the "liberal advocacy ideal" (Gordon 1988, p. 10). The essence of that concept is that the rule of law requires that all must receive the most effective possible representation in court. Lawyers do not necessarily condone their clients' actions (although there may be some "bad apples"); instead they are vindicating the rights guaranteed to all citizens. A 1928 article in the *American Law Review* argues that lawyers are being unfairly criticized, although some disreputable lawyers do exist—just as there are quacks, thieving merchants, or lying journalists (Rubin 1928). The author urges lawyers not to take cases in which they cannot in good conscience defend their client, but claims that such instances are quite rare. He further asserts that legal technicalities are designed to prevent injustice and that it is infrequent that such technicalities alter the outcome of cases. The author concludes by exhorting the bar to explain to the public that the bar should and must take unpopular causes because the best protection for society comes from securing individual justice. The author of "Certain Lay Critics" stated that although public opinion was against lawyers, the public should be educated to understand that the need to defend the guilty stems from the right to counsel guaranteed in the Constitution (Parke 1925). A 1927 Iowa bar article sounded the same theme of the need for educating the public that lawyers were not to be associated with the criminality of their clients. In addition to maintaining that clients were entitled to representation he emphasized that open immigration, not lawyers, had led to the crime wave (Byington 1927).[5]

Other bar leaders, however, did not perceive the problem as a failure of the public to understand the lawyer's role in the legal system. These leaders

5. Authors argued that despite what laymen may think, lawyers are more concerned with and supportive of law enforcement than any other profession. See Ridgway 1929, Hubbard 1930.

stressed that the public's disaffection with lawyers stemmed from substantive problems in the criminal justice system that lawyers could work to correct. Some complained of the use of "technicalities" to win acquittals for the guilty. They urged weeding out those attorneys who prevailed in criminal trials through corruption or deceit (Melton 1925; Pershing 1928; Hay 1929). A Montana lawyer and newspaper editor wrote in 1925 that modern criminals no longer feared the law, because they knew they will not be punished under it. Defense lawyers' tactics during trials were listed as the principal cause of the system's failure (Hutchens 1925; Cummings 1930). Other critics challenged the bar to provide leadership in reforming the criminal justice system itself. These bar leaders advocated legislation to modernize criminal procedure and law enforcement. In his presidential address to the Wisconsin bar in 1926 R.P. Wilcox claimed that "organized crime" should be met with an "organized bar" and that the bar's efforts to reform the criminal justice system would thwart organized crime (Wilcox 1926). An Iowa attorney began his 1927 address by calling for reforms in the conduct of trials and for the adoption of a new criminal code. He blamed the bar for making the administration of justice too slow, too technical, and too expensive to eliminate the crime wave efficiently (Swisher 1927).[6]

With the repeal of Prohibition and the onset of the Depression, discussions of criminal justice lost their prominence and became one of many issues in a list of contemporaneous problems.

The Great Depression: Autonomy from Regulation by the Market

The Depression and the New Deal produced two distinct yet overlapping sets of crises for the legal profession. The economic dislocations created conditions that threatened the market control enjoyed by the profession, while New Deal expansion of federal regulatory agencies precipitated challenges to the bar's political independence. The controversy over market controls was engendered by perceptions that the legal profession was overcrowded. This oversupply led to excessive competition, which in turn produced two socially undesirable consequences. First, with the demand for legal services down and with no reduction on the supply side, lawyers, so critics claimed, engaged in unethical practices to solicit and retain business.

6. See Daniels 1925, Lewis 1929, McNutt 1931. See also Pound 1925, who argues lawyers to take the lead in reforming the criminal justice system.

Second, as other critics charged, lawyers had abandoned any attempts to represent the interests of the middle and lower classes, who had been impoverished by the Depression. Too many lawyers were chasing the business of a few wealthy clients, and the profession as a whole had forgotten its obligation to the public. In a widely read and discussed series of articles in *Harper's Magazine* Ferdinand Lundberg called attention to the maldistribution of legal services. He began his articles by claiming that the legal profession was the only monopoly that had escaped public accountability for its role in the perpetuation of economic and social injustice in the United States (Lundberg 1938a), and in the second article of his series he discussed whether the profession should lose the monopoly privileges that had been granted it by the state.[7] He ended his first article by citing instances of the legal system's injustices and concluded: "But in cases like these, and thousands of others, the injured parties have no redress because, having no money, they have no lawyers. . . . The legal profession is the institution that is charged, under capitalism, with seeing that justice prevails for all men; and it consequently follows that it is the legal profession that must be held responsible for injustice whether overt or concealed. It is the one institution that has broken down whenever a one-sided application of the law, which is what one often sees, brings injustice" (Lundberg 1939a).

During the 1930s leaders of the bar began to acknowledge both of the effects of overcrowding. As early as 1931 articles appeared that argued that "ambulance chasers" were harming the poor through the use of unscrupulous contracts and harming the profession by tarnishing its public image (Crum 1931). In 1933 the infamous Judge Martin Manton, who later left the judiciary after receiving bribes, discussed public attitudes toward and resentment of lawyers and then urged the bar to take the lead in regulating the profession to end overcrowding (Manton 1933). In that same year a Missouri bar leader in a speech to the Kansas City Bar Association blamed public dissatisfaction with the bar on "economic pressures" that produce unethical

7. Lundberg concluded that the political autonomy the profession enjoyed was a major ingredient in preserving democratic society; however, he noted that unless the profession worked more universally for economic and social justice it would lose its privileges. He wrote: "It must be evident, in conclusion, that the structure of the legal institution and its allotted function merit approval. But the processes within the institution have, by and large, negated its ideals. The legal profession, instead of working for justice as an end, has been invoking it as a means toward the retention and attainment of power by special groups. The consequence has been that a host of independent forces have grown powerful, forces that are inimical to the future existence of the democratic state itself. But a poetic penalty awaits the legal profession in the event that its clients of the past combine to abolish the democratic state, either by force or by stealth. For upon the abolition of the democratic state will surely follow the abolition of the legal profession, as in Russia, or its reduction in status to a very mean level, as in Germany or Italy" (Lundberg 1939a).

behavior. He argued that the bar was overcrowded and that if the profession did not reform itself others would do it for them (Atwood 1933). ABA president William Ransom claimed that the Depression caused many younger men to seek entry to the legal profession and that high moral and educational standards had to be maintained in order to protect the public and shield the bar from public criticism (Ransom 1936b).[8] A 1936 article agreed with articles in *The American Mercury* and *Readers' Digest* that claimed that competition within the profession was so fierce that ethics had been abandoned (Weiss 1936). A prominent Mississippi attorney began his 1936 article with the assertion that lawyers were widely criticized by the public because high-quality legal help was inaccessible to large portions of that public. He blamed that inaccessibility both on their lack of means to pay for it and their inability to judge the competence and ethical standards of the lawyers they choose (Broadway 1936b). A 1939 address to the Commercial Law League by Edwin Otterbourg, chairman of the ABA Unauthorized Practice Committee, recounted media charges that lawyers' fees were too high and that moderate income Americans were not receiving adequate legal service (Otterbourg 1939).

Bar leaders responded to the public criticism of the bar caused by perceived overcrowding in several ways. A Missouri bar officer advised young people in 1933 to stay out of the profession (Kemp 1933); others argued that admission standards should be raised so that fewer could qualify for admission (Wormser 1929; *Missouri Bar Journal* 1931; Ragland 1933). These leaders also argued that supply should be restricted by eliminating "lay encroachment"—the unauthorized practice of law by non-attorneys. The major targets of this complaint were banks and collection agents performing repossessions and real estate transactions (Overstreet 1933; Snively 1933; Powell 1936; Pefferle 1936; Combs 1942). Others, who also sought to strengthen the monopolist position of the bar, argued that more than just control over the supply of lawyers was needed. These leaders focused on the perceived lowering of ethical standards caused by excessive competition and proposed mandatory bar membership as the solution. During the 1930's bar leaders debated in speeches and articles the establishment of "incorporated" or "unified" bar organizations. As Theodore Schneyer has pointed out in his article on unified bars, proponents of mandatory bar association membership justified their support, in part, because it would give the bar greater control over disciplining unethical practice. It would give lawyers greater political power both to stop lay persons from conducting the unauthorized practice of law, and to enable the bar to press for procedural reforms that would raise the

8. See Dawson 1936 in how misbehavior of a few tarnishes the entire profession.

public confidence in the law and lawyers (Schneyer 1983).[9] Ransom strongly advocated unified bars as part of his standard message to bar groups. He defended them as the most effective means of exercising the power to stop the unauthorized practice of law, expel unethical or incompetent lawyers from the profession, and work for procedural reforms (Ransom 1936a). That same year Ohio State University Law School dean (and future U.S. judge) Hershel Arant wrote an article extolling the virtues of integrated bars. He pointed out that in a nation of small communities voluntary bars had been successful, but that the United States now needed mandatory membership. The major benefit was the greater procedural devices and protections that such associations would have in their efforts to investigate and discipline unethical behavior (Arant 1936). Earl Warren in 1939 spoke to the Nevada bar and praised the liberal consequences of incorporation movements. He stated that the bad reputation of the bar came from the public attention given to a few misfits and to delays caused by overly complex procedural rules. The unified bar, he argued, had been successful both in increasing discipline over the unethical practitioner and in leading procedural reform (Warren 1939).

A third response to the public criticism of the effects of overcrowding in the legal profession challenged the very notion of there being too many lawyers. Instead, these critics blamed structural conditions within the profession for causing the misallocation of legal resources. This was the least prevalent view, but it was held by legal academics such as Lloyd Garrison and Karl Llewellyn (Garrison 1936; Broadway 1936b; Clark 1939). These professors, along with others such as Reginald Heber Smith, advocated empirical surveys to determine if the bar was overcrowded. What they determined from their research was that the poor and middle class were underserved. Llewellyn blamed elite lawyers for being channeled by specialization and social and ethnic stratification into providing expensive counseling that only corporate clients needed or could afford. These reformers urged the profession to retain its professional independence and its market control through establishing legal aid offices and bar association clearing houses (Smith 1939; National Lawyers Guild 1939). These would discover what

9. See Stanley 1939, who discusses how lawyers are hurt by public criticism and lay encroachment. He urges the profession to speak as a unified group, and writes that although bar associations are fighting the "illegal practice of law," they must also continue to work for procedural reform and let the public know about such work. Several articles in 1936 praised the Missouri Supreme Court for giving the organized bar full control over disbarment proceedings. In an article for the *Kansas City Law Review* of that year a Missouri practitioner stated that the court's decision would increase the power of the bar to fight lay encroachment and help overcome criticism of the profession by the public (Powell 1936).

"recurring transactions could be routinized" . . . as well as educate the public concerning what services it needs (Twining 1973, p. 352).

All of these attempts rhetorically to fight off public criticisms of the profession's autonomy over the market continued until World War II eliminated the supposed oversupply of lawyers by putting a large portion of the legal profession in uniform. Although the structural alternative received little support before the war, it remained alive and formed the basis of the postwar crisis in the 1950s.

Court-Packing and the Expansion of Federal Regulation: Autonomy from Partisan Politics

The bar's opposition to the creation of New Deal agencies and the fight against President Franklin Roosevelt's court-packing plan in 1937 is a story that has been well told by many historians, including Steve Botein, Peter Irons, Jerold Auerbach, and recent labor law historians. As the executive branch and Congress expanded the powers and reach of the federal government, lawyers became a major political force opposing such actions. Over two thousand of the most elite members of the bar joined the National Lawyers' Committee of the American Liberty League, the most politically active anti–New Deal organization. These lawyers took the lead against the creation of the agencies and the court-packing plan. The politicization of the organized bar's activities intensified after 1937 when the ABA fought for passage of the Walter-Logan Act, which attacked administrative agencies by expanding federal court review of their decisions. The act passed only to be vetoed by Roosevelt, who took the occasion to lash out at the bar. In testimony before Congress and through a national broadcast and print campaign elite lawyers railed against New Deal reforms. They were opposed by academic and government lawyers who had assisted in the design of the new agencies, planned the strategies that brought them into being, and then administered them. This political confrontation threatened to subordinate the bar to partisan politics. Some feared that the public would come to perceive the profession as merely a group of politicians, agents of the political parties with no legitimate claim to the "special privileges [they receive] from the state" (ABA 1986, p. 10). Lundberg indicated precisely this danger. In the course of discussing whether the bar should be "socialized," he stated: "Today, in a period of general crisis when throughout the world government is called upon to act more and more positively in seeking solutions to social problems, we find pitted against each other in the United States two main groups of lawyers: the able political lawyers of the reformist New Deal and their equally capable colleagues in the standpat Republican Party" (Lundberg 1939a, p. 525).

Bar leaders responded to this danger of politicization by shaping the rhetoric of their support for and against the New Deal. Steve Botein points out that the bar's opposition to F.D.R. was constrained by the public disrepute generated when the ABA crusaded against judicial referendum and recall during the Progressive Era. He argues that bar leaders modified their tactics, toned down their rhetoric, and attempted to appear less partisan. Several rhetorical strategies for this moderation appear in the writings and speeches of bar leaders during the late 1930s and early 1940s. In 1939 the president of the West Virginia Bar bemoaned the public attacks on its opposition to New Deal programs and argued that it was the role of bar associations and the individual lawyer as a public citizen to defend the Constitution. He urged, however, that the public be made to understand that role of constitutional defender, and that the political independence of the bar not be violated by partisan politics (Stathers 1939). A 1941 address by the president of the California bar similarly urged lawyers to avoid entanglements in partisan politics. He advocated a campaign to educate the public to the dangers that administrative agencies pose to "fundamental principles of democracy" (Wright 1941).[10] Bar leaders opposed to the expansion of federal regulation also attempted to justify that opposition through a second rhetorical strategy. They described the assault on civil liberties and democracy then occurring in European fascist and socialist states, and maintained that the United States needed a strong, independent bar that could serve as a bulwark against such centralization and loss of freedom. William Ransom (ABA president from 1935 to 1936) described a "sinister" conspiracy to discredit lawyers because they protect the country from European political ideas (Ransom 1936e).[11] In 1939 the president of the bar of Jacksonville, Florida, claimed that the public unfairly criticized lawyers for being too conservative. Lawyers received bad press for their opposition to court-packing, but their actions were misunderstood. They did not disapprove of social welfare programs; rather, they were fighting for the fundamental principles of separation of powers, and of civil liberties, and they opposed measures that could lead the United States toward the tyranny that European countries were enduring (Matthews 1939; Simmons 1939).

New Deal supporters also attempted to avoid making partisan political

10. See Morris 1939, who discusses the unpopularity of lawyers and concludes that lawyers have a responsibility to society to be active in public affairs, but only on questions of law.

11. See Ransom 1936d, 1936f, 1936c.

appeals and urged the bar to take seriously its professed commitment to the public interest. The National Lawyers Guild president spoke of the need to make human rights more important than property rights, and to expand the civil rights of farmers and workers (Auerbach 1976, p. 199). Paul McNutt, an Indiana bar leader and active Democrat, wrote in 1939 that it was necessary for lawyers to accept the regulatory system and to work toward curbing occasionally overzealous administrators, rather than trying to challenge the legitimacy of federal regulation (McNutt 1939). Thus, both advocates and enemies of the expansion of the administrative state accepted as paramount the need to maintain the separation of law and politics. They shared the same professional norms, but differed on the underlying substance of what adherence to the principles of the Constitution or civil liberties required.

McCarthyism: Autonomy from Clients and from Partisan Politics

Following World War II the legal profession faced two crises parallel to the two that immediately preceded the war. The fear of communism generated by the cold war spawned domestic controversies over loyalty and internal security and threatened the political autonomy of the bar. The 1950s also saw a continued challenge to the bar's autonomy over the control of the market for legal services, as signs of expanded government support for legal services developed.

The political crisis of McCarthyism arose out of the actions of the profession during the late 1940s. The organized bar played several roles in the creation of the anticommunist hysteria that characterized the times. The ABA and state bars joined in demanding that communists and their sympathizers be driven from government employment. They required loyalty oaths of applicants to the bar and threatened disciplinary sanctions against attorneys who either took the Fifth Amendment themselves or served clients who did. The two historical treatments of the legal profession's activities during this period reach markedly different conclusions about the motivation and effects of the bar's role. Jerold Auerbach, focusing primarily on the actions of the profession in the early years of McCarthyism, blames the bar for the creation and perpetuation of the anticommunist hysteria (Auerbach 1976, pp. 231–58). He argues that the organized bar used the campaign against the radicals to further purge social and political undesirables from the profession and to attempt to maintain the dominance of the elites. Terence

Halliday describes a later phase of the bar's work during this period (Halliday 1982). He argues that the Chicago Bar Association and its committees reformulated the issues of loyalty oaths and congressional investigations from substantive questions (should communists serve in government or be members of the bar) to procedural ones (due process and First and Fifth Amendment rights). In the process of transforming the debate into the "idiom of legalism" the bar secured procedural protection for victims of McCarthyism and helped bring about the end of the witchhunts.

The sample of articles included in this study supports both of these analyses, because they reflect the two phases of the legal profession's involvement in McCarthyism. From about 1945 to 1951–1952 the organized bar led a vociferous campaign against communism. The 1945 speeches hearken back to the prewar rhetoric that warned that if constitutional principles were lost America might succumb to European forms of government such as communism (Hergistod 1945). By 1948 the speeches and articles had become hyperbolic. An article in the *A.B.A.J.* that year announced that the ABA House of Delegates had adopted a resolution identifying communism as a Moscow-led "international conspiracy teaching treachery to this nation" and threatening American civil rights. The ABA vigorously opposed the "spread of Communism" and wanted "publicity" to expose communist action. The resolution urged that communists be required to register with the government and forced to tell all that they do. They should be barred from government employment, and candidates who "pander to the Communist vote" should be exposed (*A.B.A.J.* 1948b).[12] Editorials in the *A.B.A.J.* expressed regret that the Mundt-Nixon Anti-Communist Bill did not pass in Congress, and stated the need to accept an "uncompromising attitude towards the Marxist faith." The communist party was described as "an alien conspiracy," thus presumably beyond the point where toleration ends (*A.B.A.J.* 1948c). Another writer called for a "militant" anticommunist bar (Ober 1948). What is remarkable about these 1948 articles is their open call for the bar to enter into the political fray. The rhetoric hearkens back to the speeches during the referendum and recall political battles, and eschews the warnings to avoid politics made during the New Deal fights ten years earlier. A writer in 1948 urged lawyers to enter politics so that they could fight "socialized law" and centralization (Sigler 1948). Thomas Roscoe went further in his article in the *A.B.A.J.* His jeremiad began with the dangers of

12. See Wiley 1948. Wiley notes that almost all federal judges appointed since 1932 have been Democrats. He does not consider this a problem as long as these judges "don't permit any political philosophy outside of the American concepts to dominate their judicial thinking." See also *A.B.A.J.* 1948c, a polemic on the danger of communism abroad and at home and on the need for a clear and effective way to exclude communist propaganda from government, the media, and schools.

world communism, and called for an aroused public opinion to protect the United States from creeping socialism. Political parties were the key, and lawyers could help to lead those organizations and root out "incorrect thought." He implored lawyers to get involved in the real-world battles of partisan politics (Thomas 1948). An editorial in the same issue wholeheartedly endorsed this view. After running through the litany of the evils of communism, it exhorted lawyers to take party politics seriously. "Party politics are *not a game*. . . . The American lawyer at work in his party . . . has in his hands the future of his country, the hope of the world" (*A.B.A.J.* 1948a).

By 1951 the tone of the rhetoric of bar leaders shifted noticeably.[13] Gone were the outlandish, hyperbolic editorials of the *A.B.A.J.*—replaced by speeches such as that by former Texas Supreme Court Justice James Hart before the 1951 meeting of the Texas Bar Association. Hart emphasized the lawyer's duty to engage in public service activities (not politics). He received applause when he explained that communism must be fought without abridging the Bill of Rights, and he denounced "a propaganda campaign" that uses "harsh means to smear loyal and sound American institutions" (Hart 1951). Zechariah Chafee, Jr., denounced loyalty oaths and argued that in order to revitalize democracy the country needed the defense of civil liberties, not slogans (Chafee 1951). A dramatic sign of change occurred when the *A.B.A.J.* published three statements opposing loyalty oaths. The first was signed by twenty-six leading members of the bar; the second by the Bar Association of the City of New York; the third by the Massachusetts Bar Association. All denounced the oath as unnecessary, as undermining the traditions of the profession, and as potentially unconstitutional. The editorial page of the *Journal* disagreed with these arguments, but in respectful and moderate terms (*A.B.A.J.* 1951c, 1951b).

As in the other crises examined so far, bar leaders began to invoke the loss of public confidence in the bar when exhorting the bar to live up to its ideals. The president of the ABA, Cody Fowler, stated that 25 percent of the public did not respect the bar and another 50 percent had no opinion, and urged the bar to retain its leadership role. He supported loyalty oaths, but he advocated bar associations taking public stands on issues affecting the "American way of life," without advocating involvement in partisan politics (Fowler 1951b). The 1954 president-elect of the ABA, Lloyd Wright, complained of signs of decay in public respect for the bar. The cure was to work for reform

13. There were, however, some dissenting voices before 1951. Thelma Furry, writing in 1948 in the *Women Lawyers Journal*, charged that anticommunism was used to silence liberals and that the survival of democracy depended on the defense of the First Amendment (Furry 1948).

of the legal system. He urged the profession to debate controversial issues, but warned that gaining public respect through these means was not valuable if it meant refusing to defend unpopular causes (Wright 1954). That same year U.S. district judge Irving R. Kaufman defended attorneys who defend communists. He asserted that the bar must restore its leadership position by making the public understand that the defense of a client does not mean acceptance of his cause (Kaufman 1954).[14]

The clearest sign of the bar leadership's retreat from its intense politicization of anticommunism was the formation in 1952 of a Joint Conference on Professional Responsibility (*South Carolina Law Quarterly* 1958). The ABA and the Association of American Law Schools appointed the blue-ribbon panel of law professors, judges, and practitioners with a mandate to provide "a clear understanding of his [the lawyer's] obligations and of the vital connection between those obligations and the role his profession plays in society" (Joint Conference on Professional Responsibility 1959, p. 307). This panel issued a statement that reflected the profession's interest in reestablishing its political autonomy. The statement imposes on lawyers a "trusteeship for the integrity of those fundamental processes of government . . . upon which the successful functioning of our society depends." It continues: "This is a duty that attaches not only to his private practice but to his relations with the public. In this matter he is not entitled to take public opinion as a datum by which to orient and justify his actions. He has an affirmative duty to help shape the growth and development of public attitudes toward fair procedures and due process" (*South Carolina Law Quarterly* 1958, p. 313). The panel's statement also reestablished the paramount importance of the requirement to represent unpopular causes as an essential component of American democracy. For the individual the choice of clients is a matter of conscience; for the profession representation for all is mandatory: "The legal profession should in any event strive to promote and maintain a moral atmosphere in which he may render this service without ruinous cost to himself. No member of the Bar should indulge in public criticism of another lawyer because he has undertaken the representation of causes in general disfavor" (*South Carolina Law Quarterly* 1958, p. 316). Every lawyer was charged with the duty to explain to the public that lawyers were presumed to be politically independent of their clients.

Finally, the panel detailed the obligation of the lawyer as citizen. It did not urge lawyers to shirk public controversy on economic issues, rather lawyers were to assume leadership on issues, such as administrative procedures, within their special competence. Still, the bar was not to be partisan: "Law

14. See Brown 1954, p. 404, Sims 1954, p. 343.

should be so practiced that the lawyer remains free to make up his own mind how he will vote, what causes he will support, what economic and political philosophy he will espouse. . . . Distinguished examples can be cited of lawyers whose views were at variance from those of their clients, lawyers whose skill and wisdom made them valued adviser to those who had little sympathy with their views as citizens" (*South Carolina Law Quarterly* 1958, p. 317).

Thus, as Halliday has argued, the leaders of the bar used the idiom of legalism to help to bring an end to the vitriolic anticommunism that the bar itself had helped to unleash. That earlier role had politicized the bar sufficiently to jeopardize its political autonomy, and caused bar leaders once more to remind their constituents of the norms of professionalism.

The Provision of Legal Services following World War II: Autonomy over the Market

During the late 1940s and the 1950s a large number of articles appeared speaking to the need for better public relations for the bar. In 1951 an Oklahoma attorney lamented the negative portrayal of lawyers in movies, radio, and newspapers (Cleveland 1951). The *A.B.A.J.* that year noted in an editorial that the public distrusted the bar. It too called for better public relations (*A.B.A.J.* 1951a). In 1954 over one-third of the articles from the sample for this research dealt with the observation that the public image of lawyers was negative, and that the profession's top priority should be to alter that image. Both the Nebraska and the Michigan bar held symposia that year dealing with the issue. All participants in these discussions expressed the opinion that the public held the lawyer in low esteem, and that the profession should undertake a massive public relations campaign. The only exception was Albert Jenner, who did not agree that the bar was held in bad repute, but nevertheless supported better public relations.[15]

As with the other crises examined, a sudden concern with the public perception of lawyers indicated deeper concerns. There are two clues to the nature of that concern. First, a number of comparisons began to be drawn between doctors and lawyers. Second, bar leaders discussed the need to have the public understand the pro bono activities of the profession. Both of these link the public relations concern to the threat of federally-funded legal

15. See the articles on the Michigan symposium in *Michigan State Bar Journal* 1954, esp. Jenner 1954. Also see Tinkham 1954 (Tinkham was the editor of a manual for the bar on public relations).

services. Jerold Auerbach has argued that the part of the ABA's efforts to discredit the National Lawyers Guild after World War II were prompted by the Guild's call for federal funding for neighborhood legal centers (Auerbach 1976, p. 236). Mark Kessler notes: "Indeed, in the 1950s the ABA publicly condemned the idea of federal funding, charging in one resolution it passed that government funding posed a 'threat to individual freedom implicit in growing efforts to socialize the legal profession.' And a former president of the ABA argued at this time that 'the greatest threat aside from the undermining influence of Communist infiltration is the propaganda campaign for a federal subsidy to finance a nationwide plan for legal aid and low cost legal services' (Kessler 1987, pp. 5, 6). In 1951 several articles appeared discussing the British Legal Aid bill. One bar leader and legal educator denounced the British plan as a great threat to the independence of the bar. He continued: "Socialization of the medical profession in England, the British Legal Aid Act, . . . the proposal of the Lawyers Guild for federal funds to support legal aid, . . . are all 'straws in the wind' " indicating the drift toward socialization of the legal profession (Storey 1951, p. 168).[16]

The link between the bar's increased discussions of doctors and public relations stemmed from the medical profession's involvement in defeating a proposal for national health insurance in 1949. As Paul Starr has described that story, the doctors prevailed by employing the most expensive lobbying and public relations campaign in American history up to that time (Starr 1982, pp. 280–89). Bar leaders learned from the doctors both to take seriously the potential expansion of federal intervention into the provision of professional services, and the value of public relations. As early as 1945 John Bradway exhorted lawyers to begin planning action against federal legal aid modeled after national health insurance. The title of his article—"Will 'Socialized Law' Be Next?"—makes the point (Bradway 1945). During the 1954 Michigan public relations symposium one speaker carefully analyzed the AMA's successful public relations campaign, and urged the bar to copy it (L. Brown 1954).[17]

Defenders of the profession wanted no federal intervention—and no neighborhood law centers such as those proposed in the 1930s by Llewellyn and others. They believed that all that was needed was to communicate more effectively with the public about the pro bono activities of the bar. They

16. But see Freedman 1951, who disagrees with Storey about the characterization of the British plan as socialized law and insists that the plan will not destroy the independence of the English legal profession.

17. See Fowler 1951a, who exhorts lawyers to fight socialized law as doctors fight socialized medicine, and Hinshaw 1951, who explains that doctors have turned to public relations to fend off socialized medicine and the bar should follow.

employed the fear of socialism to argue that any effort to disrupt the private market for legal services threatened the independence of the bar and ultimately democracy (Storey 1951; Cleveland 1951; L. Brown 1954; Niehuss 1954; Brown 1945). Other members of the bar argued that independence required attention to the needs of the public at large, not just those who could pay. Theodore Voorhees wrote a series of articles in which he argued forcefully for lawyer reference services as the most effective way of providing legal services to the middle class. He maintained that the result would far exceed the value of public relations in convincing the American people that an independent bar was effective (Voorhees 1951, 1954a, 1954b; Pope 1957). One of the clearest expressions of the requirement of an independent profession to provide legal services is found in the Joint ABA-AALS Statement from 1958. In a section entitled "Making Legal Services Available To All" the drafters of this statement vigorously argue that the profession discharge its obligation to ensure that all people, regardless of their ability to pay, receive legal services and insists that doing so will help eliminate the "popular misconceptions" about the advocates' functions (*South Carolina Law Quarterly* 1958, p. 314). It also states: "It is of great importance, however, that both the impulse to render this service, and the plan for making that impulse effective, should arise within the legal profession itself" (*South Carolina Law Quarterly* 1958, pp. 314–15). Thus, there was agreement that the bar must maintain its autonomy over the market, but disagreement among members of the professional elite on what forms of legal services the concept of an independent bar required.

Conclusion

During these thirty-five years from 1925 to 1960 the bar's understanding of the meaning and responsibilities of being a legal professional remained relatively unchanged. The major components of that concept are those that had existed since the latter part of the nineteenth century when the major developmental stage in the bar's professionalization occurred. Knowledge, political independence, and economic autonomy were seen as central to the profession's self-definition. Political autonomy came to be formulated as autonomy from partisan politics *and* political independence from both the client and the government; economic autonomy came to mean autonomy over the market (monopoly control) *and* autonomy from the profit motives of the market.

Despite the stability in the components of the concept, there were five periods of crisis between 1925 and 1960. During those periods social, political, and economic forces external to the bar made problematic some aspect of the conditions of legal practice or the activities of the organized bar. Legal elites invoked the normative principles embedded in the concept of professionalism to exhort their fellow professionals to reestablish the norms.

Although the leaders of the profession spoke with one voice on the need to reestablish the norms threatened in each crisis period, they had different prescriptive visions for how to bring about the restoration. During Prohibition and the crises over the provision of legal services, defenders of the bar thought that the loss of public confidence could be cured by a public relations campaign justifying the bar's conduct. Critics urged that reforms take place in order to live up to professional norms—whether that be to reform the criminal justice system or to increase the provision of legal services to the poor. It must be noted that within the sample of articles read there were no radical critics. No writer, even the most radical, advocated the elimination of either the bar's political independence or its control over its market. Despite the ABA's hyperbolic claims, the National Lawyers Guild in the 1940s proposed only a limited number of federally subsidized attorneys for the poor, not socializing the profession. Lundberg, who in 1939 predicted the socialization of the bar, did so because he believed the bar's failure to assist in rendering justice for all citizens would lead to the fall of democracy in the United States. He acknowledged the superiority of a politically independent bar for the protection of civil liberties (Lundberg 1939a).

The five crises cover almost the entire thirty-five year period, which raises the question of whether there were indeed five separate crises or one continuous crisis with major "hot" points. Although this question cannot be answered definitively from the evidence in this study, it needs to be addressed, for it raises issues of theoretical importance. Continuous crisis prompts one to suspect that the structure of the profession requires crisis for its maintenance. Given public distrust of the profession and the leadership's fear of the effects of that distrust, bar elites, as the argument goes, used crisis rhetoric to discipline members of the bar and to fend off public attack. A conspiracy theory based on this interpretation of events would posit concerted activity among the elites to manipulate these crises to maintain their own dominance of the profession, as well as the profession's wealth and power. A functionalist theory would perceive the elites as carrying out the system's structural requirements, whether consciously or not. It is important to note that in this model what is contingent are the events that trigger the crisis response by elites, not crisis itself, as that is inevitable and structurally necessary. The major difference, then, between the one-crisis model versus the five is what is seen as contingent. If these crises are separate, it is crisis itself that is uncertain. One would expect periods of equilibrium in the legal profession, such as during World War II, which might be disturbed by external events that destabilize some aspect of the legal profession and the practice of law and create a crisis of professionalism.

An essay of this scope cannot accommodate the data needed to decide whether the five- or the one-crisis description seems more accurate; it would be necessary to have a "thicker" description of the different crises than is possible in this overview. Greater archival work would be necessary to examine the correspondence of the authors, as well as to analyze the role of the bar in the creation and management of these crisis periods. Nevertheless, on the evidence available, the explanation entailing five separate crises is the more compelling. First, there was a period of equilibrium during World War II, and the dating of the other periods is not meant to imply that the intensity level was uniform throughout the years studied. Toward the end of the 1950s, articles inveighing against publicly funded legal services were still being published, but infrequently. Second, as Robert Gordon and others have recently argued, functionalist arguments, which explain social phenomena as "necessary historical events," are highly questionable, as they fail to capture both the contingency of socially constructed events and the varieties of human experience (Gordon 1984b; Nelson and Trubek, Chapter 5 herein). The conspiracy model seems even less likely. In addition to the general skepticism which such arguments receive, the evidence in this study is that the elites writing these articles and speeches were a diverse and diffuse group. It would take strong and unambiguous archival evidence to make a case for collusion among such a collection of individuals.

One further point relevant to the question of whether there was one crisis or five separate crises concerns the "reality" of the crises. Did external events create public dissatisfaction with the bar which the bar then addressed, or did the bar seize on the external events to manufacture crises that did not exist? The latter would provide strong support for a single crisis explanation. Again, the evidence is not sufficient. There are only sketchy indicators (all from the last ten years of this study) of what public attitudes were. The little survey data available does not show conclusively that the public image of lawyers was affected by the actions of the bar during the 1950s. Fifty-eight percent of the respondents in a 1949 survey of Michigan residents stated that they had formed a favorable impression about lawyers from the movies; 53 percent favorable from books; 50 percent favorable from radio; while only 35 percent favorable from newspapers (Social Research Service 1949). Only 19 percent of the respondents had formed an unfavorable impression of lawyers from reading the newspapers. The Michigan survey found that the prestige of the profession was high; 57 percent said they would like to have their son (sic) become a lawyer (another 16 percent said it would be up to him), although lawyers were decidedly less respected that doctors (Social Research Service 1949, pp. 13–15). A 1952 Texas survey found that very few respondents (only 4 percent) had "a bad mental picture of lawyers. . . . Only 2 per cent conjured up a negative mental picture when they heard the word *attorney*" (State Bar of Texas Committee on Public Information 1952). Although these survey results appear to substantiate the contention that these crises were not "real," it may be that the criticisms of lawyers that appeared in highly visible media, such as films and popular magazines (as the Lundberg articles did), convinced the elites of the bar that public dissatisfaction was "real." Recall that they did not have access to survey research data.

That the elite of the legal profession might have been hypersensitive to perceptions of public dissatisfaction with the bar should not be a surprise. It is the key to understanding why if these crises are independent, contingent events, the profession was almost constantly in a crisis during the entire thirty-five years of this study. The leadership recognized that the "special privileges" the legal profession receives from the state could be removed. The monopoly over the practice of law the bar enjoys is the result of a "bargain" between the state and the profession in which the bar provides competence and access to legal services to the public, but refrains from partisan politics, and avoids the excesses of the market. In exchange the state grants the bar the right to establish the rules by which it restricts its market (including entry into the profession and the disciplining of its members) and allows it to extract monopoly rents. In each of the five crises described external events disturbed some aspect of the bar's delivery of its part of the bargain. The leadership understood that the monopoly privileges of the bar are not consistent with the egalitarian ideology of American democratic liberalism. Maintaining the uneasy legitimacy of the status of the profession required constant monitoring by its leaders. During the period of the bar's concern over the federalization of legal services an AALS conference on the "education of lawyers for their public responsibilities" was held. The 1958 report of the 1956 conference acknowledged the concern over the fragility of the bargain between the bar and the state: "If public relations fall below a certain level, the profession's position and privileges in the community will be threatened. As was said here about the lawyers, if they are going to forget about everything except the pocketbook, they would find their sphere invaded by Public Defenders in addition to Public Prosecutors; judicial jurisdiction would be taken away by dissatisfied voters acting through the legislatures" (Stone 1958, p. 1). By signaling to the rank and file of the profession that their behavior threatened the loss of public esteem and thus the profession itself, bar elites enunciated the extreme urgency of reestablishing conformance with the norms of professionalism to justify their privileges.

The five crises identified in the period from 1925 to 1960 focused on political autonomy and autonomy over the market. Very few articles expressed concern over the level of "knowledge" in the profession. There was no general perception that the public no longer considered lawyers to be "learned." The negative images in the media typically present lawyers as unethical, not incompetent.[18] The (scanty) survey data support this. Only one percent of the Michigan residents surveyed responded that lawyers were more honest than other professionals, but 39 percent answered that they were more intelligent (Social Research Service 1949, p. 13). According to one conclusion in the Texas survey, "The most important factor in public acceptance of lawyers is *the general feeling that they are experts*, for whom adequate substitutes are difficult if impossible to find" (State Bar of Texas Committee on Public Information 1952, p. 9). The commentator Andy Rooney recounts that when he worked in Hollywood as a producer's assistant he received an angry letter from the ABA complaining that "in the last 179 movies in which lawyers were portrayed they were shown as dishonest 151 times." He asked his employer, the producer, for guidance on how to respond. The producer replied: "Tell them if those figures are right, the lawyers got a break" (Roth and Roth 1989, p. 142). In short, if the rhetoric of professionalism was intended to restore the norms of professionalism, the lack of attention to the level of technical competence of the bar indicates that bar leaders were fairly confident that lawyers in general satisfy the everyday criteria of being "pros."

This article began with the ABA Commission on Professionalism's question of whether the profession had "abandoned principle for profit, professionalism for commercialism." As has been previously noted, this question makes an implicit historical comparison; answering it requires knowing what past "levels" of professionalism were. A quantification of the historical levels of professionalism is outside the scope of this article. It is certain, however, that the very asking of the question indicates that the current leaders of the bar believe the profession to be in another crisis period. Further, evidence for this is found in the report's linking its concern to evidence that "lawyers as a group are blamed for some serious public problems" such as the sharp increase in medical malpractice litigation and the rising costs of insurance (ABA 1986, p. 3). The report continues, "The public views lawyers, at best, as being of uneven character and quality. . . . The primary question for this Commission thus becomes what, if anything,

18. But see Warner Brothers' film *Body Heat* (1981).

can be done to improve both the reality and the perception of lawyer professionalism" (ABA 1986, p. 3). In addition, following the commission's report, the ABA, as in previous crises, called for a task force to study and design a public relations program for the bar to educate the public about "the justice system and the role of lawyers in society." Thus, it appears that the profession perceives itself to be in another crisis period, this time concerning the commercialization of practice.

This is not the first time that lawyers have expressed angst over law becoming a business. As early as the end of the nineteenth century and through the 1920s, 1930s, and 1940s speeches were made within the profession that accused lawyers of forgetting they were professionals for the sake of pursuing money. What is unique about the present is that concern over commercialism has become a crisis. The perception of the public's loss of confidence in the legitimacy of the profession may stem from the perceived lack of separation between law and business. Prior crises stemmed from the perceived loss of political autonomy or autonomy *over* the market, not, as currently, from the loss of autonomy *from* the market. The question becomes Why is commercialism the perceived crisis today? The answer appears to be related to the current dramatic changes in the economic structure of the practice of law. The commission details some of those changes in the section of its report entitled "Economics of Practicing Law Today." Other articles in this collection also detail more of those changes. A complete answer must, however, await more intensive empirical studies of the current conditions of law practice.

The lack of research on the effects of the normative rhetoric of professionalism on the practice of law in the past makes it difficult to use the history of past crises to predict the outcome of the current efforts of bar leaders to curb the commercialization of practice. Critical scholars, such as Abel and Larson, who believe the rhetoric was not effective in curbing past abuses (in fact it was a major tool in creating them) have no reason to doubt the continued futility of such efforts. Yet, commercialism poses new questions even for scholars such as Halliday or Gordon, who argue that the ideology of professionalism has been an important influence on shaping the bar's behavior. The bar's conduct surrounding issues of political autonomy and access to legal services, which formed the past crises, may prove to have been more amenable to influence by ideological appeals than it is today when wealth and power are so transparently at the core of the crisis. Future research on professionalism and practice will thus have to address the fundamental questions of the role of structure and ideology in explaining human behavior.

PART III
TRANSFORMING IDEALS AND PRACTICES

The chapters in this final section examine in detail a series of self-conscious attempts to deploy and revise the concept of professionalism. The authors of these essays focus on the ways professionalism has been and is being used by various actors to promote a variety of social visions.

The section opens with Robert L. Nelson and David M. Trubek's contribution to the development of a new paradigm for the analysis of professionalism. They recognize that professional ideologies are deployed by different groups for different purposes, yet argue that professional ideology cannot be dismissed as a mere facade. They find it rather a source of explicit claims about the idealized character of the roles of lawyers and a repository of unstated cultural assumptions about their professional status. So viewed, professionalism is a significant dimension of the many institutional, organizational, and community contexts in which lawyers participate.

Because Nelson and Trubek find professionalism to be important, yet complex and contradictory, they argue that it is essential to delimit and examine different "arenas of professionalism," that is, contexts in which different idealized versions of the lawyer's role are socially constructed. These versions vary with the nature of the groups involved, the nature of the arena and its audiences, and the relationships among the various arenas. This multiple arenas framework, they suggest, frees the analyst from having to choose between the "official story" that portrays professionalism as a fixed and unitary set of attributes or the "critical story" that dismisses it as a cover for self-interest. Their approach also makes it easier to understand why there are competing visions of professional work and to evaluate their moral significance and impact on everyday life. It shifts the focus of inquiry to questions about the sources and functions of professional ideology in particular contexts. Since these authors see the legal workplace as central to the life experience of lawyers and the construction of professional visions, they advocate research into the workplace ideologies of lawyers.

The two final chapters papers represent efforts by scholars to reconstruct the concept of professionalism better to serve social ends. Eliot Freidson sets forth an ideal type of professionalism which—he asserts—has advantages that ideal typical markets and bureaucracies do not possess. He believes that many of the virtues of professional institutions—including relative autonomy from clients and the state—are endangered by the current commercialization of professional services and by the increasing government regulation of professional institutions. Somewhat ironically then, Freidson, who in the 1960s reoriented the field of the sociology of the professions away from the functionalist conception toward a more critical view of professional dominance, here advocates an ideal type of professionalism to defend certain professional prerogatives. It should be noted that his position is not without critical bite. Freidson chastises professional associations for treating professionalism as an ideology, rather than taking its principles seriously. An essential part of his message is that professionals must not only pay lip service to professional ideals, they also must begin to reform professional institutions in accordance with these ideals.

Robert W. Gordon and William H. Simon, two other scholars who have also previously debunked the professional ideologies of lawyers, shift to a more constructive posture here by advocating that debates about professionalism take the concepts of professionalism more seriously. Rejecting arguments that professionalism can be explained simply as a device for preserving professional monopoly or for defending the interests of dominant economic groups in society, they suggest that the ideal of the professional work organization (in which individual practitioners control their work and govern their organization) is valuable, but that the ideal is only imperfectly realized. Moreover, they posit that professionalism is a functional necessity in a market system. Without some non-profit-seeking elements to provide a framework of fair exchange and regulation, the market could not maintain itself. They point out, however, that many current practices by law schools, law firms, and bar associations serve to undermine the professional ideal of autonomous, morally responsible practice. They recommend some practices and policies these institutions might adopt to bolster the potential for realizing professional ideals. A fundamental aspect of their position is that lawyers have considerable freedom both to remake the institutions and organizations in which they work, and to act within those contexts in a consistent and responsible manner.

CHAPTER FIVE

Arenas of Professionalism: The Professional Ideologies of Lawyers in Context

Robert L. Nelson and
David M. Trubek

In recent years there has been an outpouring of public statements alleging a serious decline in the professionalism of American lawyers.[1] Such waves of concern about declining professionalism are not new (see, e.g., Auerbach 1976, Gordon 1984b, 1988, pp. 2–6, 17–19, Solomon, Chapter 4 herein), but this one is unusual because it coincides with an economic boom in the legal services industry. Today, there are more lawyers per capita, the profession commands a higher proportion of the nation's economic resources, law firms are larger, and leading firms are more profitable than at any other time.[2] Why, then, this proclamation of crisis?

Some might be tempted to dismiss today's "professionalism crusade" as a

We thank Jerry Van Hoy and Elizabeth Chambliss for valuable research assistance and Andrew Abbott, Lisa Douglass, Wendy Espeland, William Felstiner, Mindie Lazarus-Black, Alan Paterson, Michael Powell, Rayman Solomon, Eve Spangler, and Stanton Wheeler for comments.

1. For examples of these on the national level, see Rehnquist (1987) and the Report of the American Bar Association Commission on Professionalism (ABA 1986) [often referred to as the Stanley Commission]. The Association of American Law Schools chose professionalism as the theme for its 1988 Annual Meeting: "The Law School's Opportunity to Shape the Legal Profession: Money, Morals, and Social Obligation," Miami, Florida, January 1988. At the state level see, for example, *Virginia Bar Association Journal* 1986, *Florida State Bar Journal* 1986, *Illinois Bar Journal* 1988, *New York State Bar Journal* 1988, *Washington Lawyer* 1988. At least twenty-six state and thirty-six local bar associations have taken action on professionalism (Bowser 1989, p. 12).

2. The population of lawyers more than doubled in the fifteen-year period from 1970 to 1985 (U.S. Census 1976, U.S. Department of Labor, 1986). Total receipts for legal services increased 100 percent from 1977 (17 billion) to 1982 (34 billion) (U.S. Census 1982). Profits per partner in the highest grossing law firm in the United States are currently $1,195,000; the highest profits per partner in any firm are $1,765,000. Profits per partner range from $615,000 and up in the top twenty firms to $185,000 in the hundredth-ranking law firm (*American Lawyer* 1990). (It is possible that in real dollars leading firms were more profitable in an earlier era. Nonetheless, current profit levels seem quite substantial.)

standard trope in the rhetoric of bar association leaders, something that recurs regularly without underlying cause or practical significance. It could be seen as the belated and ineffective complaints of marginalized or displaced lawyers who have lost income and status in a period when the bar—as a whole—has done extremely well. Or it might reflect a sense that the organized profession has lost control over key aspects of professional behavior.

To be sure, laments about declining professionalism have been a staple of bar association rhetoric over a long period. It is clear that there have been losers as well as winners in the period of economic expansion of the legal services industry. The bar has lost some of its power over the economic behavior of lawyers.[3] But the fact that "professionalism" is ritualistically invoked by bar leaders does not make the current resurgence of concern irrelevant. The presence of some losers among the profession does not mean that the resurgence is simply the plaint of those who have not benefited from the new prosperity. The spokespersons in the professionalism campaign are not marginal: they are a wealthy and accomplished group of lawyers. Many belong to firms that have grown and prospered in recent years.[4] Finally, although the bar has lost its ability to set fees and ban advertising altogether, it has not lost its protected position within the market for legal services.

We believe that the concerns over professionalism reflect a fundamental aspect of the American legal profession. Ideal visions of lawyering and the lawyers' role—"professional ideology"—are important. These visions affect the way lawyers organize their practices and understand their everyday life. We see the current professionalism campaign as an event in the production and reproduction of ideology, and for that reason consider it of interest to scholars of the profession. Faced with rapid change and turmoil, the architects of the current professionalism campaign have sought to articulate and defend a vision of the role of lawyers in society.

Professional ideology is an important dimension of the legal profession and worthy of careful scrutiny by sociolegal scholars. But that does not mean that one should take official statements about professionalism at face value, or that one should assume that the operative visions of lawyering that

3. Court decisions have limited the bar's ability to control advertising and set minimum fee schedules (Bates and O'Steen v. Arizona State Bar, 433 U.S. 350 [1977]; Goldfarb v. Virginia State Bar, 421 U.S. 773 [1975]; generally, see Powell 1985).

4. Van Hoy (1990, p. 16) reports that the Commission on Professionalism was dominated by partners of medium and large law firms (the two largest firms having over one hundred lawyers). Justin Stanley, the commission's chair, is a partner in Mayer, Brown, and Platt, a firm that ranks twenty-third nationally in gross earnings (*American Lawyer* 1990) and is reported to be enjoying steady growth (Middleton 1988). The commission also included such notables as former U.S. attorney general and defense bar spokesman Benjamin Civiletti.

animate lawyers in their daily lives emanate exclusively from official sources like bar associations and their official spokespersons. Quite the contrary, we think that "taking professionalism seriously" entails critical analysis of official pronouncements and careful attention to other sources of professional ideology. To do this, we believe it is necessary to create a framework for analysis that places the official professionalism rhetoric in context and attends to the full complexity of professional ideals in the American bar. That is the purpose of this chapter.

The analytic framework we have developed for the study of professional ideology asserts explicitly that lawyer professionalism is not a fixed, unitary set of values, but instead consists of multiple visions of what constitutes proper behavior by lawyers. Conceptions of lawyer professionalism reflect "the arenas" in which they are produced, that is, the particular institutional settings in which groups construct, explicitly or implicitly, models of the law and of lawyering. The arenas perspective allows for the possibility that different groups will develop different versions of the professional ideal in response to a variety of political, ideological, and situational concerns. The major analytic task set by this approach is to explain how different professional ideologies emerge in various contexts and with what effects.[5]

We illustrate our approach by juxtaposing two very different arenas of lawyer professionalism: the collective arena of bar associations and the workplace arenas of lawyers. We think the contrast between the two is enlightening. Although it is quite common for the professions literature to portray professional associations as a site in which professional ideology is produced, much less attention has been given to the production of ideology in the workplace. The emphasis on collective professional institutions as the primary source of ideology has contributed to the perception of the unitary character of professional ideals, whereas analyses of the workplace tend to reveal the divergences in the ideologies of various groups of professionals. Moreover, although studies in each of several professional locations could contribute to the intellectual project we define here, workplace studies are especially needed, for it is in the legal workplace that we find real conflicts over how practice should be organized. It is there that the presence and power of professional ideology often is least visible and least understood.

Our approach can enrich the treatment of professional ideology at the collective level. Rather than assuming that professional canons embody the ideology of the profession, as do many functionalist and critical scholars, we call for the analysis of the specific historical and political forces that shape

5. Although we confine ourselves to a discussion of lawyer professionalism, the arenas perspective could be applied to other professional occupations.

the production of professional ideology at the collective level. For this reason as well, we see the arenas approach as an advance over prior treatment of professional ideology.

Arenas and the Social Construction of Professionalism

The first task is to develop a way to think about and thus to study the phenomenon of "professionalism." We conceptualize lawyer professionalism as the process by which ideas about the appropriate role of lawyers in society and the proper methods of conducting and organizing the practice of law are constructed. From this perspective "professionalism" is not a single or unitary body of ideas or practices but rather a set of questions about which lawyers and others argue. Because the question of what lawyers should do is one that is addressed every day in many sites, we see the social production of professionalism as a complex process of interaction occurring in many arenas. Formal pronouncements, academic theorizing, public debates, and codes of ethics and their enforcement contribute to the social production of professionalism, but are neither the only nor necessarily the most significant sources of ideas about lawyering. It follows that professionalism must be studied in many arenas and in ways that take account of the relationship between the characteristics of arenas and the nature of the professional ideals constructed in them.

Alternative Strategies

There are many ways to analyze "professionalism." At one extreme, one can focus on the development and justification of an ideal of what lawyers ought to do. At the other, one could take a purely nominalistic approach, defining "professionalism" as what lawyers actually do and seeking to chart actual patterns of behavior.

Some see "professionalism" as a particular form of social organization with morally attractive features. This is the approach taken by Parsons (1968a, 1968b) and those who have followed in his footsteps. From this perspective, professionalism involves a particular set of motivations, skills, and organizational structures. A profession is an alternative to both the market and the state. Professions mediate between individuals or private organizations and society. In this view, "law" is seen as an autonomous body of norms that reflect social demands but whose interpretation and application require complex knowledge and specialized skill (Parsons 1962). Therefore, legal professionalism means the provision of services that will ensure that individual and organizational actions are consonant with social demands and norms.

It is thought that if lawyers are properly to produce knowledge of the law, they must have both autonomy and independence (see, e.g., Carr-Saunders and Wilson 1933, pp. 399–400, Parsons 1951, pp. 470–71). *Autonomy* means control of one's own work processes. It is needed because legal interpretation is complex and situational and cannot be reduced to a set of routine procedures. Only the autonomous knowledge-producer can "get it right." Thus, although it may be possible for managers to control the production of most goods and some services, the law must be the output of an individual lawyer or a collective of legal professionals who control their own activity. But autonomy is not enough: lawyers must also have independence. *Independence* means freedom from the client's definition of the situation and the client's desire for a favored outcome. If the lawyer lacks independence, and simply gives the client what he or she wants, the lawyer has failed to perform the mediating function and the society's normative system will fail to constrain behavior.

In this perspective, the problem of professionalism is to preserve autonomy and independence, while maintaining the client's trust. From the normative ideal it is possible to derive certain institutional requirements that become part of the ideal itself. These include ways to ensure that lawyers and not clients or others control the process of producing legal knowledge, advice, and advocacy, and that lawyers are free to challenge the client's goals and projects.

The alternative approach to thinking about professionalism is nominalistic. It starts from the study of what lawyers actually do and seeks to construct an idea of "professionalism" by generating an empirical picture of practice and behavior (see, e.g., Becker et al. 1961, Hughes 1958, 1984). Advocates of this approach seek to account for lawyers as social actors by learning what difference they make, and to whom. The nominalist asks questions concerning the distribution of legal services, the impact of advocacy and advice, and the mechanisms that determine how legal tasks are defined and conducted. The nominalist starts with no predetermined idea of what lawyers ought to do or not do, but seeks to develop an account of what they actually do. That—and nothing more—is what professionalism means from this point view.

Most students of the legal profession recognize that neither of these alternatives is satisfactory. It is, of course, important to develop a normative vision of the legal profession and observe the extent to which practice fulfills these ideals. But it is an idle task to construct such visions without regard to everyday practice and professional history. An ideal not grounded in real possibilities and related to everyday experience is not an ideal at all. It is also important to study what lawyers actually do. But such study cannot be divorced from a normative vision. Lawyer behavior is itself oriented toward some normative vision, official or otherwise, and is unintelligible without attention to ideals of conduct. Thus our observations of behavior make no sense unless brought together in some normative framework. Take two famous "empirical" findings about the legal profession by Heinz and Laumann (1982): that the more prestige lawyers have, the less control they have over their clients and the less they are likely to provide service to individuals. These strike us as important because of the normative vision of lawyer autonomy, independence and service. Heinz and Laumann have made an ironic comment on these ideals.

Work, Motivation, and Professional Ideologies

If one cannot study professionalism as disembodied ideal or as pure behavior, how then can one understand the relationship between ideals and conduct in legal work? We suggest that the best approach is to study exemplary moments in which lawyer roles and lawyer organizations are structured. We think there are multiple and competing visions of what it means to be a "professional." The multiplicity and the incompatability of these visions have implications for lawyer conduct and organization. We want to observe moments at which these competing visions are brought into play in a variety of settings.

Key to such an inquiry is a theory of how lawyer motivation, ideologies of professionalism, official codes of conduct and their enforcement, and workplace organization interact. There are a variety of accounts of these relationships. To explain ours, we must first look at some we have rejected.

The "official" story is the vision that lies behind much of the rhetoric on professionalism. In this account there is a strong degree of congruence among the elements we have mentioned: motivation, ideology, codes, and workplace (generally see Greenwood 1957, Goode 1957, Gordon 1988, pp. 14–30). Thus, in the official account, lawyers are individually motivated to place client interests above their own, yet to retain independence and loyalty to the law. The source of this motivation is the "professional self," which is socially constructed. There are three elements to the process of construction of a professional self: selection, education, discipline. Through self-selection and fitness requirements, persons with other-regarding and public service motivations enter the profession. This "character trait" is reinforced through an educational process that clarifies specific ethical norms and obligations and by a disciplinary structure that deters "backsliding." Formal codes of ethics delineate specific requirements and express general orientations; the study of such texts is part of the educational process; the enforcement of specific rules reinforces the educational effort.

In this account, the workplace forms part of the reinforcing structure, and the primary issues of workplace organization can be reduced to questions of professional control and lawyer autonomy. The main problems to be confronted in the legal workplace are the threat of lay control of lawyer conduct and the denial of individual autonomy in defining and carrying out tasks. As long as lawyers control their work, nothing more needs to be done at the workplace, since the "professional self" will guarantee that officially sanctioned norms of conduct are observed. If "self" discipline (including informal collegial sanctions) fails, official discipline is available to reinforce it.

There is a body of literature on the legal profession that challenges this official account at every point. These critics question the process by which a professional self is constructed and maintained. Selection is illusory. People who enter the legal profession are no more other-regarding than Americans as a whole, and may be even more self-seeking. "Fitness" screening is meaningless at best and a mode of social, racial, and political discrimination at worst (Abel 1989). Education does nothing to alter self-interested motivation, and indeed may strengthen it. Legal education fosters a cynicism about human nature in general, destroys any belief in a transcendent body of law to which professionals owe a duty, reduces professional responsibility to the question of how to avoid getting caught for violating what is actually a very undemanding set of formal requirements (Kennedy 1982). These critics characterize the codes of professional responsibility as either so general that they are meaningless, so riddled with exceptions and counterprinciples that they are illusory, or so underenforced that they are no threat to any but the most unscrupulous and careless (Abel 1981b, 1989; Rhode 1985). Finally, these critics regard the workplace as encouraging lawyer self-interest and undermining the ideal of independence. Lawyers learn on the job that the goal is to give the clients what they want if they are powerful, and to exploit them economically or psychologically if they are not (Blumberg 1967, Maccaulay 1979, Sarat and Felstiner 1986). Rewards go to those who serve the most powerful clients (Nelson 1988). Everything else is rhetoric.

These conflicting accounts have heuristic value. Neither captures fully what we know about the social construction of professionalism. Yet they point to the issues that must be examined and force us to specify mechanisms whose operations must be understood.

Take the central issue of a "professional self." The official account posits a professional self that differs from the motivations of the public at large. It makes a series of assumptions about how selection and education foster a special form of professional identity. It asserts that disciplinary agencies and collective action by the profession reinforce the professional identity created through lawyer socialization. But it focuses heavily on selection and education as mechanisms for developing professionalism. The "critical" story not only questions all these assumptions; it makes counterassumptions about the nature of entrants to the profession and the operation of education, professional culture, and discipline. The critical account identifies the workplace as the crucial determinant of lawyer behavior.

Both stories stress the unity and coherence of the mechanisms that affect professional self-identity. The official account suggests that lawyers are subjected to a uniform set of messages and pressures, all of which work together to enhance autonomy, other-regarding behavior, and independence. The critical story also stresses the coherence and congruence of the messages that lawyers receive, but insists that the hidden messages of the law school curriculum, the vacuity of professional culture, the centrality of economic motivation, the strength of workplace pressures, the ambiguity of ethical codes, and the lack of genuine commitment to disciplinary enforcement actually foster initial proclivities for self-interest and pursuit of the client's goals at any cost.

We suspect that this theme of unity and congruence has distorted the general understanding of the actual process of professionalization. We see contradiction and complexity where these accounts describe unity and coherence. We think that there are competing and contradictory pressures and messages in all the arenas that define and reproduce professional identity. Indeed, these contradictions in professional culture may be one of its dominant features. Legal education does encourage cynicism but also champions service and independence. Professional rhetoric is often vague and self-serving, but it does keep ideals of autonomy and independence alive. Disciplinary codes are often vague, contradictory, and under-enforced. They may codify lawyer self-interest and present it as other-regarding behavior. They may be enforced in a way that creates scapegoats, thus detracting attention from more basic criticisms of the legal profession. But something is going on in the disciplinary arena. Disciplinary rules are important enough to generate substantial energy and controversy; the debate over the client confidentiality provisions of the Model Rules is ample proof of how seriously lawyers take some rules (see Schneyer, Chapter 3 herein). Similarly, legal workplaces pressure lawyers to discard independence and autonomy in favor of money, status, and security, but they also are sites where such ideals are reinforced. In the various arenas lawyers find themselves embedded in a complex and contradictory cultural matrix in which little is precluded or guaranteed. Competing visions and limited constraints provide room for maneuver and opportunities for struggle. The interesting questions lie in the moments in which these opportunities are taken or not taken.

Arenas of Social Construction

The foregoing suggests that there are multiple and interacting arenas in which professionalism is produced and reproduced. Each of these arenas has its characteristic notions about the proper role of lawyers in society; the production of such notions influences what occurs in other arenas, but in a complex and indeterminant manner.

It is possible to identify a number of relatively structured settings in which issues of professionalism are salient: (1) legal education; (2) collective action on behalf of the profession (e.g., by bar associations); (3) disciplinary enforcement; and (4) the workplace. There are of course other settings in which professionalism is discussed and which may influence lawyer conduct. Both public opinion about lawyers and governmental action clearly have an influence. These areas influence "professionalism" but they are not "arenas of professionalism" in our sense, since they are not sites of systematic and regular production of ideas about lawyers' conduct.[6]

6. Arenas of professionalism cannot be defined a priori, but must be determined based on empirical investigation. DiMaggio and Powell follow a similar tack with respect to their concept of the "organizational field" (1983, pp. 148–49). Our notion of arenas also resembles Abbott's (1988) conception of "audience" and Bourdieu's more abstract notion of social "field" (1985, 1987; DiMaggio 1979, p. 1462). Abbott posits that claims of professional jurisdiction are made to three audiences: the public, the legal system, and the workplace (1988, pp. 59–65). Public jurisdictional claims are about the right (and necessity) of an occupation to control all aspects of a certain kind of work (1988, pp. 60–61). Legal jurisdictional claims occur in three places—legislatures, courts, and administrative or planning structures. Of the three audiences legal claims are the most stable over time and the most specific in content. "In the workplace, jurisdiction is a simple claim to control certain kinds of work. There is usually little debate about what tasks are or how to construct them" (1988, p. 64). Because work relationships inherently entail fuzzy lines in the division of labor among workers, workplace claims and their audiences are the most informal (1988, p. 65).

Abbott's audiences are categories of jurisdictional claims, where the content of the claim is relatively unimportant (1988, p. 59 n. 1). For Abbott audiences are important only in that they are connected to jurisdictions. The arenas approach, in contrast, not only attempts to identify general audiences for ideological claims, but analyzes the characteristics of the groups making claims, the characteristics of their audiences, and the relationships between these various players. The arenas concept is not limited to three specific audiences, but can be applied to any context in which the production of professional ideology is ongoing. Rather than focus only on jurisdictional claims, the arenas approach considers the role of professional ideology in other aspects of the organization and functioning of professional institutions. For a more extended discussion, see the introductory chapter of this book.

Bourdieu conceives of society as consisting of several professional or disciplinary "fields," which

First, it is important to note is that these arenas have some degree of internal coherence and logic. All produce notions of professionalism, and all these notions influence production in other arenas, but to some extent production in each arena is constrained and influenced by factors specific to the arena in question. Consider the law school. A major function of the law school is to produce ideas about the social role and responsibility of lawyers. These ideas are contained in formal discussions of this question, e.g. in courses on professional responsibility. But perhaps even more important are the messages implicit in all discussions of law in all courses and the "hidden" curriculum that is embodied in the way schools are organized, classes conducted, and values transmitted in informal ways. What goes on in the law schools is influenced by what is occurring in other arenas, including the collective and workplace arenas. Employer concerns are channeled into the law schools; professional rhetoric is consumed by students and teachers; codes of professional responsibility are read and studied. Yet academic pictures of lawyering, both explicit and implicit, are influenced by factors specific to the schools themselves. Legal academics are under pressure to develop accounts that are systematic and coherent, related to ideals and social visions shared by others in the university community, and congruent with their own self-images. These pressures may help explain one of the interesting aspects of contemporary academic discussion about legal ethics and the lawyer's roles, namely the tendency toward the development of two or more relatively systematic and contradictory visions. The current debate over "the lawyer's amoral role," strongly championed on libertarian grounds by some and attacked on moral grounds by others, is one illustration of these tendencies (see, e.g., Wasserstrom 1984, Luban 1984, pp. 38–171, Simon 1988,

---

are relatively separate spheres of cultural production. A field refers to "the totality of actors, institutions, and characteristic activities in a realm of cultural production and the structured, socially patterned practice of this production" (cited in Coombe 1989, pp. 105–6). The "juridical field" is one among the several fields Bourdieu has written about (Bourdieu 1977, pp. 201–9 [Translator's introduction by Richard Terdiman]). Bourdieu employs the concept of the juridical field to analyze both the internal politics of the "world of law," that is, the competition among various subgroups within the profession, and the relationship of the legal field to the broader society.

As we indicated in the introductory chapter to this book, we find Bourdieu's theory of practice as applied to professional fields potentially valuable. Although Bourdieu does not provide a clear definition of the boundaries of social fields, it is a far more global concept than our arenas notion. The two approaches are quite compatible, however. In our view professional fields contain several arenas. Each arena will to some extent embody the culture of the field as a whole, but will, depending on its specific social position within the field and its specific history, produce a distinctive version of professional ideology. This notion is implicit in Bourdieu's approach. He suggests, for example, that the very process of struggle and competition among various subsets of professional groups to define the principles of the professional field will tend to legitimate the field as a whole (Bourdieu 1987). Dezalay's research on the internationalization and restructuring of corporate law practice in Europe and the United States exemplifies this perspective (see Dezalay 1990).

Pepper 1986a, 1986b, Kaufman 1986). Another is the development of competing accounts of lawyering through the use of different and competing frameworks of analysis such as law and economics, feminism, and critical legal studies.

Second, the social production of professionalism in the various arenas we have identified is marked by the lack of a unitary vision within any arena or of any unifying ideal that ties the various arenas together. If we study each of the arenas closely, we can see multiple and often conflicting ideas about what lawyers should and should not do, how practices should and should not be organized. We have already noted this tendency in legal education and scholarship. It can also be seen in the other arenas (see Seron, Chapter 2 herein). For example, the history of the Kutak report shows that in the collective arena lawyers express very different ideals about key issues of professional role and conduct (Schneyer, Chapter 3 herein). The history of this project showed how very different ideas of proper lawyer conduct were proposed and contested. These fights continued as the states moved to enact the Model Rules. The arenas may constrain and affect the cultural process by which professionalism is defined, but not necessarily in ways that create unitary visions.

Third, arenas are neither tightly integrated nor totally distinct. The official account of the social construction of professionalism suggests both unity of vision and "tight coupling" between cultural ideals, professional norms, workplace organization, and lawyer conduct. Yet things do not seem to work this way. Each of the arenas produce multiple visions, and these affect the other arenas in indirect and complex ways. Academic discourse on professional roles and responsibilities has some impact on the collective arena and the workplace, but—perhaps in part because there is no single academic vision—this impact is limited and hard to specify. Struggles over how to define professionalism in the workplace may influence what is said in the collective arena and the schools, but again in complex and indirect ways. Perhaps one of the most interesting questions for any large-scale investigation of the social construction of professionalism is the nature and direction of these mutual influences among arenas; clearly we know very little about this except that the influences are not very direct, rarely one-directional, and never all-powerful.

Our concept of arenas of social construction posits several overlapping social "spaces" in which varied notions of lawyer professionalism are produced and reproduced. A final feature of this approach—implicit in the foregoing—is that in each arena there are ongoing struggles over all the important questions about the lawyer's role in society. The nature of professionalism is continually debated, although the degree and intensity of that debate will vary from time to time. Individuals and groups articulate and promote different visions of how lawyers should behave, how practice should be organized, and so forth, and different arenas may either mute or accentuate divergences. Different segments of the bar have championed radically diverse ideas about what should be included in codes of ethics and how these codes should be enforced. Legal academics have put forth very different ideas of the nature and purpose of legal ethics and different interpretations of the social significance of lawyer behavior. Lawyers in practice have employed notions of "professionalism" to challenge and to justify changes in the way firms and work relations are organized. Professionalism, in this view, is a site for struggle, not a fixed ideal or stable structure.

The "arenas" approach to explaining the social construction of professionalism has some advantages over other accounts. Some of the literature on this process posits very direct relationships between the "ideological" or cultural production of models of lawyer behavior and the conditions of practice. The official story asserts that professional ideals and ethical norms directly influence lawyer behavior and overcome resistances generated by economic and organizational pressures within the workplace. The critical position suggests that conditions of practice directly determine cultural production so that codes of professional responsibility are written to justify the conduct that clients will pay for. Our approach suggests that both these opinions could be correct. The presence of official norms and rhetoric can affect the ways lawyers deal with workplace conflicts, and thus may affect daily conduct—but they may not. Pressures from the workplace can influence cultural production—at least by setting in motion countervisions—but nothing says it has to be that way. Individual lawyers and collective actors are subject to constraints imposed by the arenas and specific settings in which they operate, but the very complexity and contradictory nature of the arenas and the visions they produce create opportunities for choice. Everything depends on what happens in specific contexts, so that contextual examination of micro-encounters in different arenas and settings becomes an essential part of any complete account of the social construction of professionalism.

Investigating the Collective Arena: The Stanley Report and Its Progeny

The "collective" arena is the setting for the production of views on lawyer professionalism by official representatives of the legal profession. For purposes of this chapter, we shall look only at the most recent and most general efforts to define "professionalism" by leaders of the organized bar—the Stanley Commission and some of its progeny in the states. We shall seek to account for the characteristics of this body of official rhetoric through an analysis of the nature of the collective arena itself.

At first glance the literature reflects this most recent wave of official concern with "professionalism" and gives the impression that there is a major problem to which the organized bar has turned its attention. If the amount of time devoted to the issue, the prestige of the people involved, and the attention paid to it by leaders of the bar throughout the country are any indication, one would have to conclude that the organized bar is very disturbed by the possibility that professionalism is in decline, and that it is committed to doing something about this decline. If one analyzes the reports, editorials, and commentary on professionalism in some detail, however, the situation seems less clear-cut. First, it is hard to derive any precise or concrete notion of "professionalism" from much of the literature. The definitions offered are vague; examples of "unprofessional conduct" are rare. Second, although the rhetoric suggests a decline in professionalism, no clear or convincing account is given of why that might be occurring today and what forces might lie behind alleged lapses from professional norms. Third, although a number of "remedies" are offered to curb the decline of professionalism, these are so diffuse in nature that they undermine the very idea that they deal with any coherent issue, and often seem to consist of cosmetic generalities or moralistic exhortations.

Finally, much is *not* said in the official rhetoric. It does not discuss in any detail the massive changes in the organization and economics of law practice that have occurred in the last decade. It expresses a general hostility to market relations in the delivery of legal services and shows little appreciation of the "pro-market" case. It does not deal with questions of lawyer dissatisfaction or relate ideals of professionalism to the workplace discontent of women and others who challenge the way firms have been conventionally organized. It does not give adequate attention to the question of lawyer independence.

Defining "Professionalism"

Most recent discussion of the problem of professionalism attempts to define the concept, but these definitions are very general and are rarely fleshed out with detailed descriptions of unprofessional conduct. Moreover, little if any evidence is marshaled to support the claims that there has been a major change in lawyer conduct in recent years.

The Stanley Commission did seek to define professionalism, and this definition has been influential among the state professionalism committees who have also dealt with the question in the aftermath of the Stanley Commission report. Yet the Stanley discussion is also general and ambiguous. Having noted that professionalism has many meanings and that definitions are difficult, the commission went on to offer two rather different ones (ABA 1986, p. 10). The first is based on a quotation from Roscoe Pound, who described professionalism as the "pursuit of a learned art in the spirit of a public service." The second was supplied to the commission by Eliot Freidson. His definition stresses the difficulty clients have in evaluating the quality of legal services and the need for collective self-regulation to protect clients.

The juxtaposition of these two definitions leaves the idea of "public service" ambiguous. It could be construed to refer to the lawyer's duty to ensure that client behavior conforms to the law. But, when Pound's definition is read with Freidson's client-trust concept, it could also simply mean that lawyering has a "monopoly" element created by market imperfections brought about by asymmetries in expertise. In the latter reading, "public service" would mean simply avoiding putting the lawyer's interest before the client's, not the interests of the law or the public ahead of the interests of lawyer *and* client. And it would serve as justification for preserving the lawyer monopoly, albeit with self-regulation.

To be sure, the various bar statements on professionalism do stress the lawyer's duties to the public as well as to clients. But these "public service" duties are generally construed to mean obligations of service *outside* the context of representation. Thus most of the reports and commentary stress the lawyer's duty to provide pro-bono services and to be concerned about the unrepresented (ABA 1986, pp. 47–50; *Illinois Bar Journal* 1988, p. 450; *Virginia Bar Association Journal* 1987, p. 9). But—with the sole exception of the topic of litigation abuse—there is little, if any, discussion of the potential conflict between a lawyer's duties to the public and to the client in the course of representation.

The vagueness of the current definitions of professionalism would not be too serious a problem if these definitions were accompanied by examples of "unprofessional" conduct that could flesh out a more concrete picture of the norm by tacit contrast with instances of deviance. But one can only find two areas in which leaders of the bar seem to agree about what specific conduct constitutes "unprofessional" behavior: advertising and litigation "abuse." Advertising comes in for special opprobrium in many of the reports. The Georgia Committee on Professionalism singles out advertising as both evidence of the decline of professionalism and a major cause of this decline: "The Committee shares the remorse, indeed the indignation, of much of the bar over the shameless commercialism of some advertising by lawyers. It is artless, crude, and, in a word, unprofessional." The committee notes that some see advertising as "a wedge driven between the legal profession and the esteem in which the profession was once held, it is said, by the public" (*Georgia Bar Journal* 1986, p. 15). Litigation abuses are also mentioned quite frequently. Indeed, one could argue that for many bar leaders the problem of professionalism would be solved if tasteless advertising and overzealous litigation could be controlled.

The Problem of Professionalism Today

If the bar thinks there is a real risk of decline in professionalism, and if it intends to do something about it, one might expect the reports and commentary to analyze possible causes for the decline. Of course, since relevant reports and commentaries are vague on the concept of professionalism, short on examples of unprofessional conduct, and silent on the evidence that there is more "unprofessional" conduct today than in the past, it is no real surprise to find that these reports and commentaries contain very little on why professionalism is suddenly a problem today.

The Stanley Commission may have intended to suggest some possible causes when describing changes in the legal profession in the last twenty-five years. Their report describes three changes that, it implies, are relevant to the question of professionalism: increased economic competition brought about by growing numbers of lawyers and the elimination of anti-competitive practices; the elimination of ethical aspirations from the codes of professional responsibility; and an alleged decline in the rate of return for lawyer services (ABA 1986, pp. 1–9). But it presents no evidence to support the implication that the presence of "ethical considerations" in earlier codes of ethics made any difference in lawyer conduct before the Model Rules; it provides no data to support the proposition that "profit margins" in legal practice are narrowing; it offers no proof that lawyers facing more economic pressures are likely to behave "unprofessionally," unless, of course, by that the commission *meant* they are likely to seek business more aggressively as through advertising. And the Stanley Commission very carefully avoids any direct suggestion that the factors it does identify are causes of unprofessional conduct.

Toward a Solution?

If the Stanley Commission is unclear about what professionalism really means or why it is threatened by decline, it has no shortage of recommendations for what should be done about this alleged "problem." What can we learn about the "problem" and its "causes" by examining the "remedies," which make up 80 percent of the text of the report?

The first thing to note is that most of the commission's recommendations deal with *education*. A major section is devoted to law schools; continuing education is also highlighted (ABA 1986, pp. 16–21, 24–25). This emphasis on education creates the impression that the decline in professionalism comes from a lack of understanding of what the obligations of a lawyer are, rather than from any conflict between idealized notions of desirable conduct and everyday workplace pressures. The report also emphasizes individual action and individual motivation as both the cause of and cure for any decline in behavior. Lawyers are told to be less greedy, to put clients' interests ahead of their own, and so on. The report relies heavily on the "professional self" and on voluntary choices by lawyers to behave more "professionally." To be sure, there are references to particular organizational contexts—the falsification of time records by law firm associates (1986, p. 9) and the participation of law firms in business activities with clients (1986, pp. 30–31)—and there is support for more effective disciplinary enforcement. But these receive much less attention than suggestions for more education and exhortations to change individual conduct.

Furthermore, some bar leaders who express concern about professionalism tend to see the problem as one of public relations, not a decline in lawyer conduct at all. Thus in many of the state reports and commentaries as much emphasis is placed on campaigns to change the public image of lawyers as on action to correct any "unprofessional conduct" (see, e.g., *Washington State Bar News* 1986, p. 7; *Bar Notes* 1986, p. 3; *North Carolina State Bar Quarterly* 1987, p. 13).

Left Unsaid

When one examines the recent spate of collective pronouncements on lawyer professionalism, one is struck as much by what is not mentioned as by what is specified in reports, comments, editorials. Comments made by many thoughtful observers of the legal profession are omitted or are downplayed. Issues that have surfaced in professional discourse and would seem to be related to the general question of professionalism are overlooked.

Perhaps most striking is the relative lack of attention to the major and massive changes occurring in a variety of practice settings. The vast and widely publicized changes in corporate practice are remarked on only briefly. The impact of the rapid growth of major firms, the impact of house counsel on the practice of corporate law, and the major changes in lawyer career paths in this field are touched on lightly. The problems encountered by women who seek to enter corporate law, the evidence of lawyer job dissatisfaction, the apparent "speed up" at the associate level in major firms (reflected in dramatic increases in the number of billable hours that many firms expect) are mentioned only in passing in the historical section of the report (1986, pp. 3–9). But these—and other aspects of increased workplace tension—are not dealt with at all in the commission's specific recommendations. There is a similar absence of any mention of changes in other sectors of practice.

Another issue virtually omitted is the rise of very different models of "consumer protection" in the legal services market. The report and its progeny make clear that professionalism is a way to protect the consumer of legal services. Although the Stanley Commission did not oppose lawyer advertising across the board and although it encouraged lawyers to practice in a cost-efficient manner, it continued to adhere to the model of professional monopoly and self-regulation as the sole solution to consumer protection, paying no attention to the alternative "market" model supported by some academics and entrepreneurial law firm leaders. This alternative view favors competition between lawyers and nonlawyers, accepts advertising as a desirable method for reducing information gaps, rejects the notion that clients are always unable to evaluate the quality of legal services, and asserts that some form of "deregulation" of the market for legal services is the best way to ensure that clients get the best possible service at the lowest price (see, for example, Garth 1983, Hazard, Pearce, and Stempel 1984).

Finally, the theme of lawyer "independence" receives brief consideration (ABA 1986, pp. 13, 28–29, 47). The discussion of lawyer responsibility to the public emphasizes the problem of frivolous litigation, wasteful discovery tactics, and participation in legislative activities outside the context of representation. Compare the recent reports with the earlier "declension" rhetoric collected by Robert Gordon (1988). The earlier accounts stressed the importance of maintaining lawyer independence from a client's immediate ends, and sought to preserve lawyer independence so that lawyers could perform a public role within the context of representation itself.

Towards an Account of the Collective Rhetoric

There is a great deal being said today about professionalism and the need to avert any decline in it. But the rhetoric in the collective arena is very general, the approach is individualistic and moralistic, the remedies are arguably aimed more at superficial manifestations than at basic and underlying conflicts. What accounts for the character of the collective rhetoric on professionalism?

One might argue that the absence of more sophisticated analyses or broader proposals reflects a low level of self-knowledge in the profession. Decisions must be made and conclusions drawn on the basis of sketchy and anecdotal information. There is little systematic information about changes in legal practice and lawyer behavior. Law schools have devoted little attention to these matters; the academic community that studies such questions is limited in size and lacks the resources to conduct major and regular studies of practice and its pressures (Galanter 1983).

Further, it is hard to get information even when you look for it; lawyers who confront major conflicts in their daily lives are not always forthcoming about these problems. Had the Stanley Commission and its state counterparts wanted more detailed and fundamental information about causes of professional discontent, they would have found something, but not complete or fully satisfactory information.

But gaps in the information available to bar leaders do not explain the lack of specifics or causal analysis in the official professionalism rhetoric. The various commissions and committees did not make much use of the information available about changing conditions of legal practice, lawyer dissatisfaction, and so on. Nor did they make a concerted effort to commission new studies that would bring to light fundamental problems or their causes.

The explanation for these omissions, we believe, lies in the constraints the collective arena imposes on bar presidents, commission members, and other such public actors. This rhetoric is what one would expect from these sources, even if many of the participants in the "professionalism" campaign were aware of more basic issues.

Consider the key features of this "arena": bar associations are voluntary organizations that attempt to speak for an increasingly divided and heterogeneous profession. Yet, for a variety of reasons, they must present a picture of unity and consensus. These "arena characteristics" help us understand why official rhetoric on professionalism takes the form it does.

Voluntary Association

Although there are a few integrated bars left in the United States, most associations are voluntary (Schneyer 1983, Abel 1989). And even if membership is mandatory, participation never is. Despite sizeable nonmember staffs, bar associations must enlist voluntary labor to take responsibility for associational tasks. The voluntary character of a general purpose association like the ABA not only limits the capacity to mount major projects, but also encourages the pursuit of projects that will not prove offensive to significant segments of the membership. In short, there is considerable political pressure on the ABA to avoid taking divisive stands (Powell 1979; Heinz and Laumann 1982; but see Halliday 1987, p. 312, for an argument that bar leaders can overcome divisiveness). Van Hoy (1990) reports that the Stanley Commission was extremely sensitive to objections from particular groups of lawyers and modified the early draft of the report to minimize their opposition.

An Increasingly Divided Profession with a Growing Need to Appear Unified

Despite indications that it is becoming increasingly difficult to find common ground among American lawyers, the profession may have a growing need to present a unified face to the public. Unity, professional cohesion, and commitment to self-discipline and enforcement of professional codes are promoted as essential to the preservation of the bar's monopoly over certain forms of service. In the face of an oversupply of lawyers and growing pressure from within and without the profession to deregulate legal practice, the bar must maintain at least the *image* of collective unity and a commitment to "higher" ideals (see, e.g. Auerbach 1976, pp. 11, 263–306). The remarks of Robert MacCrate, then the immediate past president of the ABA, to the American Bar Foundation's Conference on Professionalism in September 1988 illustrate the claim for the necessity of a unified bar: "For a profession to exist and survive there must be a unifying purpose collectively articulated and subscribed to by its members. The concept of the American legal profession today is of a unitary profession, educated in a common program and subject to one general licensing standard, with a shared sense of responsibility and relationship to law in all of its dimensions." These two intersecting pressures, the need for the appearance of unity and the fact of increasing fragmentation, would impel bar leaders to produce a lot of rhetoric on professionalism, but at the same time, deter efforts to make that rhetoric specific or threatening to the interests of any major segment of the profession.

Contradictions between Role and Legitimation

The production of images of lawyering in the collective arena confronts another tension: the contradiction between the public role lawyers claim and actually perform, and the fact that legal services are allocated through markets and thus their distribution is heavily skewed towards the interests of the better-off and better organized (Galanter 1974; Abel 1989). Lawyers in the American political economy occupy contradictory roles. On the one hand, they claim to be an independent estate, loyal to the law and the public as well as to specific clients. They claim the expertise to shape and influence public policy, whether they appear as representatives of specific clients or present themselves as disinterested public servants; yet the "professional knowledge" and skills that they command are for sale to the highest bidder. The result is a profession that is highly stratified in terms of the nature of clients represented, the professional status of legal specialties, and the social characteristics of lawyers (Heinz and Laumann 1982).

The collective rhetoric of the bar can be seen as a response to this dilemma. The capital value of lawyers' knowledge is increased to the degree that it is perceived as something more than the relentless pursuit of client self-interest at any cost. So official rhetoric must preserve the idea of the lawyer as something more than the agent of the client, while avoiding the creation of any true dissonance between lawyers' interests and those of their clients. Moreover, to preserve the legitimacy of American law as a unitary system, with equal justice for all, it is important for the profession to claim that it is a unitary body. As Heinz and Laumann note in the conclusion of their book, "To the extent that the public perceives the separation of lawyers into two hemispheres or two occupations, the symbolic unity of the law, and thus its legitimacy, will be weakened. . . . If lawyers of distinct social types work in distinct realms of law, serve separate sorts of clients, and deal with separate systems of courts and government agencies, symbolic unity can be maintained only with mirrors and smoke, and then unreliably" (1982, p. 385). Whether they consciously do so or not, the appeal of bar leaders to a common, if vaguely defined, set of values tends to serve a legitimating function.

Changing Situations of Legal Elites

In the introduction to this book we offered a general account of the relationship between the changing situation of legal elites and the nature of the professionalism campaign. While we think the account is instructive, it would be greatly strengthened if we could better specify the link between the professional ideologies of lawyers and the arenas of professionalism in which they participate. Both elite and non-elite lawyers may have many different reasons for participating in official bar projects. These motives include a desire to assert strongly held ideological positions concerning issues of professional self-regulation; a perceived duty to represent a particular segment of the bar in matters that may affect its interests; an effort to support friends and colleagues who are active in bar politics; an interest in advancing one's own career in bar politics; and a desire to gain broader exposure in order to benefit one's professional standing. To understand the Stanley Commission, it would be useful to possess data on the professional positions and ideological orientations of its individual participants, and to have a clear idea of the process through which the commission produced its report.

Accounts of professional arenas in action are relatively rare (but see Halliday 1987, Powell 1979, 1989), but we are fortunate to have Van Hoy's (1990) study of the Stanley Commission. Van Hoy found that the origins, operation, and eventual product of the commission reflected the general politics of the ABA. The commission began as a response by the president of the ABA to criticisms raised by then Chief Justice Burger. The composition of the commission was influenced by several factors, including which sections of the association contributed the most financial support; a perceived need to have "balanced representation" of different segments of the bar, the legal academy, and nonlawyers; and by the personal networks of the ABA president and the commission chair. The commission proceeded in that quasi-governmental style characteristic of many ABA bodies, conducting open hearings and soliciting testimony from various elements within the profession. The report and its recommendations were drafted by the chair, his assistant, and the academic reporter to the commission. It was amended in response to objections from members of the commission and liaison members representing various sections of the ABA. The chair of the commission chose not to seek approval of the report by the ABA House of Delegates, which would have subjected its contents to further scrutiny and required extensive lobbying and consultation. Instead, he succeeded in getting the House of Delegates to adopt a resolution to distribute the report and establish another commission to study the implementation of the report. This strategy allowed the ABA to conduct a sort of professionalism campaign that avoided any specific course of action that might prompt opposition within the bar.

Van Hoy's analysis of the makeup and operation of the Stanley Commission helps us understand the first and most visible arena of professionalism: the official or collective arena of bar association activity. By looking at the Stanley Commission's report in this context, we can both understand why it took the form it did and understand the constraints under which it was drafted.

The commission represented an amalgam of potentially divergent professional interests. It was led by members of the bar's corporate elite, but excluded representatives of the most aggressively entrepreneurial segment of that elite. Like most actors in the collective arena, the commission sought to avoid exposing the potential intraprofessional conflict that lurks behind any effort to articulate shared norms and visions. To this end the commission employed four primary tactics: First, it used an exceedingly general and quite conventional concept of "professionalism." Second, it muted any criticism of lawyers in general and avoided any effort to single out any segment of the bar in its description of "professional decline." Third, it avoided seeing the causes of the alleged decline of "professionalism" in structural or generic factors, but rather pointed only to individual offenders. Finally, the commission shepherded the report through the ABA in a way that minimized opportunities for the expression of dissatisfaction by organized segments of the bar. By avoiding a vote in the House of Delegates and by separating the contents of the report from the process of its implementation, the commission made it harder for opponents—if there were any—to mobilize their dissent.

The Stanley Commission showed a clear understanding of the politics of the ABA, and thus of the constraints of the collective arena. It knew that it should avoid unearthing fissures within the profession. To do that, it had to take a conventional, abstract approach to professionalism and employ an individual-deviance analysis of decline. Another commission, with different members, might have produced a different document, but these features would probably mark any product of the collective arena.

The Legal Workplace as an Arena of Professionalism

The contexts in which lawyers work represent a very different kind of professional arena from the Stanley Commission. The Stanley Commission was itself a kind of emblem of lawyer professionalism: it attempted to reaffirm professional ideals as a clearly articulated, unitary body of principles that could guide the behavior of the profession. The commission's report, although never adopted as official ABA policy, nonetheless was widely disseminated, received extensive press coverage, was imitated at the level of state and local bar associations, and led to efforts at implementation.

It may seem odd, therefore, to compare corner law offices, corporate legal departments, or large law firms to a commission charged with investigating the supposed decline in professionalism. Such contexts have no official status as organs for expressing professional principles. Nor is it likely that an observer would find the actors in these settings talking about professionalism as such. Amid the press of immediate work demands, practicing lawyers would not appear to devote much time or effort to defining the dictates of professionalism or monitoring the behavior of colleagues against a set of normative standards.

Yet the workplaces of lawyers are crucial sites in which to observe the interplay between professional ideology and the dramatic changes reshaping the practice of law in America. First, it is the workplace that has been transformed by the rapid growth in the number of lawyers, the emergence of advertising and price competition, the arrival of new forms of legal services providers, and the reorganization of corporate law firms. The collective institutions of the profession, such as bar associations, disciplinary commissions, and law schools have been involved in, and affected by, the restructuring of the market for legal services, but these collective institutions are by and large *reacting* to changes that originated in practice organizations (see Nelson 1988, pp. 22–23, Galanter and Palay, Chapter 1 herein). For the most part these collective institutions of the bar have accommodated these changes. Thus it is in the workplace that competing visions of lawyering have had their greatest effect on how legal services are organized and delivered.

Second, comparing the professional ideologies of lawyers across work settings reveals most starkly that the vision of a unitary set of professional values invoked by leaders of the bar is a fiction. Workplace contexts develop widely varying and often mutually contradictory "local versions" of professionalism. At least some of these are inconsistent with the professional ideals projected in the bar's official rhetoric. One of the implications of the diversity in professional vision one observes among lawyers at work is that the task of professional self-regulation is significantly more complex than most observers would allow. In a world of widely shared professional values, it is plausible to think that ethical canons can be interpreted, taught, and enforced in the ways envisioned by the traditional model of self-regulation. But this model breaks down when lawyers develop very different conceptions of professionalism based on the particular circumstances of their practice.

In the section that follows we begin to develop a theory of the role of professional ideology in the legal workplace. This discussion has three parts: In the first, we review two major works that demonstrate the relationship between practice settings and professionalism: Jerome Carlin's *Lawyers' Ethics* (1966) and Eve Spangler's *Lawyers for Hire* (1986). Carlin's report on the ethical orientations of the New York bar is the classic empirical refutation of the notion that lawyers possess a unified, consistent professional ideology.

Spangler's study applies theories of professional proletarianization to lawyers: because it offers a theoretical interpretation of the division of labor in the legal workplace, and its impact on the professional ideologies of lawyer-workers, Spangler's research merits extended consideration. In the second, we develop the analysis by looking at evidence that suggests that there are very different forms of "professional ideology" within and between three major workplace contexts: the corporate law firm, the corporate legal department, and legal services for the poor. Finally, we conclude by addressing a theoretical issue that is pivotal to research on the role of professional ideology in the workplace: the relationship between ideology and organizational structure in law practice.

General Studies of the Legal Workplace

Despite the existence of a considerable body of empirical research on lawyers and their work, there are relatively few studies that examine the relationship between professional ideology and the organization of the legal workplace. Much of the leading scholarship in the field concerns the social structure of the profession (see, e.g., Heinz and Laumann 1982, Ladinsky 1963). It emphasizes patterns of stratification among lawyers engaged in different kinds of practices and serving different kinds of clients, rather than the division of labor within particular practice contexts. Other studies focus on how particular types of lawyers practice.[7] Although these contain many useful insights into how lawyers work, they are not primarily concerned with the professional ideologies of the practitioners. Gordon's (1983, 1984b) historical research on turn-of the-century New York City lawyers is a helpful analytical model, for it explicitly develops the link between the practices and ideologies of elite lawyers. But no scholar has performed a similar analysis in the context of contemporary corporate law practice.

Given the limitations of the existing literature, we can provide only a preliminary analysis of the legal workplace as an arena of professionalism. We feel confident in drawing the inferences we do in support of the arenas approach, but caution that research into professional ideology in the workplace that is consciously executed with the arenas framework in mind is required before a more comprehensive theory is possible.

7. See e.g., Cain 1983, general practice solicitors; Sarat and Felstiner 1986, divorce lawyers; Macaulay 1979, consumer lawyers; Rosenthal 1974, personal injury lawyers; Mann 1985, white collar criminal defense lawyers; Flood 1987, lawyers in corporate law firms. Among the central concerns of these studies are how lawyers shaped their clients' conceptions of legal rights, the effects of lawyers' economic interests on the representation of clients, the balance of power between lawyers and clients in making decisions on settlement negotiations.

Lawyers' Ethics: Reversing the Top-Down Model of Professionalism

Jerome Carlin's *Lawyers' Ethics* (1966), a classic in research on the legal profession, is an easily overlooked example of a study of professional ideology in the legal workplace. The central focus of Carlin's study was the propensity of lawyers to violate ethical standards, and typically it is cited today for the proposition that the elite of the bar favor stricter and more strictly enforced ethical rules because such enforcement will not directly affect their practice. Carlin arrived at that finding by adopting an explicit workplace framework, that is, he sampled law firms and other groups of lawyers who shared office space rather than sampling individual lawyers; and he devoted considerable attention to the impact of practice setting on ethical orientation and behavior. He looked at the attitudes and behaviors of lawyers concerning such matters as referral fees, accepting commissions from other parties without informing the client, and not forbidding clients from attempting to pay off officials. He found that lawyers held more permissive attitudes about these practices and were more likely to admit they engaged in such actions when they worked in certain practice settings. Thus lawyers practicing in the lower-status sector of the urban bar—those working in small law firms, dealing with small business and personal clients, and appearing before lower courts and local governmental offices—were far more prone to ethical violations than other segments of the bar. These settings magnified client demands for such violations and—because they were economically marginal—made lawyers more receptive to such demands.

As a result, the ethical climates of offices correlated strongly with type of practice setting. But Carlin's research should not necessarily be read as finding that practice setting directly controlled professional ideology. Ethical climates had independent effects on the orientation and behavior of individual lawyers within the office. In "peer" organized offices, the ethical climate had the strongest effects on individual members. In "stratified offices," the lawyers in the top strata of the firm tended to have strict ethical orientations, but those in the lower strata were found to have a more permissive orientation and to report having committed ethical breaches more frequently. Thus Carlin found what Hughes had called a "moral division of labor" (1958, p. 71) in the profession; lawyers in high-status corporate practice or in the top rungs of internally stratified firms did not encounter situations in which there were pressures to commit ethical violations, because work that entailed such pressures was left to practitioners with lower-status clients or to the bottom rungs of stratified firms (Carlin 1966, p. 177).

Carlin demonstrated that a lawyer's material circumstances were a significant correlate of his or her professional ideology, not with respect to general matters of honesty and fair dealing (on which there was consensus in the sample), but with respect to attitudes about practices that would be considered ethical in business. He questioned what was (and judging from the Stanley Commission report remains) a tenet of professional self-regulation, that ethical training during the course of professional education and disciplinary machinery during the course of practice could effectively police against norm violation. "In short, neither internalization nor formal enforcement is sufficient to bring about or fully account for differences in adherence to ethical standards. *The social setting of the lawyer's work*, especially the pattern of opportunities and pressures to which he is exposed in his practice, is equally if not more important" (Carlin 1966, p. 7).

Carlin's research contradicted the top-down view of professionalism. According to Carlin, a simple deviance model cannot explain violations of the code of ethics. It is not that certain lawyers fail to learn appropriate norms or that risk of punishment was too weak, but rather that different practice contexts exhibit fundamentally different conceptions of appropriate professional conduct. In our terms, these arenas produce different conceptions of professionalism. Strengthened ethics training in law school and stricter enforcement of the profession's code would not produce uniform ethical orientations or eliminate ethical violations. If the organized bar is serious about preventing the kinds of behavior that marginal practitioners are more likely to engage in than other strata within the profession, more fundamental reforms in the organization and delivery of legal services are necessary. These include measures that will alter the basic economic conditions of representing low-status personal clients, such as the expansion of legal services for lower-income groups (Carlin 1966, p. 176–82).

Lawyers for Hire: The Proletarianization Perspective

In *Lawyers for Hire* (1986), Eve Spangler conducts a qualitative examination of four legal worksites: large law firms, corporate law departments, government law departments, and legal services offices. Her focus in each site are employed lawyers, that is, those who do not have an ownership interest in the organization where they work. Spangler's project attempts to test a prominent, if widely disputed, theory of professional work, the proletarianization thesis.[8] The thesis, which is most strongly identified with

8. Critics of the proletarianization thesis argue that the technical aspects of professional work do not easily lend themselves to routinization and deskilling. For major tenants of the theory, see Freidson 1973, 1986, Larson 1977, 1980, and Derber 1982.

Charles Derber (1982; also Derber and Schwartz 1983), asserts that the professions in contemporary society are being subjected to a transformation of the work process that parallels the transformation of the labor process of craft workers during the industrial revolution. According to proletarianization theorists, just as industrial workers increasingly lost control over the work process due to the introduction of mass production and the corresponding deskilling of labor, professional workers, an increasing proportion of whom work as employees rather than as independent producers, are being deskilled—and alienated—by the redesign of professional work.

Proletarianization theory predicts that professionals will lose control of their work in three ways: (1) tasks will be decomposed and divided up among increasingly less skilled professionals or para-professionals ("technical proletarianization"); (2) professional workers will be subject to administrative rules that will dictate how they carry out tasks ("bureaucratic control"); and (3) professional workers will lose control of the ends to which their work and its products are put ("ideological proletarianization").

In *Lawyers for Hire*, Spangler argues that to one degree or another all four work settings she studied show the operation of these processes. We have found her descriptive accounts immensely useful, but we question whether she has demonstrated the validity of the proletarianization theory. And we have reservations about the value of the theory itself for an understanding of the role of ideology in the contemporary legal workplace.

The central thrust of the general theory of professional proletarianization on which Spangler relies is the analysis of the relationship between professional workers and capital. This relationship is assumed, a priori, to be both fixed and antagonistic. These assumptions make the question of ideology less salient than we believe it to be. To be sure, Charles Derber and other proponents of professional proleterianization recognize that the process has an ideological component. But the deterministic aspects of the theory make it appear that the ideological dimension is not central to the explanation of actual relationships in the workplace. Because proletarianization is posited as unavoidable, the theory gives little if any attention to the ways in which professional workers and owners struggle about definitions of what is or is not proper work for professionals, and the proper way that professional work should be performed and governed. We consider such struggle the very heart of the problem.

Michael Burawoy's critique of Harry Braverman's theory of deskilling in industrial organizations states the problem succinctly. Burawoy contends that Braverman portrays the degradation of work as "a cancerous growth" that has a momentum of [its] own (1985, pp. 54–55). If workers and capital are seen as locked in a fixed, antagonistic relationship, there would be little value in investigating the ideology they bring to the relationship: "[T]he crucial issue is that the interests that organize the daily life of workers are not given irrevocably; they cannot be imputed; they are produced and reproduced in particular ways. To assume, without further specification, that the interests of capital and labor are opposed leads to serious misunderstandings of the nature of capitalist control, if only because it provides an excuse to ignore the ideological terrain on which interests are organized" (Burawoy 1985, p. 29).

If ignorance of the ideological terrain leads to the failure of the deskilling theory as applied to industrial organizations, it is even more problematic in the realm of professional service firms. In professional firms, where associates can become partners and partners continue to function as workers, the relationship between "capital" and "workers" is far more complicated than in the industrial setting. Several dimensions of the professional organization are strongly connected to institutionally defined status systems. Elite corporate law firms, for example, hire from elite law schools, represent resourceful corporate actors, engage in high-status fields of law, and maintain distinctive patterns of work, career, and reward. These patterns reflect the character of cultural authority through which professionals establish claims over particular kinds of problems and institutional environments (see Starr 1982, pp. 32–59, Abbott 1988, Freidson 1986, pp. 209–30). The work life inside professional organizations reflects and reproduces these cultural patterns in numerous ways. Analyses that ignore the world views of professionals in these contexts risk misinterpreting the determinants of organizational structure and practice (see, e.g., Bosk 1979, pp. 188–92).

Perhaps it is for this reason that Spangler's observations do not appear to support her argument. The descriptions of the work process in the various settings do not identify a process of deskilling. Despite the use of forms, increasing computerization, and substantive specialization, work is organized in collegial fashion. In many work contexts these tendencies indicate rising skill levels rather than deskilling. Thus the proletarianization theory may misinterpret the technical changes occurring in the work processes of lawyers. Moreover, the proletarianization theory cannot readily explain what motivates lawyers to work so hard. Something other than bureaucratic control is responsible for the long hours and enthusiastic commitment that Spangler's lawyers exhibit.

Spangler's perspective is valuable because it focuses on processes of social change in the professional workplace. It is limited, however, because it fails to analyze the workplace ideologies of lawyers. In the sections that follow we offer preliminary versions of such analyses drawn from the existing literature.

Professional Ideology in Three Workplace Contexts

The legal workplace is an arena of professionalism in the sense that the specific organizational contexts in which lawyers work produce and reflect particular visions of professional ideals. These visions, what we refer to as workplace ideologies, correspond to the external relationships between the work organization and its environment, relationships among lawyers inside the organization, and the lawyerly roles actors adopt within the specific fields in which they practice. Although we do not have any empirical studies that apply the arena approach to legal work settings explicitly, the existing literature on corporate law firms, corporate legal departments, and legal services offices demonstrates the validity of this framework.

The Large Law Firm

Since the mid-1970s, the market for the services of large law firms has changed dramatically, the firms have grown rapidly, and their internal organization has been significantly altered (Nelson 1988; Galanter and Palay, Chapter 1 herein, and 1991). The shift to increasingly bureaucratic internal structures and to a more competitive, transaction-oriented market poses a serious challenge to the traditional ideology of large firms. Competing visions of how law firms should be organized have become apparent both in intense rivalry among firms, in which each claims to possess distinctive advantages in organization or style over the others, and in numerous conflicts inside firms over organizational policies, many of which have led to defections and leadership changes.

One of us recently completed a study of these transformations in large law firms, *Partners with Power* (Nelson 1988). The research focused on four large Chicago law firms, two that had developed bureaucratic structures by the early 1980s and two that had not. Despite many similarities in organizational structure and practice, Nelson found that the firms had developed different ideologies of professionalism that reflected their client bases and influenced internal patterns of management and work. In the two firms that had failed to develop the internal administrative and informational services characteristic of a bureaucratic organization, the leaders of the firms had criticized such arrangements as inconsistent with "professionalism." Among the two bureaucratic firms, only one had self-consciously adopted a "bureaucratic ideology" in the sense that its official policies explicitly promoted a formal managerial hierarchy, departmentalization, and substantive specialization. These policies had their origin in the founding of the firm, which occurred much later than for the other firms, and were in large part a strategy for gaining a market niche by offering corporate clients highly specialized, cost-effective services. Similar practices had developed in the other bureaucratic firm, primarily due to the powerful centralizing effects of representing a small number of very large corporate clients, but the expressed ideology of this firm opposed bureaucratic organization. The professional ideology of the firm exalted professional tradition and effectively cloaked what had taken place in practice, the construction of a bureaucratic organizational infrastructure.

The variations in workplace ideologies were apparent in the recruitment process, where firms competed with each other directly. One of the firms with a traditional organizational ideology represented to law students that they would not have to specialize quickly, that the firm saw itself as recruiting the most able law students who were more likely to thrive in a less structured work environment. The self-consciously bureaucratic firm, by contrast, hired associates directly into departments on the theory that it allowed the new hires a more rapid "professional" development by enabling them to become skilled specialists more quickly. Both firms appealed to students in the idiom of professionalism, even though both pursued opposing strategies.

The organization of work in the four firms also reflected appeals to norms of professionalism. Contrary to the proletarianization thesis, Nelson found that the work process in the firms had not been deskilled through the decomposition of jobs into constituent parts, but rather, that there had been an intensification of the traditional, status-based division of labor between partners and associates (1988, pp. 159–89). (Spangler reports a similar pattern in the Boston firms she studied [1986, p. 44].) The firms had successfully inculcated young lawyers with a high degree of commitment to their work, even though a large proportion of associates were unsure whether they planned to stay on after making partner. But there were significant differences in workplace norms across the firms. Lawyers in the two traditionally organized firms reported working significantly more hours than their counterparts in the two bureaucratic firms. Given that lawyers of comparable seniority earned similar incomes at the four firms, it was clear that the organizations had constructed different definitions of acceptable output levels corresponding to different ideals of what constituted an appropriate professional work life.

Nelson's findings contradicted Smigel's (1964) analysis of the role of professional values in the organization of the large law firm. In his study of Wall Street law firms of the 1950s, Smigel observed relatively little internal conflict and infrequent recourse to formal rules of policy and operation. In an interpretation quite similar to the "official" story of professionalism, Smigel attributed the informality and lack of conflict to the operation of official professional values. He posited that all members of the firms shared a set of values, derived from (or at least codified in) the code of professional responsibility, which shaped their behavior and obviated the need for internal regulation. Nelson found a very different picture. He found differences in professional ideology between partners and associates in the same firm, and between firms. Nelson concluded that official norms—such as the Code of Professional Responsibility—were not the source for the professional values of the firms he examined. He argued instead that "*professional values related to organizational policies arise inside the firm and reflect the managerial ideology of the elite in power*" (1988, p. 220). Thus "[i]t is possible for firms to tailor the meaning of professionalism to accommodate bureaucratic administrative and work-group structures" (1988, p. 226). Professionalism did not determine the organizational practice, but was constructed within in each firm according to its particular history and the interests of its most powerful partners.

Corporate Counsel

The work context of corporate legal counsel is an interesting and increasingly important arena of professionalism. Inside counsel have grown in numbers and status in recent years and show a new propensity for collective action within the organized bar (Rosen 1989; Lieber 1984; Mayer 1984). In the increasingly competitive market for corporate legal services, the top legal officers of corporations have become powerful figures because they control which law firms get selected for various projects (Nelson 1988, pp. 56–58). Despite these manifestations of rising status and power, corporate counsel occupy an ambiguous position both within the legal profession and within their employing organization. This raises particular problems for their conceptions of professionalism. Within the corporate sector of the profession they continue to suffer from the relatively lower status attached to working as employees of corporations. Lawyers in outside law firms question the ability of inside counsel to exercise the kind of independence from client demands that remains part of the official account of lawyer professionalism (Nelson 1988, pp. 83–85).[9] Nor is it clear whether management fully

9. Numerous articles in the legal press suggest that inside counsel are no longer considered status inferiors (e.g., Mager 1984, Lieber 1984, Ayer 1982). Yet the same articles that proclaim the "arrival" of corporate law departments as the status equivalents of corporate law firms take the law firm as their point of departure and unintentionally convey the opposite message. For example, when discussing recruiting standards for the legal departments of corporations Ayer states, "The 'real' lawyers are no longer just on the outside. Recruiting standards at Boise Cascade Corp. and many

accepts inside counsel as members of key corporate decision-making groups (Rosen 1984; Chayes and Chayes 1985).

The literature suggests that corporate counsel have dealt with these tensions by developing a professional ideology that combines a strong identification with the employer and an organization of work that reproduces traditional patterns of collegial control and a craft-like division of labor. Corporate counsel maintain the appearances and internal rhythms of a law firm: they look and act like lawyers, they have their own law offices within their corporations, and these offices are managed by lawyers. In this way they preserve their self-image as autonomous professionals. At the same time, the way inside counsel are recruited and rewarded insures that they will be sympathetic to the viewpoint of the management they work with.

The legal departments of corporations attract and socialize lawyers into a business ideology. As Spangler reports, many of the lawyers recruited into house counsel positions are lawyers departing corporate law firms (1986, p. 80). She suggests that these recruits "have no qualms about serving business interests," and that a more salient concern for most is the stigma that law firm attorneys attach to house counsel (Spangler 1986, pp. 80, 105). The lawyers who head legal departments and enjoy "near dictatorial" power over them identify strongly with the client. One general counsel informed Spangler that "I always feel I have one hat, and this is: I am a corporate officer who is a lawyer" (1986, pp. 74, 98–99). The career structure in corporations reinforces the business orientation. The corporate ranking system promotes staff lawyers at set intervals until a ceiling is reached. At that point the only way to move up in the organization is to advance into one of a limited number of supervisory positions in the legal department or to move out of the law department into a business executive position (Spangler 1986, pp. 82–87).

Corporate legal departments reflect the corporate cultures in which they exist. But outside of some obvious differences from autonomous practice that flow from organizational life in large bureaucratic organizations, such as the participation of lawyers in the centralized personnel policies of the corporation, and some greater tendency for bureaucratic work rules concerning the use of document forms, the organization of work in corporate legal departments seems quite similar to that encountered in autonomous professional firms. Most law departments are collegial enclaves within the corporation. Spangler reports, "Given a choice between controlling staff by de-

---

other corporations parallel those of private law firms" (1982, p. 10); and Lieber asserts that "the increase in volume and complexity of legal work performed by in-house counsel has had the effect of making in-house practice as exciting and vital as law firm practice" (1984, p. 23).

skilling them and controlling them by motivating them, law department supervisors clearly have chosen the latter strategy" (1986, p. 89). Work expectations are dramatically different from those in corporate law firms; in-house lawyers work fewer hours on a more predictable basis. As a result, corporate law departments may be a particularly attractive setting for female attorneys with child-rearing responsibilities. But like the large law firms we discussed above, corporate law departments rely on a culture of professional work to insure that lawyers are committed to their tasks.

Although corporate counsel appear less interested in independence from their employers than in involvement in their affairs, studies suggest that corporate counsel can play either of two distinct functions within a corporation. Robert Rosen (1984) labels these *legal risk analysis* and *decision consulting* (see also Slovak 1979, Chayes and Chayes 1985, p. 281, Spangler 1986, p. 93). The former entails a relatively circumscribed role for the lawyer, in that he or she produces data on legal risks for use by the responsible businesspersons in the firm, but does not otherwise attempt to influence the decision. In decision consulting, however, lawyers blend legal advice with business advice. The lawyer thus "draws upon the corporation's conception of itself embedded in its cultures and policies [to become] an influential member of the corporation" (Rosen 1984, pp. 257–58).

Rosen recognizes the paradox that confronts house counsel. Professional autonomy is gained at the expense of influence in corporate decisions. He argues that a resolution of the paradox is possible if lawyers engage in decision consulting, but maintain a strong posture of ethical independence. "[C]orporations need professionals to exercise influence. They want professionals to elaborate corporate interests and commitments. . . . But professionalism is in tension with inward-looking bureaucratization. It fights bureaucracy in the name of improved methods and professional autonomy" (1984, pp. 316–17). Thus Rosen asserts that lawyers can use professionalism strategically to enhance the rationality and fairness of corporate decision making.

Rosen's analysis is intriguing. It is not clear to what extent he actually observed the two roles being played by corporate counsel in the corporations he studied. Whether his analysis is empirical or normative, he offers only a vague interpretation of the kinds of professional training or institutional structures necessary for achieving the twofold goal of influence and professional autonomy. What these analyses suggest, however, is that even within a workplace that is thought of as rather strictly constraining professional independence, it may be possible for lawyers to construct quite different models of the lawyerly role.

Again it is obvious that more research is needed to develop a better understanding of the professional ideology and work of corporate counsel. What research exists, however, underscores the significance of issues involving professionalism. How lawyers are motivated to work and the role they take in corporate decision making are discussed and must be understood in terms of professionalism. Despite Rosen's optimism about the prospects for blending professional autonomy and influence, it appears that the workplace ideology of lawyering inside a corporation favors compliance with management over the assertion of independent professional judgment. Whether, how often, and with what exceptions this is in fact the case remain topics for further inquiry.

Legal Services for the Poor

The significance of professionalism in the legal workplace is not limited to the private sector. Indeed, one of the clearest instances of the link between work, motivation, and professional ideology appears among lawyers for the poor.

In *Poor People's Lawyers in Transition* (1982), Jack Katz provides an account of the history and social organization of legal services in Chicago. Katz describes the competition between two organizational models for civil representation of the poor. The first was the "legal aid" model that dominated the local scene prior to the war on poverty. This model provided "day-in-court" representation and recruited lawyers with low-status credentials who had no better career opportunities. Legal aid lawyers adopted a working ideology of "reasonableness": they sought to work with state welfare and lower court officials without challenging the system's treatment of poor people as a category. They drew satisfaction from acceptance into this subcommunity, as well as from easing (however temporarily) the circumstances of individuals in trouble.

The "legal services" model, in contrast, was born in the Office of Economic Opportunity and emphasized reform. It addressed the problems of the poor as a group rather than as individuals. Legal services attracted lawyers who had the credentials necessary to pursue careers in corporate law firms, but who chose legal services careers for political reasons. (Many had been active in social movements in the sixties.) Katz found that even though they had a strong ideological commitment, legal services attorneys had to break out of the routine and continuous representation of clients in the neighborhoods or they quickly suffered "burnout." This led them to seek cases or activities that were "professionally significant" due to the complexity of legal issues or the magnitude of the political or fiscal stakes involved.

During the period Katz examined (roughly 1965 to 1974), the legal services model eventually won out over the legal aid model. In Chicago, the legal services group became the sole recipient of federal funding; legal aid was re-established as an agency of United Charities. In the 1970s, legal services grew quite dramatically in staff and budget and differentiated organizationally, developing specialized appellate and subject matter units and reorganizing neighborhood offices to provide lawyers with more control over client intake and caseloads. Limited funding combined with the activist orientation of lawyers pursuing legal services careers has contributed to serious tensions within the organization. Staff attorneys are unionized; strikes over salaries and working conditions occur frequently.

Katz's study of the differences between legal aid and legal services in Chicago in the 1970s illustrates the impact of professional ideology on the legal workplace. The two groups of Chicago lawyers Katz studied performed the same general function, but they developed different working styles, different organizational forms, and different representational strategies that reflected the very different professional visions these two groups brought to their work.

Structure and Ideology in the Legal Workplace

These brief analyses of workplace contexts suggest that lawyers possess widely varying conceptions of professional ideals that correspond to the historical and practical circumstances of their work. One interpretation of the patterns we have sketched is that the organizational structures of practice determine the professional ideologies of lawyers. This is too simplistic an explanation and is at odds with our conception of workplaces as arenas in which professional ideals are constantly formed and reformed by the lawyers who work there. It is not surprising that ideology will tend to reproduce the social structure that created it. That does not imply, however, that social structure consistently produces ideology, but ideology never influences social structure.

Perhaps the clearest instance of the effect of ideology in the cases we studied here is the history of the formation of legal services. The ideology of legal reform associated with the war on poverty gave rise to a fundamentally different mode of organizing legal services for the poor. In a similar but less visible fashion, the organizational structures of corporate law firms and corporate legal departments were shaped by the professional ideologies of founding partners and managers. These structures and ideologies have been reproduced and reshaped by succeeding generations of lawyers in response to changes in the material circumstances of practice and shifts in the intellectual climate surrounding the practice of law but often still bear a remarkable resemblance to the structures and ideologies present at the time of formation. Practices that reflected the ideology of earlier generations, once embedded in institutional structure, may appear as given or inherent in the nature of the work or the organization itself. Ideological product thus becomes material reality.

Bourdieu quotes Durkheim to this effect:

> [I]n each of us in varying proportions, there is part of yesterday's man; it is yesterday's man who inevitably predominates in us, since the present amounts to little compared with the long past in the course of which we were formed and from which we result. Yet we do not sense this man of the past, because he is inveterate in us; he makes up the unconscious part of ourselves.
>
> Consequently we are led to take no account of him, any more than we take account of his legitimate demands. Conversely, we are very much aware of the most recent attainments of civilization, because, being recent, they have not yet had time to settle into our unconscious. [1977, p. 79]

Organizational sociology has in recent years become sensitive to the possibility that many aspects of the formal structures of organizations are rooted in symbolic processes rather than in the technical requirements for organizational practice. To gain legitimacy, organizations sometimes imitate the structures and rules of other organizations in the institutional environment (Meyer and Rowan 1978). Organizations often collect far more information than they can process, in part, it is argued, as a means of making symbolic commitments to certain values (Feldman and March 1981). Some scholars suggest that these ideological processes are particularly significant for professional organizations, where professional education is seen as "provid[ing] members with a common culture, in the sense of shared definitions of problems and common repertoires for managing those problems" (Tolbert 1988, p. 104; see also DiMaggio and Powell 1983).

Although we might disagree with the centrality this implies for professional education, we agree with the more fundamental assertion that the core technology of a professional field such as the law is heavily dependent on the manipulation of information, language, and symbols, and thus is substantially ideological in content. Robert Gordon has given the most articulate statement of the ideological model of practice. After arguing that shifts in large-scale ideology could be linked to changes in the legal field of reorganization, he reflects:

> When talking to lawyers about this project, I frequently come across a deeply ingrained suspicion of the notion that they should be depicted as a species of intellectuals producing ideology. Very few of them are self-consciously any-

> thing of the kind. Naturally they think of themselves as practical persons occupied with practical affairs, and doubtless this attitude helps to explain the tenacity of legal-technological and interest-group explanations of what they do. Yet when a lawyer helps a client arrange a transaction so as to take maximum advantage of the current legal framework, he or she becomes one of the army of agents who confirm that framework by reinforcement and extend it by interpretation into many niches of social life. The framework is an ideological one, i.e., a set of assertions, arguments, and implicit assumptions about power and right. [1983, p. 110]

Just as Gordon argues that lawyers are ideological agents in the work they perform, we suggest they are agents of professional ideology in the workplace. In reinforcing or resisting organizational practices they encounter in the workplace, they shape the very organizational structures through which legal services are delivered.

Conclusion

In this chapter we moved from the analysis of the production of professional ideology in the collective arena of official bar politics to the examination of professional ideology in the arenas of legal practice. Although this has been only a brief foray, the insights we have gained suggest the value of studying the arenas of professionalism. From the arenas perspective we can better understand that the official rhetoric of the bar offers only a partial account of the transformations occurring in the legal profession. The professionalism crusade reflects the continuing need for the myth of a unitary profession. The largely symbolic character of the crusade has been dictated by the constraints on concerted action inherent in the politics of bar associations. The studies of the legal workplace we reviewed imply that the professional ideologies lawyers develop in the workplace are critical to the continued reproduction of the professional organization, to the sense of satisfaction or alienation lawyers derive from practice, and to the roles they play with respect to clients and the legal system. Yet they also revealed that workplace ideologies often served some groups more than others in the organization and legitimated practices that arguably are harmful to the larger society.

The arenas approach thus explicates the relationship between professional ideology and social power. Lawyers' visions of their working life and working relationships are intimately related to the kinds of organizations they construct and the roles they play in political, economic, and social exchange.

Scholarship on the legal profession must examine the construction and deployment of professional ideology in the myriad of contexts in which lawyers appear, not just the arenas that are most visibly associated with the power of the professional group. By doing so it will advance a broader understanding of how the practices of lawyers reflect, reproduce, and alter the social order.

Chapter Six

Professionalism as Model and Ideology

Eliot Freidson

Professionalism is under attack. The legal profession is accused by radicals and liberals of elitism, discriminating against minorities in recruitment, training, and employment, and failing to protect the interests of the poor and the underprivileged. Its members are charged by, for example, Auerbach (1976), with being 'hired guns' who protect the interests only of those able to pay them handsomely—namely, the rich and the powerful. Others, far more politically influential over the past decade or so, argue from the point of view of both the consumer movement and that of neoclassical economics that law is a business like any other and should be stripped of special privileges and subjected to free competition in the marketplace. When the leaders of the profession invoke ethics and the values of professionalism, critics declare that invocation the promotion of a self-serving ideology masking naked self-interest. At their most charitable, they consider professionalism to be an antiquated survival from an earlier time irrelevant to the work of those called professionals today. Does the idea of professionalism have any relevance to us?[1] Is it at all defensible in light of the patent deficiencies of its institutions?

These questions cannot be answered easily because much of the debate about professionalism is clouded by unstated assumptions and inconsistent and incomplete usages. Most important, it is not informed by a systematic method of thinking. I hope to clarify the issues by first distinguishing the characteristic limitations of the most common usages employed in the debate

Revision of a paper read at the annual meeting of the American Association of Law Schools, Miami Beach, 30, January 1988.

1. Another question of some intrinsic value is why all this criticism of professionalism arose when it did. For a lively chronicle of the rise of such criticism among sociologists and historians, and a tentative explanation of it, see Metzger (1987).

and noting the absence of a systematic analytic or ideal model of professionalism. I will then sketch such a model and discuss its relationship to the alternatives implied by most attacks on the professions. Finally, I will discuss how the professions can be defended by the use of an analytic model and the implications an effective defense would have for the regulation of the professions.

Versions of Professionalism

The idea of profession or professionalism is developed in a number of distinctly different ways.[2]

First of all, it is a naturally created social label applied to a limited number of occupations considered to be in some way superior to ordinary occupations. This is the lay or folk idea (Becker 1970, p. 92). It is a very loosely organized construct, including within it criteria of relatively high prestige, extended, specialized training, and being paid for one's work. It might be useful to call it the *commonsense* idea of professionalism.

The commonsense idea of professionalism is developed passively: it is not elaborated, systematized, or refined self-consciously so much as it grows out of everyday, social usage. Among professionals themselves, as Nelson and Trubek rightly argue, its substance varies with the arenas in which they work and their perspectives on them (Chapter 5 herein). When it is expanded and articulated by those who think about it self-consciously, it changes. In English-speaking nations, where professions have often been self-organized rather than created by the state, the idea of profession is elaborated by the leaders of a profession in the course of making a claim to professional standing and used as a political tool for dealing with legislatures, the media, and the public at large. It is this larger policy arena that concerns me here, for at this level "professionalism" is used not only to represent the profession to outsiders, but also to its own members. Commonsense usage is expanded to emphasize those characteristics of an occupation that justify special standing and privilege: it becomes a *profession's* portrayal of profession. Its content is largely determined by the political and ceremonial needs of the profession, and its function is primarily to advance and defend its position. While many versions of the term emphasize the same things—for example, probity and public service—its ideological character, particularly in those substantive areas where the profession's internal politics or self-interest is threatened, precludes its development into a systematic and consistent whole.

2. For an extensive review of the varied usages of "profession," see Freidson 1986, pp. 20–62.

Most of the debate that surrounds professions compares the actual performance of their members with either the ideological claims made by those supporting them or the commonsense expectations of the public and the commentators. Comparison between promise and performance reveals discrepancies that lead some critics, for example, Roth (1974), to reject the relevance of the idea of profession for understanding occupations with professional standing and others to attack professional standing itself. But what is rejected is either commonsense professionalism or ideological professionalism, neither of which is developed as a model or analytic concept.

The needs of analysis are different from those of either commonsense thinking or ideology, for neither of the latter is compelled to create a systematic, logically coherent model of all essential characteristics based on a stated rationale or principle. Commonsense thinking need not concern itself with contradictions between various usages so long as it can segregate them by invoking them in different contexts. Ideological and ceremonial conceptions of professionalism are shaped primarily by convenience and necessity and need include only those elements that defend threatened interests by denying characteristics deserving condemnation and claiming virtues worthy of praise. This variation in emphasis by those who speak for professions is clearly shown by Solomon's analysis of the responses of leaders of the bar to the crises they perceived over a thirty-five-year period (Chapter 4 herein).

By contrast, an analytic model attempts to seek out and resolve contradictions and to include within its framework all that is necessary to create a systematic whole. It can be a model only when it does not attempt to describe reality but instead creates a conceptual yardstick against which the empirical world can be compared. Modeling is a systematic way of thinking about reality by selecting what is most consequential or important. It is most satisfying when its terms explain what they address, but if they don't, then it is sufficient if they show plausibly how the model works.

Models of Professionalism

An important but often overlooked characteristic of analytic models in the social sciences is that although they can be used in a purely neutral fashion, they can also be used prescriptively to represent what should exist and to guide practical efforts to realize them. They can also serve as ideologies to focus and organize political activity. Indeed, the most effective ideologies are those based on models sufficiently abstract to be applicable to a wide range of issues and circumstances. Those models can thus explain systematically what is wrong with the world and stand as guidelines by which wrong can be righted. The most persuasive attacks on professions come from people who themselves, explicitly or implicitly, are advancing an ideology based on an analytic model. They attack the professions not merely for deficiencies in performance but because their existence stands in the way of realizing another, more desirable model.

The basic policy question underlying discussions of professionalism is *how the work of those we now call professionals should be organized and controlled*. Two quite different models for organizing work stand behind the most powerful criticisms of professionalism today. One is advanced by neoclassical economists who attack professionalism as a barrier to what *should* exist—namely, the individual freedom of workers in the marketplace to offer whatever goods and services they desire and of consumers to buy whatever they wish.[3] The wholly logical and utopian analytic model active here is the free market. Another, quite different model is implicit in critiques of professionalism that stress order, efficiency, and comprehensive service: many conservative and some radical critics attack professionalism as a barrier to the attainment of a planned system of efficient services that would exist if it were subject to the centralized, monocratic control of either private corporate capital firms or (representing the people) agencies of the state. The underlying model here is that of rational-legal bureaucracy.

There is in theory a third model implied by the position of some of those who criticize the professions for elitism. These commentators advance an egalitarian ideal whereby all workers collectively, rather than managers or experts, determine what work is to be done, who is to do it, and how.[4] Unfortunately for their argument, a plausible model for the exercise of collective or egalitarian control over work seems to presuppose a very simple division of labor in which all work is sufficiently unskilled to be easily learned and performed by all workers. There is no provision for the elaborate specialization characteristic of large, complex societies with advanced standards of living.[5] Perhaps this theoretical difficulty is responsible for the

3. The best known exponent of this position is Milton Friedman (1962, pp. 137–60), who urges the elimination of professional licensing.

4. See, for example, Gordon 1977. In Wright's considerably more sophisticated analysis, expertise is recognized as a source of exploitation, but it is not considered *intrinsically* exploitative so long as "ownership rights in skills have been equalized . . . [when] differential incomes and control over the social surplus cease to be linked to differential skills" (Wright 1985, p. 85). This position is extremely rare among left-oriented critics.

5. Rothschild and Russell's review of studies of democratic participatory productive organizations (1986) notes that they all tend to have a simple division of labor. My guess is that the primary sources of difficulty for exponents of egalitarianism are their inability to recognize that functional differentiation need not represent inequality and their conflation of two quite different things—the authority of political, economic, and administrative power with the authority of expertise. While

paradox that much of the criticism of professionalism by radicals seems to advance the implicit alternative of the individualistic free market that underlies capitalism (e.g., Collins 1979, pp. 197–204). Without having a plausible alternative model of their own, egalitarian and populist critics sustain their position solely by rhetoric.

There are, then, two clear alternatives for envisioning how professional services could be organized after eliminating professional privileges—Adam Smith's free market and Max Weber's monocratic, rational-legal bureaucracy. But no analogous model of professionalism figures in policy debates in the same way and on the same level of abstraction. Nonetheless, as Gordon and Simon note in this volume, professionalism can be conceived of as a distinct alternative to the free market and bureaucracy. Let me sketch out the essentials of such a model and then discuss its relevance to the debate.

An Ideal-Typical Model of Professionalism

Professionalism, like the free market and bureaucracy, represents a method of organizing the performance of work. It differs from the free market and from bureaucracy in that it revolves around *the central principle that the members of a specialized occupation control their own work* (cf. Johnson 1972, p. 45). By control, I mean that the members of the occupation determine the content of the work they do. Absolute control presupposes controlling the goals, terms, and conditions of work as well as the criteria by which it can be legitimately evaluated. By contrast, in the free market, consumer demand and the free competition of workers for consumer choice determine what work will be done, who shall do what work, how, and for how much pay. In bureaucracy, the market for labor and its products is institutionalized by rational-legal methods: the executives of organizations decide what product will be made or service offered, who shall make it, by what methods, and how it shall be offered to consumers.

Given this fundamental criterion of occupational control over work, one can build a model around the circumstances and characteristics necessary for occupations to gain and maintain such control. This requires attention to methods of controlling recruitment and training, entrance into the labor market under conditions that allow gaining a living from performing the

---

many, Foucault (e.g. 1980, pp. 146–65) being the most prominent, would impute "power" to expertise, they refer to the influence of discourse or persuasion and semantically conflate it with the power of material sanctions, which they recognize as quite different.

work, and the procedures and criteria by which performance is organized and evaluated at work. In the professional model, both individual consumers and executives or managers (who are corporate or organizational consumers of labor) are excluded from such control. But since specialized knowledge and skill have no intrinsic connection with material (as opposed to cultural) capital or power, an occupation can fend off control of their work by individual or corporate consumers only by having power delegated to it by the state. An essential element of an analytic model of professionalism must therefore be to specify the activities and institutions that obtain the delegation of state power and subsequently maintain the conditions that assure its continuation.

In order to have power delegated to it, an occupation must be organized as an identifiable group: it cannot be a mere aggregation of individuals who claim to have the same set of skills. Only if it is an organized group, or if someone speaking for it manages to establish a corporate identity for its members, can it be dealt with collectively as a defined social category. The profession becomes an organized, corporate body either by the action of its own members independently of the state, as has commonly been the case in English-speaking nations, or by the actions of the state in creating specialized civil servants, as was more common in countries on the European continent. However the occupation becomes organized, those holding power must be persuaded that the body of knowledge and skill ascribed to the occupation is of such a special character to warrant privilege. A number of claims provide the grounds for privilege—the functional importance of the body of knowledge and skill for the well-being of some significant segment of society, its intrinsic cultural importance, its unusually complex and esoteric character, and its superiority over the knowledge and skill claimed by competing occupations. Perhaps the most powerful claim is that there would be grave danger to the public if there were no control over those who offer their services—that the work provides access to "guilty knowledge" (Hughes 1971, p. 288) that only those who can be trusted should have, and that serious consequences to the individual or the public at large can result from poor work. Central to effective claims is the idea that the profession's skills are so complex and esoteric that lay people are not well enough informed to be able to perform the work themselves, or to choose the competent over the incompetent, or to judge the quality of the work and even its outcome.

Beyond being persuaded that the occupation's body of knowledge and skill merits special protection, the state must also be persuaded that the occupation as a corporate body is able to control itself without abusing its privilege. In short, the occupation must display institutional arrangements that make self-regulation plausible. Such arrangements include methods of recruiting new members selectively and restrictively by using screening criteria of ability or probity, and the maintenance of training institutions that are sufficiently standardized to permit assuming that all who complete their training successfully will be of at least minimally acceptable competence. Additional assurance can be provided by requiring examinations of those who have completed their training before allowing them to work. Not only competence, but trustworthiness must also be assured. The claim may be that recruits are selected who have "good character" in addition to potential competence. Codes of ethics may be created both to display concern for the issue and to provide members with guides to proper performance at work. Peer or collegial review to assure adequate performance at work may be established, as may regulatory institutions such as disciplinary committees. Floating above all such claims and activities, of course, is the ceremonial rhetoric of the leadership.

With their material interests secured by their control over their work and their protected position in the marketplace, members of professions are able to develop a deep, lifelong commitment to and identification with their work: it becomes a "central life-interest" (Dubin, Hedley, and Taveggia 1976, pp. 281–341). Concerned with advancing the discipline to which they have become committed, some will experiment, innovate, and do research to expand their body of knowledge and skill both for its own sake and to find new practical applications for it. To protect the integrity of their profession and its work, they will monitor and correct each other's work and discipline or even expel deviants when necessary.

Collegiality is a central element of the professional model (Waters 1989). It distinguishes professionalism from both the unfettered individualistic competition among workers in a free market and the formal hierarchies of rational-legal bureaucracy. Protection from competition allows the development and maintenance of such collegiality, of course, but bitter competition between members themselves and between various specialties within the profession is always possible. In order to promote a professional community professions attempt to limit potentially divisive economic competition among their members by promulgating rules designed both to temper the spirit and substance of intraprofessional competition and to establish a basic income floor for all its members. Established within the profession is an egalitarian, collegial atmosphere in which the greatest rewards are symbolic. As Parsons (1939, pp. 185–99) pointed out some time ago, professionals are not distinguished from people in business by being altruistic rather than self-interested. They, too, are self-interested, but for them success depends more on gaining the symbolic rewards offered by their colleagues than on gaining a high income. Professional honors are accorded to those who advance the discipline by unusual achievement in its daily practice, by innovation, and by employing it to make an important contribution to the public good.

The Virtues of Professionalism

All this should sound familiar, for it is an argument assembled from bits and pieces freely borrowed from the major writers on the professions.[6] But here those bits and pieces are brought together in a systematic way, and are not advanced as fact, but as a model of the elements that together allow people to control their own highly specialized work in the spirit of service to others and the advancement of their discipline. The model specifies the conditions for professionalism, just as those of the free market and rational-legal bureaucracy specify the conditions for universal opulence (in Adam Smith's terms) or formal rationality. None of those models faithfully describes the way professions, markets, and bureaucracies actually perform. All are ideological and analytic in character, advancing a desired ideal as well as an analytic construct.

Both economists and planners for state and corporate enterprises are well aware of the way empirical versions of the professional model obstruct their aims. Understandably, they have not dwelt on its virtues. Rather, they dwell on the virtues of what will be gained by their own alternatives once the obstruction of professionalism is removed—more goods and services at lower prices and greater variety, more innovation, more predictability and reliability, greater efficiency, and the like. In contrast, those speaking for the professions today have employed a purely reactive, mostly commonsense and ceremonial defense. But once one conceives of professionalism as a model, one can identify potential virtues that commonsense thinking alone overlooks.[7]

The professional model is based on the democratic notion that people are capable of controlling themselves by cooperative, collective means and that in the case of complex work, those who perform it are in the best position to make sure that it is done well. It contains within it the assumption that when

6. Space requires me to limit my references to those from whom I have borrowed most liberally: Carr-Saunders and Wilson 1933, Parsons 1968b, Goode 1957, 1960, 1969, Hughes 1971, Moore 1970, Johnson 1972, Larson 1977, and Abbott 1988. Some of my own contributions may be found in Freidson 1970 and Freidson 1986.

7. For some examples of past conceptions of the virtues of professionalism, see Spencer 1896, Tawney 1920, Carr-Saunders and Wilson 1933, T.H. Marshall 1939, Parsons 1968. For a recent discussion of the ideal of professionalism in law in the light of the approach of economists, see Simon 1985.

people can control their own work, and when their work, while specialized, is complex and challenging, they will be committed to it rather than alienated from it. According to the terms of the model, people find intrinsic value and interest in the work itself, which leads them to want to do it well. Furthermore, they constitute a kind of community in that they interact on grounds of strongly held common interests both in maintaining their professional position and in performing the work they do (Goode 1957). Thus, they are alienated neither from their work nor from each other, nor, insofar as they believe they advance the good of others through their work, are they alienated from society. In short, as Gordon and Simon observe in this volume, the ideal of professionalism provides many of the conditions that neutralize Marx's analysis of alienation from work under capitalism (Chapter 7 herein).[8]

Professionalism encourages an additional activity of some importance. It provides a milieu favorable to intellectual innovation—the development of new knowledge, skills, and ideas. But that innovation is not restricted merely to developing new modes of satisfying the perceived needs or demands of consumers in a marketplace or the demands of those who control organizations. More important, because it is insulated from the need to respond immediately to the demands of others, it can transcend the status quo and received opinion to an extent that can only be considered revolutionary. The innovations made possible are richer and more varied than would be the case under a free market or a rational-legal bureaucracy. Research and theorizing that threaten the foundation of the practical work of "normal science" (Kuhn 1962) become possible, as does questioning the legitimacy of conventional practices and policies.

It may seem inappropriate to impute to professionalism the function of critical thinking and the creation of new ideas and knowledge. The former function is usually assigned to those whom social scientists call intellectuals,[9] while the latter is assigned to scholars and scientists. To many, the professional is someone who merely applies available knowledge to the solution of practical problems—the practicing doctor and lawyer being prominent exemplars.[10] Intellectuals, scholars, and scientists, in turn, are

8. For a brief statement of Marx's position, see Marx 1972, pp. 69–80, 116–25. Also see Arendt 1959, pp. 71–117, for a penetrating critique of Marx's conception of work and Haworth 1977 for a conception of a society oriented toward satisfying work rather than consumption, a conception organized around professionalism.

9. For a brief review of the most prominent writings on intellectuals, see Freidson 1986, pp. 9–15.

10. They too, however, are in a position in which they can exercise judgment independent of their clients, balancing the interest of the individual client against that of other clients and the public at large. For a sophisticated and sensitive analysis of the independence of practicing lawyers, see Gordon 1988.

not considered to be professionals. How one chooses to use a word is of course somewhat arbitrary, but if we wish to take into account the institutions that make such activities as the "disinterested" pursuit of knowledge for its own sake possible on a regular and predictable basis by a large number of people, then we must include scholars and scientists among professionals. They could not exist without such institutions. Neither could most intellectuals.

Ever since the nineteenth century and the decline of the gentlemanly amateur scholar/scientists who relied on personal resources or patronage for their livings, the institutions of professionalism, tied to universities, have been the shelters within which modern intellectuals, scholars, and scientists work. Like the practicing professions, they control the recruitment, training, and employment of their members. Furthermore, most cannot make a living by scholarship or research any more than most intellectuals can do so by their writing. The university teaching jobs that they control provide them with their living. Those jobs require daily engagement with the issues of scholarship and research and provide the free time in which to pursue rather than merely teach them. Following Parsons (1969) then, I would include scholars and scientists among those occupations today that resemble the ideal model of professionalism.

There is more to the building of an analytical model of professionalism than including scholars and scientists among the professions, however. It must also be recognized that the conventional practicing professions also produce new knowledge and techniques by exploring their own concepts and theories rather than merely passively serving others' demands. The traditional professions have been graced in the past by individual practitioners who made new discoveries or who have raised their voices against the accepted practices of their time, and there remain some who do so today. But the closer reality comes to the model of professionalism, the more such activity becomes possible on a routine, institutionalized basis primarily by members of the profession who serve in the special role of teaching.

Practitioners, of course, are heavily involved in the day to day activity of serving others, so one cannot expect most of them to be routinely engaged in scholarship, research, or the like.[11] But professions control the recruitment, training, and certification of their own members, and insofar as the process is institutionalized to ensure some standardization of the outcome, formal schools will perform those functions, with special members of the profession serving as faculty. Insofar as they are full-time faculty, those in professional

11. The fact of having no full-time instructors explains some of the past and present weakness of the crafts: they have been unable to prevent others' innovations by anticipating and controlling them, depending almost entirely on the frail reed of trade secrets, or, in medieval terms, "mysterys."

schools are in the same position as conventional scientists and scholars in universities—supported economically by the practice of teaching in circumstances that leave them a fair amount of free time to theorize and do research. They, too, are insulated from the practical demands and needs of the outside world and in a position to develop ideas and make discoveries somewhat independently of it. Like scholars and scientists in universities, concerned with the development and practice of their specialized body of knowledge and skill, committed to the goals or purposes of their craft, they may pursue the unexamined logical implications of what is known and extend them well past immediate practical necessity.

While these institutional grounds for independent thought and research that professionalism provides are much too important to ignore, it is obviously dangerous to exaggerate the degree of independence that is possible. Quite apart from the impossibility of ever being entirely free of the perspectives and prejudices of one's historical time and place, a practical limit on independence is posed by the impotence of knowledge and the dependence of its bearers on the dominant powers for their protection. What they do collectively, therefore, cannot deviate so far from the interests of those powers that they threaten them overtly. But the collectivity provides a general shelter within which highly critical modes of thought can develop well past what is conventionally accepted.

These innovative cognitive activities characteristic of professionalism provide a source of growth and enrichment in knowledge, values and technique that could not be produced by workers wholly dependent on satisfying the demands that others formulate or primarily concerned with serving their own material interests. While the extension of old ideas and the creation of new may lead to the creation of new demands that increase the number and value of professional jobs, it is only the most vulgar view that implies deliberate intention to do so. In any case, without meaning to imply that professions have a corner on the market for Truth, their capacity to pursue new knowledge, techniques, values, and ideas from a relatively independent point of view is a virtue. It can make an important contribution to the possibility of developing a more humane, richer, and more effectively functioning society.

The Inadequacy of the Present Defense

This conceptual construct, professionalism, advances a kind of blueprint for organizing work in a manner that can be defended as more desirable than the available alternatives. It is coherent in design, shows how and why it deviates from the models based on free competition and rational order, and justifies its deviation by its virtues. It shows the interrelationship among various attitudes, activities and institutions, and given ends. Thus, it provides the raw material not only for a defensive ideology employed merely to fend off criticism, but also for an aggressive or offensive ideology directed at extending and strengthening professionalism in the real world in the direction of the ideal model and its benefits.

In current debate, few if any from outside the professions have defended them. Indeed, most who are not members of conventionally recognized professions have joined in the attack even though a great many of them are academics whose own positions are sheltered by professional institutions. Among academics, most sociologists attack professions for exclusionary practices that contribute to inequality. Those critics often sound like the economists, who understandly attack them as monopolists who interfere with the operation of the free market. Political scientists (e.g., Gilb 1966) attack them as private governments unresponsive to public needs. Historians (e.g., Auerbach 1976) attack the elitist and exclusionary nature of their past activities. Those prominent in practical policy affairs—planners and heads of state agencies in the public sector, and executives, managers and investors in the private sector—more often than not see the professions as obstacles between them and their goals.

Most of those who attempt to reply to such criticism have been members of the conventionally recognized practicing professions—some in their capacity as officials of professional associations, and some especially prominent in other ways. This has encouraged a focus on individual professions rather than on the principle of professionalism, and reactive and defensive rather than assertive tactics. Those who defend their own profession do not defend other professions and may even join others in attacking them—representatives of medicine and law, for example, often attack each other publicly. They are not aware that all professions share a common interest that is threatened by exponents of the alternative models. Furthermore, because the defenders are usually official or quasi-official representatives of their professions, they cannot escape being prisoners of the politics of their own associations. They can neither openly concede patently indefensible abuses as anything other than anomolous or rare, nor propose or agree to corrective actions that are unacceptable to some important bloc of their profession. The consequence is that their defenses have been weak, partial, inconsistent, and in some cases even misleading.

Because all professions in the United States today can count on a fair degree of respect and trust, albeit ambivalent and varying in degree from one to another, many of their claims are likely to be accepted by the public and the politicians who sanction their privileges. But when the position of the professions seriously interferes with the economic and political interests of capital or the state, capital and the state have the power to change public opinion and reduce support for professional institutions. Like all workers, intellectual or no, professionals have no tangible power of their own. They possess only their knowledge and skill, the essence of their labor. Therefore, the professions are highly vulnerable to political and economic pressures. Medicine, the most prestigious and wealthy of them all, provides an instructive example of ultimate weakness in the face of the power of the state and of capital. It is being forced to change in ways that were inconceivable twenty years ago,[12] and it is possible (though not probable) that law will share its fate in the future.[13] Although I certainly do not believe that the professions are on the way to settling into the position of a true industrial proletariat—indeed, not even industrial workers in the United States may be said to be in such a position—it is quite possible that the conditions of professional work will move further away from those specified by the ideal-typical model I have sketched here. A decline in relative income is likely, but that has little relevance to professionalism as such so long as it does not drop to truly penurious levels.

Present defenses, I believe, can do little to prevent the changes going on in the United States today. I have already noted that the leaders of the professions are the intellectual prisoners of a purely reactive ideology as well as the political prisoners of the conflicting interests that characterize their associations. As Schneyer's analysis (Chapter 3 herein) of the process of creating the 1983 ABA Model Rules of Professional Conduct shows, the official reforms have been limited mostly to what is acceptable to a heterogeneous membership. They are also limited by an ideology that is insufficiently systematic to provide adequate intellectual guidance, and seriously distorted by reliance on elaborations of traditional, commonsense conceptions of professionalism. The ideology they employ is an intellectual patchwork created from selected fragments of idealized history, moral precepts, pious exhortations, optimistic interpretations of the profession's members' capacity and inclination to serve the public good generously, and obsession with symbolic matters of tradition, convention, and propriety such as advertising, unionization, and the like. The worn thread that holds the patchwork to-

12. For appraisals of the present position of medicine in the United States, see Freidson 1989, Relman 1980, Starr 1982, and McKinlay and Stoeckle 1988.

13. For appraisals of the present position of law in the United States, see Schwartz 1980b, Rothman 1984, Powell 1985, Abel 1989.

gether is almost always spun from a naïve, commonsense conception of human action in which the knowledge, values, and attitudes of individuals provide the major source of motivation and direction for their behavior. And so their main emphasis is on reforming the way recruits are selected and trained while paying little attention to changing the institutional and economic structures within which their members do their work. As the model of professionalism specifies, the two are interdependent: the latter provides the resources that either corrupt or reinforce the consequences of the former.

I wish to suggest that an aggressive ideology advancing the terms of the analytic model of professionalism can defend the professions far more effectively than a commonsense version. It can do so, first of all, because it is better equipped to argue the greater desirability of professionalism than the alternatives implied or asserted by exponents of the free market or of rationalized corporate or state authority. It is able to acknowledge monopoly without apology, for monopoly in and of itself is a vice only if one assumes that a free market is a virtue, and that a monopoly exercised by an independent body of specialized workers cannot serve the public interest better than a monopoly of authority exercised by functionaries of capital or the state. It can observe that there is no reasonable basis for expecting people to serve the public good if they cannot be assured of a reasonably secure (but by no means necessarily luxurious) income for themselves and their families. And it can argue that a monopoly held by an occupation whose members are committed to maintaining the integrity of a craft that is of value to others is a more desirable and less destructive solution to an important social problem than is the free play of unbridled material interest or the reduction of all to formally specified procedure proposed by its critics. The practical issue then becomes regulating the conduct of those who possess the monopoly to assure adequate performance, not eliminating monopoly itself.

Following the model, however, a truly consistent and principled ideologue will go on to specify what must be done by the professions in order to come closer to realizing the virtues claimed for their ideal model. A principled ideologue for the free market cannot serve as an apologist for concentrations of economic power that prevent the free play of individual choices to produce, offer, and buy services and goods on the basis of material interest. A principled ideologue of rational-legal bureaucracy cannot condone the use of anything other than competence to decide who shall hold a position or any exception to the rule-governed exercise of authority employed to gain the ends specified by the ultimate authorities. By the same token, a principled ideologue of professionalism cannot condone a monopoly that serves primarily to protect rather than seek out and control the incompetent, the venal, and the negligent among its members, any more than condone a monopoly in which all are free to maximize their incomes at the expense of a public with nowhere else to turn.

A principled defense of the professions, in short, is offensive as well as defensive. By contrasting its ideal-typical model with those of its critics, it can promote itself as no more or less utopian than they and demonstrate that the characteristic pathologies of the empirical forms of the other models are even less desirable than those to be found in professionalism. It can aggressively join the attack on the pathologies that stem from material self-interest in the marketplace and from the reduction of work and its products to formal bureaucratic procedure. But it can no less aggressively attack the practices of professionals that compromise the integrity of the model. Only by maintaining its own integrity can it succeed in leaving no doubt of its superiority over the free play of individual self-interest or the iron cage of formal rationality.

CHAPTER SEVEN

The Redemption of Professionalism?

Robert W. Gordon and
William H. Simon

Lawyers have long viewed the ideal of professionalism as a source of inspiration and a guide to reform. Academics have tended to be more skeptical. In recent years they have portrayed this ideal as a mask for projects of professional or class domination or as simple hypocrisy. (For the most powerful statements of this point of view, see Abel 1989 and Auerbach 1976.) We have contributed to this debunking vein ourselves (see Simon 1978, Gordon 1988), but here we offer some qualifications to its more extreme implications. We want to suggest, albeit guardedly, some reasons for taking the professional ideal seriously on its own terms, and to speculate about the conditions on which its redemption might depend.

TAKING PROFESSIONALISM SERIOUSLY

The traditional ideal of professionalism involves an institutional element and a moral element. The institutional element is the commitment to autonomy in work. From the larger perspective, this means occupational self-regulation, which in turn has meant some immunity from the pressures of the market and some provisions designed to secure high-quality practice. From the perspective of the particular enterprise, it has meant a decentralized, informal, egalitarian workplace where individual workers retain a broad range of responsibility and enjoy the trust of their peers. The moral element of the ideal is a learned disposition on the part of individual lawyers to

Some portions of this essay have been adapted from Robert W. Gordon, "Corporate Law Practice as a Public Calling," *Maryland Law Review* 49 (1990).

contribute to the social goals to which the profession is committed and to comply with social norms.

The social theory that accompanies this ideal, the moral element, social commitment, makes possible the institutional element, autonomy, and compensates for the inability of conventional market forces or government agencies to regulate an activity of such specialized complexity and low visibility (see, e.g., Parsons 1954).

There is a lot to be said for treating the ideal as something to be debunked rather than redeemed, as the profession's more uncompromising critics suggest. Nevertheless, our sense is that after both the weaknesses of the ideal and the bar's faithlessness to it are acknowledged there remains a residuum of the professional vision with significant normative appeal and, though this is far more speculative, social potency.

To the extent that the critics reduce professionalism entirely to economic interests, they surely go too far. There are two variations on the reductionist critique: one emphasizes the subservience of professionalism to the bar's own economic interests; the other emphasizes its subservience to the interests of wealthy clients.

The first variation sees professionalism as a project of cartelization. It sees the ethical rhetoric as mere rationalization for the institutional features of the professional ideal that secure immunity from the market—entry restrictions, preclusion of lay practice, prohibition of advertising and solicitation, and price fixing (see generally Abel 1989).

There is obviously much truth to this view. Many lawyers have turned to professional rhetoric as a defense against competitive pressures, and bar associations have often behaved as if they were concerned primarily with alleviating such pressures. But these facts do not provide a complete account of the appeal and preeminence of professional rhetoric. The cartelization project appears to have been important largely to the lower middle tier of the profession—sole and small-firm lawyers with largely local practices and individual clients. The privileged economic position of elite practitioners—mainly large-firm lawyers with regional or national practices and business clients—does not seem to have depended on any of the distinctive institutions of self-regulation justified by the professional ideal. The elite's basic strategy has rather been a kind of product differentiation involving the cultivation of long-term client relations and the exploitation of hierarchical status distinctions of ethnicity and schooling. This strategy may have depended on the inhibition of competition, but such inhibition did not require the formal institutions of professional regulation.[1] Yet, although elite law-

1. This needs some qualification. It is not hard to make the case that where elite lawyers have controlled the bar's disciplinary machinery, they have used it as a means of reinforcing their own

yers appear to have had little to gain from economic self-regulatory aspects of professionalism in terms of shoring up their market position, they have been the most enthusiastic proponents of professionalism.

The other theme of the reductionist account sees professionalism as serving the economic interests of wealthy clients. The bar's posture of independence and altruistic commitment has been interpreted in terms of the interests of the wealthy in two ways. First, professionalism might serve the wealthy as a class by enabling lawyers to constrain actions by particular wealthy clients that, while individually advantageous, would threaten class interests either by violating important requirements of intraclass stability or by threatening the legitimacy of the social structure in the eyes of outsiders by outraging popular morality (see, e.g., Balbus 1973). Client efforts to frustrate the reasonable expectations of trading partners might threaten class interest in the first way; egregious violations of public norms about the environment or consumer safety or labor might threaten class interest in the second. To the extent that the professional stance of independence and public commitment helps lawyers to discourage such activities, it will enable lawyers to constrain shortsighted deviance among the wealthy in the interest of their long-term class interests. Second, vis-à-vis the non-wealthy, professionalism might serve the wealthy by clothing its privileges in an aura of neutrality and inevitability (see, e.g., Ehrenreich and Ehrenreich 1979). The bar's posture of independence, in this view, substantiates the claims of the legal system to secure justice rather than to serve the interests of any particular group.

Again there is much truth in such accounts. Legal services, especially elite legal services, are rendered disproportionately to the wealthy, and lawyer values overlap substantially with those of business elites. Lawyers do produce ideology that tends to legitimate established hierarchical institutions, and they do directly manipulate non-wealthy clients in ways that sometimes make those clients less militant about pursuing their interests than they might otherwise be. On the other hand, the extreme claim that the sole or principal social significance of professionalism is to protect the wealthy cannot be sustained. If the interests of the wealthy are defined in abstract terms, the contention that lawyers coordinate the activities of the wealthy to protect long-term class interest is likely to become a tautology. Anything lawyers do that does not directly and unambiguously benefit the wealthy can always be rationalized in terms of some long-term interest, say, as strategic concessions to forestall popular radicalism.

Yet when the interests of the wealthy are defined more narrowly and

---

status pretensions by stigmatizing and scapegoating lower-status practitioners—as for example through campaigns against ambulance-chasing and the contingent fee (see Carlin 1966).

concretely, it seems hard to square important categories of lawyers' activities with them. Lawyers, for example, have sometimes exaggerated but nevertheless significant commitments to substantive norms of civil liberty and to access to the legal system for the non-wealthy that do not unambiguously serve the economic interests of the wealthy. Moreover, if the wealthy had the power to unilaterally design institutions to serve their economic interests, they would almost certainly have chosen more informal and flexible instruments of coordination than those lawyers tend to bring to bear. The longstanding and recently intensified complaints at all levels of society about the legal system's cumbersome approaches to planning, negotiation, regulation, and dispute resolution point up the respects in which contemporary lawyering has been ill-suited to the task of smoothly coordinating the interests and activities of any single group. It is hard to account for the survival of many of these procedures without assuming that to some extent they are designed (however ineffectually) to curb the power of the wealthy, as well as to serve their interests.

The contribution of the professionalism project to reconciling the nonwealthy to hierarchy is also hard to demonstrate. We are inclined to believe that legal ideology does influence lay people in generally conservative ways, but the nature of this influence remains to be demonstrated, and it probably does not depend on the professional posture of independence and public commitment. Lawyers often do pacify or "cool out" lower-status clients, but they seem to do so more often by inducing a sense of cynical hopelessness than by convincing them of the justice of their lot (see, e.g., Felstiner and Sarat 1986). There is little evidence that clients are mystified by lawyers' claims of professionalism. On the contrary, the lay public seems to be nearly as cynical about the neutrality of the legal system and the independence of lawyers as the reductionist critics themselves (see Sarat 1977). It is striking that the people who find the claims of professionalism most convincing are the professionals themselves. If professionalism is simply ideology, then the professionals are its principal victims.

One could of course agree that professionalism is not strictly reducible to the economic interests of lawyers or their wealthy clients and still conclude that the professional project is without promise. Some skeptics might dismiss professionalism as hypocritical self-congratulation without any substantial practical social influence. Others might doubt that the conception of public interest likely to emerge from even the sincere efforts of contemporary lawyers, even if it transcended economic self-interest, would be an attractive one. These more modest forms of skepticism are more difficult to respond to. A full-scale response would require the formulation of an acceptable definition of public interest, an examination of the elusive motivations of a heterogeneous group of people, and some counterfactual analysis of the various possible trajectories of professional evolution. We are not prepared to offer such an analysis here, but until someone does, we think that there are two somewhat more speculative grounds for taking professionalism seriously—albeit with cautions and qualifications—as a set of legitimate and socially desirable aspirations. It is interesting that these grounds are deeply rooted in the two traditions from which the reductionist critiques themselves originate—those of socialism and market liberalism.

The first ground is the ethical plausibility of the professional ideal of work as an activity that combines self-expression and public service and that transcends the distinction between work that merely executes prescribed tasks and the activity of reinterpretation and reinvention of tasks. The utopian core of professionalism exalts a kind of work that fosters both the individual development of the worker and socially valuable production. It suggests that this goal can be accomplished through the design of work roles to emphasize creative discretion and the design of communities of workers that emphasize collegial solidarity and pride in work. This aspect of the professional conception of work corresponds precisely to a central feature of the ideal of work in the socialist tradition. It is perhaps ironic that the elite professional firm of the twentieth century is one of the two settings in American history in which the socialist ideal of work has come closest to being institutionalized. (The other—the nineteenth-century artisan's workshop—succumbed to economic pressures similar to those that now confront the professional firm, though many contemporary analogues survive today.)

In some respects, contemporary professional doctrines portray autonomy and responsibility in work in a manner that is far more concrete and practical than anything developed in the literature of socialism. For instance, the literature of legal decision making such as Henry Hart and Albert Sacks's theory of "reasoned elaboration" is surely one of the most ambitious efforts ever undertaken to illustrate a kind of work that both involves individual creativity and is governed by social norms (Hart and Sacks 1958).

It is strange that writers committed to the socialist ideal should summarily dismiss as mere pretense the professed aspirations of elite professionals for autonomy, solidarity, and responsibility in work. The socialist tradition has resolutely imputed such aspirations to industrial workers (even in the face of objections from the workers themselves). Why should it be so incredible that elite workers might share these aspirations?

The other ground for taking professionalism seriously is its potential contribution to a basic problem of free market liberalism. This brand of liberalism seeks to accommodate a broad range of individual self-seeking, but it depends on compliance by self-seekers with the boundaries imposed by the rules of the market. Some of the classic formulations of this liberal vision have suggested that this compliance could only be achieved through a sense of virtuous self-restraint on the part of the citizenry. The less compromising forms of free market liberalism have tended to dispense with reliance on generalized virtue and to look to coercively administered sanctions to bring self-interest into line with the collective interest defined by the market. But any version of free market liberalism must rely on the civic virtue of at least some actors in the system, such as those who administer the sanctions. The most uncompromising free market liberal must deplore the prospect that police officers or prosecutors or judges might behave self-seekingly in their roles and sell their actions to the highest bidders. And even private lawyers committed to unswerving loyalty to client interests still must assume a quasi-public responsibility for honest observance of the basic rules and procedures of the framework, even in the face of the many opportunities they have to ignore the rules with impunity. Once this is acknowledged, the free market liberal faces the problem of how such islands of civic virtue might be secured in a world of generalized self-seeking. It is unlikely that he will be able to come up with a better answer than the one offered by professionalism.

We are not suggesting that the failures and betrayals of professionalism be ignored. We merely propose that the professionalism project be taken seriously in two ways. First, we ought to consider that an important part of the explanation for the emergence of professional rhetoric and institutions may lie in a sincere (and to some extent, normatively plausible) aspiration for autonomy, solidarity, and responsibility in the workplace. Second, we ought to consider the professional tradition as a source of inspiration and ideas for the reform of lawyering.

These suggestions are subject to important qualifications. It is important to take full account, not only of the failure of professionals to live up to their ideals, but of the extent to which the ideals themselves have been bound up with the rationalization of hierarchy inside and outside the profession. The professionalism project ought to be considered relatively more promising where it is not directly committed to practices and structures of hierarchy and exclusion.

Professional Institutions

The proponents of professional redemption, such as the ABA Commission on Professionalism, assign the major institutional roles in this project to the law schools and the bar associations. Here we consider some ambiguities and problems in the roles of these institutions.

Law Schools: Conformity versus Judgment

There is an ambiguity in the rhetoric of professionalism about the kind of ethical dispositions associated with professionalism. Much of the conduct widely cited as evidence of the decline of professionalism represents fairly clear violations of legal rules. The criminal behavior of some of the Watergate lawyers, which did so much to fuel current efforts to teach professional responsibility, is an example. Moreover, it is quite common for lawyers to condemn as unprofessional behavior that fails to show respect for informal structures of workplace authority. For an associate to go over a supervisor's head in a large firm or to compare salaries with colleagues, for example, may be condemned by superiors as a failure of professionalism. Such complaints implicitly associate professional ethics with either compliance with established rules or deference to constituted authority.

At the same time, however, professionalism is associated with a quite different ethical orientation, one that emphasizes reflective—that is, complex and autonomous—judgment. While the goal of reflective judgment is not necessarily incompatible with the goal of compliance with rules and deference to authority, there is a potential tension between them. The goal of conformity could lead to efforts to foster unreflective acquiescence. And the goal of reflective judgment might inspire the questioning and criticism that subverts established rules and institutions.

The most ambitious and distinctive goals of the professionalism project are bound up with the orientation of reflective judgment rather than that of conformity. For example, the rationalization for the professional institutions of self-regulation depends on the premise that such judgment is fundamental and pervasive in practice. Yet strikingly, most of the contemporary efforts at teaching professional responsibility seem to understand professionalism in terms of unreflective conformity.

The Stanley Commission's report on professionalism, like many proposals to redeem the concept, calls for more attention to professional responsibility in legal education. The call, however, is essentially a quantitative one. The report says little about what the content of these efforts ought to be. If the recommendation is interpreted as urging the expansion of efforts in the style of the currently prevailing approaches, its influence will more likely frustrate than advance the more ethically ambitious interpretations of the professionalism project.

Contemporary efforts to teach professional responsibility are ill suited to encouraging reflective judgment and indeed often inimical to doing so. The efforts of the past two decades have gone a long way toward collapsing that subject into that of disciplinary rule enforcement. The professional responsibility portions of bar examinations are exclusively concerned with testing knowledge of disciplinary rules. In part because of the influence of the bar exams, nearly all law school courses on professional responsibility focus on these rules, probably a majority exclusively so.

Moreover, the discussion of ethical issues even in the narrow context of disciplinary regulation tends to take place at a level of sophistication and complexity below that of most other legal subjects. This reflects in part the conscious goal of the drafters of the most recent code to provide "black letter" norms that would obviate complex judgment for any particular issue (see, e.g., Hazard 1982). Indeed, one of the most frequently voiced complaints about ethical codes is that they fail to go far enough in providing the kind of categorical specificity that would make it unnecessary for lawyers to reflect at all. The Multistate Professional Responsibility Examination exacerbates the tendency to conflate legal ethics with unreflective rule following by using a multiple choice format, which rewards only rote memorization.

A further obstacle to any law school effort to contribute to the more ambitious aspirations of professionalism is the conventional pedagogy of the law school classroom. The traditional "Socratic" method was ironically misnamed. A true dialogue in the spirit of Socrates might be a good way to promote reflective judgment. But the Kingsfieldian terrorism that misappropriated Socrates' name is an entirely different affair. Far from being an open-ended conversation that respects the autonomy of the junior participants, it is a highly authoritarian and manipulative proceeding in which students compete to please the teacher with glib responses within rigid time constraints. Even the liberalized contemporary versions of this pedagogy remain at best passive and at worst infantilizing. To be sure, students are often invited to speculate on broader policy and moral issues. But at least in the large classes, both the range of acceptable answers and the opportunities given students to develop them are narrowly limited. For the purposes of imparting purely technical aptitude and doctrinal knowledge, the passive, regimented character of this pedagogy is not necessarily fatal; indeed it may be necessary to efficient instruction. But this is not a mode of instruction compatible with the cultivation of reflective judgment.

Thus, a critical prerequisite to the revival of the professionalism project is to end the subordination of professional responsibility education to exhortation and instruction in disciplinary rules. Perhaps this could best be accomplished by separating the study of the disciplinary rules from the study of legal ethics or professional responsibility entirely. At the least, it would require broadening and deepening the current approaches in several ways, to include the following:

First, courses in professional responsibility need more jurisprudence and more social theory. Serious reflection about legal ethics has to be grounded in theoretical understanding of the nature of legality and the goals of the legal system, and of how lawyers' practices may serve or subvert those goals. Yet when courses in contemporary professional responsibility venture beyond the parsing of disciplinary rules, they are likely to invite students to reflect on their private and personal values, to consider the extent to which "role morality" can legitimately constrain their personal inclinations, and to be more sensitive to the interpersonal aspects of relations with clients and others. These are important matters, but before the legitimacy of the claims of role and legality are assessed, some attention needs to be paid to the content of those claims themselves. Contemporary material on professional responsibility materials (with some exceptions see, e.g., Rhode and Luban 1991) have astonishingly little to say about such matters and rarely attempts to draw on the rich jurisprudential literature that bears on the topic. Part of this failure has to be attributed to the tendency of jurisprudence to focus almost obsessively on the judicial role. The task of applying jurisprudence to the lawyering role is relatively undeveloped and should be on the agenda of teachers of professional responsibility.

Second, instruction in professional responsibility should include the sociology of everyday practice settings. Students are typically unengaged by intellectually ambitious ethical discourse in the classroom. Teachers often take this as evidence of philistinism or vocationalism, but it probably reflects in part a valid insight about the limits of ethical discourse not grounded in the contexts of practice.[2]

To begin with, professional responsibility discourse at its most ambitious talks about the good, but has little to say about the possible. Yet students are acutely aware that their decisions in practice will depend heavily on such factors as what partners, clients, and powerful third parties will expect and tolerate from them. Ethical discussion abstracted from such factors has an academic, ineffectual quality. In the absence of attempts to confront practical constraints, many students tacitly assume that they will have virtually no autonomy in practice, that the partners must do as the clients say, and that they as associates must do as their partners say, without any slack for cavil or maneuver, at peril of losing their jobs. In other words, students assume that practical considerations will almost always trump ethical ones in the "real world," that the constraints of practice will leave the lawyer so little discretion that ambitious reflection would be pointless. We are inclined to believe

2. For a similar critique of the training of lawyers who plan to work with and on behalf of subordinated groups, see Lopez 1989, who emphasizes the need for education that situates practice tasks in social context.

that this pessimism is both pervasive and empirically exaggerated. Yet the matter necessarily remains speculative since there has been so little systematic consideration of the practical circumstances of lawyer autonomy in ethical decision making. Clearly what is required here for teaching purposes is something like the Harvard Business School's case approach, complete with accounts of practice situations thickly and realistically described, which call upon students to develop a range of strategic and ethical responses.[3]

Even more basic, the cultivation of reflective judgment about law practice demands both some empirical understanding of the effects of that practice and the ability to assess how well current practices are serving the social norms of the legal system. In this arena law schools have a curiously mixed record. Law teachers, compared to the profession as a whole, have used their freedom from the constraints of practice to take up at least mildly critical and reformist stances toward the legal system and its operations. In many courses it is common for teachers to point to failures of the current system and to recommend reforms in doctrine, institutions, or practices. (On occasion, though more rarely, they have even conducted empirical studies of lawyers' practices and their effects.)

A teacher might for example argue to his Corporations class that most of the ingenious devices to thwart take-overs—poison pills, shark repellents, and the like—invented in recent years by the mergers-and-acquisitions defense bar are pernicious in their economic consequences, since they prevent or raise the costs of transactions that would increase shareholder and social welfare. A teacher could also argue that not all take-overs are beneficial to the shareholder or society, but that current rules and practices fail adequately to discriminate. A Torts teacher is likely to point to the huge administrative costs of the current tort litigation system, and to recommend alternative institutions or settlement modes (no-fault, alternative dispute resolution, and the like) that save money for both plaintiffs and defendants. A Labor Law teacher may criticize the deficiencies of an enforcement system that rewards blatantly illegal anti-union tactics by opposing them with sanctions that are so weak and so long delayed that they can be disregarded. Yet our impression is that law teachers in their reformist mode mostly see themselves as addressing policymakers, judges, other legal academics, and perhaps also those students who may some day assume such roles, not students as prospective practitioners.[4] The upshot is that we do little to

3. A useful start has been made with Heymann and Liebman 1988.

4. For a rare exception, see Cooper 1980. This is an article framed as a dispute between a senior and a junior partner over whether tax advice that the junior is proposing to give a client constitutes proper avoidance or improper evasion.

prepare our students to perceive what opportunities there may be to engage in reflective judgment and institutional reform from within the practice roles themselves—even when, as in the examples just given, it is apparent that the behavior of lawyers is a contributing cause of the social problem.

Finally, the teaching of professional responsibility should look to pedagogical approaches more conducive to the cultivation of reflective judgment than the conventional methods of instruction in law school. This means attempting to overcome the regimented aspects of even the liberal post-Socratic classroom. Small classes and seminar formats would help. As many have argued, clinical courses in which students are responsible for actual cases and clients are well suited for raising ethical issues, not only because they provide a rich practical context, but because they encourage active student involvement.

Another promising approach that would not require exceptional resource commitments would be to focus a substantial portion of the professional responsibility on the role of the law school and legal education in the legal system and the society. Students might be encouraged to consider their own institution and experience in the light of broader published interpretations of the significance of law schools, such as those of Scott Turow, Robert Stevens, and Richard Abel (Turow 1977; Stevens 1983; Abel 1989). Currently debated issues within the institution over matters such as grading, admissions, and placement policies might be discussed against the broader interpretations provided by the readings. The idea would be to provide a clinical experience in reflective practical thinking in a context that is relatively dense and in which the student has a stake and a status that might inspire intellectual autonomy. The fact that students know so little about law practice makes them vulnerable in professional responsibility discussions both to myths fueled by their own fears and hopes and to the authority of the teacher. But students have a good deal of practical knowledge about law schools. This background should make it possible for them to experiment in the kind of thinking that relates general interpretations to particular institutional contexts. It also should give them a degree of self-confidence that they could not easily achieve in an exercise focused on a subject area. Moreover, the law school, by encouraging critical reflection on the part of its students, would provide an example of the institutionalization of the kind of reflective judgment to which the professionalism project aspires.

Bar Associations

In the vision of professionalism the professional life is simultaneously collective and individual. The norms of the profession are collectively articulated, but their articulation is not exhaustively or permanently specified. The norms are general and to some extent revisable, so there remains a need for interpretation and even innovation by individual lawyers in particular circumstances. A lawyer making an ethical decision in practice is in a position similar to that of a judge applying a particular norm of the common law. The norms are binding on the judge, but they are often ambiguous, and prior interpretations are open to revision. Individual decisions are grounded in past decisions, but they also contribute to the elaboration of future decisions by other decision makers.

But the project of elaborating a professional normative vision has repeatedly run up against a dilemma. Normative precepts formulated at a level sufficiently abstract to command widespread assent throughout the organized bar have too little substance to constitute a credible ethical vision. When the bar attempts to formulate collective commitments more concretely, it is blocked by dissensus and controversy. Indeed, the current malaise about professionalism is most often associated with the changing economic conditions of practice, but it may also be a function of the increasingly intense controversy in areas in which the bar has traditionally focused efforts to concretize its public responsibilities. The principal such areas have been:

Disclosure

Disclosure has long been the most hotly contested area of professional responsibility. The problem has been to reconcile the bar's simultaneous commitment to client confidentiality and responsibility to substantive legal norms. The bar has never achieved a stable reconciliation. All the lines drawn between these competing norms have been controversial. However, in the late 1970s some people detected an emerging consensus among elite lawyers that the established norms were insufficiently responsive to public concerns. The Kutak Commission was formed to propose a revision of the *Code of Professional Responsibility* in the expectation that it would implement this view. In the event, its proposal for a fairly modest expansion of disclosure obligations proved violently controversial within the American Bar Association membership and was voted down by the House of Delegates (see Theodore Schneyer's essay, Chapter 3 herein).

Procedural integrity

One of the oldest aspirations of professional responsibility discourse has been to define and enforce ground rules of fair and efficient dispute resolution. This has meant both norms of good practice within the established procedural frameworks and reform efforts to improve the frameworks.

Norms of good practice include notably the prohibitions of tactics designed to achieve advantage through delay or imposing or threatening to impose litigation costs on the opposing party. Although the norms governing these matters have remained vague and general, most lawyers can probably agree on what constitutes this kind of abuse when they see it. The problems of enforcement probably have more to do with an inability to achieve consensus on or at least secure agreement for effective sanctions for breaches. The most recent effort to put teeth in these prohibitions—the revised Rule ll of the Federal Rules of Civil Procedure—has come, not from the bar associations, but from the judiciary.

At the level of procedural reform the problem of defining norms and goals remains severe. The bar's traditional models of fair procedure have focused on elaborate judicial adversary proceedings. Throughout this century, first in connection with the expansion of the welfare-regulatory state and more recently in connection with the alternative dispute resolution movement, these proceedings have been challenged as wasteful and alienating to lay claimants by proponents of more informal, less lawyer-dominated ones. While some segments of the bar have acknowledged the merits of these challenges and accommodated their practice to some of the proposed reforms, the challenges remain controversial with others. The challenges threaten both economic interests of many practitioners and the traditional cultural attachment to the adversarial judicial process. Moreover, in many areas, such as proposals to curtail negligence adjudication in favor of no-fault systems, procedural reform is linked to substantive changes that are deeply controversial in themselves.

Access

Another long-standing professional responsibility precept has been the duty to extend legal services to those unable to pay for them. Until recently, however, most efforts to do so in any more than a marginal and routine fashion were condemned by some segments of the bar as violations of solicitation or champerty norms. An important development of the 1960s was the rejection of the interpretations of the solicitation and champerty norms that had supported these attacks and the support of the organized bar for government-subsidized legal services for the poor (see, e.g., In re *Primus* 1978, Cramton 1981). The organized bar did not initiate these developments; the judiciary took the lead in reinterpreting the solicitation and maintenance rules, and the federal executive took the lead in promoting subsidized legal services. But the bar's support for legal services beginning in the l970s played an important role in legitimating it within the profession and in securing political support for the subsidies.

Still, the bar has been unable to extend this effective consensus beyond a general support for government subsidies. The Kutak proposal for mandatory no-fee service was soundly defeated. And although the level of subsidized legal services remains tiny relative to the need, efforts to set priorities among different types of substantive claims are typically controversial. When the California State Bar recently decided to devote efforts to extending representation to prisoners challenging the conditions of their confinement, conservative members of the lawyer-dominated legislature forced it to back off by threatening to block a bar fee increase that required legislative approval.

Regulation

In 1962 Adolph Berle suggested that New Deal regulatory programs and their progeny would eventually liberate "the bulk of the corporate bar from the profitable but mostly undistinguished bondage in which most of it lives" (Berle 1962). The idea was that this body of regulation would form an objective basis for elite lawyers to concretize their public commitments. If these regulations were elaborated and enforced effectively enough, client self-interest would be brought into line with the public interest, and lawyers, simply by advising clients on self-interested compliance, might feel that they had a valuable role in implementing important national programs.

This view has turned out to be astonishingly naïve both in assuming that lawyers would come to regard regulation as uncontroversially legitimate and in predicting that public enforcement would eliminate client opportunities for self-interested deviance. Today it seems that lawyers and clients influence substantially the implementation of regulatory programs, and a broad segment of the bar continues to resist the idea that lawyers have any responsibilities beyond those prescribed unambiguously in the positive law. Still another segment promotes the perspective of Holmes's "bad man" (as very few lawyers did in Holmes's day), which urges that even clear legal prohibitions may legitimately be violated so long as the violator remains ready to pay whatever penalties the law prescribes if prosecuted.

This pervasive dissensus at the level of even moderate concreteness makes the prospect of fleshing out the professionalism project at the level of national or state-wide bar associations seem remote. We wonder whether the prospect might be more promising among smaller, more homogeneous professional groups. In the last twenty years there has been an increase in both official and unofficial lawyers' associations. Some of them are associated with women's and minority groups or with particular clienteles. But others have more diverse memberships, and even those recruited from particular segments of the bar usually define at least part of their mission quite broadly in terms of public service.

In the late 1960s, for example, a group of younger lawyers of the Chicago bar broke off from the Chicago Bar Association to found an alternative bar association, the Chicago Council of Lawyers. The CCL was able to persuade several highly respected elite lawyers to join it and endorse its reformist public-interest agenda. After some struggle the CCL has succeeded in establishing itself as an official rival to the CBA, taking independent positions on judicial appointments and issues of legal policy (Powell 1979). In 1969 younger lawyers in large New York City firms formed the New York Council of Law Associates "to represent their concerns about the distribution of legal services and to organize opportunities for them and their firms to undertake *pro bono publico* work" (Powell 1988). Some of these groups have been concerned with professional responsibility, even to the point of promulgating alternative codes of ethics. The organized tax bar, for instance, has attempted to specify when avoidance becomes evasion and to set ethical standards for tax opinions. On occasion it has even taken policy positions on tax reform issues—such as opposing current proposals to cut capital-gains rates—that work against the interests of major clients.[5]

Lawyers concerned with the professionalism project might do well to think about working at it through one of these alternative organizations or by forming one of their own. In addition to the public-interest projects commonly undertaken by some of them, such an organization might (as a few have) promulgate its own norms of ethical practice. It might seek to enforce them against its own members, through internal sanctions and the threat of expulsion. And it might seek to influence the practice of nonmembers by lobbying courts and legislatures in competition with established bar associations to enact its rules or simply by publicly criticizing the practice of nonmembers.

One function of such groups is to give collegial support to members in developing their own conceptions of responsible practice. Another is to serve as a political base for broader professional reform. The two functions are closely related, since lawyers who attempt to implement any ethically ambitious vision of practice on their own risk being marginalized. The political success of such an organization would require that the vision of practice it advocates become attractive to a significant range of lawyers and clients, so that association with the organization would confer status on its members. By doing so, the organization would be able to provide its members with a collective good that would induce loyalty, the threatened loss of which would lend force to internal sanctions.

It is often asserted that efforts to raise the standards of practice through any

5. For details, see Gordon 1990, p. 274 n. 113.

means other than profession-wide disciplinary rules will be ineffective because less ethically ambitious lawyers will lure clients away with promises of greater willingness to serve the clients' selfish interests. Here the image is of a "race to the bottom" in which moral entrepreneurs will undercut others in a competitive process that will push standards down to their least common denominator.

To the extent that clients shop for lawyers in terms of their willingness to do the clients' bidding, there is some reality to this view. But to the extent that clients value high ethical standards in lawyers, the view ignores countervailing pressures. Clients might value high ethical standards in lawyers because they themselves have such standards and prefer to associate with people who share their views. They may value high standards because they believe such standards are associated with an especially sophisticated type of legal judgment that is less likely to sacrifice the client's long-term interests to short-term gain. They may value them because association with lawyers with a reputation for high standards lends the client valuable status or credibility with third parties with whom the client has to deal.

If high standards have economic value in this sense, lawyers have practical reason to institutionalize them through organizations like bar associations and to give them credibility by conferring powers to certify and enforce them on such associations. Thus, one might imagine a "race to the top" in which entrepreneurs make their services more attractive by associating them with a credible reputation for high ethical standards, thus creating competitive pressures for others to follow suit. As more lawyers follow suit, association with those who do not will carry an increasingly costly stigma that deters clients and marginalizes this type of practice. Of course, this vision is no more plausible than the "race to the bottom." It seems likely that any market for legal services will involve pressures pushing ethical standards in many directions. The point is that these conflicting pressures may leave ambitious lawyers some room for institutional innovation that furthers their ethical ideals.

Although the national and state-wide bar associations seem too large and heterogeneous to pursue effectively projects of ethical renovation, an "alternative" association would almost certainly be ineffective also if it were extremely small and homogeneous. This is especially true of groups identified in terms of a particular area of practice and clientele, such as the associations of personal injury plaintiff's lawyers and of the insurance defense bar. Such groups have a tendency both to focus on matters of narrow self-interest and to be associated in the minds of outsiders with such matters to the exclusion of other, broader questions.

Perhaps the most notable example of a bar association that has self-consciously undertaken a project of ethical reform of the sort envisioned here is the Association of the Bar of the City of New York. It was founded in 1870 for the express purpose of contributing to the elaboration and enforcement of an ethically more ambitious vision of practice than the one implicit in the then prevailing practices of the New York bar. It was founded as, and has remained even as its formal admissions policies have relaxed, an elite organization. Through its own initiative it achieved and maintained for many decades a semi-official role in the disciplinary enforcement practices of the New York courts. It has also engaged in a variety of unofficial critiques and debates on matters of professional responsibility. The ABCNY has hardly lived up to the most grandiose ambitions of its founders to set standards and enforce discipline for the elite bar itself. It has been fairly criticized for focusing its ethical zeal on the practices of non-elite, nonmember lawyers; and for taking policy positions (support for no-fault insurance plans, resistance to expanded corporate liabilities and disclosure obligations, etc.) in forms that all too purely reflect the interests of corporate clients. Nonetheless, the ABCNY has willing in some notable instances to scrutinize elite practices. One of its earliest investigations concerned the conduct of David Dudley Field in the Erie Railroad litigation of the 1860s. Some of its functions have been displaced by state courts adopting their own ethical codes and official enforcement procedures, but even today it remains a forum in which standards higher than those of the enacted codes are debated and applied at least in discussion.

The ABCNY has also shown some talent for self-regeneration. A reform-minded leadership foreclosed a revolt of Young Turks in the 1970s by opening up governance positions to younger lawyers, women, and minorities; creating new policy committees on such matters as the Environment, Consumer Affairs, and Sex and the Law; and staffing some of the standing special committees with new members of diverse backgrounds (governmental, public-interest, law teaching). The result has been some surprising departures from conventional professional policy proposals. The ABCNY has recommended dismantling restrictions on lawyer advertising and archaic and useless "character and fitness" standards for bar admission. It opposed the Vietnam War and the invasion of Cambodia and supported civil rights legislation, legal rights of the mentally ill, and divorce reform. It has also promoted some positions plainly adverse to the interests of clients of some leading ABCNY lawyers, such as support for strengthening environmental,[6] antitrust, and trade regulation.[7]

6. Two ABCNY committees split on these issues; the leadership allowed both positions to be recommended to the legislature.

7. For a comprehensive account of ABCNY, its organizational changes and policy positions, see Powell 1988.

As another, quite different example, consider the National Lawyers Guild. It was founded in 1937 as an organization of lawyers serving dissidents and the economically disadvantaged. It began as a coalition of liberal and radical lawyers aspiring to be more inclusive than the major bar associations (to admit Jews, women, and blacks without discrimination), to improve the distribution of legal services, and to function as an organized counterweight to the conservative politics of the ABA. The coalition promptly fell apart when the center-liberals tried and failed to exclude communist members; for after that schism the Guild gave up the plan to become a broad national umbrella organization for left-of-dead-center lawyers—leaving an organizational space that is still unfilled (on the Guild's founding and schism, see Auerbach 1976, pp. 201–4). Thus the Guild's visions of practice have always been much more explicitly political than those of most bar associations, and although its general projects of social transformation have always been much more ambitious than that of the ABCNY, its intraprofessional projects have been less ambitious. Instead of trying to reform the bar as a whole, it has sought to create a more secure space for lawyers engaged in labor, civil rights, and poverty practice. It has done so by providing a setting of collegial support and information exchange, by maintaining referral and consultation networks, by sponsoring and publishing instructional literature on relevant areas of practice, and by taking public positions on matters of concern to members. The Guild has had little or negative prestige within the elite sectors that constitute the ABCNY's reference group, but it has influenced significantly civil rights and left oriented political groups.[8]

The Guild never conceived of its role in terms of the professionalism project. Most of its members have probably been skeptical, if not contemptuous, of the profession and of the rhetoric and values of professionalism. Perhaps for that reason, it has never tried to elaborate or enforce a vision of practice that addressed concretely issues of the sort with which the bar's professional responsibility doctrine is concerned. However some sympathetic observers might conclude both that it has been in a position to do so and that it has suffered for failing to do so. The Guild's tendency to focus its efforts on broad issues of substantive policy and doctrine has often been associated with the tacit embrace of unexamined conventional norms of practice.

The ABCNY and the Guild interest us, not because the particular substantive visions of lawyering they have espoused are invariably plausible or appealing, but because they are examples of professional associations that seem to have been small and homogeneous enough to have developed visions of practice more ambitious and more concrete than those of the

8. For an good sampler of Guild activity, see the documents collected in Ginger and Tobin 1988.

national and statewide associations and yet large and heterogenous enough to have had some success either in strengthening their members' abilities to implement their ideals or in influencing outsiders to adopt their vision. Such groups seem the most promising settings for ambitious professional reform.

An Illustrative Context: Corporate Counseling

As an illustration of the limits of the disciplinary code's approach to instilling and institutionalizing professional values and conduct, and of the promise of working through alternative associations sketched here, consider the constraints and opportunities of a commonplace legal task, that of helping corporate clients deal with government regulation. Corporate lawyers do not always agree on what "professionalism" demands in the performance of this task, and the more specific the discussion becomes the more violently they disagree; but there is a strong, respectable view that the norms and practices of adversary advocacy do not give adequate or appropriate content to the lawyer's role in this context, at least not until the company has been caught in a violation and has definitively rejected any response save that of minimizing its liability.

Until then, the respectable view holds, the professionally responsible lawyer will direct his or her advice not just to the defensive aim of minimizing exposure, but to the affirmative one of promoting compliance with the regulation's purposes. In the debates over the Kutak Commission's recommendations, it was striking that even those lawyers who resisted any obligation—or even discretion—to disclose a client's ongoing crimes or frauds paid some homage to this ideal of a professional function going beyond that of adversary advocacy. In fact their main argument against allowing lawyers to breach confidences was that it would impair their effectiveness as compliance counselors, since lawyers who could not be relied on not to go to the authorities would be cut out of the company's information loops and would never find out about illegal conduct until it was too late to stop it (see, e.g., Hoffman 1978, Higginbotham 1982).

Regulation of corporate activity normally registers—among other, haphazardly miscellaneous interests and purposes—social judgments about how to promote competition and fair dealing in markets (antitrust, labor law, laws against deceptive practices and bribery, or discrimination in hiring) or how to prevent and pay for the social costs of corporate activity (damage to the environment or to worker health and safety, discrimination, sexual harassment, or economic dislocation); and obviously these are purposes that may, at least in the short run, appear as obstacles to the pursuit of profit. The view of the lawyer as compliance counselor is one in which the lawyer is to function, in Talcott Parsons's words, as "a kind of buffer between the illegitimate desires of his client and the social interest. Here he 'represents' the law rather than the client" (Parsons 1954, p. 384).

Sometimes the lawyer's two aims of minimizing client exposure and promoting compliance with regulatory goals may be in harmony but obviously they need not be: from management's point of view, substantive compliance may be the surest way to avoid liability, but may cost much more than creative avoidance. In any actual corporate organization, there will be considerable discrepancies between the moral and policy norms expressed in regulation (the "myth-system") and the company's routine practices (its "operational code") (Reisman 1979). Again from management's point of view, the company's lawyers have the job of managing these discrepancies so that they do not become so glaring that they interfere with or raise the cost of business as usual.

Trying to condition the company into compliance is one way of closing the gap; but so are other, less idealistic strategies such as adopting the most restrictive conceivable interpretations of what the law demands, constructing devices that will formally satisfy the regulation while defeating its substance, designing the cosmetic appearance of compliance (e.g. the publication of paper directives that everyone will ignore because nothing turns on disobeying them), concealing violations when they do occur, playing the audit lottery, stonewalling or counterattacking enforcers, or simply paying fines or settling cases as they come up as a continuing cost of doing business. To reduce these options to a crude typology, corporate counsel can and do choose among actual compliance, cosmetic compliance, nullification-by-resistance, or the "Holmesian bad man's" strategy of violate-and-pay, or any combination of these.

The ideal of the professional as a transmitter of the moral norms enforced in law generally recommends promoting actual compliance so far as it is practically feasible for the lawyer to do so—not dumb, literal obedience to every rule but creative forms of compliance that, although aiming to minimize cost and disruption to the company, still effectively realize the regulations' basic purposes. It is undoubtedly too much to ask that a counselor refuse to compromise the goal of substantial compliance to the point of running up against implacable resistance at the company's highest decision-making levels—one can take only so many causes to the CEO or board, threaten to resign only so many times—but it doesn't seem unreasonable to ask that he or she spend political capital shrewdly for as much compliance as possible.

But why on earth *would* a corporate counsel choose this course rather than alternatives that usually occasion less conflict with and more rewards from the client organization? Skeptics about the practicality of the professional ideal find it easy to list reasons why advocating compliance won't work in real-world settings. Corporations notoriously draw sharp organizational boundaries between themselves and outsiders, reinforced by bonds of loyalty that induce tremendous stress and dissonance in employees trying to serve both the social norms of their professions and company policies. The ideology of the business world depreciates many regulatory goals as populist folly or special-interest selfishness enforced by unreasonable and ignorant bureaucrats. Expressions of moral concern in moral terms in such a context can sound hypocritical and inappropriate. The punishments dealt to the conscientious whistleblowers can be savage—isolation, demotion, and social death if they stay with the company, scapegoating and unemployability if they are fired or resign. Executives who remain "loyal" suffer no stigma and may even get their old jobs back when they get out of jail (on the self-protectiveness of corporate cultures, see Reisman 1979, Jackall 1988, Westin 1981).

The basic problem—the skeptic continues—with tasking lawyers to initiate and supervise compliance efforts in resistance to pressures generated by cultures of profitability, loyalty, and antiregulatory ideologies, is that they are subject to most of the same constraints as other corporate agents. In-house lawyers, who are most familiar with the details of the business, are part of the management team, and their personal fortunes may well rise and fall with that of their colleagues. Outside lawyers, besides wishing to avoid gratuitious offense to an important source of fees, especially under recent conditions of ferocious competition for corporate business, may know too little about a client's operations to see developing problems and devise creative ways of correcting them. Even more important, and of greatest relevance to our project here, is that the professional ideal, as currently articulated and institutionalized in corporate law practice, does not give lawyers resources sufficient to overcome these constraints. The ideal is in fact so elastic that it defeats its own purposes.

The counselor's ethic may recommend an active role in promoting and monitoring compliance, but the ethic is a sickly one that at the first sign of resistance is apt to dissolve into the adversary's goal of minimizing exposure through any plausibly legal means available, which means include, of course, high technical virtuosity in casuistic interpretation and procedural manipulation.[9] The disciplinary codes give almost no support to the com-

9. Some legal doctrines actually turn the lawyer's monitoring function from a sword into a shield by allowing corporate managers facing liability for "intentional" or "bad faith" conduct to plead reliance on advice of counsel as a defense.

pliance counselor's role. The ABA's Model Rules of Professional Conduct were drafted (largely at the instance of the trial bar) to give primacy to the advocate's role and to reduce dissonance between the law and the immediate interests of the client by encouraging acquiescence to the client.

The skeptic's final point is that corporate willingness to comply with regulatory norms really depends upon external political and economic conditions over which the company's lawyers have little or no control. The degree of a corporation's "social responsibility," its concern for goals beyond maximizing short-term profit, is a function of the structure of its market and its position in that market. The other main inducement to compliance is the threat of heavy sanctions, predictably enforced, which in turn is a function of political support for regulation and the power of countervailing constituencies, especially labor unions. In recent years most U.S. companies have experienced severe pressure from international competition to cut costs. The amazing new volatility of the market for corporate control has increased the inter-firm mobility of corporate managers, severed their traditional ties to local communities, and brought to power a breed of portfolio managers oblivious to audiences outside the securities markets, whose priorities put great pressure on middle managers to cut legal corners in order to make profit targets. At the same time, at the federal level (and in many states too) the climate of regulatory enforcement in such fields as environmental, safety and health, employment discrimination, and labor regulation has been relatively permissive. Labor unions have reached their postwar nadir in membership and influence.

The main response to the skeptic—whose claims have undeniable force—has to be that there are actually enormous variations in the responsiveness of American corporations to the social norms reflected in regulation[10]; and the variations don't seem to be tied in any very tightly determined way to external variables such as market structure and regulatory climate (see, e.g., Lane 1977, Kagan and Scholz 1984). Conditions of imperfect competition (oligopoly), for example, may have a lot to do with creating opportunities for socially responsible conduct, but cannot explain the degree to which a company takes advantage of such opportunities. Even for companies determined to behave as perfect economic persons, amoral calculators, the most basic terms of the calculus—both "profit-maximizing" and "costs" of liability or regulatory sanctions—are far too amorphous to dictate uniform responses. (This is effectively demonstrated by the often disastrous miscalculations of morally indifferent managers, resulting in huge liabilities for harms that much less costly recall or correction in mid-production could have averted [Kagan and Scholz 1984].)

10. For a survey of the social policies of 130 large U.S. corporations, see Lydenberg et al. 1986.

Thus, for explanations of variation in law-abiding corporate conduct, a growing body of work is inclined to look to variations in corporate strategies, structures, and "cultures"; and nearly all of this work, some of it in detail, is neccessarily concerned to examine what will strengthen the advisory and monitoring capabilities of—among other potential monitors such as competitors, independent directors, shareholders, "private attorneys general," etc.—the corporation's lawyers (see especially Coleman 1985, Stone 1985, Krankman 1985, Stone 1975, Coffee 1977, 1981, Kagan and Sholz 1984, Rosen 1984).

The recent work of Robert Rosen on the sociology of house counsel's work (Rosen 1989) is particularly suggestive in its grouping of corporate legal departments into two general types, one of which takes a very narrow view of the lawyer's role in corporate decision making, the other a much broader view, each finding a fit into their companies' organizational structures in ways that reflect those views. Legal departments adopting the narrow view sharply distinguish legal from business advice and confine the lawyer's role to the strictly legal; their advice is reactive, neutral risk analysis, given only when sought, accepting as the "client" whatever manager at whatever level consults it, and accepting the "problem" and the corporation's "interest" as defined by that manager. They don't ask what happens when the "client" leaves their office—unless required to perform monitoring or auditing functions, in which case they will confine themselves to formal questions and formal responses. Under attack by regulators or civil adversaries, they will see their function as simply minimizing liability in every case.

The A.H. Robins company that has had to devote most of its resources to compensating victims of its catastrophic decisions to market and then conceal mounting evidence of the dangers of Dalkon Shield, probably exemplifies an extreme version of this narrow model and its perils. At Robins the medical and legal departments were, apparently by design, kept insulated from one another, so that lawyers defending the mounting flow of tort suits had no access to doctor's reports on dangers of the shield; while the medical department in turn was deprived of new medical information generated in the suits. The lawyers also seem to have destroyed or permitted the destruction of key documents; and engaged in ferociously adversary litigation tactics, cross-examining plaintiffs on details of their sexual practices to deter suits, hiding important documents from discovery in mountains of trivial ones, and coaching top executives to forget virtually all details of management decisions relating to the Shield (see Mintz 1985).

Legal departments adopting the broader view see their role as that of building compliance goals and prevention-and-monitoring mechanisms to reach those goals into the company's own strategies and routine operations, so that compliance becomes not a grudging response to a lawyer-policeman muttering vague threats of state terror, but company policy, implemented through its regular divisions. A nice set of examples comes from Allied Chemical's restructuring after it was caught dumping Kepone into Chesapeake Bay. Allied created a Toxic Risk Assessment Committee and a new executive position reporting to top management, rerouted information on toxic production and waste so it would reach these new monitors, and tied one-third of the compensation of plant managers to their safety records.[11]

This broad role is a obviously much more demanding than the other. To perform it the lawyers need to be able to report directly to the CEO, maintain personal ties to the CEO and the board and have the authority to investigate and intervene at any level, in any division. They need discretion to define the "client" and its "problems" and "interests" more broadly than particular divisions or levels may wish. Above all, they need sufficient knowledge of the business operations of the company so that they can work with middle managers to devise means of institutionalizing preventive compliance with regulatory norms that those middle managers can accept,[12] sufficient trust so that problems will be brought to their attention before it is too late to dislodge the policies or investment decisions that caused them, sufficient prestige to influence changes at middle management levels without actually having to spend the political capital of running to the CEO, and sufficient authority to summon independent forces, such as outside lawyers or consultants or "audit committees," to recommend or monitor changes.

To return now to where we started: Assuming that the broad counseling function is the best way of realizing the professional ideal in corporate law practice, what kinds of organized professional activity could be undertaken that would usefully support the ideal? Generally speaking, what corporate lawyers need to do is to develop independent views of the purposes of the regulatory laws and regulations that concern them; and then work to institutionalize conditions of their practices to be in a position to make their advice effective.

The disciplinary codes, as earlier mentioned, contribute very little to this project. They may even undermine it. The Kutak Commission pressed the organized bar to express a vision of lawyers' obligations sufficiently ample to

11. See Coffee 1981, pp. 451, 456, and for a particularly interesting set of case studies of restructuring consent orders (FTC), see Solomon and Nowak 1980.

12. A manufacturer ordered by the FTC to improve its warranty service, for example, instituted sweeping changes in quality control procedures, construction materials, and manufacturing techniques in order to reduce its repair costs, and reported that "the cost of the changes was less than the benefits received in the form of savings in repair costs and increased good will" (Solomon and Nowak 1980, p. 139).

promote the social purposes reflected in law. The bar responded by enacting into the codes a narrow view of professional responsibility. For example, under the Model Rules of Professional Conduct, lawyers are not to abet clients in criminal or fraudulent conduct (Rule 1.2), but neither are they required to urge clients to obey the law. They are not required to go beyond "purely technical" advice (Rule 2.1, Comment) such as "bad-man's" risk-analysis or value-neutral description of formal-legal sanctions and the likelihood they will be imposed if that's all the client wants (Rule 2.1).[13] Should they wish to assume the "broad role," they have virtually no formal leverage over clients who persist in illegal conduct, since they may disclose misconduct to outsiders only to avert death or serious bodily harm (Rule 1.6[b][1]) and may not even resign unless the company's highest authority resolves to proceed with a "clear" violation of law likely to result in "substantial injury" to the organization (Rule 1.13). In short, a lawyer may exercise near total indifference to the morality or legality of a client's intentions and actions without even bending any of the rules of this so-called disciplinary code.

Still, it is doubtful whether reforms in the disciplinary rules could have lent much support to the counseling function anyway. The major reform proposed concerned increasing a lawyer's discretion or obligation to disclose ongoing harmful conduct. The opponents of disclosure, with support from more objective observers (see, e.g., Coffee 1977, p. 1146), argued that the only effect a mandatory disclosure rule was likely to have would be to prevent the lawyers or possibly *any* responsible corporate officers from learning of possibly shady or risky operations going on in a company. The argument was surely overstated. Of course bad clients won't knowingly reveal dubious conduct to lawyers if the lawyers must disclose it. But some clients, realizing that the only way they can get legal help will require disclosure, will clean up their act, and even bad clients may disclose inadvertantly (see Luban 1988, pp. 206–34, Zacharias 1989). In any event, the politics of the ABA closed off even this narrow avenue to reform.

If the threat of disclosure is rarely available to corporate lawyers trying to institutionalize the counseling function, what is? To bargain with managers for compliance, lawyers need both plausible threats of damage to the corporation and plausible promises of benefits. Benefits are more important because it is often difficult to induce managers to invest in simply avoiding losses, especially losses that are inevitably speculative because the risk of

13. In a rare and grudging concession to the broad view of counseling, the Rules say that lawyers "may refer . . . to moral, economic, social and political factors, that may be relevant to the client's situation" (Rule 2.1), though the comments reject the idea that the lawyer is a "moral advisor as such," and emphasize that he is not (usually) obliged to give "unwanted" advice.

harms to others and the risk of regulatory detection and enforcement are always so uncertain. The best way for corporate lawyers to promote this function would be to use professional associations such as the American Corporate Counsel Association, practitioners' seminars, and widely read journals like the *Business Lawyer* to instruct one another in success stories of compliance strategies and models of compliance structures.[14] It is also crucial that counsel for the more law-abiding and socially responsible companies articulate informal standards of good practice. In this way lawyers fighting for marginal changes in their own work settings can point to highly respectable examples of appropriate practice. It would also help, at least slightly, if there were continuing emphasis, even if only in the usual form of highminded rhetoric on the President's Page, from the major bar associations on lawyers' social responsibilities.

Clearly, however, lawyers need sticks as well as carrots. The ideal regulatory regime from the compliance lawyer's point of view is one that has potentially severe sanctions for violations, but is willing to be flexible in negotiating compliance systems or consent decrees to prevent and remedy violations. This would give counsel something draconian to bargain with, but the promise of extracting a sweet deal for his company, a conversion from "unreasonable" to "reasonable" regulation.[15] Regulation, it has often been said, is the "businessman's best friend" so long as it is taken as a more or less objective constraint, something that must be incorporated into the firm's strategies because it is *inevitable*. In this view, no manager can be blamed for having made a "losing" investment in compliance (see Jackall 1988, p. 160). When doubts arise about the seriousness of regulatory intentions or adequacy of enforcement, there are enormous temptations to "badman" strategies, cosmetic compliance, or outright nullification.[16] The regulatory enforcement climate, especially at the level of the small decisions that are critical in practical terms but concealed from political view, is something that corporate lawyers can help to influence as members of

14. In many fields of course they do this already—e.g. hold seminars to instruct managers or other lawyers in how to design a corporate sexual harassment policy and grievance procedure. The threat is that of potential vicarious liability for harassment if they lack such a policy; the benefit is the improvement in employee morale from an harassment-free work atmosphere.

15. For an extended argument that regulatory "unreasonableness"—inability to distinguish between unwitting technical violators and genuine "bad apples," between major substantive and trivial formal violations—is a contributing cause of noncompliance, see Bardach and Kagan 1982 on OSHA enforcement during the Carter Administration. But see, e.g., Noble 1987 for how non-confrontational "cooperative" enforcement policies of Reagan Administration vitiated the purposes of the act.

16. The weakness of NLRB enforcement, for example, has led to increasingly aggressive union-busting tactics in the knowledge that penalties if any will be light and imposed far too late to help an organizing campaign. See Weiler 1983.

powerful policymaking elites; as participants in rulemaking and regulatory-negotiation proceedings; and as drafters of consent decrees restructuring deliquent businesses. Indeed, the most efficient regulatory regime for some contexts may be one that creates "gatekeeper" obligations, one that directly conscripts the lawyers as regulatory agents by requiring them to monitor certain company transactions, investigate underlying facts, certify conditions, and disclose violations of law; and imposes liability on the gatekeepers as well as their clients for negligence or nondisclosure (see Krankman 1985, pp. 178, 200–204).

Lawyers do of course frequently and unfortunately deploy their influence in ways that are actually antithetical to their professional interests, that is, in reflexive and mindless antiregulatory lobbying. This is to some degree inevitable given the immersion of lawyers in the cultures and ideologies of their clienteles. It does not seem likely that organizations of industry counsel as such will press vigorously for strengthening of outside regulatory regimes—as opposed to strengthening of inside preventive and monitoring systems, which they can be expected to support. It seems virtually certain that such groups would even more fiercely resist regulation imposing disclosure requirements or gatekeeper liabilities on lawyers themselves. They have always done so in the past.

But there are other kinds of institutions—the bar association committee or task force or law-reform group, governmental or foundation commissions and advisory bodies, nonprofit public-policy centers—in which the same lawyers can serve. In such settings the members may to some extent escape both the parochialism of their usual associates and the narrow advocacy roles and be freed to articulate more disinterested views of ethics and policy. If the group includes lawyers from diverse business sectors, they will have cross-cutting interests anyway: insurance-industry lawyers will urge preventive regimes on counsel for potential mass-tort defendants, house counsel will press mechanisms for reducing litigation costs on law-firm litigators, outside-firm lawyers can suggest mechanisms for damage control after corporate violations have been discovered that will bring them in as outside monitors and reduce the dangers of cover-ups and suppression of evidence; lawyers for capital-intensive industries can take a more detached view of labor and employment laws, and so forth. Even if such groups' ties effectively disable them from initiating proposals for strong and effective outside regulation, experience suggests that they can play an important part in deciding how to respond to outside initiatives—whether to try to cripple the initiative, or make it palatable to major business interests while preserving its basic purposes—and thus to mediate between regulatory and business constituencies.

In the currently emerging conditions of corporate practice, it may be that outside-firm lawyers may be able to contribute more to the provision of relatively disinterested ethical and policy advice, without feeling that they are betraying their clients or risking loss of business. This is because companies now less often retain the same firm to represent all their interests than they did fifteen years ago, and more often spread legal business among several firms. A law firm thus has less to lose if one of its lawyers risks offending a client (see, e.g., Chayes and Chayes 1985). Organized bar groups, besides providing forums of their own for professional policymaking, can support such efforts in several ways.

Specifically, it would be useful if the ABA and big city bar associations were to adopt policies that would concretely back up their commitments to public service by the bar, and serve as sources of influence to counter the economic pressures of private practice that severely discourage engagement in non-billable ventures of any kind. They might, for example, issue ethical opinions regarding merely "positional" conflicts, to the effect that law firms and general counsel's office may do nothing to inhibit partners or associates from writing articles or otherwise being active in policy-formation causes simply on the ground that their clients might object (see *Business Law* 1978, p. 1495). They could also helpfully recommend, for it is probably politically impossible for them to require, firms to count time spent in public-interest activity toward billable-hours quotas and to give it full credit in partnership decisions. They can, as some bar associations are already doing, pass rules or recommend that firms contribute some set minimum proportion of time or income to public-interest or public-policy organizations.

We are obviously not arguing here that regulation is always good and business resistance to it bad, so that lawyers should always deploy their individual and collective influence to secure compliance. Of course much regulation is inefficient; much results simply from protectionist rent seeking, or registers far-from-admirable compromises among interests; and lawyers may sometimes in fact promote both their clients' and general social interests by pressing for its reform. Our point is simply that regulatory schemes usually, however imperfectly, also give expression to general social and moral norms. Fidelity to the general purposes recorded in law, and the obligation to try to give them practical effect in the rules and practices of one's ordinary working conditions, is at the heart of the professional ideal.

References

Abbott, Andrew. 1989. "The New Occupational Structure: What Are the Questions?" *Work and Occupations* 16:273–91.

——. 1988. *The System of Professions*. Chicago: University of Chicago Press.

Abel, Richard. 1989. *American Lawyers*. New York: Oxford University Press.

——. 1988a. "England and Wales: A Comparison of the Professional Projects of Barristers and Solicitors." In Richard Abel and Philip S. C. Lewis, ed., *Lawyers and Society: The Common Law World*. Berkeley and Los Angeles: University of California Press.

——. 1988b. "United States: The Contradictions of Professionalism." In Richard Abel and Philip S. C. Lewis, eds., *Lawyers in Society: The Common Law World*. Berkeley and Los Angeles: University of California Press.

——. 1987. "Lawyers." In Leon Lipson and Stanton Wheeler, eds., *Law and the Social Sciences*. New York: Russell Sage Foundation.

——. 1986. "The Transformation of the American Legal Profession." *Law and Society Review* 20:7–19.

——. 1985a. "Comparative Sociology of the Legal Profession: An Exploratory Essay." *American Bar Foundation Research Journal* 1985:3–79.

——. 1985b. "Law without Politics: Legal Aid Under Advanced Capitalism." *UCLA Law Review* 32:474.

——. 1981a. "Toward a Political Economy of Lawyers." *Wisconsin Law Review* 1981: 1117–87.

——. 1981b. "Why Does the American Bar Association Promulgate Ethical Rules?" *Texas Law Review* 59:639.

Abel, Richard, and Philip S. C. Lewis, eds. 1989. *Lawyers and Society: Comparative Theories*. Berkeley and Los Angeles: University of California Press.

——. 1988a. *Lawyers and Society: The Common Law World*. Berkeley and Los Angeles: University of California Press.

——. 1988b. *Lawyers and Society: The Civil Law World*. Berkeley: University of California Press.

Adams, Edward. 1989. "Longer Partnership Odds at N.Y. Firms." *New York Law Journal* 202(10):1, 6.
Aguilar, Louis, 11 July 1990. "Survey: Law Firms Slow to Add Minority Partners." *Chicago Tribune*, section 3, p. 1.
Alvesson, Mats. 1987. *Organization Theory and Technocratic Consciousness*. New York: Walter de Gruyter.
American Bar Association. 1986. *In the Spirit of Public Service: A Blueprint for the Rekindling of Lawyer Professionalism*. Chicago: American Bar Association.
——. 1983. *Model Rules of Professional Conduct*. Chicago: American Bar Association.
——. 1982. *Legal Clinics: Merely Advertising Law Firms?* Chicago: American Bar Association.
——. 1979. *Model Code of Professional Responsibility*. Chicago: American Bar Association.
——. 1969. *Canons of Professional Ethics*. Chicago: American Bar Association.
——. 1959. *Lawyers' Economic Problems and Some Bar Association Solutions*. Chicago: American Bar Association, Special Committee on the Economics of Law Practice.
American Bar Association Center for Professional Responsibility. 1987. *The Legislative History of the Model Rules of Professional Conduct: Their Development in the ABA House of Delegates*. Chicago: American Bar Association.
American Bar Association Journal. 1951a. "The Bar and the Public Trust." 37:752.
——. 1951b. "The Lawyer's Loyalty Oath." 37:128.
——. 1951c. "The Proposed Anti-Communist Oath: Opposition Expressed." 37:123.
——. 1948a. "Challenge to the Lawyer Citizen." 34:916.
——. 1948b. "Communists in the U.S.: Registration Urged." 34:381.
——. 1948c. "The Point Where Toleration Ends." 34:696.
——. 1948d. "To Ensure Domestic Tranquility." 34:44.
American Bar Association Section of Legal Education and Admissions to the Bar. 1931. "Overcrowding of the Legal Profession." *Missouri Bar Journal* 2:11.
American College of Trial Lawyers. 2 April 1982. Report of the Legal Ethics Committee on the 30 May 1981 Proposed Final Draft of the Model Rules of Professional Conduct.
American Law Institute. 1989. *Restatement of the Law Governing Lawyers, Tentative Draft No. 2*. Philadelphia: American Law Institute.
The American Lawyer. July/August 1990. "The AM LAW 100." Special Pull-Out Section.
——. July/August 1989. "The AM LAW 100." Special Pull-Out Section.
Andrews, Champ. 1907. "The Law—A Business or a Profession?" *Yale Law Journal* 17:602–10.
Arant, H. W. 1936. "Making Disciplinary Procedures More Effective." *American Bar Association Journal* 22:188.
Arendt, Hannah. 1959. *The Human Condition*. Garden City, N.J.: Doubleday Anchor.
Arrow, K. J. 1963. "Uncertainty and the Welfare Economics of Health Care." *American Economic Review* 53:941–73.
Ash, Robert. 1948. "What Should Be the Lawyer's Concept of Professional Service in Our Changing World?" *The Lawyer and Law Notes* 2:6.
ATLA Commission on Professional Reponsibility. June 1980. *The American Lawyer's*

Code of Conduct. Washington, D.C.: The Roscoe Pound American Trial Lawyers Foundation.

Atwood, Frank. 1933. "Responsibilities and Powers of Bench and Bar." *Missouri Bar Journal* 4:179.

Auerbach, Jerold. 1976. *Unequal Justice: Lawyers and Social Change*. New York: Oxford University Press.

Austin, Edwin. 1957. "Some Comments on Large Law Firms." *Law Practice Forum* 3(4):8–16.

Ayer, Randolph J. 15 February 1982. "In House—Better Than Ever." *The National Law Journal*, p. 11.

Balbus, Isaac. 1973. *The Dialectics of Legal Repression*. New York: Russell Sage Foundation.

Bardach, Eugene, and Robert A. Kagan. 1982. *Going by the Book: The Problem of Regulatory Unreasonableness*. Philadelphia: Temple University Press.

Bar Notes. October/November 1986. "President's Comments," p. 3.

Becker, Howard S. 1970. "The Nature of a Profession." In Howard S. Becker, ed., *Sociological Work*. Chicago: Aldine.

Becker, Howard S., Blanch Geer, Everett C. Hughes, and Anselm Strauss. 1961. *Boys in White: Student Culture in Medical School*. Chicago: University of Chicago Press.

Bellon, Lee Ann. 18 January 1988. "Southeast Boasts an Expanding Legal Community." *The National Law Journal*, pp. 19–20.

Bendix, Reinhard. 1956. *Work and Authority in Industry: Ideologies of Management in the Course of Industrialization*. Berkeley and Los Angeles: University of California Press.

Bergman, Andrew. 1971. *We're in the Money: Depression America and Its Films*. New York: New York University Press.

Berkman, Barbara. 24 March 1988. "Temporarily Yours: Associates for Hire." *The American Lawyer*, pp. 26–27.

Berlant, Jeffrey. 1975. *Profession and Monopoly: A Study of Medicine in the United States and Great Britain*. Berkeley and Los Angeles: University of California Press.

Berle, Adolph. 1962. "Book Review." *Harvard Law Review* 76:430–32.

Berman, Jerry, and Edgar Cahn. 1970. "Bargaining for Justice: The Law Students' Challenge to Law Firms." *Harvard Civil Rights—Civil Liberties Law Review* 5:16–31.

Bernstein, Peter. August 1982. "Profit Pressures on the Big Law Firms." *Fortune*, pp. 84–100.

Blau, Judith. 1984. *Architects and Firms*. Cambridge: MIT Press.

Bledstein, Burton. 1976. *The Culture of Professionalism*. New York: W. W. Norton.

Blum, Bill, and Gina Lobaco. 1988. "When Associates Don't Make Partner." *California Lawyer* 8(1):51–54.

Blumberg, A. S. 1967. *Criminal Justice*. Chicago: Quadrangle Books.

Bodine, Larry. 12 March 1979. "Law Firm Ladder Gets New Rung." *The National Law Journal*, pp. 1, 17.

Bolman, Lee, and Terrence E. Deal. 1984. *Modern Approaches to Understanding and Managing Organizations*. San Francisco, Calif.: Jossey-Bass.

Bosk, Charles L. 1979. *Forgive and Remember*. Chicago: University of Chicago Press.

Botein, Stephen. 1983. " 'What We Shall Meet Afterwards in Heaven': Judgeship as a Symbol for Modern American Lawyers." In Gerald L. Geison, ed., *Professions and Professional Ideologies in America*. Chapel Hill: University of North Carolina Press.

Bourdieu, Pierre. 1987. "The Force of Law: Toward a Sociology of the Juridical Field." *Hastings Law Journal* 38:805–53.

——. 1985. "The Social Space and the Genesis of Groups." *Theory and Society* 14:723.

——. 1977. *Outline of a Theory of Practice*. Trans. Richard Nice. Cambridge: Cambridge University Press.

Bowles, Samuel and Herbert Gintis. 1976. *Schooling in Capitalist America: Educational Reform and the Contradictions of Economic Life*. New York: Basic Books.

Bowser, Nancy. May/June 1989. "The Pros of Being a Pro: Trend toward Enhanced Professionalism Grows." *Bar Leader*, p. 12.

Bradway, John. 1945. "Will Socialized Law Be Next?" *Journal of the American Judicature Society* 28:13.

Brandeis, Louis. 1914. *Business—A Profession*. Boston: Small, Maynard, and Co.

Braverman, Harry. 1974. *Labor and Monopoly Capital*. New York: Monthly Review Press.

Brill, Steven. June 1989. "The Law Business in the Year 2000." *The American Lawyer*, p. 10.

Bristol, George. 1913. "The Passing of the Legal Profession." *Yale Law Journal* 22:590–613.

Broadway, John. 1936a. "Legal Standards." *Mississippi Law Journal* 8:349.

——. 1936b. "A National Bar Survey." *Boston University Law Review* 16:662.

Brogan, Thomas. 1936. "The Judiciary and the Bar." *New Jersey State Bar Association Quarterly* 3:210.

Brown, Brendon. 1945. "The Lawyer and the American System." *North Carolina Law Review* 24:33.

Brown, Leo. 1954. "Bar PR: A Professional Appraisal." *Michigan State Bar Journal* 33:53.

Brown, Ralph S. 1954. "Lawyers and the Fifth Amendment: A Dissent." *American Bar Association Journal* 40:404.

Burawoy, Michael. 1985. *The Politics of Production*. London: Verso.

Business Disputing Group. 1989. "Corporation in Court: Trends in American Business Litigation." Report prepared for Arthur Andersen & Co. by M. Galanter, Stewart Macaulay, Thomas Palay, and Joel Rogers, University of Wisconsin Law School, Madison, Wisconsin.

Business Week. 13 January 1968. "Why Law Is a Growth Industry." Pp. 78–79.

Byington, O. A. 1927. "Lo! The Poor Lawyer." *Iowa State Bar Association* 1927:73.

Cain, Maureen. 1983. "The General Practice Lawyer and the Client: Towards a Radical Conception." In Robert Dingwall and Philip S. C. Lewis, eds., *The Sociology of the Professions*. New York: St. Martin's Press.

Carlin, Jerome. 1966. *Lawyers' Ethics—A Survey of the New York City Bar*. New York: Russell Sage Foundation.

——. 1962. *Lawyers on Their Own*. New Brunswick: Rutgers University Press.

Carr-Saunders, A. M., and P. A. Wilson. 1933. *The Professions*. Oxford: Oxford University Press.

Chafee, Zechariah, Jr. 1951. "Purge Trials Are for Russian Lawyers." *New York Law Journal* 74:161.

Chambers, David. 1989a. Presentation to the annual meeting of the Law and Society Association, Madison, Wisconsin, 8–11 June.

——. 1989b. "Accommodation and Satisfaction: Women and Men Lawyers and the Balance of Work and Family." *Law and Social Inquiry* 14:251–87.

Chandler, Alfred D. 1977. *The Visible Hand: The Managerial Revolution in American Business*. Cambridge: Harvard University Press.

Chayes, Abram, and Antonia Chayes. 1985. "Corporate Counsel and the Elite Law Firm." *Stanford Law Review* 32:277–300.

Chicago Tribune. 19 April 1988. "Isham Lincoln to Be Dissolved: Chicago's Second Oldest Law Firm." P. 7.

Clark, Charles. 1939. "The Bar and Recent Reform of Federal Procedure." *American Bar Association Journal* 25:22.

Cleveland, Chester. 1951. "The Value of Public Relations." *The Journal of the Oklahoma Bar Association* 22:204.

Coffee, John. 1981. "No Soul to Damn, No Body to Kick: An Unscandalized Inquiry into the Problem of Corporate Punishment." *Michigan Law Review* 79:386.

——. 1977. "Beyond the Shut-Eyed Sentry." *Virginia Law Review* 63:1099.

Cohen, J. H. 1926. "Tendencies in the Legal Profession." *Rhode Island Bar Association Journal* 1926:56.

——. 1924. *The Law: Business or Profession?* New York: G. A. Jennings.

Coleman, James S. 1985. "Responsibility in Corporate Action: A Sociologist's View." In Klaus J. Hopt and Gunther Teubner, eds., *Corporate Governance and Directors' Liabilities: Legal, Economic, and Sociological Analyses on Corporate Social Responsibility*. New York: Walter de Gruyter.

Collins, Randall. 1979. *The Credential Society: An Historical Sociology of Education and Stratification*. New York: Academic Press.

Combs, Hugh. 1942. "Lawyers Should Do More Work for Insurance Companies." *Ohio Bar* 15:517.

Coombe, Rosemary J. 1989. "Room for Manoeuver: Toward a Theory of Practice in Critical Legal Studies." *Law and Social Inquiry* 14:69–121.

Cooper, George. 1980. "The Avoidance Dynamic: A Tale of Tax Planning, Tax Ethics, and Tax Reform." *Columbia Law Review* 80:1553.

Couric, Emily. 1 August 1988. "New Relationships, New Rules." *The National Law Journal*. Pullout-Supplement 2.

Cramton, Roger. 1981. "Crisis in Legal Services for the Poor." *Villanova Law Review* 26:521.

Crawford, Coe I. 1924. "Bench and Bar in Territorial Days." *South Dakota Bar Association* 1924:140–51.

Croly, Herbert D. 1965. *The Promise of American Life*. Cambridge: Harvard University Press, Belknap Press.

Crum, Bartley. 1931. "Clean Up the Legal Profession." *Commercial Law Journal* 36:235.

Cummings, A. M. 1930. "Elimination of the Incapable." *Michigan State Bar Journal* 9:108.

Curley, John. 6 February 1981. "Lawyers Squabble About a New Code of Ethics." *Wall Street Journal*. P. 44.
Curran, Barbara A. 1986. "American Lawyers in the 1980s: A Profession in Transition." *Law and Society Review* 20:19–53.
Curran, Barbara A., Katherine Rosich, Clara Carson, and Mark Puccetti. 1985a. *Lawyer Statistical Report: A Statistical Profile of the U.S. Legal Profession in the 1980s*. Chicago: American Bar Foundation.
——. 1985b. *Supplement to the Lawyer Statistical Report: The U.S. Legal Profession in 1985*. Chicago: American Bar Foundation.
Daniels, Frank. 1925. "The Lawyer as Citizen—His Duty to the Public." *North Carolina Law Review* 1925:156.
Darby, D. Weston. 1985. "Are You Keeping Up Financially?" *American Bar Association Journal* 71:66–68.
Dawson, Mitchell. 1936. "More Bar to Bar." *Case and Comment* 42:6.
——. March 1930. "Frankenstein, Inc." *American Mercury*, pp. 274–80.
Derber, Charles. 1982. "The Proletarianization of the Professional: A Review Essay." In Charles Derber, ed., *Professionals as Workers: Mental Labor in Advanced Capitalism*. Boston: G. K. Hall.
Derber, Charles, and William Schwartz. 1983. "Toward a Theory of Worker Participation." *Social Inquiry* 53:61–78.
de Tocqueville, Alexis. 1972. "Money Talks: Why It Shouts to Some Lawyers and Whispers to Others." *Juris Doctor* 2(4):55–57.
Dezalay, Yves. July 1990. "The Big Bang and the Law: The Internationalization and Restructuration of the Legal Field." *Theory, Culture, and Society* 7:253.
Dickerson, Harvey. 1954. "The Responsibilities of the Bar." *Nevada State Bar Journal* 19:12.
DiMaggio, Paul J. 1979. "Review Essay on Pierre Bourdieu." *American Journal of Sociology* 84:1460.
DiMaggio, Paul J., and Walter W. Powell. 1983. "The Iron Cage Revisited: Institutional Isomorphism and Collective Rationality in Organizational Fields." *American Sociological Review* 48:147–60.
The Docket. March 1926. "Loophole Lawyers." 3:3008–9.
Dockser, Amy. 19 October 1988. "Midsize Law Firms Struggle to Survive." *Wall Street Journal*, p. 31.
Doerfler, Christian. 1927. "An Ancient and Honorable Profession." *Marquette Law Review* 11:113.
Douglas, William O. 1948. "Law in Eruption: A Concept of Lawyer's Duty in a Time of Change." *American Bar Association Journal* 34:647.
Drew, Elizabeth. 7 October 1973. "The Rule of Lawyers." *New York Times Magazine*, p. 16.
Dubin, Robert, R. Alan Hedley, and Thomas C. Taveggia. 1976. "Attachment to Work." In Robert Dubin, ed., *Handbook of Work, Organization, and Society*. Chicago: Rand McNally College Publishing.
Durkheim, Emile. 1958. *Professional Ethics and Civic Morals*. Trans. Cornelia Brookfield. London: Routledge and Kegan Paul.
Earle, Walter. 1963. *Mr. Shearman and Mr. Sterling and How They Grew: Being Annals of Their Law Firms*. New Haven: Yale University Press.

Edelman Murray. 1971. *Politics as Symbolic Action*. Chicago: Markman Press.

Edwards, Richard. 1979. *Contested Terrain: The Transformation of the Workplace in the Twentieth Century*. New York: Basic Books.

Ehrenreich, Barbara, and John Ehreneich. 1979. "The Professional-Managerial Class." In Pat Walker, ed., *Between Labor and Capital*. Boston: South End Press.

——. 1977a. "The Professional-Managerial Class, Part 1." *Radical America* 11:7–31.

——. 1977b. "The Professional-Managerial Class, Part 2" *Radical America* 11:7–22.

Elliot, P. 1972. *The Sociology of the Professions*. London: Macmillan.

Epstein, Cynthia Fuchs. 1981. *Women in Law*. New York: Basic Books.

Etzioni, Amitai. 1969. *The Semi-Professions and Their Organization*. New York: Basic Books.

Falk, Carol. 29 May 1970. "Many Lawyers Take Up Political, Social Causes on Their Firms' Time." *Wall Street Journal*, pp. 1, 15.

Farnum, George. 1936. "A Word for the Lawyers." *Boston University Law Review* 16:887.

Feldman, Martha S., and James March. 1981. "Information in Organizations as Signal and Symbol." *Administrative Science Quarterly* 26:171–86.

Felstiner, William L. F., and Austin Sarat. "Law and Strategy in the Divorce Lawyer's Office." *Law and Society Review* 20:93–134.

Fisk, Margaret. 26 September 1988. "What Does the Future Have in Store?" *The National Law Journal*, pp. 49–50.

Fitzpatrick, James. 1989. "Legal Future Shock: The Role of Large Law Firms by the End of the Century." *Indiana Law Journal* 64:461–71.

Flaharty, Francis. 31 Octeber 1983. "Comparison Shopping Hits the Law: Companies Cut Costs." *The National Law Journal*, pp. 9–11.

Fletcher, G. P. 1981. "Two Modes of Legal Thought." *Yale Law Journal* 90:970–1003.

Flood, John. 1987. "Anatomy of Lawyering: An Ethnography of a Corporate Law Firm." PhD. diss., Northwestern University.

Florida State Bar Journal. 4 February 1986. "President's Page." P. 3.

Fortune. 25 April 1988a. "The Fortune 500 Largest U.S. Industrial Corporations." Pp. D11–60.

——. 6 June 1988b. "The 500 Largest Service Corporations." Pp. D7–38.

——. July 1960a. "The Fortune Directory: The 500 Largest U.S. Industrial Corporations." Pp. 131–50.

——. August 1960b. "The Fortune Directory Part II." Pp. 135–44.

Foucault, Michel. 1980. *Power/Knowledge. Selected Interviews and Other Writings, 1972–1977*. New York: Pantheon Books.

Fowler, Cody. 1951a. "Address." *Nebraska Law Review* 30:239.

——. 1951b. "The American Lawyer and His Problem." In *New Jersey State Bar Association Yearbook*. New Jersey: New Jersey Bar Association.

Frank, J. L. 1976. "Legal Service for Citizens of Moderate Income." In Murray Schwartz, ed., *Law and the American Future*. Englewood Cliffs, N.J.: Prentice-Hall.

——. 1965. "The Legal Ethics of Louis D. Brandeis." *Stanford Law Review* 17:683–709.

Frankel, Marvin. 1975. "The Search for Truth: An Umpireal View." *University of Pennsylvania Law Review* 123:1031–59.

Freedman, Warren. 1951. "The Legal Profession and Socialization: A Reply to Dean Robert G. Storey." *American Bar Association Journal* 37:333.
Freeman, Martha. 1987. "Alternatives to the Old Up or Out." *California Lawyer* 7(12): 44–45, 104–5.
Freidson, Eliot. 1989. *Medical Work in America*. New Haven: Yale University Press.
——. 1986. *Professional Powers: A Study of the Institutionalization of Formal Knowledge*. Chicago: University of Chicago Press.
——. 1983. "The Reorganization of the Professions by Regulation." *Law and Human Behavior* 7:279–90.
——. 1975. *Doctoring Together*. Chicago: University of Chicago Press.
——. 1973. *Professions and Their Prospects*. Beverly Hills, Calif.: Sage Publications.
——. 1972. *The Profession of Medicine*. New York: Dodd, Mead.
——. 1970. *Professional Dominance: The Social Structure of Medical Care*. Chicago: Aldine.
Fried, Charles. 1976. "The Lawyer as Friend: The Moral Foundations of the Lawyer-Client Relation." *Yale Law Journal* 85:1060.
Friedman, Lawrence. 1985. *Total Justice*. New York: Russell Sage Foundation.
——. 1973. *A History of American Law*. New York: Simon and Schuster.
Friedman, Lawrence, and Zigurds Zile. 1964. "Soviet Legal Profession: Recent Developments in Law and Practice." *Wisconsin Law Review* 1964:32–77.
Friedman, Milton. 1962. *Capitalism & Freedom*. Chicago: University of Chicago Press.
Friedman, Stephen J. 1978. "Limitations on the Corporate Lawyer's and Law Firm's Freedom to Serve the Public Interest." *Business Lawyer* 33:1475–1506.
Furry, Thelma. 1948. "Civil Rights and the Legal Profession." *Women Lawyers Journal* 34:21.
Galante, Mary Ann. 22 August 1983a. "Firms Look Closer at How to Create Lawyer Categories." *Los Angeles Daily Journal*, pp. 1, 14.
——. 24 October 1983b. "Meet the Permanent Associate." *The National Law Journal*, pp. 1, 28, 30.
Galanter, Marc. 1983. "Larger than Life: Mega-Law and Mega-Lawyering in the Contemporary United States." In Robert Dingwall and Philip S. C. Lewis, eds., *The Sociology of the Professions: Lawyers, Doctors, and Others*. London: Macmillan.
——. 1974. "Why the Haves Come Out Ahead: Speculation on the Limits of Legal Change." *Law and Society Review* 9:95–160.
Galanter, Marc, and Thomas Palay. 1990a. "The Size of Large Law Firms: Data on One Hundred Firms." Unpublished Paper, University of Wisconsin Law School.
——. 1990b. "Data on Associate Promotion Rates." Unpublished Paper, University of Wisconsin Law School.
——. 1990c. "Why the Big Get Bigger: The Promotion-to-Partner Tournament and the Growth of Large Law Firms." *Virginia Law Review* 76(4):747–811.
——. 1991. *Tournament of Lawyers: The Growth and Transformation of the Big Law Firm*. Chicago: University of Chicago Press.
Galanter, Marc, and Joel Rogers. 1988. "The Transformation of American Business Disputing? Some Preliminary Observations." Paper presented to the annual meeting of the Law and Society Association, Vail, Colorado, 9–12 June.
Gandossy, Robert P. 1985. *Bad Business: The OPM Scandal and the Seduction of the Establishment*. New York: Basic Books.

Garceau, Oliver. 1961. *The Political Life of the American Medical Association*. Hamden, Conn.: Archon.

Garrison, Lloyd. 1936. "Is the Bar Overcrowded?" *Dickinson Law Review* 40:179.

Garth, Bryant. 1983. "Rethinking the Legal Profession's Approach to Collective Self-Improvement: Competence and the Consumer Perspective." *Wisconsin Law Review* 1983:639–87.

Gartner, Michael. 1973. "Guest Opinion: Are Outside Directors Taking Outside Chances?" *Juris Doctor* 3(3):4–5, 37.

Gawalt, Gerard. 1984. *The New High Priests: Lawyers in Post–Civil War America*. Westport, Conn.: Greenwood Press.

Geison, Gerald L. 1983. *Professions and Professional Ideologies in America*. Chapel Hill: University of North Carolina Press.

Georgia Bar Journal. 1986. "Report of the Committee on Professionalism." 23:14–17.

Gibson, Nathan. 1933. "After Graduation—What?" *Oklahoma State Bar Journal* 4:64.

Gilb, Corine L. 1966. *Hidden Hierarchies: The Professions and Government*. New York: Harper & Row.

Gilson, Ronald, and Robert Mnookin. 1989. "Coming of Age in the Corporate Law Firm: The Economics of Associate Career Patterns." *Stanford Law Review* 41:567–95.

——. 1985. "Sharing among the Human Capitalists: An Economic Inquiry into the Corporate Law Firm and How Partners Split Profits." *Stanford Law Review* 37:313–92.

Ginger, Eugene, and Ann Tobin. 1988. *The National Lawyers Guild: From Roosevelt through Reagan*. Philadelphia: Temple University Press.

Goode, William J. 1969. "The Theoretical Limits of Professionalization." In Amitai Etzioni, ed., *The Semi-Professions and Their Organization*. New York: The Free Press.

——. 1960. "Encroachment, Charlatanism, and the Emerging Professions: Psychology, Sociology, and Medicine." *American Sociological Review* 25:902–14.

——. 1957. "Community within a Community: The Professions." *American Sociological Review* 22:194.

Gordon, David M. 1977. "Capitalist Efficiency and Socialist Efficiency." *Monthly Review* 29:19–39.

Gordon, Robert W. 1990. "Corporate Law Practice as a Public Calling." *Maryland Law Review* 49:255.

——. 1988. "The Independence of Lawyers." *Boston University Law Review* 68:1–83.

——. 1984a. "Critical Legal Histories." *Stanford Law Review* 36:57.

——. 1984b. "The Ideal and the Actual." In Gerard Gawalt, ed., *The New High Priests: Lawyers in Post–Civil War America*. Westport, Conn.: Greenwood Press.

——. 1983. "Legal Thought and Legal Practice in the Age of American Enterprise, 1870–1920." In Gerald Geison, ed., *Professions and Professional Ideologies in America*. Chapel Hill: University of North Carolina Press.

——. 1982. "New Developments in Legal Theory." In David Kairys, ed., *The Politics of Law: A Progressive Critique*. New York: Pantheon Books.

Gouldner, Alvin. 1950. *Studies in Leadership*. New York: Harper & Row.

Graham, Deborah. 1983. "New 'Senior' Attorney Program Draws Attention at Davis Polk." *Legal Times* 5(37):3, 7.

Grau, Charles W. 1978. *Judicial Rulemaking: Administration, Access, and Accountability*. Chicago: American Judicature Society.
Green, Mark. 1970. "Law Graduates: The New Breed." *The Nation* 210:658–60.
Greenhouse, Linda. 2 February 1980. "Lawyers' Group Offers a Revision in Code of Ethics: Draft Says Client Interests Could Be Placed Second." *New York Times*, p. 6.
Greenwood, E. 1957. "Attributes of a Profession." *Social Work* 2:44–55.
Griggs, Peter, and Daviryne McNeill. 1987–88. "Upper Ranks Add Heft at Most Big D.C. Firms." *Legal Times* 10(30):4.
Hall, Richard. 1968. "Professionalization and Bureaucratization." *American Sociological Review* 69:92–104.
Hallam, Kirk. 18 March 1983. "Big Firms Search for Alternatives to Traditional Form." *Los Angeles Daily Journal*, pp. 1, 14.
Halliday, Terence C. 1987. *Beyond Monopoly: Lawyers, State Crises, and Professional Empowerment*. Chicago: University of Chicago Press.
——. 1982. "The Idiom of Legalism in Bar Politics: Lawyers, McCarthyism, and the Civil Rights Era." *American Bar Foundation Research Journal* 1982:911.
Halpern, Sydney A. 1988. *American Pediatrics: The Social Dynamics of Professionalism, 1880–1980*. Berkeley and Los Angeles: University of California Press.
Harley, H. 1922. "Group Organization among Lawyers." *Annals of the American Academy of Political and Social Science* 101:33.
Hart, Henry M., and Albert M. Sacks. 1958. *The Legal Process*. (No publisher listed.)
Hart, James P. 1951. "The Law—A Learned Profession." *Texas Bar Journal* 14:498.
Haserot, Phyllis. 19 October 1987. "Multiprofessional Mixes Are Proliferating." *The National Law Journal*, pp. 16, 18.
——. 25 August 1986. "How to Get Associates into the Act." *The National Law Journal*, pp. 15, 21.
Haug, Marie R. 1977. "Computer Technology and the Obsolescence of the Concept of Profession." In M. R. Haug and Jacques Dofny, eds., *Work and Technology*. Beverly Hills, Calif.: Sage Publications.
——. 1975. "The Deprofessionalization of Everyone?" *Sociological Focus* 8 (August): 197–213.
——. 1973. "Deprofessionalization: An Alternative Hypothesis for the Future." *Sociological Review Monograph* 20:195–211.
Haworth, Lawrence. 1977. *Decadence and Objectivity*. Toronto: University of Toronto Press.
Hay, Charles. 1929. "The Place of the Lawyer in American Government." *Colorado Bar Association* 32:114.
Hazard, Geoffrey C. 19 December 1988. "Male Culture Still Dominates the Profession." *The National Law Journal*, p. 13.
——. 1982. "Legal Ethics: Legal Rules and Professional Aspirations." *Cleveland State Law Review* 30:571, 574.
——. 1979. "The Legal and Ethical Position of the Code of Professional Responsibility." In Louis Hodges, ed., *Social Responsibility: Journalism, Law, Medicine*. Lexington, Va.: Washington & Lee University, distributed by W.S. Hein, Buffalo, N.Y.
Hazard, Geoffrey C., Russell G. Pearce, and Jeffrey W. Stempel. 1984. "Why Lawyers

Should Be Allowed to Advertise: A Market Analysis of Legal Services." *New York University Law Review* 58:1084–1109.

Heintz, Bruce. 26 December 1983. "Elements of Law Firm Competition." *The National Law Journal*, pp. 15, 19, 42.

——. 1982. "New Trends in Partner Profit Distribution." *Wisconsin Bar Bulletin* 55(10): 24–26, 45.

Heinz, John. 1983. "The Power of Lawyers." *Georgia Law Review* 17:891.

Heinz, John, and Edward Laumann. 1982. *Chicago Lawyers: The Social Structure of the Bar*. New York and Chicago: Russell Sage Foundation and American Bar Foundation.

Hergistod, O. B. 1945. "The Lawyer in the Post-War Era." *North Dakota Bar Review Briefs* 21:15.

Heydebrand, Wolf. 1989. "New Organizational Forms." *Work and Occupations* 16:323–57.

——. 1973. "The Study of Organizations." In Wolf Heydebrand, ed., *Comparative Organizations*. Englewood Cliffs, N.J. Prentice-Hall.

Heymann, Philip B., and Lance Liebman. 1988. *The Social Responsibility of Lawyers: Case Studies*. Westbury, N.Y.: Foundation Press.

Higginbotham, F. Michael. 1982. " 'See No Evil, Hear No Evil'—Developing a Policy for Disclosure by Counsel to Public Corporations." *Journal of Corporation Law* 7:285.

Hinshaw, Joseph. 1951. "Public Relations." *Illinois Bar Journal* 40:37.

Hirsch, Ronald L. 1989. "Will Women Leave the Law?" *Barrister* 16:22–29.

——. 1985. "Are You on Target?" 12(1):17–20, 49–50.

Hirschhorn, Larry. 1988. "The Post-Industrial Economy: Labour, Skills, and the New Mode of Production." *The Services Industries Journal* 8:19–38.

——. 1984. *Beyond Mechanization*. Cambridge: MIT Press.

Hirschhorn, Larry, and Katherine Farquhar. 1985. "Productivity, Technology, and the Decline of the Autonomous Professional." *Office: Technology and People* 2:245–65.

Hobson, Wayne. 1986. *The American Legal Profession and the Organizational Society 1890–1930*. New York: Garland Publishing.

Hochschild, Arlie. 1989. *The Second Shift*. New York: Penguin Books.

Hoffman, Junius. 1978. "On Learning of a Corporate Client's Crime or Fraud—The Lawyer's Dilemma." *Business Lawyer* 33: 1389.

Hoffman, Paul. 1973. *Lions in the Street: The Inside Story of the Great Wall Street Firms*. New York: Saturday Review Press.

Hofstadter, Richard. 1955. *The Age of Reform: From Bryan to F.D.R.*. New York: Knopf.

Holmes, Deborah. 1988. "Structural Causes of Dissatisfaction among Large-Firm Attorneys: A Feminist Perspective." Working Paper, Institute for Legal Studies.

Hubbard, Nelson. 1930. "President's Annual Address." *South Dakota Bar Association* 31:203.

Huggins, W. O. 1933. "The Editor Talks to the Lawyers." *Commercial Law Journal* 38:292.

Hughes, Everett. 1984. "The Humble and the Proud: The Comparative Study of Occupations." In Everett Hughes, ed., *The Sociological Eye*. New Brunswick, N.J.: Transaction Books.

——. 1971. *The Sociological Eye: Selected Papers*. Chicago: Aldine.

——. 1958. *Men and Their Work*. Glencoe, Ill.: The Free Press.
Hurst, James Willard. 1950. *The Growth of American Law: The Lawmakers*. Boston: Little, Brown.
Hutchens, Martin. 1925. "The Relation of the Lawyer to the Public." *Montana Bar Association* 1925:108.
Illinois Bar Journal. 1988. "Illinois State Bar Association Report of the Special Committee on Professionalism." 76:441–52.
Jackall, Robert. 1988. *Moral Mazes: The World of Corporate Managers*. New York: Oxford University Press.
Jaffe, Louis, L. 1937. "Law Making by Private Groups." *Harvard Law Review* 51:201.
Jenner, Albert E. 1954. "The State Association." *Michigan State Bar Journal* 33:48.
Jensen, Rita. 19 February 1990. "Minorities Didn't Share in Firm Growth." *The National Law Journal*, pp. 28–31, 35.
—— 18 January 1988. "Banking Clients More Willing to Shop for Firms." *The National Law Journal*, pp. 1, 18.
——. 10 August 1987a. "Partners Work Harder to Stay Even." *The National Law Journal*, p. 12.
——. 5 October 1987b. "The Rainmakers." *The National Law Journal*, pp. 1, 28, 30.
Johnson, O. Stanley. 1942. "Leadership and Legal Training." *Rocky Mountain Law Review* 15:87.
Johnson, Terence C. 1972. *Professions and Power*. London: Macmillan.
Johnstone, Quintin, and Dan Hopson, Jr. 1967. *Lawyers and Their Work: An Analysis of the Legal Profession in the United States and England*. Indianapolis: Bobbs-Merrill.
Joint Conference on Professional Responsibility. 1959. "Professional Responsibility: A Statement." *South Carolina Law Quarterly 11*:306–20.
Kagan, Robert, and John Scholz. 1984. "The Criminology of the Corporation and Regulatory Enforcement Strategies." In Keith Hawkins and John Thomas, eds., *Enforcing Regulation*. Hingham, Mass.: Kluwer Boston.
Kahler, Kathryn. 2 December 1988. "Women Lawyers Bailing Out: Family Issues and Sexual Discrimination Are Forcing Many into Other Careers." *Chicago Sun-Times*, p. 39.
Kanter, Rosabeth Moss. 1983. *The Change Masters: Innovation and Entrepreneurship in the American Corporation*. New York: Simon and Schuster.
——. 1977. *Men and Women of the Corporation*. New York: Basic Books.
Kariel, Henry S. 1961. *The Decline of American Pluralism*. Stanford: Stanford University Press.
Karmel, Roberta. 1972. "Attorneys' Securities Law Liabilities." *Business Lawyer* 27: 1153–64.
Katz, Jack. 1982. *Poor People's Lawyers in Transition*. New Brunswick: Rutgers University Press.
Kaufman, Andrew L. 1986. "A Commentary on Pepper's 'The Lawyer's Amoral Role.' " *American Bar Foundation Research Journal* 1986:651.
Kaufman, Irving R. 1954. "Representation by Counsel: A Threatened Right." *American Bar Association Journal* 40:299.
Kemp, William. 1933. "A Review of *I Want to Be a Lawyer*." *Missouri Bar Journal* 4:5.
Kennedy, Duncan. 1982. "Legal Education as Training for Hierarchy." In David Kairys, ed., *The Politics of Law*. David Kairys, ed. New York: Pantheon.

Kessel, Reuben. 1958. "Price Discrimination in Medicine." *Law and Economics* 1:20–53.
Kessler, Mark. 1987. *Legal Services for the Poor: A Comparative and Contemporary Analysis of Interorganizational Politics*. New York: Greenwood Press.
Kiechel, Walter. 23 October 1978. "Growing Up at Kutak Rock & Huie." *Fortune*, pp. 112–20.
Kingson, Jennifer. 8 August 1988. "Women in the Law Say Path Is Limited By 'Mommy Track.'" *New York Times*, pp. 1, 15.
Klaw, Spencer. February 1958. "The Wall Street Lawyers." *Fortune*, pp. 140–44, 192–98, 202.
Klemesrud, Judy. 9 August 1985. "Women in the Law: Many Are Getting Out." *New York Times*, p. 14.
Kornhauser, William. 1962. *Scientists in Industry*. Berkeley and Los Angeles: University of California Press.
Koskoff, Theodore. August 1980. "Introduction to the *American Lawyer's Code of Conduct*." *Trial*, pp. 46–47.
Kotter, John. 1982. *The General Managers*. New York: The Free Press.
Krankman, Rainier. 1985. "The Economic Functions of Corporate Liability." In Klaus Hopt and Gunther Teubner eds., *Corporate Governance and Directors' Liabilities*. New York: Walter de Gruyter.
Kramer, Victor. 1979. "Clients' Frauds and Their Lawyers' Obligations: A Study in Professional Irresponsibility." *Georgetown Law Journal* 67:991–1003.
Labaton, Stephen. 18 April 1988. "Lawyers Debate Temporary Work." *New York Times*, p. D2.
Ladinsky, Jack. 1963. "Careers of Lawyers: Law Practice and Legal Institutions." *American Sociological Review* 28:47–54.
Landon, Donald D. 1990. *Country Lawyers: The Impact of Context on Professional Practice*. New York: Praeger Publishers.
Lane, Robert E. 1977. "Why Businessmen Violate the Law." In Gilbert Geis and Robert F. Meier, eds., *White Collar Crime*, New York: The Free Press.
Larson, Magali Sarfatti. 1980. "Proletarianization and Educated Labor." *Theory and Society* 9:131–75.
——. 1977. *The Rise of Professionalism*. Berkeley and Los Angeles: University of California Press.
Lasch, Christopher. 1977. *Haven in a Heartless World*. New York: Basic Books.
Lauter, David. 26 January 1984. " 'Outsiders' Who Work for Firms." *The National Law Journal*, pp. 1, 32.
Law and Society Review. 1988. "Special Issue: Law and Ideology." Ed. Robert L. Kidder. 22:623.
Levy, Beryl. 1961. *Corporation Lawyer: Saint or Sinner*. Philadelphia: Chilton.
Lewin, Tamar. 11 February 1987. "Outside Ventures Transform Law Firms." *New York Times*, pp. D1, D7.
——. 18 April 1986. "At Cravath, $65,000 to Start." *New York Times*, pp. D1, D18.
——. 4 October 1984. "The New National Law Firms." *New York Times*, pp. D1, D6.
Lewis, John. 1929. "Some Duties and Responsibilities of the Legal Profession." *Commercial Law League Journal* 34:747.
Lieber, Carol N. Summer 1984. "Corporate Law: Where the Action Is." *Barrister* p. 23.

Lieberman, Jethro. 1978. *Crisis at the Bar: Lawyer's Unethical Ethics and What to Do about It*. New York: W. W. Norton.

Liggio, Carl. 1984. Remarks in Federal Bar Council, conference proceedings of the 1984 Bench and Bar Conference, Dorado, Puerto Rico, 29 January—5 February.

Lipset, Seymour, Martin A. Trow, and James S. Coleman. 1956. *Union Democracy: The Internal Politics of the International Typographical Union*. Glencoe, Ill.: The Free Press.

Lipsky, Michael. 1980. *Street-level Bureaucracy: Dilemmas of the Individual in Public Service*. New York: Russell Sage Foundation.

Lisagor, Nancy, and Frank Lipsius. 1988. *A Law unto Itself: The Untold Story of the Law Firm Sullivan and Cromwell*. New York: William Morrow.

Lopez, Gerald. 1989. "Training Future Lawyers to Work with the Politically and Socially Subordinated: Anti-Generic Legal Education." *West Virginia Law Review* 91:305.

Luban, David. 1988. *Lawyers and Justice*. Princeton: Princeton University Press.

——. 1984. *The Good Lawyer*. Totowa, N.J.: Rowman & Allanheld.

——. 1983. "The Adversary System Excuse." In David Luban, ed., *The Good Lawyer: Lawyers' Roles and Lawyers' Ethics*. Totowa, N.J.: Rowman & Allanheld.

Lubove, Roy. 1965. *The Professional Altruist: The Emergence of Social Work as a Career*. Cambridge: Harvard University Press.

Lumbard, Thomas. 1981. "Setting Standards: The Courts, the Bar, and the Lawyers' Code of Conduct." *Catholic University Law Review* 30:249–71.

Lundberg, Ferdinand. April 1939a. "The Priesthood of the Law." *Harper's Magazine*, pp. 515, 526.

——. July 1939b. "The Law Factories: Brains of the Status Quo." *Harper's Magazine*, pp. 180–92.

——. December 1938. "The Legal Profession: A Social Phenomenon." *Harper's Magazine*, p. 1.

Lydenberg, Steven, Alice Tepper Marlin, Sean O'Brien Strub, and the Council on Economic Priorities. 1986. *Rating America's Corporate Conscience*. Reading, Mass.: Addison-Wesley.

Lyons, James. October 1985. "Baker & McKenzie: The Belittled Giant." *The American Lawyer*, pp. 115–22.

Macaulay, Stewart. 1979. "Lawyers and Consumer Protection Laws." *Law and Society Review* 14:115–71.

——. 1963. "Non-Contractual Relations in Business." *American Sociological Review* 28:55–76.

MacCrate, Robert. 1988. "Perspectives on Professionalism." Speech to the American Bar Foundation's Conference on Professionalism, Ethics and Economic Change in the American Legal Profession, Evanston, Illinois, 23, September.

MacDonald, Keith, and George Ritzer. 1988. "The Sociology of the Professions: Dead or Alive?" *Work and Occupations* 15:251–72.

Mairs, Patricia. 14 March 1988. "Bringing Up Baby." *The National Law Journal*, pp. 1, 7–8.

Mann, Kenneth. 1985. *Defending White Collar Crime: A Portrait of Attorneys at Work*. New Haven: Yale University Press.

Mansnerus, Laura. 2 June 1989. "Rule on Temporary Lawyers Changes Again." *New York Times*, p. B6.

Manton, Martin. 1933. "A 'New Deal' for Lawyers." *American Bar Association Journal* 19:599.
Marcus, Ruth. 13 March 1986. "Lawyers Branch Out from the Law." *Washington Post*, pp. A1, A17.
Martin, Clarence. 1933. "The Law in Retrospect and Prospect." *American Bar Association Journal* 19:137.
Marx, Karl. 1972. *The Essential Writings*. Ed. Frederic L. Bender. New York: Harper & Row.
Mather, Lynn, and Barbara Yngvesson. 1981. "Language, Audience, and the Transformation of Disputes." *Law and Society Review* 15:775–822.
Matthews, John. 1939. "Public Duties and Responsibilities of Lawyers." *Florida Law Journal* 13:184.
Maxwell, David F. 1957. "The Public View of the Legal Profession." *American Bar Association Journal* 42:785.
Mayer, Charles. 1984. "Corporate Counsel Come in from the Cold." *California Lawyer* 4(3):43.
Mayer, Martin. 1966. *The Lawyers*. New York: Harper & Row.
——. January 1956a. "The Wall Street Lawyers, Part I: The Elite Corps of American Business." *Harper's Magazine*, pp. 31–45.
——. February 1956b. "Keepers of the Business Conscience: The Wall Street Lawyers, Part II." *Harper's Magazine*, pp. 50–56.
McGregor, Douglas. 1960. *The Human Side of Enterprise*. New York: McGraw-Hill.
McIntyre, Lisa J. 1987. *The Public Defender: The Practice of Law in the Shadows of Repute*. Chicago: University of Chicago Press.
McKinlay, John B., and J. D. Stoeckle. 1988. "Corporatization and the Social Transformation of Doctoring." *International Journal of Health Services* 18:191–205.
McNutt, Paul. 1939. "The Lawyer in Government." *Federal Bar Association Journal* 3:359.
——. 1931. "The Triumvirate of the Profession of the Law." *Illinois State Bar Association* 1931:268.
Meadow, Robert, and Carrie Menkel-Meadow. 1982. "Personalized or Bureaucratized Justice in Legal Services: Resolving Sociological Ambivalence in the Delivery of Legal Aid to the Poor." *Law and Human Behavior* 9:397–413.
Melone, Albert P. 1977. *Lawyers, Public Policy, and Interest Group Politics*. Washington, D.C.: University Press of America.
Melton, Alger. 1925. "Lawyers, Judges, and Courts." *Oklahoma State Bar Association* 157.
Menkel-Meadow, Carrie. 1989. "Feminization of the Legal Profession: The Comparative Sociology of Lawyers." In Richard Abel and Philip S. C. Lewis, ed., *Lawyers and Society: Comparative Theories*. Berkeley and Los Angeles: University of California Press.
——. 1985. "Portia in a Different Voice: Speculations on a Women's Lawyering Process." *Berkeley Women's Law Journal* 1:39.
——. 1979. *The 59th Street Legal Clinic: Evaluation of the Experiment*. Chicago: American Bar Association.
Menkel-Meadow, Carrie, and Robert Meadow. 1983. "Resource Allocation in Legal Services." *Law and Policy Quarterly* 5:237–56.

Merry, Sally. 1990. *Getting Justice and Getting Even: Legal Consciousness among Working-Class Americans*. Chicago: University of Chicago Press.

Merton, Robert. 1968. *Social Theory and Social Structure*. 3d ed. New York: The Free Press.

Mertz, Elizabeth. 1988. "The Uses of History: Language, Ideology, and Law in the United States and South Africa." *Law and Society Review* 22:661–85.

Metzger, Walter P. 1987. "A Spectre Is Haunting American Scholars: The Spectre of 'Professionalism.' " *Educational Researcher* 16:10–19.

Meyer, John, and Brian Rowan. 1978. "Institutional Organizations: Formal Structure as Myth and Ceremony." *American Journal of Sociology* 83:340–63.

Michels, Robert. 1949. *Political Parties*. Glencoe, Ill.: The Free Press.

Michigan State Bar Journal. 1954. Symposium. 33: 33.

Middleton, Martha. 4 July 1988. "A Centenarian Firm Grows-Up Fast." *The National Law Journal*, pp. 38–39.

——. 4 June 1984. "Getting Support." *The National Law Journal*, pp. 1, 26, 28.

Mintz, Morton. 1985. *At Any Cost*. New York: Pantheon Books.

Mintzberg, Henry. 1973. *The Nature of Managerial Work*. New York: Harper & Row.

Montagna, Paul. 1973. "The Public Accounting Profession: Organization, Ideology, and Social Power." In Eliot Freidson, ed., *The Professions and Their Prospects*, Beverly Hills, Calif.: Sage Publications.

Moore, Wilbert. 1970. *The Professions: Roles and Rules*. New York: Russell Sage Foundation.

Morgan, Thomas. 1977. "The Evolving Concept of Professional Responsibility." *Harvard Law Review* 90:702–43.

Morris, George. 1939. "The Lawyers and the Public." *New Hampshire Bar Association* 7:9.

Murphy, J. D. 1926. "Reminiscences of Bench and Bar in a Lighter Vein." *North Carolina Bar Association* 28:61–78.

Nader, Ralph, and Mark Green, eds. 1976. *Verdicts on Lawyers*. New York: Thomas Y. Crowell.

National Industrial Conference Board. 1959. "Organization of Legal Work." *The Conference Board Business Record*.

——. 9 July 1990b. "The Long Rise and Quick Fall of Marshall Manley." Pp. 1, 26–27.

——. 12 June 1989a. "Legal Search Profession Annual Survey." Pp. S1–52.

——. 24 July 1989b. "Mass Firing in Seattle." P. 2.

——. 26 September 1988. "The NLJ 250." Pp. S1–28.

National Lawyers Guild. 1939. "The Neighborhood Law Office Plan." *National Lawyers Guild Quarterly* 2:140.

National Organization of Bar Counsel. 8 Aug. 1981. *Proposed Amended Disciplinary Rules to the ABA Model Code of Professional Responsibility*. New Orleans: National Organization of Bar Counsel.

Nelson, Robert. 1990. "Analysis of Hirsch Data by Robert L. Nelson." In Geoffrey C. Hazard and Susan P. Koniak, eds., *The Law and Ethics of Lawyering*. Westbury, N.Y.: Foundation Press.

——. 1988. *Partners with Power: The Social Transformation of the Large Law Firm*. Berkeley and Los Angeles: University of California Press.

——. 1987. "Ideology, Scholarship, and Social Change: Lessons from Galanter and the Litigation Crisis." *Law and Society Review* 21:676–93.

Nelson, Robert L., John P. Heinz, Edward O. Laumann, and Robert H. Salisbury. 1987. "Private Representation in Washington: Surveying the Structure of Influence." *American Bar Foundation Research Journal* 1987:141.

New York Times. 2 June 1989a. "New Partner in the Firm: The Marketing Director." P. B6.

——. 9 June 1989b. "Law Firms Moving Rapidly into New Businesses." P. 27.

——. 21 September 1988. "Big Exodus of Lawyers at Top Firm." P. 27.

——. 11 February 1983. "Lawyers for Hire for Anything"? P. A26.

——. 7 May 1957. "Bar Group Backs Bid by Stevenson." P. 38.

Newton, Lisa. 1983. "Professionalism: The Intractable Plurality of Values." In Wade L. Robinson, Michael S. Pritchard, and Joseph Ellin, eds., *Profits and Professions: Essays in Business and Professional Ethics*. Clifton, N.J.: Humana Press.

——. 1981. "Lawgiving for Professional Life: Reflections on the Place of the Professional Code." *Business and Professional Ethics Journal* 1:41.

Niehuss, Marvin L. 1954. "It's What You Do." *Michigan State Bar Journal* 33:7.

Noble, Charles. 1987. *Liberalism at Work: The Rise and Fall of OSHA*. Philadelphia: Temple University Press.

Noble, David. 1977. *America by Design: Science, Technology, and the Rise of Corporate Capitalism*. Oxford: Oxford University Press.

North Carolina State Bar Quarterly. 1987. "Commercialism versus Professionalism." 34:13–20.

O'Barr, William, and John Conley. 1985. "Litigant Satisfaction versus Legal Adequacy in Small Claims Court Narratives." *Law and Society Review* 19:661.

Ober, Frank. 1948. "Communism vs. the Constitution." *American Bar Association Journal* 34:645.

Of Counsel. 1989. "Of Counsel 500." 8(8):18–20.

O'Neill, Suzanne. 16 January 1989. "Associates Can Attract Clients Too." *The National Law Journal*, pp. 17, 20.

Oppenheimer, Martin. 1973. "The Proletarianization of the Professional." *Sociological Review Monograph* 20:213–27.

Orey, Michael. September 1987. "Staff Attorneys: Basic Work at Bargain Prices." *The American Lawyer*, p. 20.

Otterbourg, Edwin M. 1948. "New National Statement of Principles between Life Underwriters and Lawyers." *Trusts and Estates* 86:291.

——. 1939. "Address in Answer to Recent Criticism of the Bar." *Law Society Journal* 8:270.

Ouchi, William. 1984. *Theory Z*. Reading, Mass.: Addison-Wesley.

Overstreet, Carl Lee. 1933. "The Inquiring Laymen." *Missouri Bar Journal* 7:301.

Parke, Neal. 1925. "Certain Lay Critics." *Maryland State Bar Association* 1925:3.

Parsons, Talcott. 1969. " 'The Intellectual': A Social Role Category." In Philip Rieff, ed., *On Intellectuals*. New York: Doubleday Anchor.

——. 1968a. *The Structure of Social Action*. New York: The Free Press.

——. 1968b. "Professions." In David L. Sills, ed., *International Enclopedia of the Social Sciences, XII*. New York: The Free Press.

——. 1962. "The Legal Profession." In William M. Evan, ed., *Law and Sociology*. Glencoe, Ill.: The Free Press.

——. 1954. *Essays in Sociological Theory*. Glencoe, Ill.: The Free Press.

——. 1951. *The Social System*. Glencoe, Ill.: The Free Press.

——. 1939. "The Professions and Social Structure." *Social Forces* 17:457–67.

Pashigian, B. Peter. 1978. "The Number and Earnings of Lawyers: Some Recent Findings." *American Bar Foundation Research Journal* 1978:51.

Payne, John 1977. "The Weakness of Bar Associations." *Journal of the Legal Profession* 2:55–76.

Pefferle, Leslie George. 1936. "Why Attack the Legal Profession?" *Illinois Bar Journal* 25:99.

Pepper, Stephen L. 1986a. "The Lawyer's Amoral Role: A Defense, A Problem, and Some Possibilities." *American Bar Foundation Research Journal* 1986:613.

——. 1986b. "A Rejoinder to Professors Kaufman and Luban." *American Bar Foundation Research Journal* 1986:657.

Pershing, J. J. 1928. "Obligations of the Bar to the State and the People." *American Bar Association Journal* 14:65.

Pfennigstorf, Werner, and Spencer L. Kimball. 1977. *Legal Service Plans: Approaches to Regulation*. Chicago: American Bar Foundation.

Pinansky, Thomas. 1986–87. "The Emergence of Law Firms in the American Legal Profession." *University of Arkansas at Little Rock Law Review* 9:593–640.

Pope, Jack. 1957. "The Duties of the Profession: What the Organized Bar Owes to the Public." *American Bar Association Journal* 43:801–4.

Postema, Gerald. 1980. "Moral Responsibility in Professional Ethics." *New York University Law Review* 55:63–89.

Pound, Roscoe. 1909. "The Etiquette of Justice." *Proceedings of the Nebraska State Bar Association* 3:231–51.

Powell, Elmer. 1936. "The Lawyer—His Problem and Responsibility." *Kansas City Law Review* 4:83.

Powell, Michael. 1988. *From Patrician to Professional Elite: The Transformation of the New York City Bar Association*. New York: Russell Sage Foundation.

——. 1987. "Professional Innovation: Corporate Lawyers and Private Lawmaking." Unpublished manuscript on file at the American Bar Foundation.

——. 1986. "Professional Divestiture: The Cession of Responsibility for Lawyer Discipline." *American Bar Foundation Research Journal*. 1986:31–54.

——. 1985. "Developments in the Regulation of Lawyers: Competing Segments and Market, Client, and Government Control." *Social Forces* 64:281–305.

——. 1979. "Anatomy of a Counter-Bar Association: The Chicago Council of Lawyers." *American Bar Foundation Research Journal* 1979:501–41.

Practicing Law Institute. 1965. "Managing Law Offices." In the edited transcript of the proceedings of the Practicing Law Institute Forum, Statler Hilton Hotel, New York, 20–21 May.

Price-Waterhouse. 1989. Trends Presentation to the American Bar Foundation by James Rabenhorst. Chicago, Illinois.

Quinlan, Edward. 1942. "The Lawyers' Relation to the Public." *Connecticut Bar Journal* 16:117.

Ragland, Rawlings. 1933. "Learning to be Lawyers." *Kentucky Bar Association Journal* 1933:120.

Ransom, William. 1936a. "The Bar's Duty to the Public." *New Jersey State Bar Association Quarterly* 3:15. Reprint of a speech to the Indiana State Bar.

——. 1936b. "Entering the Profession of Law." *American Bar Association Journal* 22:563. Reprint of an address to the Albany Law School.

——. 1936c. "The Lawyer in a Time of Change." *American Bar Association Journal* 22:389.

——. 1936d. "Lawyers and Government." *Washington Law Review* 11:251.

——. 1936e. "Next Steps for Bar Associations and the Bar." *Pennsylvania Bar Association* 42:398.

——. 1936f. "Which Road for the Legal Profession?" *American Bar Association Journal*. 22:21.

Rehnquist, William H. 1987. "The Legal Profession Today." *Indiana Law Journal* 62:151–52.

Reid, Thomas R. 1954. "Your Stake in Civil Affairs." *Wisconsin Bar Bulletin* 27:7.

Reisman, W. M. 1979. *Folded Lies: Bribery, Crusades, and Reforms*. London: Collier Macmillan.

Relman, Arnold S. 1980. "The New Medical-Industrial Complex." *New England Journal of Medicine* 303:963–70.

Rhode, Deborah. 1985. "Ethical Perspectives on Legal Practice." *Stanford Law Review* 37:589–652.

——. 1981. "Why the ABA Bothers: A Functional Perspective on Professional Codes." *Texas Law Review* 59:689–721.

Rhode, Deborah, and David Luban. Forthcoming. *Legal Ethics*. New York: Foundation Press.

Ridgway, Thomas. 1929. "Assuming Our Responsibilities." *California State Bar Association* 2:44.

Ritzer, George and David Walczak. 1988. "Rationalization and the Deprofessionalization of Physicians." *Social Forces* 67:1–20.

Robinson, T. 4 February 1980. "Proposed Ethics Code Gives Clients a Clean Break." *Washington Post*, p. C1.

Rosen, Robert. 1989. "The Inside Counsel Movement, Professional Judgement, and Organizational Representation." *Indiana Law Journal* 64:479–90.

——. 1984. *Lawyers in Corporate Decision Making*. Ph.D. diss., University of California, Berkeley.

Rosenthal, Douglas. 1974. *Lawyer and Client: Who's in Charge*? New York: Russell Sage Foundation.

Roth, Andrew, and Jonathan Roth. 1989. *The Unnatural History of Lawyers*. Berkeley, Calif.: Nolo Press.

Roth, Julius A. 1974. "Professionalism: The Sociologist's Decoy." *Sociology of Work and Occupations* 1:6–23.

Rothman, Robert. 1984. "Deprofessionalization: The Case of Law in America." *Work and Occupations* 11:183–206.

Rothschild, Joyce, and Raymond Russell. 1986. "Alternatives to Bureaucracy: Democratic Participation in the Economy." *Annual Review of Sociology* 12:307–28.

Rotunda, Ronald. 1983. "The Notice of Withdrawal and the New Model Rules of Professional Conduct." *Oregon Law Review* 63:455–84.

Rubin, Samuel. 1928. "The Public Defender an Aid to Criminal Justice." *American Law Review* 62:385.

Salisbury, R. H. 1979. "Why No Corporatism in America?" In Phillipe C. Schmitter and Gerhard Lehmbruch, eds., *Trends toward Corporatist Intermediation*. Beverly Hills, Calif.: Sage Publication.

Salter, Leonard. 1942. "In Time to Come—From the Lawyer's Viewpoint." *Commercial Law Journal* 47:135.

Saltonstall, Susan, and Page Lane. 6 June 1988. "Consultancies Develop with Specialties, Client Needs." *The National Law Journal*, pp. 25, 28–29.

Sander, Richard H., and Douglas Williams. 1989. "Why Are There So Many Lawyers? Perspectives on a Turbulent Market." *Law and Social Inquiry* 14:431–79.

Sarat, Austin. 1977. "Studying American Legal Cultures: An Assessment of Survey Evidence." *Law and Society Review* 11:427–67.

Sarat, Austin, and William L. F. Felstiner. 1988. "Law and Social Relations: Vocabularies of Motive in Lawyer/Client Interaction." *Law and Society Review* 22:709–36.

Schaefer, C. B. 1982. "Proposed Model Rule 5.4: Is It Necessary for Corporate Staff Counsel?" *Creighton Law Review* 15:639–49.

Schmidt, Sally. 25 August 1986. "Firm Development Mobilized by a 'New Breed' of Resource." *The National Law Journal*, pp. 15, 17, 19.

Schneyer, Theodore 1989. "Professionalism as Bar Politics: The Making of the Model Rules of Professional Conduct." *Law and Social Inquiry* 14:677–737.

——. 1988. "Professionalism and Public Policy: The Case of House Counsel." *Georgetown Journal of Legal Ethics* 2:449–84.

——. 1983. "The Incoherence of the Unified Bar Concept: Generalizing from the Wisconsin Case." *American Bar Foundation Research Journal* 1983:1–108.

Schwartz, Murray L. 1980a. "The Death and Regeneration of Ethics." *American Bar Foundation Research Journal* 1980:953–63.

——. 1980b. "The Reorganization of the Legal Profession." *Texas Law Review* 58: 1269–90.

——. 1978. "The Professionalism and Accountability of Lawyers." *California Law Review* 66:669.

Scott, James C. 1987. "Protest and Profanation: Agrarian Revolt and the Little Tradition." *Theory and Society* 4:1–38, 211–46.

Scott, Richard. 1969. "Professional Employees in a Bureaucratic Structure: Social Work." In Amitai Etzioni, ed., *The Semi-Professions and Their Organization*. New York: The Free Press.

——. 1965. "Reactions to Supervision in a Heteronomous Professional Organization." *Administrative Science Quarterly* 10:65–81.

Shaffer, T. L. 1981. *On Being a Christian and a Lawyer*. Provo, Utah: Brigham Young University Press.

Shklar, Judith N. 1964. *Legalism*. Cambridge: Harvard University Press.

Shuchman, Philip. 1968. "Ethics and Legal Ethics: The Propriety of the Canons as a Group Moral Code." *George Washington Law Review* 37:244–69.

Siconolfi, Michael. 18 November 1985. "Law Firms Aren't Simply for Law as Attempts to Diversify Begin." *Wall Street Journal*, p. 33.

Siddall, Roger B. 1956. *A Survey of Large Law Firms in the United States*. New York: Vantage Press.

Sigler, Kim. 1948. "How the Legal Profession Can Aid the Cause of Good Government." *Dicta* 25:235.

Silas, Faye. 1986. "Diversification." *American Bar Association Journal* 72:17–18.

Silbey, Susan S., and Sally E. Merry. 1986. "Mediator Settlement Strategies." *Law and Policy* 8:7.

Simmons, D. A. 1939. The Responsibility of the Lawyer in a Democracy." *New Mexico State Bar*, p. 121.

Simon, Ruth. 4 July 1988. "Paralegals: The Hottest Job Market." *The National Law Journal*, p. 1.

Simon, William. 1988. "Ethical Discretion in Lawyering." *Harvard Law Review* 101: 1083–1145.

——. 1985. "Babbitt v. Brandeis: The Decline of the Professional Ideal." *Stanford Law Review* 37:565–87.

——. 1978. "The Ideology of Advocacy: Procedural Justice and Professional Ethics." *Wisconsin Law Review* 1978:29–144.

Sims, Cecil. 1954. "The Lawyer and the Classics." *Arkansas Law Review* 8:343.

Singer, Amy. January/February 1987. "Senior Attorney Programs: Half a Loaf." *The American Lawyer*, p. 12.

Singsen, Gary. 1985. "Personal Legal Services: Problems and Possibilities in the Marketplace." Unpublished manuscript.

——. 1984. "New Providers in the Marketplace: Prepaid, Mass Market, and Clinical Legal Services." Unpublished manuscript.

Slovak, Jeffrey S. 1979. "Working for Corporate Actors: Social Change and Elite Attorneys in Chicago." *American Bar Foundation Research Journal* 1979:465–500.

Smigel, Erwin O. 1964. *The Wall Street Lawyer: Professional Organization Man?* New York: The Free Press.

Smith, Beverly. 1925. "The Business-Getter." *American Mercury* 5(18):199–201.

Smith, Chesterfield. 1976. "Lawyers Who Take Must Put—At Least a Bit." *Journal of the Legal Profession* 1:27–31.

Smith, Larry. 1989. "National Study: Lateral Hiring Continues Unabated." *Lawyer Hiring and Training Report* 9(13):6–8.

Smith, Reginald Heber. 1941. "Law Office Organization III." *American Bar Association Journal* 26:610–16.

——. 1939. "The Bar Association Law Office for Persons of Moderate Means." *Boston University Law Review* 19:226.

Snively, John. 1933. "Review of Recent Activities to Eliminate Lay Encroachments." *American Bar Association Journal* 19:177.

Social Research Service. 1949. *The State Bar of Michigan Survey: Report on a Pilot Study*. Michigan State University.

Solicitor's Journal. 1926. "George III and Lawyers." 70:991.

Solomon, Lewis D., and Nancy Stein Nowak. 1980. "Managerial Restructuring: Prospects for a New Regulatory Tool." *Notre Dame Law Review* 56:120.

Solomon, Rayman. 1985. "Regulating the Regulators: Prohibition in the Seventh Circuit." In David E. Kyvig, ed., *Law, Alcohol, and Order: Perspectives on National Prohibition*. Westport, Conn.: Greenwood Press.

South Carolina Law Quarterly. 1958. "Professional Responsibility: A Statement." 11:306.

Spangler, Eve. 1986. *Lawyers for Hire: Salaried Professionals at Work*. New Haven: Yale University Press.

Spencer, Herbert. 1896. *The Principles of Sociology*. Vol. 3. New York: D. Appleton.

Stanley, W. A. 1939. "Will the Public Listen?" *Journal of the Bar Association of Kansas* 8:211.

Starr, Paul. 1982. *The Social Transformation of American Medicine*. New York: Basic Books.

State Bar of Texas Committee on Public Information. 1952. *What Texans Think of Lawyers*. Austin, Tex.: Joe Belden and Associates.

Stathers, William. 1939. "The Law—An Appraisement." *West Virginia Law Quarterly* 46:5.

Stevens, Mark. 1987. *Power of Attorney: The Rise of the Giant Law Firms*. New York: McGraw-Hill.

Stevens, Robert B. 1983. *Law School: Legal Education in America from the 1850s to the 1980s*. Chapel Hill: University of North Carolina Press.

Stevenson, Tom. 1973. "The Talent Peddlers." *Juris Doctor* 3(7):12, 13.

Stewart, James B. 1983. *The Partners: Inside America's Most Powerful Law Firms*. New York: Simon and Schuster.

Stille, Alexander. 21 October 1985. "When Law Firms Start Their Own Businesses." *The National Law Journal*, pp. 1, 20–22.

Stone, Christopher D. 1985. "Public Interest Representation: Economic and Social Policy Inside the Enterprise." In Klaus Hopt and Gunther Teubner, eds., *Corporate Governance and Directors' Liabilities*. New York: Walter de Gruyter.

——. 1975. *Where the Law Ends*. New York: Harper & Row.

Stone, Julius. 1958. *Two Hundred and Fifty Thousand Lawyers*. Committee on Education for Professional Responsibility, Association of American Law Schools.

Stone, Robert. 1942. "To Do or Not to Do." *Journal of the Bar Association of Kansas* 10:273.

Storey, Robert. 1951. "The Legal Profession versus Regimentation: A Program to Counter Socialization." *American Bar Association Journal* 37:168.

Strong, Theron. 1914. *Landmarks of a Lawyer's Lifetime*. New York: Dodd, Mead.

Sugarman, David. 1991. "Lawyers and Business in England, 1750–1950." Paper presented to Working Group on Corporate Practitioners. Centre de Recherche Interdisciplinaire de Vaucresson. Vaucresson, France.

Swaine, Robert. 1946. *The Cravath Firm and Its Predecessors, 1819–1947*. Vol. 1. New York: Ad Press.

Swisher, B. F. 1927. "The Lawyer of the Centuries." *Iowa State Bar Association* 1927:18.

Szeleyni, Ivan, and Bill Martin. 1989. "The Legal Profession and the Rise and Fall of the New Class." In Richard Abel and Philip S. C. Lewis, eds., *Lawyers in Society: Comparative Theories*. Berkeley and Los Angeles: University of California Press.

Taggart, Jay P. 1945. "The Bar and the Bench." *The Ohio Bar* 18:425.
Tawney, R. H. 1920. *The Acquisitive Society*. New York: Harcourt Brace.
Thomas, Roscoe P. 1948. "Challenge to the Lawyer-Citizen: All Should Enroll in Party Organizations." *American Bar Association Journal* 34:891.
Thrift, J. E. 1927. "The Lawyer's Elbows." *Oklahoma State Bar Association Journal* 21:144.
Tinckham, Richard P. 1954. "The Public Relations of the Bar." *Nebraska Law Review* 33:348.
Tolbert, Pamela S. 1988. "Institutional Sources of Organizational Culture in Major Law Firms." In Lynne G. Zucker, ed., *Institutional Patterns and Organizations*. Cambridge, Mass.: Ballinger Publishing.
Tucker, Marilyn, Laurie A. Albright, and Patricia Busk. 1989. "What Ever Happened to the Class of 1983?" *Georgetown Law Journal* 78:153–95.
Tucker, Marna. 1976. "Pro Bono ABA?." In Ralph Nader and Mark Green, eds., *Verdicts on Lawyers*. New York: Thomas Y. Crowell.
Turow, Scott. 1977. *One-L*. New York: Putnam.
Twining, William. 1973. *Karl Llewellyn and the Realist Movement*. Norman: University of Oklahoma Press.
Tybor, Joseph. 2 November 1981. "Bad Day at Kutak Rock." *The National Law Journal*, pp. 8–9.
Unger, Roberto. 1987. *Politics: False Necessity*. New York: Cambridge University Press.
United States Census Bureau. 1982. *Census of Service Industries*. Washington, D.C.: U.S. Government Printing Office.
——. 1976. *Historical Statistics of the United States*. Washington, D.C.: U.S. Government Printing Office.
United States Department of Health, Education, and Welfare. 1973. *Report of the Secretary's Commission on Medical Malpractice*. Washington, D.C.: U.S. Government Printing Office.
United States Department of Labor. January 1986. *Employment and Earnings*. Washington, D.C.: U.S. Government Printing Office.
Van Hoy, Jerry. 1990. "The Politics of Professionalism: A Test Case." Paper presented at the annual meeting of the Midwest Sociological Society, Chicago, IL, 16 April.
Virginia Bar Association Journal. 1987. "Special Report on Lawyer Professionalism." 13:14–17.
——. 1986. "President's Page." 12:3.
Voorhees, Theodore. 1954a. "Lawyer Referral Service in 1954: Legal Advice for Those with Jobs." *American Bar Association Journal* 40:578–81.
——. 1954b. "The Lawyer Referral Service: Medium-Sized and Smaller Communities." *American Bar Association Journal* 40:578–81.
——. 1951. "Publicizing the Lawyer's Reference Service." *American Bar Association Journal* 37:187.
Wall Street Journal. 29 July 1988. "The Strange Case of the Vanishing Firms." P. 17.
Warren, Earl. 1939. "The Responsibilities of the Legal Profession." *Nevada State Bar Journal* 4:182.
Washington Lawyer. March/April 1988. "President's Page." P. 6.
Washington State Bar News. October 1986. "The President's Corner." P. 7.

Wasserstrom, Richard. 1984. "Roles and Morality." In David Luban, ed., *The Good Lawyer*. Totowa, N.J.: Rowman and Allenheld.

——. 1975. "Lawyers as Professionals: Some Moral Issues." *Human Rights* 5:1–24.

Waters, Malcolm. 1989. "Collegiality, Bureaucratization, and Professionalization: A Weberian Analysis." *American Journal of Sociology* 94:945–72.

Weiler, Paul. 1983. "Promises to Keep: Securing Workers' Right to Self-Organization under the NLRA." *Harvard Law Review* 96:1769.

Weisenhaus, Doreen. 8 February 1988. "Still a Long Way to Go for Women, Minorities." *National Law Journal*, pp. 1, 48, 50, 53.

Weiss, Sol. 1936. "Law League of Lawyer's League." *Commercial Law Journal* 41:299.

Weklar, Diane. 1 August 1988. "Strategies for Legal Marketing." *The National Law Journal*, pp. 22, 26.

Westin, Alan F. 1981. *Whistle-Blowing*. New York: McGraw-Hill.

Wiebe, Robert H. 1967. *The Search for Order: 1877–1920*. New York: Hill & Wang.

Wilcox, Roy P. 1926. "President's Address." *Proceedings of the State Bar Association of Wisconsin* 16:161.

Wiley, Alexander. 1948. "A Free Judiciary: American System Contrasted with Society." *American Bar Association Journal* 34:441.

Wise, Daniel. 26 October 1987. "Pssst! Wanna Make Partner?" *The National Law Journal*, pp. 32–33.

Wolfram, Charles H. 1986. *Modern Legal Ethics*. St. Paul, Minn.: West Publishing Co.

——. 1978. "Barriers to Effective Public Participation in Regulation of the Legal Profession." *Minnesota Law Review* 62:619–47.

Wormser, I. M. 1929. "Fewer Lawyers and Better Ones." *New York State Bar Association* 52:352.

Wright, Erik Olin. 1985. *Classes*. London: Verso, 1985.

Wright, Lloyd. 1954. "Public Relations—Are We Meeting Our Obligations?" *Detroit Lawyer* 22:105.

——. 1941. "The Bar at the Crossroads." In *The State Bar of California—Proceedings of the Fourteenth Annual Meeting*. P.I.

Wuthnow, Robert. 1987. *Meaning and Moral Order: Explorations in Cultural Analysis*. Berkeley and Los Angeles: University of California Press.

Yale Law Journal. 1964. "The Jewish Law Student and the New York Jobs—Discriminatory Effects in Law Firm Hiring Practices." 73:625–60.

Zacharias, Fred C. 1989. "Rethinking Confidentiality." *Iowa Law Review* 74:351.

Zion, Sidney. 15 February 1968a. "New Lawyers to Find Salary Market Bullish." *New York Times*, p. 45.

——. 17 February 1968b. "Law Firms across U.S. Raising Pay." *New York Times*, p. 31.

Zuboff, Shoshana. 1988. *In the Age of the Smart Machine: The Future of Work and Power*. New York: Basic Books.

Zussman, Robert. 1985. *Mechanics of the Middle Class: Work and Politics among American Engineers*. Berkeley and Los Angeles: University of California Press.

Cases

Bates v. State Bar of Arizona. 1977. 433 U.S. 350.

Brotherhood of Railroad Trainmen v. Virginia State Bar. 1964. 377 U.S. 1.

Garner v. Wolfinger. 1970. 430 F.2d 1093 (5th Cir. 1970), cert. denied 401 U.S. 974.
Goldfarb v. Virginia State Bar. 1975. 421 U.S. 733.
In re Primus. 1978. 436 U.S. 412.
In re R.M. J. 1982. 455 U.S. 191.
NAACP v. Button. 1963. 371 U.S. 415.
Ohralik v. Ohio State Bar Association. 1978. 436 U.S. 447.
Shapero v. Kentucky Bar Association. 1988. 486 U.S. 466.
Tarasoff v. Regents of University of California. 1976. 17 Cal. 3d 425, 551 P. 2d 334.
United Mine Workers of America, District 12 v. Illinois State Bar Association. 1967. 389 U.S. 217.
United Transportation Union v. State Bar of Michigan. 1971. 401 U.S. 576.
Zauderer v. Office of Disciplinary Council. 1985. 471 U.S. 626.

Index